1. *PRINCIPAL CRUISING ROUTES*

World Cruising Routes

Jimmy Cornell

INTERNATIONAL MARINE PUBLISHING COMPANY
Camden, Maine

Published simultaneously in Great Britain
by Adlard Coles Limited, 8 Grafton Street, London W1X 3LA

Published by International Marine Publishing Company
21 Elm Street, Camden, Maine 04843
(207) 236-4342

Library of Congress Cataloging-in-Publication Data
.

ISBN 0-87742-246-X

To Dottie and Albert Fletcher
of *Duen*
who in a 14 year circumnavigation of over 100,000 miles
left a legacy of goodwill and friendship
wherever they sailed.

Contents

Acknowledgements   viii

Author's Note   ix

List of Maps and Diagrams   x

Introduction   xii

1. Route planning   1

2. Principal world cruising routes   6

3. Winds and currents of the world   13

ATLANTIC OCEAN

4. Winds and currents of the North Atlantic   34

5. Regional weather of the North Atlantic   40
    Iberian Peninsula   40
    North-west Africa   41
    West Africa   41
    Azores   43
    Madeira   44
    Canary Islands   45
    Cape Verde Islands   47
    Guyanas   48
    Venezuela and the ABC Islands   48
    Trinidad   50
    Lesser Antilles   51
    Virgin Islands   53
    Greater Antilles   54

	East coast of Central America	56
	Gulf of Mexico	56
	Bahamas	57
	US coast from Florida to Cape Hatteras	59
	Cape Hatteras to Cape Cod	59
	Cape Cod to Newfoundland	60
	Bermuda	60
6.	Routes in the North Atlantic	62
	AN10 Routes from North Europe	62
	AN20 Routes from Portugal	69
	AN30 Routes from Gibraltar	71
	AN40 Routes from the Canary Islands and West Africa	74
	AN50 Routes from the Azores	79
	AN60 Routes from Bermuda	82
	AN70 Routes from USA	87
	AN80 Routes from the Bahamas and Virgin Islands	94
	AN90 Routes in the Caribbean Sea and from Panama	102
	AN100 Routes from the Lesser Antilles	109
	AN110 Routes from the ABC Islands	114
7.	Transequatorial routes in the Atlantic	117
8.	Winds and currents of the South Atlantic	131
9.	Regional weather in the South Atlantic	134
	South Africa	134
	Magellan Straits to Rio de la Plata	134
	Rio de la Plata	138
	Brazil	138
	St Helena	139
	Ascension	139
	Falkland Islands	140
10.	Routes in the South Atlantic	142

PACIFIC OCEAN

11.	Winds and currents of the North Pacific	149
12.	Regional weather of the North Pacific	156
	Alaska	156
	British Columbia	156

US west coast 157
California 157
Mexico 158
Central America 159
Hawaii 159
Line Islands 160
Marshall Islands 160
Kiribati 161
Caroline Islands 162
Palau 163
Mariana Islands 163
Philippine Islands 166
Hong Kong 168
Japan 168

13. Routes in the North Pacific 171
PN10 Routes from the west coast of North America 171
PN20 Routes from Panama 177
PN30 Routes from Hawaii, Marshalls and Kiribati 183
PN40 Routes from the Philippines and Singapore 194
PN50 Routes from Hong Kong 198
PN60 Routes from Japan 202
PN70 Routes in Micronesia 206

14. Transequatorial routes in the Pacific 209

15. Winds and currents of the South Pacific 226

16. Regional weather of the South Pacific 232
South American Coast 232
Juan Fernandez 233
Galapagos 233
Easter Island 234
Pitcairn Island 234
Gambier Islands 236
Tuamotu Archipelago 236
Marquesas 237
Society Islands 237
Austral Islands 239
Cook Islands 240
Samoan Islands 240

Wallis and Futuna 241
Tuvalu 242
Tonga 243
Fiji 244
New Zealand 245
Tasmania 247
New South Wales 247
Queensland 247
New Caledonia 248
Vanuatu 251
Solomon Islands 251
New Guinea 254
Papua 254
Louisiade and Trobriand Islands 256
Bismarck Archipelago 256
Manus Islands 256

17. Routes in the South Pacific 258
PS10 Routes in the Eastern South Pacific 263
PS20 Routes from the Society and Cook Islands 268
PS30 Routes from Samoa and Tonga 276
PS40 Routes from Fiji, Tuvalu and Wallis 282
PS50 Routes from New Zealand 288
PS60 Routes from New Caledonia, Vanuatu and
        Solomon Islands 299
PS70 Routes from Australia and Papua New Guinea 306

INDIAN OCEAN

18. Winds and currents of the North Indian Ocean 316

19. Regional weather of the North Indian Ocean 320
Singapore 320
Malacca Straits and Malaysian west coast 320
Thailand 321
Bay of Bengal 321
Sri Lanka 322
Arabian Sea 322
Gulf of Aden 323
Maldives 323

20. Routes in the North Indian Ocean 325

21. Transequatorial routes in the Indian Ocean 336

22. Winds and currents of the South Indian Ocean 344

23. Regional weather of the South Indian Ocean 348
    Northern Australia 348
    Arafura and Timor Seas 348
    Indonesia 349
    Western Australia 350
    Christmas Island 350
    Cocos Keeling 350
    Chagos Archipelago 351
    Rodriguez 353
    Mauritius 353
    Réunion 353
    Madagascar 353
    Comoro Islands 354
    Seychelles 355
    East Africa 356
    South Africa 356

24. Routes in South Indian Ocean 357

RED SEA

25. Winds, currents and routes in the Red Sea 380
    RN Northbound routes 384
    RS Southbound routes 386

MEDITERRANEAN SEA

26. Winds, currents and routes in the Mediterranean Sea 388
    M10 West to east routes 395
    M30 East to west routes 405

27. Canals and cruising regulations 412

Bibliography 425

Index to routes
    in numerical order 428
    in alphabetical order 430

Acknowledgements

In writing this book I have drawn on the experience of many of my friends, particularly those who have sailed on routes which I have not. Norma and Chester Lemon, who circumnavigated both the Pacific and Indian Oceans on *Honeymead*, and Illa and Herbert Gieseking of *Lou V*, now on their second world voyage after circumnavigating on *Lou IV*, have written many informative letters about the routes they have sailed. A similar special mention must also go to Muriel and Erick Bouteleux for information on routes covered during their circumnavigation on *Calao*. Other circumnavigators I wish to thank for their contribution are:

Liz and Bruce MacDonald of *Horizon*
Marg and Bob Miller of *Galatea IV*
Julie and Doncho Papazov of *Tivia*
Waltraud and Robert Bittner, formerly of *Vamos*, now sailing on *Lorebella*

My thanks also to other long distance voyagers who have supplied information on specific areas or topics:

Sandra and Paul Ewing of *Maamari*
Gunter Gross of *Hägar the Horrible*
Peter Noble of *Artemis*
Kim Prowd of *Tarrawarra*
Margaret and Charles Pickering of *Keegenoo*
Pierre Ribes of *Sphinx*
Nina and Juan Ribas of *Abuelo III*
Frances and Bill Stocks of *Kleena Kleene II*
Saskia and John Whitehead of *Cornelia*

I am most grateful to Chris Bonnet of the *Ocean Appletiser Sailing Academy*, Durban, for the wealth of information he supplied concerning sailing conditions in South African waters.

I would also like to thank the following for their help in various ways:

The Librarians at the National Maritime Museum, Greenwich.
Sue Brown and Jean-Claude Bachelier of UTA French Airlines.
John Wilkinson of IBERIA Airlines.
National Bureau of Standards, US Department of Commerce.
Peter Parker of the Barbados Port Authority.
Arturo Molina Suarez and *El Patronato de Turismo*, Las Palmas.

The US Defense Mapping Agency.
J.D. Potter Ltd, Admiralty Agents for charts and nautical publications.
The Cruising Association.
MAGNAVOX for information on great circle sailing by satellite navigation.
Dick Johnson and all at *Yachting World* for their continuing support.

Author's Note

This book has been compiled from a great variety of both official and private sources, as well as the author's personal ocean cruising experience. The sketch maps accompanying the text are simple diagrams to show approximate positions of routes only. While every effort has been made to ensure the accuracy of the data included in this volume, neither the publishers nor the author can assume any responsibility for possible errors made in these pages.

List of Maps and Diagrams

1.	Principal cruising routes	*end papers*
2.	Prevailing wind systems January to March	16–17
3.	April to June	18–19
4.	July to September	20–21
5.	October to December	22–3
6.	World distribution of tropical storms	26–7
7.	Tropical storm tactics northern hemisphere	29
8.	Tropical storm tactics southern hemisphere	30
9.	North Atlantic currents	38
10.	West Africa	42
11.	The Azores	44
12.	Madeira	45
13.	Canary Islands	46
14.	Cape Verde Islands	47
15.	Venezuela and the ABC Islands	49
16.	Trinidad and Venezuelan Islands	50
17.	Lesser Antilles	52
18.	Virgin Islands	53
19.	Central America and the Gulf of Mexico	56
20.	Bahamas, Turks and Caicos Islands	58
21.	Bermuda	61
22.	Transatlantic routes east to west	63
23.	Atlantic routes from Western Europe	68
24.	Transatlantic routes west to east	82
25.	Routes between the US East Coast and the Caribbean	87
26.	Routes between the Caribbean and the US East Coast	96
27.	Routes to and from the Bahamas	99
28.	Caribbean routes to and from Panama	103
29.	Routes in the Eastern Caribbean	110
30.	Transequatorial routes in the Atlantic	118
31.	South Atlantic currents	132
32.	Islands in the South Atlantic	135
33.	Magellan Straits and Cape Horn	136–7
34.	Falkland Islands	140
35.	South Atlantic routes	142
36.	North Pacific currents	154–5
37.	Hawaii	160
38.	Marshall Islands	161
39.	Kiribati	162

40.	Caroline Islands	164–5
41.	Mariana Islands	166
42.	Philippines	167
43.	Japan	169
44.	Routes in the North-East Pacific	172–3
45.	North Pacific routes	184–5
46.	Routes in the Far East	193
47.	Routes between Papua New Guinea and Micronesia	207
48.	Routes in the Eastern Pacific	210–11
49.	South Pacific currents	230–31
50.	Galapagos Islands	233
51.	Islands in the South-East Pacific	235
52.	Marquesas	238
53.	Society Islands	239
54.	Samoan Islands	241
55.	Islands in the Central Pacific	242
56.	Tonga	243
57.	Fiji	245
58.	New Zealand	246
59.	New Caledonia	249
60.	Vanuatu	250
61.	Solomon Islands	252–3
62.	Papua New Guinea	255
63.	Routes in the South Pacific	260–61
64.	Routes in Eastern Polynesia	269
65.	Routes in the Central Pacific	278
66.	Routes from New Zealand	290–91
67.	Routes in the Coral Sea	300–301
68.	Indian Ocean currents during North-East monsoon	317
69.	Maldives	324
70.	Indian Ocean routes	326
71.	Indian Ocean currents during South-West monsoon	346
72.	Islands in the South Indian Ocean	351
73.	Mascarene Islands	352
74.	Comoros	354
75.	Seychelles	355
76.	Routes to Singapore and Indonesia	358–9
77.	Routes in the West Indian Ocean	364
78.	Routes in the Red Sea	381
79.	Routes in the Western Mediterranean	396
80.	Routes in the Eastern Mediterranean	406
81.	Panama Canal Atlantic Ocean entrance	414–15
82.	Panama Canal Pacific Ocean entrance	416–17
83.	Suez Canal Approaches to Port Said	419
84.	Suez Canal Approaches to Suez	420

Introduction

As a young boy growing up in Romania, caged in by an iron curtain which separated me from the rest of the world, planning imaginary journeys was the only way I was allowed to travel. I relieved my frustrations by making dream voyages to exotic places, tracing my finger along the routes I would take on an old atlas of the world. Route planning fascinated me then and has continued to do so, even after I obtained my freedom and the world lay before me. Routes across Europe became miraculously transformed into the reality of railroads and motorways, as later on, pencil marks on charts were to become sailing tracks across the oceans.

As a voyage around the world passed from being a dream into becoming a possibility, a finger tracing a line on a chart was no longer sufficient and I started planning my voyage in earnest. Trying to translate dreams into concrete plans was not so easy and although the shelves were full of books on almost every aspect of cruising under sail, I found very little on route planning aimed specifically at the small boat voyager. This gap, although annoying, was not enough to deter me from setting off, as so many others have also done. However, during my six-year circumnavigation of 60,000 miles, including some of the remotest areas of the world, I retained an interest in routeing and collected information as I went along.

This book attempts to fill that gap by providing essential information on winds, currents, regional and seasonal weather, as well as details of nearly 300 cruising routes. With the help of the information contained in this book, I hope to make it much easier for anyone who intends to undertake an ocean voyage to do all forward planning from the comfort of their home. Once the voyage has started, the book will continue to be useful in suggesting alternatives or detours from the main itinerary.

World Cruising Routes is a guide to cruising routes, not a comprehensive pilot for the entire world, and its users are urged to refer to the relevant sailing directions, pilot charts and regional publications, before undertaking a particular passage. Because of the vast area included in the book, only the basic data needed for planning an extensive cruise could be included, as it would have been physically impossible to include in one single volume detailed information about every route. I had to limit myself to giving only general directions on how to get from one destination to the next. These directions mention safe and dangerous seasons, prevailing winds, the kind of weather to be expected, as well as other factors that ought to be known by a small boat voyager. Whenever a particular aspect was debatable or variable, such as the beginning or end of a hurricane season, the strength of a particular current or the frequency of gales in a specific area, I have preferred to err on the side of caution. For the same reason, I have concentrated more on giving details for what is considered to be the safe cruising season and less on weather conditions during unfavourable seasons. I believe that cruising should be a pleasurable activity and as many unpleasant sailing conditions can be avoided with a bit of planning, this aspect is emphasised throughout the book. I have no intention of encouraging anyone to look for tough routes and foul weather. Therefore the book concentrates on the warmer regions of the world, where most sailors intend to cruise or dream of cruising one day, rather than on how to prepare for a gale swept mid-winter crossing of the North Atlantic.

The primary aim of this book is to enable the reader to plan a voyage from beginning to end, and the information needed to do this is threefold: general offshore weather conditions, regional weather in cruising areas and descriptions of actual routes. The regional weather information contained in the book does not comprise an exhaustive list. Areas which are seldom visited by sailing boats have either been omitted or described only briefly. The regional weather is only intended as a rough guide to what weather conditions can be expected in certain areas by those planning to cruise there.

As an example, if a one-year stay is envisaged in the South Pacific as part of a longer voyage and a cruise is planned among the islands of Fiji, details can be found in the relevant sections on general weather conditions in the South Pacific, when and where tropical storms can be expected, ways of avoiding the dangerous season, regional weather and the best time of year for cruising in Fiji, how to get there, and finally how and when to leave.

As the majority of routes in any ocean keep to one hemisphere, the cruising routes are subdivided into six main areas of the world, coinciding with the six hemispheres of the three oceans. I consider this to be a more logical way of organising the routes than dealing with each ocean as a whole, mainly because all routes in a certain hemisphere are governed by similar weather considerations. Because of the seasons being opposite, weather conditions usually differ considerably between hemispheres. Every route is identified by two letters and a number, the two letters showing the ocean and the hemisphere – A for Atlantic, P for Pacific and I for Indian Ocean, and the letter N or S relating to whether the route is in the northern or southern hemisphere of that particular ocean. Transequatorial routes in each ocean are dealt with separately and carry the letter T after the initial letter of the ocean in question.

Every route mentions the best time for a passage to be made along that route and the season when tropical storms affect that particular region. The extent of the hurricane season is given for the entire route, even if the point of departure or that of arrival are not themselves subject to tropical storms, but when the threat of hurricanes does exist in some area along that route. Also given are the great circle distances between principal ports, but as these distances are only meant for guidance, they are approximate, especially when the suggested route is not direct. Also indicated at the beginning of each route are the charts and sailing directions (pilots) relevant to that part of the world. As this book deals with offshore passages, only small scale charts are indicated. Although the sailing directions deal mainly with pilotage in coastal areas and their use on ocean passages is limited, it is advisable to have on board pilots of adjacent areas to those sailed through, in case an emergency landfall has to be made in an area for which charts are not carried. The US Pilots indicated are those published by the US Defense Mapping Agency. Those dealing with US coastal waters published by the National Ocean Service have not been quoted. Both American and British charts and publications are indicated as certain parts of the world are covered better by one or other hydrographic office. As a general rule British charts are better for areas which were once part of the former British Empire, whereas American charts tend to be more accurate in areas of prime US interest, such as the North Pacific. Although chart and pilot numbers were correct at the time of going to press, some numbers are changed occasionally and this should be borne in mind especially when ordering charts suggested at the beginning of each route.

For reasons of space, but also because certain well-sailed areas of the world are already more than adequately covered by other publications, I have kept to a minimum the information on cruising routes within North America, Northern Europe, Australia and the Mediterranean. The few routes mentioned for those areas are only meant for general guidance for outsiders who plan to cruise in those countries, and not as a cruising guide for local sailors. In a similar way, the book gives routes on how to get to a certain area, for example the Bahamas, but is not a guide to cruising between islands within that area.

In the preparation of this book I have drawn extensively on older publications and even on logs kept by the captains of sailing ships, which contain a wealth of information on ocean passages and prevailing sailing conditions. These conditions have changed little since the heyday of sailing vessels, when ships' captains were under tremendous pressure from their owners to make the fastest passages possible. Unfortunately this valuable information is rarely included in current publications, as it is not considered to be essential for the powered vessels that ply the oceans today. Even so, this information is often of little use to a cruising yacht, as the routes popular now seldom coincide with those sailed by the square riggers of yesteryear, especially since the opening of the Panama and Suez canals. The South Pacific is the best example in this respect, as there is hardly any information available on the sailing routes of that increasingly popular cruising area.

I hope to be forgiven if I have missed out or overlooked some route.

Several times I have decided to omit a little frequented route when I knew, for instance, that there is rarely more than one cruising boat per year sailing from Tuvalu to the Solomon Islands direct. In such cases I considered that there was sufficient information which could be taken from adjacent routes, where conditions are similar.

There are probably some people who expect a book of this kind to provide precise solutions for all their needs. Obviously this would be impossible, especially when dealing with something as inconsistent as winds and weather. Every so often there occurs freak weather which can affect even the normally dependable routes. There is an infinite variety of circumstances which render it impossible to lay down any fixed rule which can be followed to advantage at all times. Therefore, in those cases in which a certain course is pointed out as the best to be pursued, but this proves impossible to accomplish, it is always better to follow one's own instincts, even if it results in a detour or delay.

As well as drawing on a large variety of sources, much of the material included in the book was provided from my own voyaging. I have also received enormous help from my many sailing friends, particularly those who have ventured where I have not. In those areas, the faculty learnt in my youth of transposing myself to unknown places has served me in good stead. I am still tracing my finger along routes on charts, but this time with a little help from my friends.

1   Route planning

Some voyages start as a dream, but end as a nightmare, usually due to a lack of planning and inadequate preparation. Almost any well found modern sailing boat is able to travel from point A to point B under most conditions, provided the length of time it takes does not matter. Whether this is worth doing or not is highly debatable. Captain Bligh nearly had a mutiny on his hands when he stubbornly tried to round Cape Horn from east to west in the middle of winter. He finally gave up and turned around, only to find an even greater challenge in the Tahitian *vahines*. Evidently, even the best forward planning could not have foreseen that kind of danger.

Fortunately the factors that have to be taken into account when planning an extended voyage nowadays are more predictable and most of the dangers that can threaten a cruise are well known. The wise navigator planning an offshore voyage will try to take full advantage of the favourable winds and currents and avoid encountering any extreme weather. An offshore cruising boat should be well enough constructed to be able to withstand the average gale, and fortunately along the routes described in this volume, the frequency of violent storms is extremely low during the accepted 'safe' cruising season. The main dangers to watch out for are tropical revolving storms, whether these are called hurricanes, cyclones, typhoons or willy-willies, but as they affect known areas during certain times of the year, they can easily be avoided. This is where advance route planning has a major role to play, as it is perfectly possible to plan a voyage to any popular cruising area of the world without running the risk of encountering a hurricane, cyclone or typhoon. Another element that must be taken into account when planning a voyage are the few areas of the world considered to be dangerous because of piracy, drug running or high criminality. Because of their human nature such dangers are more difficult to predict than natural phenomena, although the areas to be avoided are usually known and the sailing grapevine sounds warnings about areas that should be given a wide berth, be it Colombia, islands between Indonesia and the Philippines, or parts of the Red Sea.

Yet in spite of all the information available today and the fact that so much more is known about the weather systems of the world, small boats still come to grief every year because their skippers ignore all warnings and decide to spend the hurricane season in an area known to be hit by these violent storms. Less traumatic but nevertheless uncomfortable is the realisation made each year by owners of boats from the west coast of America, who find themselves in some South Pacific island at the end of a nice downwind cruise without the foggiest idea of how to get back home. Eventually some of them choose the logical solution and carry on westwards, adding thousands of miles to a cruise, which willy-nilly has turned into a circumnavigation. A certain degree of advance planning could have made life easier. Such lack of forward planning is the main reason why there are always boats for sale in Caribbean ports, their disenchanted European owners not relishing the return voyage across the Atlantic.

On the other hand there are obviously instances where either by force or by choice one has to fight the elements to reach a certain point. After transiting the Panama Canal in *Aventura* we decided to visit Peru and the west coast of South America, before starting our cruise among the islands of the South Pacific. As we were very determined to sail to Peru, the only alternative to a long beat against contrary winds and the Humboldt Current would have been an even longer detour around Cape Horn or through the Magellan Straits. Our decision to go against the weather was only taken because of our wish to visit a particular place. When planning a longer voyage, however, the most important thing is to make the best use of favourable winds and to avoid bad weather by choosing a suitable course and, above all, by being in the right place at the right time.

When starting to plan a voyage, one of the first requirements in the planning stages is a gnomonic chart for the area where the intended cruise will take place. Regional charts do not have to be acquired at this stage and in fact it is better if they are only bought after the itinerary of the cruise has been finalised. A gnomonic chart is necessary because the ordinary navigational charts, based on the Mercator projection, cannot be used for planning an offshore voyage of more than a few hundred miles. On the Mercator charts all meridians are represented as straight parallel lines that do not converge at the poles, as meridians do in reality. This means that any straight line drawn between two points on one of these charts is not necessarily the shortest distance between those two points and although a ship that sails such a course will reach its destination, it will not be by the shortest route. To be able to sail more efficiently it is necessary to establish the great circle route, which is the shortest distance between two points on the surface of the earth.

The principles of great circle sailing have been known for a long time and it is believed that great navigators such as Columbus and Magellan were already acquainted with the subject. The advantages of sailing along a great circle route were first mentioned in a work by the Spanish navigator Pedro Nuñez in 1537. They were brought to the attention of British seamen in the book *The Arte of Navigation*, translated into English by Richard Eden in 1561. Other works also referred to the applications of great circle sailing, but the term itself appears to have been coined by John Davis in a book published in 1594 under the title *Seaman's Secrets*, which described 'three Kinds of Sayling – Horizontall, Paradoxall and *Sayling upon a Great Circle*'.

It was at about the same time that the Dutch mathematician Gerhard Mercator published a universal map on a projection that now bears his name. A course represented by a straight line on a Mercator chart is called a rhumb line and for short voyages sailing along such a line between the port of departure and that of arrival makes a minimal difference. In order to find the shortest route for a longer passage, the same straight line will have to be drawn on a gnomonic chart, which uses a different projection with meridians converging at the poles and parallels of latitude represented by curved lines. Any straight line on a gnomonic chart is part of a great circle and is indeed the shortest distance between the two points joined by that line. Because gnomonic charts cannot be used for navigation, the great circle track drawn on such a chart has to be transferred to a Mercator chart. This is done by making a note of the latitudes at which the great circle route intersects successive meridians which have been selected at convenient intervals, usually at 5°. These positions are transferred to the corresponding Mercator chart and joined by straight lines. This succession of rhumb lines approximates very closely the actual great circle track for that route.

This rather cumbersome method of finding the great circle track for any chosen route can be avoided by solving the problem not graphically but mathematically. There are several ways of calculating both the initial great circle course and the great circle distance between two given points and one of the simplest methods is described at the beginning of the sight reduction tables for marine navigation. The problem can also be solved by using an electronic calculator, while some satnav models display the great circle course and distance between two chosen points at the push of a button.

The purchase of gnomonic charts is therefore no longer absolutely necessary for those who intend to calculate their great circle course by other means, although acquiring the pilot charts for the oceans that will be crossed is essential. These routeing charts are published by the US Department of Defense Hydrographic Center and the British Admiralty Hydrographic Department and can be obtained from the usual chart agents. Pilot charts are issued for all oceans of the world and give monthly or quarterly averages of wind direction and strength, currents, percentages of calms and gales, limits of ice, tropical storm tracks and other kinds of information. The data contained in these charts is based on observations made by ships that have passed through those areas and although they give an accurate overall picture of weather conditions for a certain time of year, they are only averages and must be regarded as such. Other publications that might be useful at the planning stage are *Ocean Passages for the World*, published by the British Hydrographic Department and the *Planning Guides*, published by the US Defense Mapping Agency. Both these publications are meant primarily for ships and their use for sailing boats is limited. The *Planning Guides* contain general information on each ocean and are meant to be used in conjunction with the respective Sailing

Directions. They cover the following areas: North Atlantic (140), South Atlantic (121), North Pacific (152), Far East (160), South Pacific (122), Indian Ocean (170) and Mediterranean (130).

With the help of the relevant pilot charts for the area to be cruised and the directions contained in this book, planning a voyage can start in earnest. In order to make it simpler to draw up the general outline of a longer cruise, some hypothetical voyages are described in the next chapter. These examples are only meant to show what can be done in a given amount of time. Both short-term and long-term planning are finally the responsibility of the skipper who knows best what are the capabilities and limitations of his or her crew and boat.

The importance of long-term or forward planning can be seen from the following example. Presuming that a cruise of a few months is planned in the Lesser Antilles, the order in which the islands are visited should be determined by subsequent plans. Most people leave from the Canaries concerned only with crossing the Atlantic by the fastest and most convenient route, their landfall in the Caribbean being decided by many factors, but not always by long-term considerations. If one is planning to return to Europe or the USA at the end of the cruising season in the Caribbean, the logical way to cruise through the islands is from south to north, so that the same ground will not be covered twice. On the other hand, if the voyage will continue in the Pacific and a transiting of the Panama Canal is planned, it makes more sense to end the transatlantic crossing in one of the islands further north, such as Antigua or Martinique, and then sail down the chain of islands towards Grenada or Venezuela. Such a route would ensure better winds when sailing among the Lesser Antilles and also a shorter passage to Panama when the time arrives. The passage across the Caribbean Sea can be extremely rough at the end of winter and a start from one of the ABC islands off Venezuela (Aruba, Bonaire and Curaçao) would make that leg shorter and more pleasant. An additional advantage is the fact that the southernmost part of the Caribbean is outside the hurricane zone so that if the cruise is delayed for any reason, the boat will be in a safe place.

Equally important when forward planning is to allow certain subjective factors to influence the choice of routes. An order of priorities has to be decided and this is usually the point at which one must be prepared to face up to one's own limitations. Some people are ashamed to admit to others, and even to themselves, that they are afraid of a certain passage. A good example is the rounding of the Cape of Good Hope, more aptly called the Cape of Storms, which is indeed a very dangerous area, especially if one is not too confident that the boat could take a knockdown or capsize, which is an eventuality that must be faced by all those who take this route. There is absolutely nothing wrong in avoiding such a passage and this can be done easily by choosing the Red Sea route instead. However, this decision must be made well in advance, ideally before going through the Torres Strait and not on the eve of departure from Mauritius.

Another area in which subjective factors should be allowed to play their part is in the continuing dispute between purists and realists. All too often, using the engine except for manoeuvring in port is still frowned upon, sometimes by people who would not walk to their corner shop when they can drive. Unfortunately for the purists, engines have become an indispensable part of a modern cruising boat's equipment and many routes described in this book would be very difficult to accomplish without the help of an engine. After all, we live in a technological age, and however satisfying it may be to be able to sail out the anchor or tack into a crowded port, there is nothing wrong in turning on the engine to get out of the way of a tanker bearing down on you. Reliance on auxiliary engines has become an accepted part of modern cruising and this is the reason why on certain routes skippers are advised to have a good reserve of fuel as this can make a great difference to the length of the passage. The convenience of being able to motor through the doldrums and not be becalmed for days or weeks is one such instance, as is the ability to power against a strong outflowing current to enter a lagoon, which otherwise could not be entered.

These are only some of the factors that can influence planning, both in the short and long term. What is needed at all times, however, once the cruise has started, is a good dose of common sense, which will help overcome most problems. For example, if one is not too sure about the position of a certain reef, island or any other danger, it is generally safer to assume that the latitude stated is more accurate than the longitude. The coordinates of most of these dangers were fixed by navigators before the advent of precise modern instruments, and many charts of remote areas have yet to be corrected. This is why it is still perfectly valid to use the practice of the masters of the sailing ships, who always tried to 'run down' the latitude of a given place, so as to maximise the chances of finding it. On the other hand, if one wishes to avoid a certain danger, the main thing to avoid is its latitude. As many ocean passages along the popular cruising routes are from east to west, this means that it should not be too difficult to choose a safe latitude and stay on it when approaching a known danger.

The influence that such common sense can have on good seamanship is shown by some of the examples mentioned in my book *Ocean Cruising Survey*, where one of the conclusions drawn after talking to a great number of experienced sailors was that one of the most important qualities to have while sailing is patience. A little bit of humility and respect for the powers of nature are perhaps just as important and this is probably the explanation why superstitious sailors preferred to say that they were 'bound for' their destination. Many things can happen to stop a ship from reaching its desired destination and careful planning has a major part to play in bringing a ship safely home.

2 Principal world cruising routes

Planning an extended cruise is not a simple matter, as many factors have to be taken into consideration. The most important factor to be considered is the safety of the vessel and its crew, and therefore it is crucial to ensure that the route will avoid areas of known danger and also that as much as possible of the sailing will be done during favourable seasons. The majority of the cruising routes described in this book are in the tropics, which is where world voyagers spend much of their time. However, many tropical areas are only safe for six or seven months of the year, the remaining months being liable to tropical storms. In the following pages I shall try to give some examples of typical world cruises that can be done with maximum safety. The suggested routes are shown on the world map depicted on the end papers of this book.

Voyage A: A two-year circumnavigation from Europe or the US east coast

The shortest time in which a cruise around the world can be accomplished in a small sailing boat is probably two years, anything less being hardly a cruise, but more a feat of endurance. If the point of departure is Scandinavia, Britain or Northern Europe, the recommended time for leaving would be early summer when optimum conditions can be expected in the North Sea, English Channel and across the Bay of Biscay. Departures from Mediterranean ports and Gibraltar can be left as late as October. This is also the time when boats should be on their way to the Canaries, whether sailing direct or via Madeira.

The best time for an Atlantic crossing along the NE trade wind route is late in November, as such a departure ensures that landfall is made in one of the Caribbean islands before Christmas, at the beginning of the safe cruising season.

For boats leaving on a two year circumnavigation from the east coast of the USA, the timing of departure is crucial and the margins less generous. If some time is to be spent in the Lesser Antilles, an attempt should be made to leave by the first week of November, sailing directly to the Virgin Islands. For those planning to sail straight to Panama, there are two alternatives, either via the Bahamas and the Windward Passage, or through the Intracoastal Waterway to Florida and thence to Panama. In the latter case, a later departure is possible.

Whether the initial port of departure is in Europe or the USA, the Panama Canal should be transited in January or early February. This avoids arriving in the Marquesas before the end of March when the islands of French Polynesia are still subject to tropical cyclones. Because of the limited time available, Tahiti should be left in early June so as to arrive in Fiji by July. As these are the months when the SE trades are at their most constant, these long passages can usually be made in good times. Passages from Fiji onwards should be timed to pass through the Torres Strait before the end of August or early in September.

The passage across the South Indian Ocean will have to be made in a similar rhythm, with long periods at sea and little time to spend in the islands en route. The start of the cyclone season in December indicates a departure from Mauritius for the passage to Durban not later than the end of October. The next leg to Cape Town is best made in January or February, when conditions around the tip of Africa are considered to be the most favourable.

Those planning to return to the Mediterranean via the Red Sea have the choice of either calling in at Bali and carrying on to Singapore, or making their way to Sri Lanka via Christmas Island. A cruising permit is required for those wishing to pass through Indonesia, which probably dictates the choice of route. The advantage of a passage across the North Indian Ocean is that this can be done in January or February, which allows longer time to be spent in the Pacific, negotiating the Torres Strait only in September or even early October.

Those returning via the Cape of Good Hope can either sail directly to the Azores, if bound for Europe, or to Brazil and the Lesser Antilles, if bound for the east coast of the USA. An arrival in the Azores in April or May would enable a return to the point of departure exactly two years after leaving home. Those returning to the US east coast can accomplish this circumnavigation in even less time, although few people do. There are so many temptations lying in wait en route, for Americans and Europeans alike, which invariably means that even with the best of intentions, such quick voyages end up by stretching into three and even four years. However, this hypothetical example shows how it is possible to plan a two-year circumnavigation so as to always be in the right place at the right time.

Voyage B: A three-year circumnavigation from Europe or the US east coast

The previous voyage can be made much more enjoyable if more time is available. Although the additional mileage covered during a three-year long circumnavigation would only amount to about 4000 miles, the extra year allows more time to be spent in places en route and thus makes the entire voyage more enjoyable.

The first part of the voyage either from Europe or North America would be similar to the one described in the previous example. More time can be spent in the Caribbean, but the Panama Canal should be transited by early March so as to arrive in the Marquesas before the end of April. The following three months can be spent in French Polynesia, allowing one to be there for the unique 14 July celebrations. Leaving the Society Islands before the end of July makes it possible to spend some time in all the island groups en route to Fiji. Because of the approaching cyclone season (December to March), a decision must be made whether to spend this in Tonga (Vava'u), American Samoa (Pago Pago) or New Zealand. Although a number of boats hole up in one of the first two places, these anchorages are in the cyclone area and the vast majority of those cruising the South Pacific make their way to New Zealand, which is outside the cyclone belt. A stay in Fiji is not recommended as the number of safe anchorages is small and they fill up quickly in an emergency.

The passage from Fiji to New Zealand is normally undertaken in November. Most people spend the entire cyclone season in New Zealand and leave for the Torres Strait and Indian Ocean early in April. Such a departure allows them to visit some of the island groups bordering on the Coral Sea before reaching the Indian Ocean. Another alternative is to sail across the Tasman Sea from New Zealand to Australia in February or March and then sail up the east coast of Australia towards the Torres Strait.

An earlier arrival in the Indian Ocean allows more time to be spent en route, whether in Darwin or Indonesia, if a cruising permit has been obtained beforehand. The rest of the voyage is virtually the same as that described in Voyage A.

Voyage C: A three-year circumnavigation from the west coast of North America

If a circumnavigation is planned from California or British Columbia, at least three years should be allowed. The primary destination for almost all of those who undertake this voyage is Tahiti, which can be reached via either Hawaii or the Marquesas. The time of departure is less crucial for the Hawaiian route, but a late April or early May departure is recommended for those intending to sail to the Marquesas first.

Whichever route is chosen, it is unlikely that Tahiti will be reached before July or August, which means that the coming cyclone season (December to March) is best spent in the Society Islands. This certainly applies to those who leave California in November and sail direct to the Marquesas, as a number of boats have done in recent years. For those who decide to stay in Tahiti or any of the other Society Islands there are several safe anchorages available, but one must make sure that one is close enough to them in case a cyclone comes that way. The islands of French Polynesia are not visited by cyclones every year and this has lulled many people into a false sense of security, which was shattered in 1983 when Tahiti was struck by two violent cyclones and several boats were lost. One way to avoid spending the cyclone season in French Polynesia is to leave California in November and spend the winter either in Hawaii or Mexico and Central America. The voyage to Tahiti can then be made in March, allowing one to arrive there at the start of the safe season. The rest of the South Pacific cruise could follow the pattern described in either voyage A or B.

Those who are in a hurry to return home in the shortest time possible should follow the previously suggested timetable across the South Indian Ocean so as to arrive in Cape Town not long after Christmas. This would allow them to arrive in the Lesser Antilles by February and in Panama by March or April. Once through the Panama Canal the choice is between a bash along the coast of Central America, if one can rely on a powerful engine, or a detour to Hawaii in the hope of finding favourable winds for the return voyage. The timing of one's arrival in Panama is crucial if one is planning to sail to California along the coast, because Cabo San Lucas should be cleared before the onset of the hurricane season in June.

Because of this tight scheduling and other considerations, many West Coast sailors are put off by the South African route and choose the Red Sea route instead. As described in Voyage A, the passage across the North Indian Ocean can be done as late as February, which allows a more relaxed pace earlier on. But the main attraction of this alternative route is the chance to spend some time in the Mediterranean. Arriving there through the Suez Canal in April one has about six summer months in which to sail to Gibraltar and visit some interesting places on the way. The passage from Gibraltar to the Canaries can easily be done in October and the subsequent crossing of the Atlantic will also take place at the best of times. Having arrived in Barbados or some other Caribbean island before Christmas, the voyage to Panama and beyond can be undertaken in a more leisurely fashion than if one had arrived there straight from South Africa. With more time in hand, even the difficulty of the return passage along the Pacific coast of Central America can be faced with more detachment.

Voyage D: A four-year circumnavigation from the west coast of North America

Some of the factors mentioned in the previous example point to the advantage in allowing more time for a circumnavigation originating from the Pacific coast of North America. Many successful voyages in recent years have been accomplished in four years, which seems an ideal span, although those with more time available have often spent considerably longer on such a voyage.

The initial stages would not differ from those described in Voyage C and in spite of my natural reluctance to suggest spending the cyclone season in French Polynesia, such a course of action is difficult to avoid, and it is therefore recommended to take careful precautions. Spending some time sailing in Tahiti and the other Society Islands during the safe season will make it possible to investigate the best anchorages for the forthcoming cyclone season. There are several hurricane holes dotted about the Society Islands, so that it is possible to continue cruising during the cyclone season, provided one is never too far from one of these anchorages and weather forecasts are listened to regularly. However, it must be pointed out that the better anchorages get very crowded with both local and visiting boats and this restricts the choice of anchorage considerably.

An early start from French Polynesia after the end of the cyclone season allows a leisurely cruise through the various island groups to Fiji, where a choice has to be made concerning the next cyclone season. The course of action taken in recent years by the majority of those cruising in the South Pacific is to spend this season in New Zealand. Another alternative is to carry on from Fiji to Australia, preferably to ports in New South Wales or southern Queensland which are also outside the cyclone belt. An increasing number of boats spend the season cruising in Papua New Guinea waters, where only the very south eastern islands lie in the cyclone area. Yet another possibility is to remain in Fiji, American Samoa (Pago Pago) or Tonga (Vava'u), where relatively safe anchorages can be found, although still in the cyclone area.

The itinerary of the voyage after this second cyclone season can take many shapes and the permutations are almost infinite. For those who contemplate a complete voyage around the world, including a return to the west coast of the United States or Canada, voyage C spells out the alternatives very clearly. For West Coast sailors with less time on their hands, voyage E may suggest an even more attractive alternative.

Voyage E: A round Pacific voyage

Probably the greatest disadvantage of the Pacific Ocean from a cruising point of view is that it does not lend itself to an obvious circumnavigation, a fact recognised as early as the 16th century by the Spanish navigators. Today's voyagers are faced with almost the same dilemma, but at least the improved windward-going capability of their craft makes the problem somewhat easier.

Because the South Pacific and its myriad islands continue to be the principal attraction of a Pacific cruise, the return voyage to the West Coast will be considered from somewhere in the South West Pacific, New Zealand being the most likely place for the start of such a voyage. The most logical return itinerary is via Tahiti with the help of westerly winds found below latitude 35°S. This return voyage to Tahiti is best made at the end of the cyclone season, in April or May, before the onset of the southern winter. If a prompt departure is made from New Zealand, there is sufficient time to reach the West Coast via Hawaii long before winter also arrives in the northern hemisphere. Such a return trip to Tahiti allows those who had sailed quickly through these islands on their outward voyage to see more of French Polynesia the second time around. The other alternative is to sail from New Zealand to Hawaii via the Cook Islands by following the same time schedule.

For those who are determined to complete a circumnavigation of the Pacific, there is always the possibility of continuing a South Pacific cruise to the Far East. This is best accomplished by sailing from Papua New Guinea to the Philippines or Hong Kong and thence to Japan. The voyage can then be continued via the Aleutian Islands to Alaska, British Columbia and beyond. Such a detour requires careful planning, so as to sail among the islands of the Far East at the most favourable time, but such a northern sweep can be accomplished even if it takes longer than the return route via Tahiti and Hawaii.

Other itineraries for a return to the West Coast have also been tried out, although far less successfully, because of the high proportion of head winds encountered on the way to Hawaii, particularly in the case of voyages starting from Micronesia. Many of these attempts had to be abandoned and those who managed to complete them vowed never to make such an error of judgement again. This is why the importance of properly planning a return voyage to the West Coast cannot be emphasised strongly enough and the various alternatives outlined in these examples should be considered, preferably before leaving home.

Voyage F: A round Atlantic voyage

Compared to the Pacific Ocean, a circumnavigation of the North Atlantic is much easier to accomplish and it is in fact a voyage undertaken by an increasing number of people, who only have time for a one-year offshore cruise.

A late spring or summer start is recommended for those leaving from Northern or Western Europe, so as to cross the Bay of Biscay before the middle of August. Such a timing allows some time to be spent cruising along the coasts of the Iberian peninsula before heading for the Canary Islands, either direct or via Madeira. The crossing of the Atlantic can be made in November or early December along the trade wind route, arriving in the Caribbean before the end of the year. The next four months can be spent cruising among the Lesser Antilles, preferably from south to north, to avoid covering the same ground twice. The return voyage to Europe should start in April or early May and usually includes a stopover in Bermuda, although a few people sail directly to the Azores. The Azores provide a convenient springboard in mid-Atlantic for a return passage to reach the home port almost one year after leaving.

A similar round trip of the North Atlantic can also be undertaken from the east coast of either the USA or Canada. The best time for leaving is also the late spring or early summer when Western Europe can be reached either direct or via the Azores. Unfortunately such a timing does not allow too much time to be spent in any of the more northerly ports of Europe as one has to head south before the onset of the autumn gales. However, more time can be spent in Portugal, Gibraltar or Madeira before joining the other boats preparing the cross to the Caribbean from the Canaries. If one is short of time it is perfectly possible to cross to the Caribbean directly from Madeira.

The return voyage from the Caribbean to ports on the East Coast offers far more choices than those available to European sailors. The quickest way is to sail directly to the East Coast at the end of winter (April), either from the Virgins or Antigua, and to make landfall in one of the ports south of Cape Hatteras. Alternatively one can sail to Bermuda, from where it might be easier to reach ports lying further north along the East Coast. Yet another possibility is to sail to Florida via the Bahamas and return home through the Intracoastal Waterway.

An extended Atlantic circumnavigation has taken shape in recent years with an increasing number of boats sailing from the Canary Islands to Brazil, either direct or via the Cape Verde Islands and West Africa. Such a detour usually adds another year to the voyage which from Brazil continues along the coast of South America to the Caribbean where it rejoins the routes mentioned above.

3 Winds and currents of the world

Ever since man first ventured offshore in craft powered by the wind, he has looked for patterns in the winds' behaviour. Such observations may have led the early fishermen to use an offshore breeze to take their canoes to favourite fishing spots in the morning and the onshore breeze to waft them back home later in the day. These patterns are still made use of in some parts of the world where fishermen continue to use sailing craft as their forefathers have done over countless generations. Discovering a similar regularity for offshore voyaging was more complicated and some remote places in the world might have remained unpopulated until much later if early voyagers had been able to find a favourable wind to return home. The fact that there was a regular pattern to the winds was already recognised in ancient times and seasonal sailing routes were a common feature in the ancient world. The Chinese established such routes in the Far East, the Greeks used them in the Aegean, the Polynesians were helped by them to colonise the far flung islands of the Pacific, while Arab traders used the monsoons of the Indian Ocean to establish a regular link between India and East Africa.

This reliance on favourable winds for most offshore voyages lasted until the last century, when the greatly improved windward-going capabilities of sailing ships freed their masters of the shackles imposed by having to follow a route governed by the wind alone. However, in spite of being able to sail closer to the wind, neither the masters of the old clippers nor the skippers of modern yachts enjoy battling against head winds and most would still make a detour to pick up a fair wind. Even in a well designed yacht it is often wiser to cover a longer distance with better winds than to stubbornly try to follow the direct route between two points. This is the reason why it is so important to understand the prevailing wind systems of the world, which dictate most of the cruising routes described in the following pages.

The importance of defining the prevailing winds in certain areas of the world was already recognised by the Spanish and Portuguese navigators of the 15th and 16th centuries and their findings were kept a closely guarded secret for a long time. The first transatlantic voyage by Christopher Columbus showed his followers that a detour to the south was the best route to the newly discovered islands of the Caribbean, whereas a northerly sweep was to be preferred for the return voyage to Europe. Similarly in the Pacific, Magellan and other early navigators demonstrated that the voyage from east to west across the South Pacific was a relatively easy matter if one stayed within the south-easterly trades. However, a return voyage against the same trades proved impossible until finally the Spanish navigator Urganeta discovered the westerly winds of higher latitudes, which came to be called the anti-trades.

This world-wide wind pattern has thus been known for a long time and countless navigators have made use of this knowledge over the centuries. In his *Memoir of the Northern Atlantic Ocean*, published in its 13th edition in 1873, Alexander George Findlay succinctly describes this wind pattern in the following words:

'It has been well observed that the wind systems of our globe naturally govern the tracks of ships crossing the oceans, the trade winds carrying them from East to West within the tropics, while anti-trade or passage winds will bring them back again eastward beyond the tropics. If it were not for the intervening belt of calms, sailing directions for vessels going into opposite hemispheres would be of the simplest kind; but the well-known Equatorial embarrassments – "the doldrums" – generally make a very different matter of it, and cause many considerations to enter into the problem of shaping a course.'

The three main factors that influence the formation and direction of the wind are atmospheric pressure, air temperature and the rotation of the earth. The primary cause of wind is a difference of temperature. This in its turn leads to a difference in atmospheric pressure mainly because of the tendency of warm air to rise, which is then replaced by cold air drawn from elsewhere. Air also tends to flow from an area of high pressure to one of low pressure. Consistent areas of high pressure are situated between approximately the latitudes of 20° and 40°, both north and south of the equator. On either side of these belts of high pressure there are areas of low pressure. If it were not for the rotation of the earth, the wind direction would be either north or south, but because the earth is rotating on its axis in an easterly direction, air which is drawn towards a centre of low pressure is deflected to the right in the northern hemisphere and to the left in the southern one. The result of this movement in the northern hemisphere is the anticlockwise circulation of wind around a low pressure area and the clockwise rotation of wind around a high pressure area. The opposite is the case in the southern hemisphere, where the wind circulates in a clockwise direction around a low pressure area and in an anticlockwise direction around a high pressure area.

Maps 2 to 5 show the way in which winds on the equatorial side of the high pressure belts blow towards the equator from a NE direction in the northern hemisphere and from a SE direction in the southern hemisphere. North and south of those belts of high pressure the winds in both hemispheres are predominantly westerly.

In many areas these systems are distorted by land masses, which are subjected to more pronounced differences of temperature and barometric pressure than the oceans. The wind systems are also affected by the seasons since the annual movement of the sun causes the belts of high pressure to move towards the poles in the summer. Because of this movement, the wind systems associated with these areas of high pressure, particularly the trade winds, tend to shift a few degrees south or north with the sun.

Trade winds

These steady winds which blow on either side of the equatorial doldrums were so called because of the assistance they gave to the trade of sailing ships. They are usually NE in the northern hemisphere and SE in the southern hemisphere. They rarely reach gale force and on average blow at force 4 to 5. The weather associated with the trade winds is very pleasant, with blue skies and fluffy cumulus clouds. The barometric pressure within the trade wind belt is steady, interrupted only by a pressure wave, which causes a slight rise and fall of the barometer every 12 hours. If the diurnal movement of the barometer ceases or if it is very pronounced, a tropical disturbance can be expected. The entire trade wind belt, including the doldrum zone that lies between the two systems, moves north and south during the year. This movement is influenced by the movement of the sun, although there can be a delay of up to two months between the movement of the sun itself and that of the trade winds. The trade winds are less steady in the vicinity of the Intertropical Convergence Zone.

Intertropical Convergence Zone

This area of low barometric pressure lying between the trade wind regions of the two hemispheres is known as the Intertropical Convergence Zone (ITCZ), the equatorial trough, or more commonly the doldrums. The winds in this area are either light or non-existent and the weather is sultry and hot. The only interruptions are occasional squalls and thunderstorms, when rain can be very heavy. The extent of the doldrums varies greatly from year to year and season to season. Although the doldrums have earned their bad reputation because of the frequent calms that could delay ships for days on end, doldrum weather can sometimes be particularly unpleasant, with violent squalls and raging thunderstorms. Weather in the doldrums tends to be worse when the trade winds blow at their strongest.

Variable winds

A zone of light and variable winds extends on the polar sides of the trade winds, corresponding more or less with the high pressure areas of the two

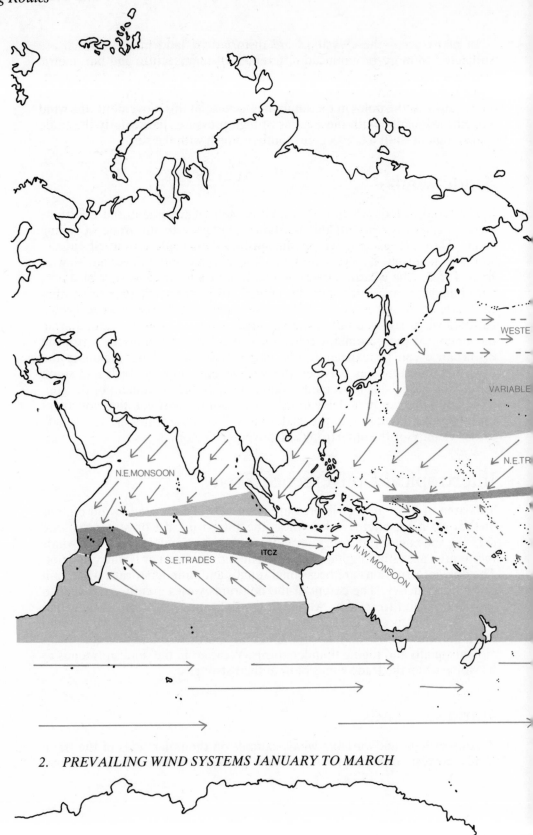

2. *PREVAILING WIND SYSTEMS JANUARY TO MARCH*

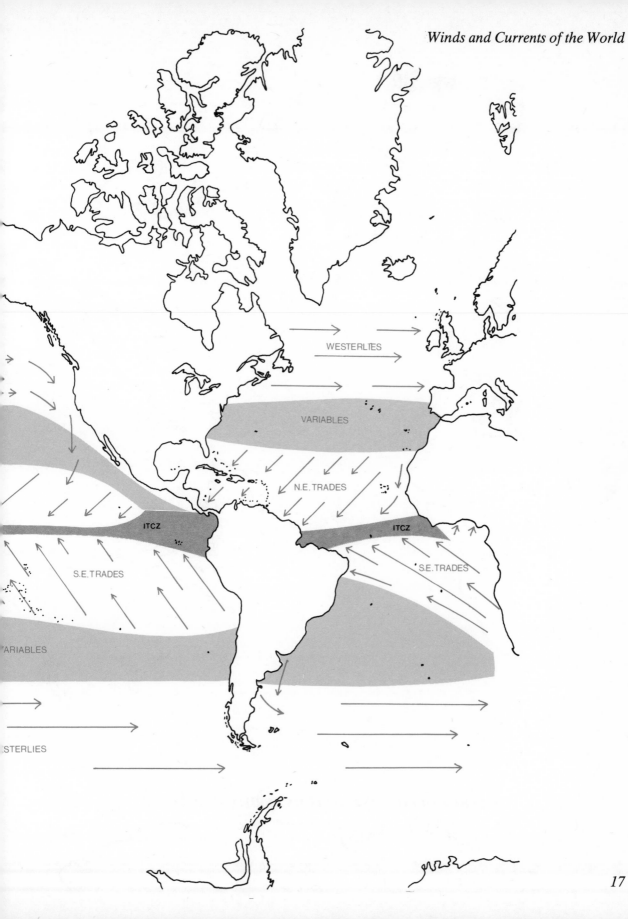

WESTERLIES

VARIABLES

N.E. TRADES

ITCZ

ITCZ

S.E. TRADES

S.E. TRADES

VARIABLES

STERLIES

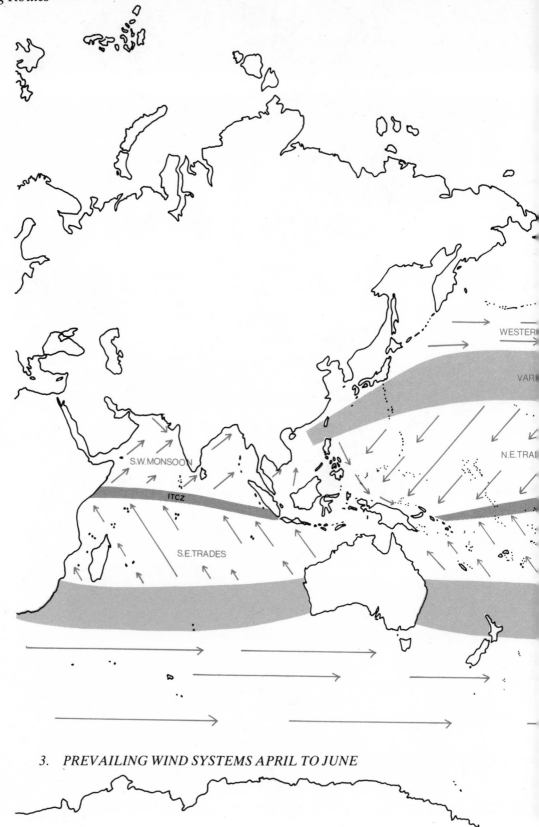

WESTER

VAR

N.E.TRA

S.W.MONSOON

ITCZ

S.E.TRADES

3. *PREVAILING WIND SYSTEMS APRIL TO JUNE*

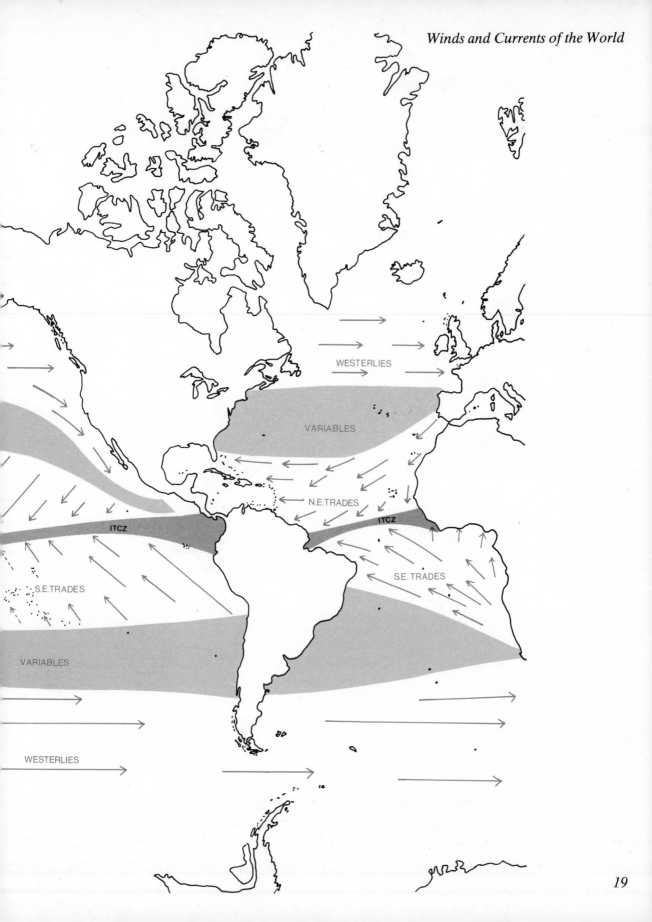

WESTERLIES

VARIABLES

N.E.TRADES

ITCZ

ITCZ

S.E.TRADES

S.E.TRADES

VARIABLES

WESTERLIES

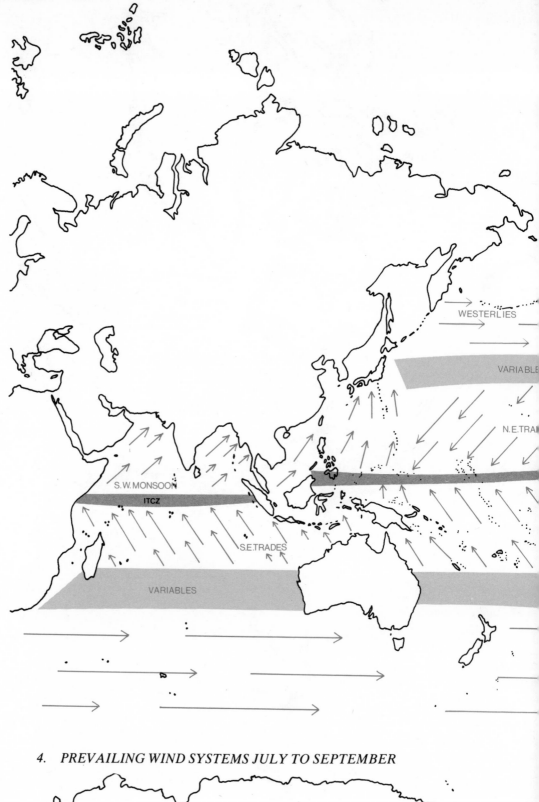

4. *PREVAILING WIND SYSTEMS JULY TO SEPTEMBER*

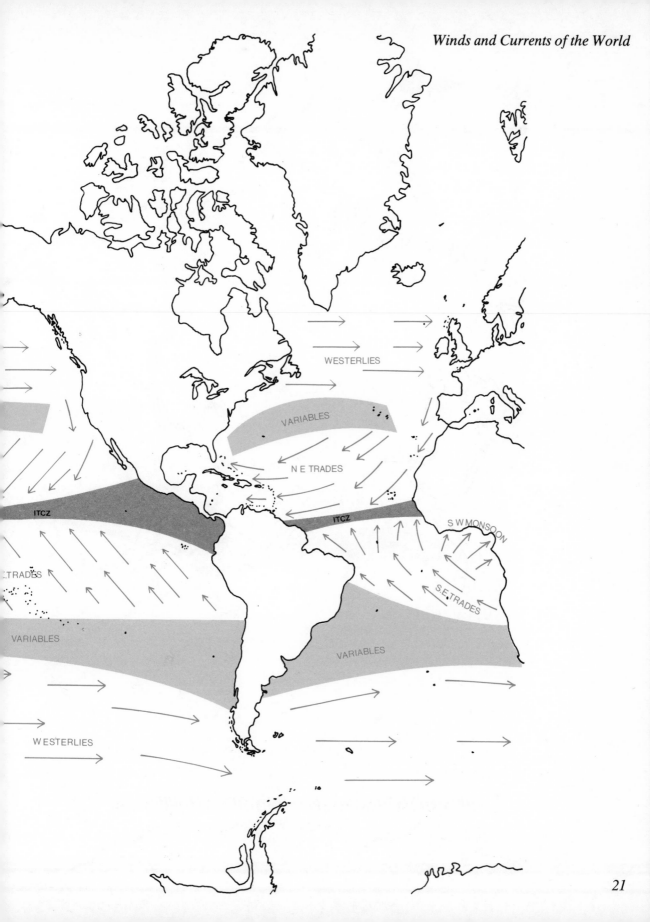

WESTERLIES

VARIABLES

N E TRADES

ITCZ

ITCZ

S W MONSOON

S.E.TRADES

.E.TRADES

VARIABLES

VARIABLES

W ESTERLIES

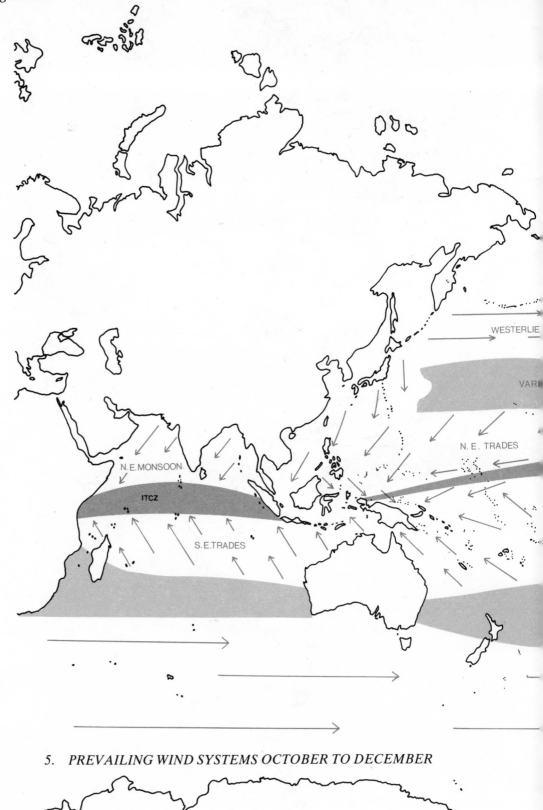

5. PREVAILING WIND SYSTEMS OCTOBER TO DECEMBER

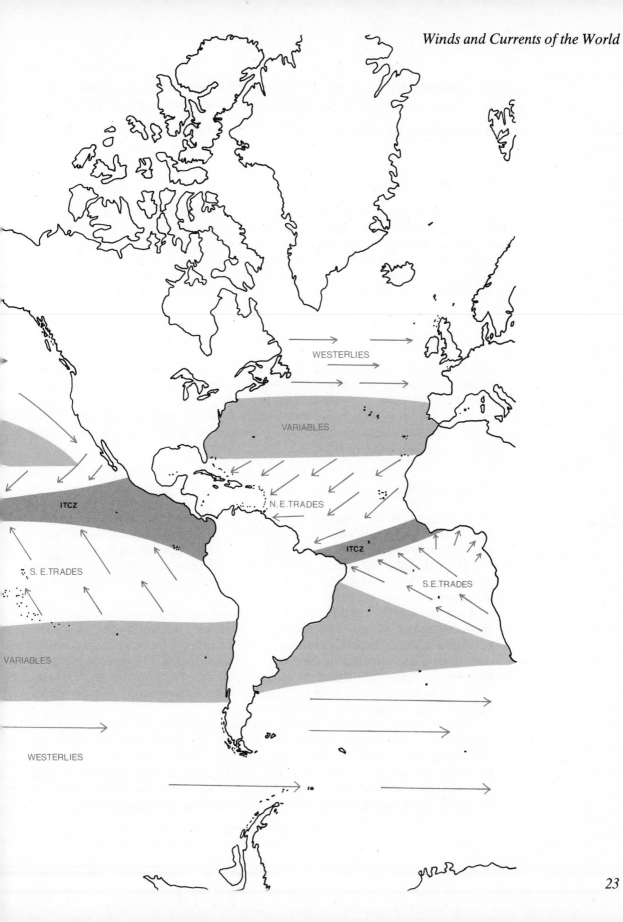

Winds and Currents of the World

WESTERLIES

VARIABLES

ITCZ

N.E.TRADES

ITCZ

S. E.TRADES

S.E.TRADES

VARIABLES

WESTERLIES

hemispheres, between latitudes 25° and 35° approximately. These zones were given the name of Horse Latitudes, because sailing ships that were becalmed in these areas were sometimes forced to kill the animals on board due to the lack of drinking water.

Westerly winds

The higher latitudes of both hemispheres have an increased proportion of westerly winds, which prevail north and south of latitude 35°. Westerly winds are stronger and more predominant in the southern ocean, where they often blow with gale force from the same direction for several days. Because of the more extensive land masses in the northern hemisphere, the westerlies of the northern oceans are lighter and less consistent.

Monsoons

Seasonal winds are experienced in several areas of the world, the name monsoon deriving from the Arabic word meaning 'season'. Such winds blow consistently from one direction for one season, and after a short interruption blow with equal consistency from the opposite direction. The most important regions affected by such seasonal winds are the Indian Ocean and West Pacific Ocean.

Depressions

A depression is an area of low barometric pressure, which is usually responsible for periods of unsettled weather, although not all depressions are accompanied by strong winds. Depressions occur most frequently in middle and higher latitudes, although the most severe storms encountered at sea are those formed in the low latitudes and of a revolving nature, discussed in the next section.

As stated earlier, winds in the northern hemisphere blow around low pressure areas in an anticlockwise direction, while in the southern hemisphere the direction is clockwise. Most depressions move in an easterly direction, a few moving in other directions at times. The speed at which they move can vary from very little to 40 knots or more. Usually depressions last about four to five days and their movement gradually slows down as they fill and the pressure rises.

The strength of the wind generated by a depression is dictated by the closeness of the isobars, which can be seen on a synoptic chart as lines joining areas of equal barometric pressure. The closer the isobars lie together the stronger the wind. The approach of a depression is always indicated by a falling barometer and usually by a change in the aspect of the sky and cloud formation. It may be worthwhile studying this aspect of meteorology, so as to be able to predict the kind of wind and weather to expect both on passage and at anchor.

Tropical revolving storms

Tropical revolving storms are the most violent storms that can be encountered at sea and it is prudent to try to avoid the areas and seasons where such storms occur. The extremely strong winds generated by these storms and the huge seas they raise can easily overwhelm a boat. Depending in which part of the world they occur, these storms are known as hurricanes, cyclones, typhoons or willy-willies. They blow around an area of low pressure, the rotation being anticlockwise in the northern hemisphere and clockwise in the southern hemisphere. The wind does not move around the centre in concentric circles but has a spiral movement, being sucked in towards the core of the storm.

As a rule these storms occur on the western sides of the oceans, although they are also found in other parts of the world. They usually form between latitudes 7° and 15° either side of the equator, but there have been many instances when tropical storms were formed closer to the equator. The breeding ground of tropical storms is the Intertropical Convergence Zone, where the two opposing trade wind systems converge. Under certain conditions of barometric pressure, temperature and moisture, the resulting whirlpool of air created at the point of convergence can develop into a severe tropical revolving storm. The most dangerous areas affected by such storms are the western North Atlantic from Grenada to Cape Hatteras, the western North Pacific from Guam to Japan, the South Pacific from the Marquesas to the Coral Sea, the north and north west coasts of Australia, the south west Indian Ocean and the Bay of Bengal. In some of these areas tropical storms occur several times a year, while others are only hit about once every ten years.

In addition to their circular motion, tropical revolving storms also have a forward movement. In the northern hemisphere the movement is initially WNW, storms recurving gradually to the N and NE as they reach higher latitudes. In the southern hemisphere the initial movement is WSW, storms recurving to the SE as they approach latitude 20°S. Sometimes a storm does not recurve but continues in a WNW direction in the northern hemisphere, or WSW direction in the southern hemisphere, until it hits the continental land mass where it gradually breaks up after causing a lot of damage. Occasionally the storms meander erratically and their direction is always impossible to predict with certainty. The speed of a storm is normally about 10 knots in the early stages and accelerates after recurving.

Any boat lying in the path of a storm, particularly its centre, will be in serious danger. The wind remains constant in direction until the eye has passed, then after a brief calm, the wind returns from the opposite direction, possibly with greater violence creating a rough and confused sea

MAY-JUNE
OCT-NOV

MAY-NOV

JUNE-DEC

DEC-APRIL

DEC-MARCH

DEC-MARCH

6. *WORLD DISTRIBUTION OF TROPICAL STORMS*

JUNE-NOV

JUNE-OCT

or putting vessels at anchor on a dangerous lee shore. Every storm has two sides, or semicircles, known as the navigable semicircle and the dangerous semicircle. In the northern hemisphere, the dangerous semicircle is the half of the storm lying on the right-hand side of the track in the direction in which the storm is moving. In the southern hemisphere, the dangerous semicircle is on the left.

The detection and tracking of tropical storms has greatly improved since the advent of weather satellites. Stations WWV in Fort Collins, Colorado, and WWVH in Kauai, Hawaii, broadcast hourly reports of tropical storms, their coordinates, speed of movement and wind strength. Tropical storm warnings for the Atlantic Ocean are broadcast at 8 minutes past each hour by WWV on 2.5, 5, 10, 15 and 20 MHz. Warnings for the Pacific are broadcast by WWVH at 48 minutes past the hour on 2.5, 5, 10 and 15 MHz. From the information obtained from these stations it is possible to plot the course of an approaching storm and take the best avoiding action. The path of the storm in relation to the vessel's latest position will show the degree of danger. If one is at sea, the best course of action is as follows:

(a) Northern hemisphere

When facing the wind, the centre of the storm will be between 90° and 135° on the right of the observer. If the wind veers, i.e. shifts to the right, the boat is in the right-hand semicircle, which is the dangerous semicircle. A backing wind is associated with the navigable semicircle. If the direction of the wind is constant, its strength increases and the barometer falls, the boat is exactly in the path of the storm. If the direction of the wind is not changing, but its strength decreases while the barometer slowly rises, the boat is directly behind the centre.

The generally accepted tactic for vessels caught in the path of a tropical storm is to run off on the starboard tack by keeping the wind on the starboard quarter. The same tactic should be applied if the boat is in the navigable semicircle when one should try to follow a course at right angles to the assumed track of the storm. Depending on the boat's behaviour in a quartering sea, one should try to run either under bare poles or storm jib. If the boat is in the dangerous semicircle one should heave to on the starboard tack or, if possible, sail close hauled on the same tack, with the object of moving away from the storm centre.

(b) Southern hemisphere

South of the equator, the centre of a tropical storm is between 90° and 135° on the left of the observer. If the wind is backing, the boat is in the dangerous semicircle; if it veers, the boat is in the navigable semicircle. The vessel is directly in the path of the storm if the wind is constant in direction. An increasing velocity combined with a falling barometer means that the

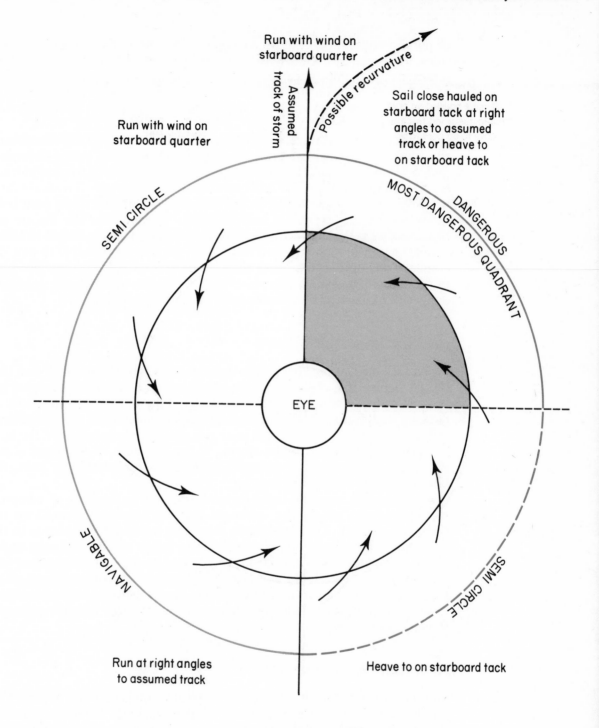

Run with wind on
starboard quarter

Assumed
track of storm

Possible recurvature

Sail close hauled on
starboard tack at right
angles to assumed
track or heave to
on starboard tack

Run with wind on
starboard quarter

SEMI CIRCLE

MOST DANGEROUS QUADRANT

DANGEROUS

EYE

NAVIGABLE

SEMI CIRCLE

Run at right angles
to assumed track

Heave to on starboard tack

7.   *TROPICAL STORM TACTICS*
NORTHERN HEMISPHERE

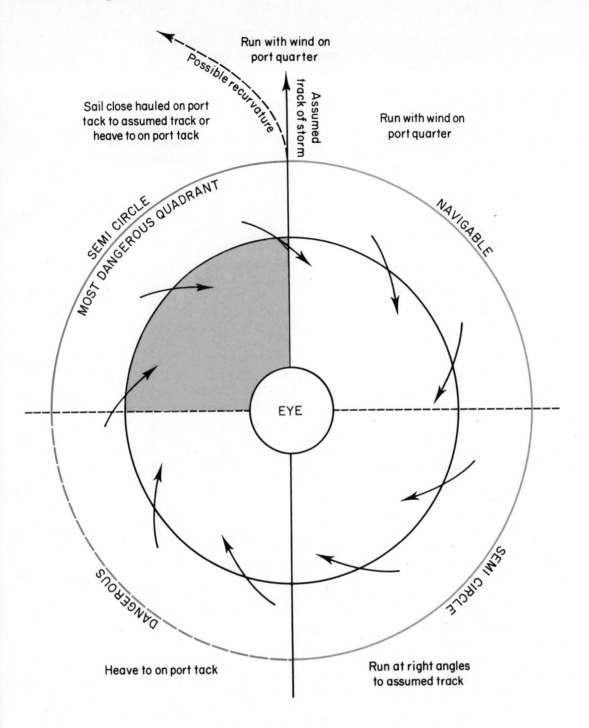

Run with wind on
port quarter

Assumed
track of storm

Possible recurvature

Sail close hauled on port
tack to assumed track or
heave to on port tack

Run with wind on
port quarter

SEMI CIRCLE

MOST DANGEROUS QUADRANT

NAVIGABLE

EYE

SEMI CIRCLE

DANGEROUS

Heave to on port tack

Run at right angles
to assumed track

8.   *TROPICAL STORM TACTICS*
SOUTHERN HEMISPHERE

boat is in front of the storm, a decreasing wind speed and a rising barometer means that the observer is behind the centre.

The best tactic if one is directly in front of the storm is to run with the wind on the port quarter. The same tactic should be applied if the boat is in the navigable semicircle, by trying to run away from the storm at right angles to its assumed track, also with the wind on the port quarter. If the boat is in the dangerous semicircle, one should try to sail close hauled on the port tack so as to proceed away from the storm centre. If this is not possible, the boat should heave to on the port tack.

Although these general rules are applicable in most situations, there can be circumstances when they should not be followed without question. Tropical storm strategy depends on many factors, such as the lack of sea room or the behaviour of a particular boat when hove to in strong winds or running before big quartering seas. Such considerations will dictate a different approach to the problem and there is unfortunately no fast rule that can be applied at all times. There is no doubt that the safest course of action is to avoid altogether the areas where hurricanes are likely to occur. Therefore the most important consideration when drawing up plans for a voyage is to make sure that the boat will not be in an area affected by tropical storms during the dangerous season. If one plans to pass through an area which is never entirely free from tropical storms, one should at least attempt to sail during the months of lowest frequency. Such a strategy is not too complicated to follow and many boats have spent several years cruising in the tropics without ever being in the wrong place at the wrong time, simply by leaving the hurricane zone for the dangerous season and returning at the end of it. The directions given for various cruising routes mention the hurricane-prone months, so that these can be avoided when planning a cruise along those routes.

Tropical storms are most frequent during the late summer or early autumn in both hemispheres. The safe season in the northern hemisphere is from mid-November to mid-June, whereas the safe season for the southern hemisphere lasts from about May until mid-November. The only tropical area entirely free of hurricanes is the South Atlantic. In the Western North Pacific no month is considered to be entirely safe, although typhoons are extremely rare in winter. In the Arabian Sea, cyclones do not occur in summer, but at the change of the monsoon, either in May–June or in October–November. Map 6 shows the world distribution of tropical storms and the months when they are most likely to occur.

It is not uncommon for tropical storms to develop outside the official seasons and the early part of the safe season should be treated with caution. The tropical storm seasons around the world are as follows:

Area	*Season*	*Highest frequency*
West Indies	June to November	September
NE Pacific	May to November	July–September

Area	Season	Highest frequency
NW Pacific	All year	July–October
Bay of Bengal	May to December	October–November
Arabian Sea	April to December	April–May, October–November
S Indian	November to May	December–April
S Pacific	November to April	January–March

Prevailing winds

Regional weather conditions will be described in greater detail at the beginning of individual chapters on each ocean, but it may be useful to summarise here the wind patterns of the principal six areas of the world as they appear on Diagrams 2 to 5.

North Atlantic: The NE trades blow roughly between latitudes 2°N and 25°N in winter, 10°N and 30°N in summer. In the northern part of the ocean, the winds are predominantly W becoming SW near the North American coast. Between the trades and westerlies there is an area of variable winds, known as the Horse Latitudes.

South Atlantic: The SE trades cover a wide belt roughly from the equator to 30°S during the southern summer. They move north during winter (July) when they are found between 5°N and 25°S. There are virtually no doldrums south of the equator. Constant westerly winds are to be found in higher latitudes, but they tend to become NW and even N on the South American side of the ocean, especially during the southern summer.

North Pacific: During the summer months the NE trades blow between latitudes 12°N and 30°N, but move down to an area comprised between latitudes 4°N or 5°N and 25°N in winter. Between latitudes 35°N and 55°N the winds are W or NW. The doldrums are less well defined.

South Pacific: The SE trades are less constant and reliable than in other oceans. At the height of winter (June to August) they blow in a belt stretching approximately from 5°N to 25°S. During the southern summer the trades are even less constant and blow south of the equator as far as latitude 30°S. Westerly winds blow consistently south of 30°S in winter and 40°S in summer.

North Indian: The winds are dominated by the two monsoons, NE in winter (November to March) and SW in summer (May to September).

South Indian: The SE trade wind extends from the equator to latitude 25°S in winter (July). During the southern summer (January), the SE trades can be found between about 10°S and 30°S and the NE monsoon also makes itself felt south of the equator as far as 10°S, but is deflected to the left by the rotation of the earth and becomes the NW monsoon. To the south of the

SE trade wind belt there is a zone of variable winds. The higher latitudes are known for their strong westerly winds.

Currents of the world

Currents occur at all depths of the oceans, but the only ones of real interest to the small boat voyager are the surface currents. Because the main cause of surface currents is the direction of the wind, there is a close relationship between their direction and that of the prevailing wind. Constant winds, such as the trade winds, create some of the most constant currents, although these do not always follow exactly the direction of the wind that has generated them. As in the case of the winds, the rotation of the earth has an effect on currents too and therefore in the northern hemisphere currents tend to flow to the right of the direction of the wind, in the southern hemisphere to the left. This is the reason why in the northern hemisphere the currents flow in a clockwise direction, while in the southern hemisphere currents generally tend to flow in an anticlockwise direction. Currents will be discussed in more detail in the individual chapters dealing with the three oceans.

4 Winds and currents of the North Atlantic

Maps 2 to 6

North-east trade winds

The NE trade winds extend in a wide belt north of the equator reaching from the west coast of Africa to the Caribbean Sea. They blow for most of the year on the south side of the anticyclone which is situated in about latitude 30°N, known as the Azores high. The northern limit of the trade winds is around latitude 25°N in winter and 30°N in summer, although the constancy of the trades cannot be relied on near their northern limits. Therefore when making a transatlantic passage it is advisable to be certain the trade winds are reached before turning west.

The constancy of the trades improves during the winter months, as does their strength. Although the average strength of these trades is force 3–4, it is not uncommon for them to reach force 6 and even 7 during January to March. The trades tend to be lighter and less consistent in summer, which is also the hurricane season. They have more of a northerly component in the eastern part of the ocean and become increasingly easterly in the Caribbean.

The consistency and reliability of the NE trades is of particular interest to those who intend to make a transatlantic voyage along the classic route starting in the Canaries. Although the winter months are reputed to have the most consistent winds, there are years in which these winds are found in lower latitudes than normal and it is not unusual for boats to cover almost half the distance to the Caribbean before falling in with steady winds.

Also described as trade winds are the Portuguese Trades which blow from between NE and NW off the western coast of the Iberian peninsula from April to September or October. Another regional variation of the NE trades is the *harmattan*. This is a hot and dry wind, created by the NE trades blowing over the deserts of Africa and reaching the sea laden with dust. Around latitude 20°N it is encountered only in the vicinity of the African coast, but as one moves further south, the *harmattan* can be experienced farther offshore, covering boats in a fine reddish dust and reducing visibility. This easterly wind normally occurs between November and February.

Another regional phenomenon associated with the area which is normally under the influence of the NE trades are *northers*. During the winter months vast anticyclones develop over the North American continent occasionally reaching as far as the Gulf of Mexico. A strong northerly flow of cold air develops ahead of this area of high pressure, and becomes a violent *norther* which is sometimes felt as far away as the Caribbean. The progress of a *norther* is usually checked by the higher islands of Hispaniola and Cuba, but to the north of these islands they can be particularly dangerous, mainly because of the steep seas which are created when a strong *norther* hits the north flowing Gulf Stream. The approach of a *norther* is usually heralded by a heavy bank of cloud on the N or NW horizon.

Intertropical Convergence Zone

The extent of the trade winds at all times of the year is influenced by the position of the Intertropical Convergence Zone (ITCZ) or doldrums. The ITCZ stays north of the equator throughout the year, although its position varies greatly, mainly in accordance with the seasonal movement of the sun, but also on a diurnal basis. The width of the doldrums is also variable and averages between 200 and 300 miles, although it tends to be wider near the African coast and narrower near Brazil. The weather inside the doldrum belt is more turbulent in the wider eastern region than in the west, with frequent squalls and thunderstorms occurring.

South-west monsoon

The heat generated by the land mass of Africa during the summer lowers the barometric pressure over that area and causes the ITCZ to be deflected towards the north. The SE trade wind of the South Atlantic is thus drawn across the equator and arrives off the coast of Africa as the SW monsoon. It lasts from June to October between the equator and latitude 15°N, but in the Gulf of Guinea light SW winds prevail throughout the year.

Line squalls

This is a common phenomenon encountered in the tropics, especially below latitude 20°N and near the African coast. These linear disturbances travel from east to west at 20–25 knots and are usually perpendicular to the direction of the prevailing wind. They are accompanied by thundery and squally weather. The first indication of an approaching line squall is a heavy band of cumulo-nimbus to the east. The wind is usually light or calm and the atmosphere oppressive. As the cloud approaches it becomes dark and menacing with the occasional thunder and lightning. The bottom of the cloud has the appearance of a straight line but it sometimes changes to an arch as it passes overhead. Suddenly there is a blast of wind from an easterly direction, which on average rises to 20 or 25 knots, although occasionally it can be much stronger. Shortly after the blast of wind, it starts to rain heavily. Such squalls last on average about half an hour, although sometimes they may last longer. The barometer does not indicate their approach, therefore they can only be detected visually. As some of these squalls can be quite vicious, it may be prudent in squall-prone areas to reduce sail at night, when their approach is more difficult to detect. Line squalls occur especially at the beginning and end of the rainy season (May to October) and are particularly violent near the African coast.

Variables

A band of variable winds extends across the Atlantic to the north of the NE trade winds. This is the area of high atmospheric pressure which straddles the 30th parallel, being situated slightly to the north of it in summer and to the south in winter. The winds in the eastern half of this area are usually northerly and can be regarded as an extension of the trade winds. In the western part of the ocean the winds are often very light and long periods of calms can be expected. This is the area of the feared Sargasso Sea where sailing ships used to be becalmed for weeks on end.

Westerlies

Westerly winds predominate in the northern part of the Atlantic Ocean, where the weather is often unsettled, mainly due to the almost continuous passage of depressions that race across the ocean in an easterly direction. The winds in these higher latitudes are less constant in direction than those of the Roaring Forties of the Southern Ocean, although the predominant direction is westerly.

Hurricanes

A large area of the western North Atlantic is affected by tropical revolving storms, which can theoretically occur at any time as hurricanes have been recorded over the last few centuries in every month of the year, although extremely rarely in some months. The normal hurricane season is from late May until early December, the highest frequency occurring from August to October, with a lower number occurring in the rest of the season. September has the highest frequency, with an average of two hurricanes per month over a period of 100 years, although in some years the number of hurricanes recorded in September was much higher. In fact both the frequency and intensity of hurricanes vary greatly from year to year, some years being extremely bad with up to 15 hurricanes, while other years go by with hardly any being recorded. A West Indian rhyme describes the season as follows:

'June too soon,
July standby,
August look out you must,
September remember,
October all over!'

Most hurricanes are born in the doldrum area west of the Cape Verde Islands. They usually travel west towards the Caribbean, their tracks moving clockwise around the perimeter of areas of high pressure. The area most affected by hurricanes is the Caribbean Basin, particularly the northern part of the Lesser Antilles, the Virgins, Bahamas, Bermuda, the Gulf of Mexico and Florida. At the beginning and at the end of the hurricane season, these storms sometimes develop in the Western Caribbean, from where they move in a northerly direction, affecting mainly the southern states of the USA. The later months of the season are particularly dangerous for those sailing in the Caribbean, as September and October hurricanes usually develop locally and warnings are shorter. Therefore if one intends to sail in the Caribbean during the hurricane season, especially among the Lesser Antilles, it would be safer to plan to be there at the beginning of the hurricane season (May to June) rather than towards its end (October to early November). Another useful tip concerning West Indian hurricanes is that if during May, June and July the wind remains above average strength, the rainfall below average and the humidity also low, less than two hurricanes can be expected to hit the Eastern Caribbean during August and September.

Tornadoes

Tornadoes and waterspouts occur in the same areas and during the same season as hurricanes. They usually travel in the same direction as the prevailing wind and their approach can normally be seen, especially as they rarely form at night. The wind generated by a tornado can be extremely violent, but as the actual area covered is very small, the likelihood of being hit by such a whirlwind at sea is quite remote. Waterspouts sometimes occur during afternoon thunderstorms in the vicinity of the coast, the ocean side of Chesapeake Bay being particularly vulnerable during the summer months.

Currents

The currents of the North Atlantic are part of a vast clockwise-moving system that occupies the entire ocean south of latitude 40°N. The NE trade

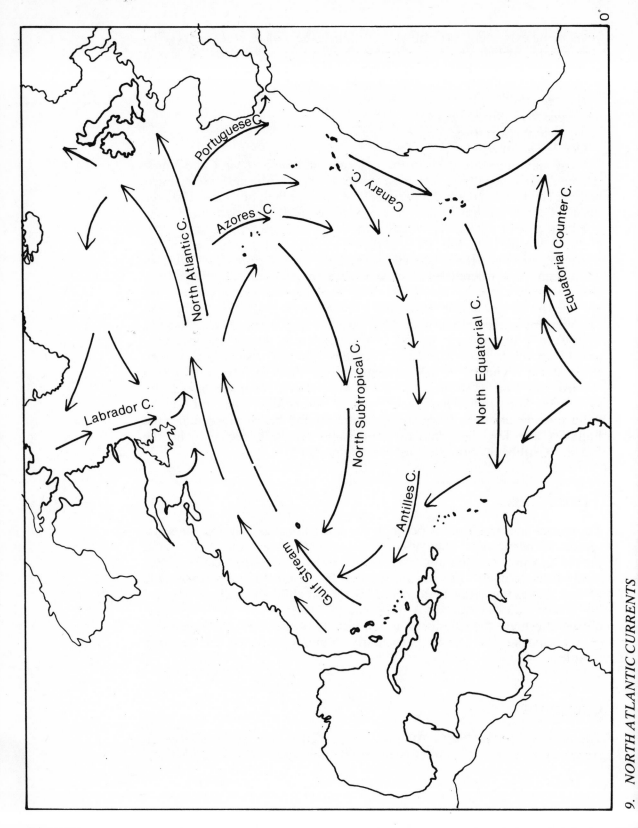

9. *NORTH ATLANTIC CURRENTS*

winds create the North Equatorial Current, which sets westward from the Cape Verde Islands to the Caribbean. Running to the north of it is the weaker North Subtropical Current. Part of the North Equatorial Current sets into the Caribbean Sea, while another branch flows northward along the Lesser Antilles and is known as the Antilles Current.

The mainspring of the North Atlantic circulation is the Gulf Stream, which in spite of its name does not originate in the Gulf of Mexico but is a continuation of the North Equatorial Current. The wide band of warm water sweeps along the eastern side of North America until it meets the cold Labrador Current, which forces it to flow in an easterly direction. From about longitude 45°W it ceases to be so strong and continues eastwards as the North Atlantic Current. In the eastern part of the ocean the currents are less well defined, the North Atlantic Current fanning out into different directions to form the south setting Azores Current and, further east, the Portugal Current. This current sets along the Iberian peninsula, one branch being deflected through the Straits of Gibraltar into the Mediterranean, while the other sets SW along the African coast to become the Canary Current. Ultimately this current turns west to join the North Equatorial Current, thus completing the clockwise system of the North Atlantic currents.

South of latitude 10°N the pattern of the currents is more complex. Between the two westward setting equatorial currents is the Equatorial Countercurrent. In winter this eastward setting countercurrent is most noticeable along latitude 6°N east of about longitude 45°W, but it diminishes in strength towards the South American continent where it disappears altogether. The South Equatorial Current combines in this region with the North Equatorial Current to form a strong westward flowing current which is deflected in a northerly direction along the coast of South America towards the Lesser Antilles.

5   Regional weather of the North Atlantic

Iberian Peninsula

The most significant constant feature of this area for sailing boats is the Portuguese Trades, which blow steadily down the coast during summer months. The prevailing wind is northerly from April to September and in June and July can extend as far as Madeira. The north western coasts of the peninsula experience more variable winds although there is also a more northerly component in the summer. In fine summer weather there are land and sea breezes along the coast although the northerly trades do modify the sea breezes to some extent. There is also more sea fog in summer near the coast, associated with calm or light weather. The climate is usually dry and hot, especially farther south.

In winter the winds are more variable along the entire coast, although winds from the western sector dominate. The number of gales, strong winds and amount of rain increase in winter with the highest frequency off the north west coast of Spain, where frost can occur in coastal areas. Squalls are also more common from November to March and are associated particularly with cold fronts from the W or NW. In mountainous areas these squalls can be very severe when they hit the coast.

In the southern part of the Iberian peninsula from Cape St Vincent to Gibraltar the winds are more variable in all months, the Portuguese Trades being less felt in this area, which allows a SW or W sea breeze to blow onshore. Sailing conditions close to the Straits of Gibraltar are affected by the highly individual nature of these Straits. The wind usually either blows into or out of the Straits and can be quite strong at times. The strong E wind is called a *Levanter* and when this blows hard against the prevailing east setting current flowing through the Straits into the Mediterranean, it creates a short sharp sea making entry to Gibraltar from the Atlantic difficult. The opposing *Poniente* which is a strong W or SW wind can make it almost as difficult to sail in the opposite direction, out of Gibraltar into the Atlantic. In the Straits there are frequent changes of *Levanter* and *Poniente*, although the *Levanter* occurs most frequently from July to October and is associated with rain and poor visibility. Also in the summer the occasional small depression moves north from Morocco towards Gibraltar.

North-west Africa

Although few gales hit this area and the weather is generally benign, only a few boats cruise the Moroccan coast on their way to the Canaries, the only port, with limited facilities for yachts, being Casablanca.

NE winds prevail over this area, being strongest in summer. The northerly Portuguese trades blow constantly along the Atlantic coast of Morocco in summer months, although land and sea breezes along the coast do have an effect on the trades. A sea breeze starting a few hours after sunrise pulls the wind to the NW where it increases to a maximum in the afternoon and drops at sunset. A land breeze from NE to SE blows late at night and in the early morning. The sea breeze starts later in the day in winter. In the late summer months a hot dusty wind can blow off the land from the S or SE.

In the winter the NE trades can be affected by depressions moving across the Atlantic or from the Canaries bringing N or S winds. The strongest winds come after the low has moved across, but these lows are not very common nor very strong. There are very few gales.

Further south the weather is affected by the position of the Intertropical Convergence Zone, which moves north in summer bringing northerly winds into coastal areas. In winter, when the trades extend further south, NE and E winds prevail, although some fairly strong W to SW winds can occur from October to March.

Although northern Morocco can be quite cold in winter, down to 8°C, the summer temperatures are hot, around 27°C when a sea breeze is blowing, but much more when the wind is off the land. Even 47°C has been recorded at Rabat! June to September are dry, with most rain falling in winter, often as short heavy showers, especially when one of the small depressions is passing over. As the coast tends south from Casablanca, there is less and less rain, and high temperatures all year round. In summer months there is often coastal fog in the early morning, especially where the land breeze blows over colder Atlantic water.

West Africa

For a taste of Africa, some of the best cruising on that continent is to be found in Senegal and Gambia with the possibility of navigating the larger rivers in this area. Although cruising in West Africa is usually incorporated into a longer voyage by those making a more southerly transatlantic passage to Brazil, one outstanding yachtsman, Pierre Ribes, has been sailing in his 26 ft *Sphinx* from France to Senegal and back for many years in order to distribute medical supplies as part of the aid programme he founded.

The main factor influencing weather in this region is the position of the Intertropical Convergence Zone, which moves north from January to July and south from July until December. In the more northerly areas of this

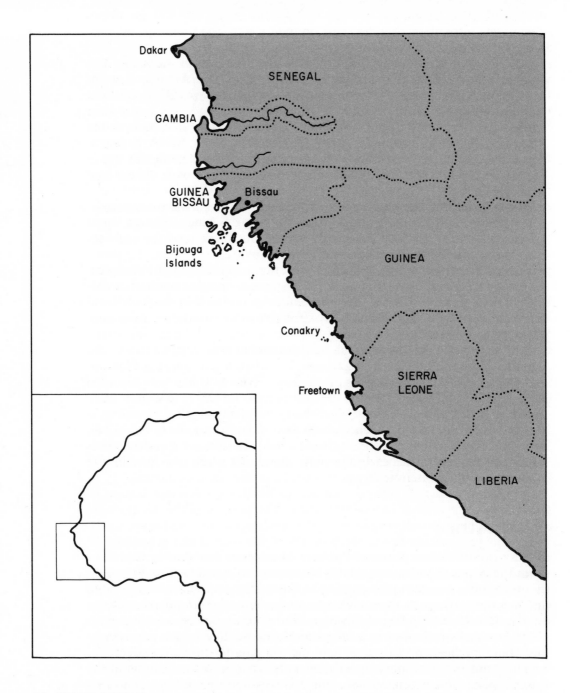

10. WEST AFRICA

coast the NE trades prevail for most of the year, although usually deflected as northerly winds along the coast. A short SW monsoon occurs in summer months. Further south the picture is opposite, with the SW monsoon prevailing for most of the year and the NE trades penetrating briefly in January. At points in between the proportion of NE trades and SW monsoon varies accordingly, while in the ITCZ zone itself the winds are variable. Around Dakar for example, seasonal north winds prevail from October to April, while from June to August the winds are usually from a westerly direction.

A feature of winter months when the NE trades are further south is the easterly *harmattan*. These hot winds can interrupt the trades between November and February and cause the temperature to rise as high as 40°C. The particles of dust carried by the *harmattan* produce a haze, which can cover large areas of coastal waters and as far out as the Cape Verde Islands, reducing visibility considerably, to as little as 50 yards on some occasions.

Gales and strong winds are almost unknown in this area, although West African weather is characterised by the line squalls which move from east to west. These thundery squalls can pack strong winds up to 30 knots for short periods and are usually followed by heavy rain for an hour or two. They can occur at any time during the wet summer season, most commonly at the beginning and end of the season. Temperatures are high in this area with little variation between the seasons, although winter months are drier and less sultry. As the coast tends south the wet season gets longer and starts earlier. Most rain falls during squalls and thunderstorms.

Azores

This group of rugged volcanic islands spread out in the middle of the North Atlantic do not have a lot of safe harbours, but these few are appreciated by sailors on long transatlantic voyages. The islands are also a popular cruising destination for yachts from Western Europe in the summer months.

The Azores boast an Atlantic climate, of which the dominant feature is the area of high pressure named after them. The position of the Azores high varies with the season, being more to the north in October and more south in February. It usually lies to the S or SW of the islands and in summer is often stationary, when prolonged periods of calm can be expected. At other times the winds are very variable in both strength and direction, although those from the western sector are slightly more frequent. Close to the land the wind is deflected, especially where the coastline is steep, and the direction of the wind varies from island to island and place to place.

The weather in the Azores is also affected by the lows which pass across the Atlantic from west to east. These usually pass to the north, except in winter when they can pass directly over the islands. When one of these fronts passes, the winds change quickly, veering from SW to NW and bringing rain. Rain occurs in all months, although more falls in winter,

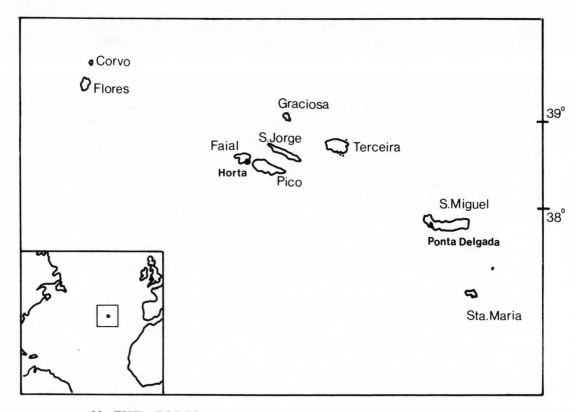

11. THE AZORES

especially associated with the Atlantic lows. The air temperature varies with the wind direction, but even in summer the nights can be quite cold.

Although not in the hurricane belt, extremely rarely a rogue hurricane has taken an abnormal path to pass near the Azores, but is generally weakened by the time it reaches that far. There is a moderate frequency of gales over the Azores, of which more occur in winter months.

Madeira

Lying over 350 miles off the coast of Morocco, Madeira is the main island of this group of mountainous islands of volcanic origin, famous for its dessert wine. The climate is warm in summer with mild winters and a variable rainfall which can sometimes be quite heavy.

The prevailing wind is north easterly, but because of the height of Madeira, the wind funnels around and can blow from the SW on the southern coast when it is NE offshore. The smaller island of Porto Santo is also very high and the NE wind accelerates down the mountain, blowing in gusts in its lee.

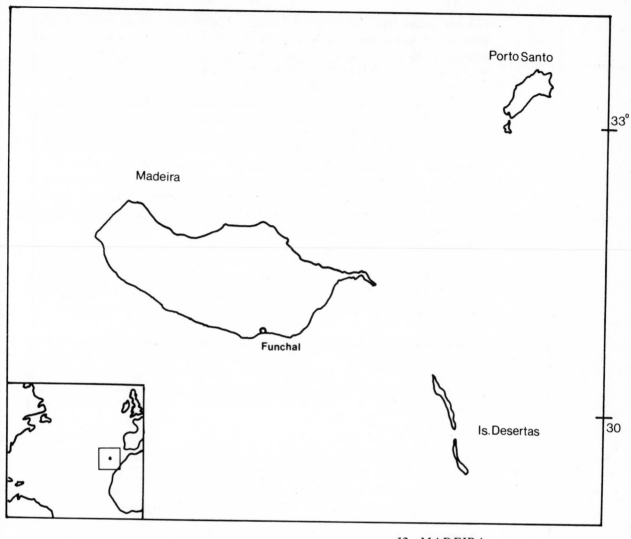

Porto Santo

33°

Madeira

Funchal

Is. Desertas

30

12. MADEIRA

   In winter the winds are more variable and come from all directions. The North Atlantic fronts that pass across the ocean from west to east occasionally pass more to the south and affect the island, but their effect is less strong than in the Azores. Dust hazes, which reduce visibility, can occur when easterly winds blow from the African continent.

Canary Islands

This archipelago close to the coast of Africa has been the traditional springboard for a transatlantic passage ever since Columbus started the fashion some five hundred years ago. Today the islands offer a large number of ports and facilities both for repairs and provisioning. Their popularity as a departure point has overshadowed the fact that it is possible to cruise in the Canaries all year round and few cruising boats are seen here apart from between September and December.

The prevailing winds are north easterly throughout the year, being strongest in July and August and lightest in October and November. The high volcanic islands however do cause local variations in the winds. As a rule there are different winds in the lee of the islands compared to the coasts exposed to the trade winds. When the NE trades are blowing strongly, an opposing wind usually blows on the other side of the island, varying in strength with the strength of the trade wind. A funnelling effect is also felt along the coasts of some of the mountainous islands and the trades can be accelerated by up to 15 knots in places.

The Atlantic lows rarely come as far south as the Canaries, although small lows do develop near the islands themselves and move north east towards Gibraltar or east towards Africa. Gales are rare, although occasionally these local depressions bring strong S and W winds. In summer months a strong easterly wind can blow hot from Africa.

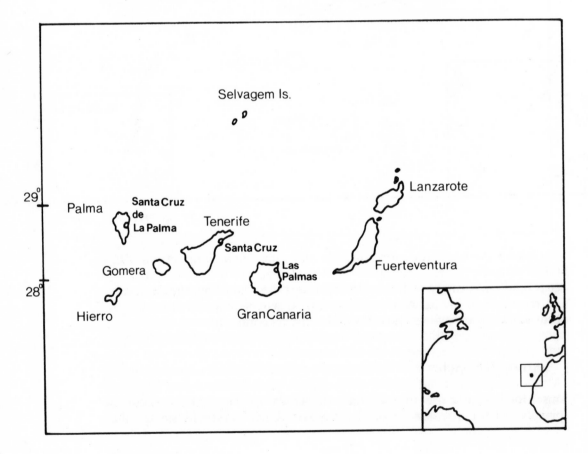

13. CANARY ISLANDS

The climate is very equable, being not too hot in summer and pleasant in winter. The rainfall varies enormously from place to place and as the high mountains trap moisture, the higher islands such as Tenerife, Palma and Gran Canaria have the highest rainfall. Lanzarote and Fuerteventura have little rain at any time. The southern coasts of all the islands are sunnier and warmer than the northern coasts which can be cool and cloudy.

Cape Verde Islands

This group of small islands two hundred miles off the coast of West Africa used to be a busy coaling station frequented by intercontinental steamers. They are being rediscovered as a convenient stopover for those wishing to shorten their transatlantic passage to the Caribbean or planning to make

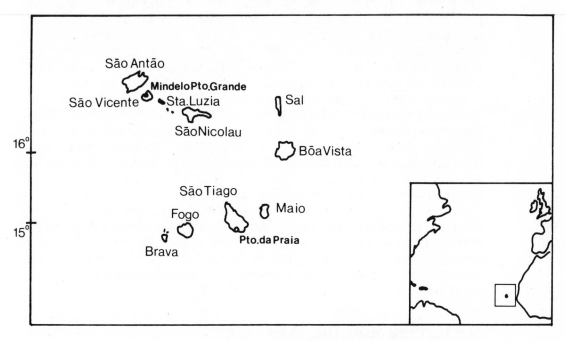

14. CAPE VERDE ISLANDS

their landfall in Brazil. Lying in the NE trade wind belt, the prevailing wind is NE most of the year, being stronger from February to June (15–25 knots). There are more variable winds as the convergence zone moves to its most northerly position in summer months, with fresh southerlies in August and September, the time of the SW monsoon.

Between December and February the strong NE trades blowing across Africa can produce *harmattan* winds. These often create a dust haze and cover the boat and sails in reddish dust. Distinguished by a yellow sky and a blurred horizon, this haze not only reduces visibility to a few hundred yards, but even when the visibility is several miles it makes it very difficult to estimate distances at sea until land or an object is seen. Therefore great care must be taken when approaching the Cape Verde Islands during these conditions.

Gales are rare in the archipelago, although squalls can blow down the valleys between hills and winds are much stronger on the trade wind coasts than on the lee coasts. The rainfall varies between the islands, occurring mostly between August and October, but in many areas there is little rain and long periods of drought do occur.

Guyanas

This region of the South American coast from Venezuela down to Brazil lies mainly in the belt of the NE trades, although the SE trade winds do penetrate into the area from August to October when the convergence zone moves north. The temperature is warm and varies little from 26–28°C throughout the year. May to July is the wettest season, September and October the driest months, the climate being wetter further south and east, with the wet season occurring earlier in the year and lasting longer.

The NE trade is strongest from January to March (15 knots) with a more northerly component earlier in the season and more easterly later on. From May through to July there are more calms and frequent squalls as the winds gradually change through ENE to ESE. The SE trade winds when established are not very strong (7–8 knots) and the change back to the NE in November occurs more suddenly and without the squalls that characterise the other change of season.

Near to the coast the winds decrease at night and pick up again in the morning; usually the earlier in the day this occurs the stronger the wind will be that day. Land breezes from SW to NW can occur close to the coast, especially towards the latter part of the year, but they do not last long. Squalls over the land are fairly common, bringing thunder and rain along the coast.

Venezuela and the ABC Islands

The fact that Venezuela and the offshore islands lie to the south of the hurricane belt, while still being in the trade wind zone, is the attraction of this area for cruising during the summer months when the risk of hurricanes hangs over the rest of the Caribbean. Although outside of the hurricane area, very rarely a rogue storm has been known to head this way and heavy swells can be experienced when a hurricane is passing further north. The offshore islands of Venezuela and the Dutch territories of Aruba, Bonaire and Curaçao are all under the influence of the NE trade winds for most of the year and enjoy similar weather conditions to the more southern islands of the Lesser Antilles.

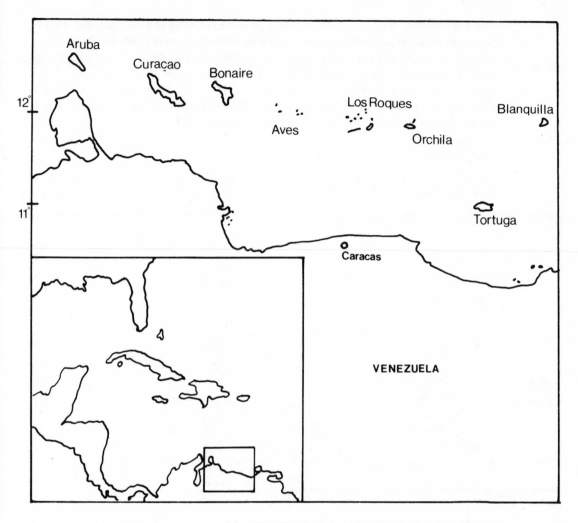

Aruba

Curaçao

Bonaire

Los Roques

Blanquilla

Aves

Orchila

12°

11°

Tortuga

Caracas

VENEZUELA

15. VENEZUELA AND THE ABC ISLANDS

The weather along continental Venezuela is influenced by the land mass of the South American continent. The NE trade winds have a much more easterly component along this coast, particularly from March to June. The season of the strongest winds is December to April when the trades blow NE to E. From June to September, when most people choose to cruise this area, the winds are lighter and more variable. The land mass causes easterly breezes which usually blow in the daytime and die out at night, it often being quite calm at dawn. The day breeze picks up during the morning and by mid-afternoon can blow quite strongly.

Venezuela is slightly cooler than the Lesser Antilles and can be as low as 18°C on a winter night. This is the driest part of the coast, the climate becoming progressively wetter both towards Panama and south east towards Brazil. The rain falls mainly in squalls along the mountains. From May to November, these are strong southerly squalls which lose their intensity as they blow offshore. In the Maracaibo area local afternoon squalls called *chubascos* can blow with up to 50 knots of wind. In the same area strong winds build up in the winter due to the desert heating up and drawing in the wind off the water. In the autumn hot short blasts called *calderatas* blow down the mountains from time to time.

Trinidad

Slightly apart from the rest of the West Indian islands, Trinidad attracts cruising boats particularly to its carnival, which is one of the most

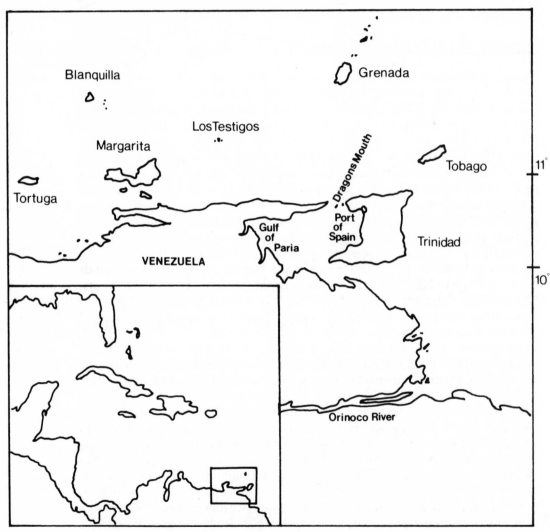

16. TRINIDAD AND VENEZUELAN ISLANDS

spectacular in the Caribbean. Although enjoying NE trade winds for most of the year, the more southerly position of Trinidad and its proximity to the Venezuelan coast does lessen their effect in the summer months from June to November, which is also the rainy season. A SE wind sweeps across the plains bordering the Gulf of Paria, building up a sea every afternoon in the gulf. Sea conditions are generally rough near the island due to the clashing of winds and currents setting strongly out of the Gulf of Paria and around the north coast of the island. The current in the Dragon's Mouth can set north 5 knots at times and seldom sets south.

Being south of the hurricane area, Trinidad rarely suffers any serious storms and this century only one wayward tropical storm has affected the island.

Lesser Antilles

These islands, which stretch in an arc from the coast of South America to Puerto Rico, are renowned for their consistently fine weather and excellent sailing conditions. Their greatest attraction is the steady winds and pleasant weather, with no extremes of heat or humidity. During winter months the NE trades blow with regularity and both day and night temperatures are pleasantly warm. In fact, the average temperature rarely varies from 26–28°C throughout the year. In late summer and autumn, when the trades ease up, the threat of hurricanes spoils this perfection. Few people carry on cruising during this period for fear of being caught out by a hurricane, although it is possible, provided some basic precautions are observed. The bumper season is the winter, when hundreds of boats arrive from over the ocean to join the fleets of charter boats based in the area.

From the middle of December until the end of April, the trade winds blow between NE and ENE, usually at a constant 15–20 knots. Occasionally these increase to 25–30 knots for a few days and can gust up to 45 knots at times, especially in late January and early February. Extended *northers* sometimes reach as far as the upper islands.

As summer approaches the wind tends to veer SE and even S, gradually returning to the E and NE towards the end of the year. In summer months the winds are lighter, from 12–15 knots in June through to September. This is the rainy season, particularly from August on into November. The higher islands are much wetter as they collect moisture from the trades and so are liable to heavy rain squalls at all times of the year. The lower southern islands such as the Grenadines are much drier, as are Antigua and other low northerly islands.

Squalls can occur throughout the year but are normally short lived, lasting from 5 to 20 minutes. Although most squalls rarely exceed 30 knots, the wind can reach 50 knots, while other squalls have no wind but much rain. As it is impossible to tell how much wind an approaching squall will bring, experienced sailors in the Antilles recommend shortening or

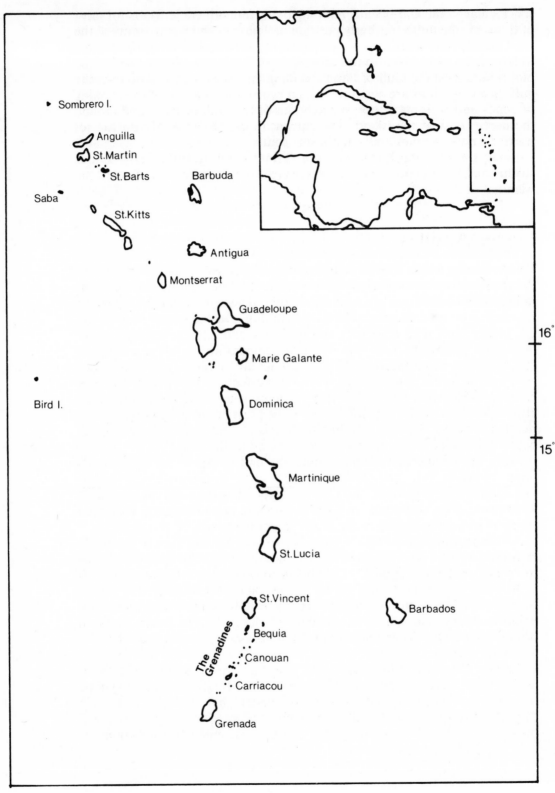

17. *LESSER ANTILLES*

dropping sails for *all* squalls. Squalls are more common in unsettled weather and are considerably affected by local conditions, especially close to the high islands. These high islands can block the trades completely in their lee and here the wind may shift around up to 180° at times. Winds blocked by the hills and then funnelling down larger valleys can hit a boat very suddenly.

Occasionally the weather is interrupted by an *Easterly Wave*, a low pressure trough which moves westward and can develop into a hurricane. Whenever the wind shifts to the north during the summer months, a stiff blow can be expected. West Indian hurricanes usually form about 800 miles to the east of Barbados and track north and west. Hurricanes are more frequent in the northern Leeward than the southern Windward Islands and rarely strike the most southerly islands such as Grenada. The further south and east one is at the height of the season the less likelihood of experiencing such a storm. A common path is for the hurricane to pass about the latitude of Guadeloupe or further north and then move along the Leeward Islands before turning north. The hurricane season is from June to November, with the greatest number occurring in September. Very rarely a hurricane strikes in May or December.

Virgin Islands

These smaller, lower islands to the east of Puerto Rico and north of the Lesser Antilles are an extremely popular cruising ground enjoying very similar weather conditions to the Lesser Antilles. The prevailing wind tends to be easterly, the trade winds being slightly north of east in winter and south of east in summer. The trades are stronger in winter months, around 20 knots, gusting occasionally over 30 knots. *Northers* can also affect the

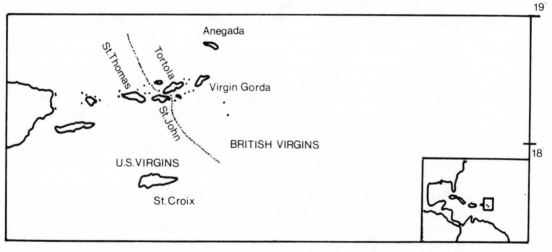

18. VIRGIN ISLANDS

islands in winter, although not so frequently nor so strongly as in other areas. Due to their position and comparatively low height, the islands tend to be dry with little rainfall. The Virgin Islands lie in the hurricane area and they can be affected by tropical storms every year.

Greater Antilles

Not such a popular cruising ground as the Lesser Antilles, the large islands of Cuba, Hispaniola, Puerto Rico and Jamaica are still visited by many yachts en route to other places. While experiencing the typical Caribbean weather pattern of winters dominated by the NE trades, punctuated by *northers*, and summers threatened by hurricanes, these large islands do affect local weather conditions considerably due to their height and position. Normally the winds along the coasts moderate at night as cooled air flows off the hills and out to sea. This land breeze can be quite strong at night off all the islands, which thus counteracts the tradewinds completely and gives calm conditions.

In winter months, the prevailing NE trades can become more easterly along northern coasts. During this period the islands are affected by *northers*, which bring strong N or more often NW winds and cold temperatures to the north and west coasts of the islands. The south coasts of the islands are shielded from the effect of these gales. These winds come without much warning out of a clear sky, although some indication may be the wind shifting around through S and SW beforehand.

In summer the trade wind has a more southerly component and is much lighter, the sea and land breezes being prominent. Thundery squalls are common over the whole area, especially in the late afternoon close to land. Some of the most violent squalls in the Caribbean, short but sharp with lightning and heavy rain, occur off the south coast of Cuba. But because the high islands block the passage of N winds, line squalls are more associated with the northern coasts of Hispaniola and Cuba. Jamaica is a little more sheltered than the other islands and has less seasonal change, the winds being generally lighter and more variable.

The Greater Antilles are in the middle of the hurricane belt and hurricanes accelerating through the Caribbean frequently hit the shores of these islands on their curved path northward. Their eastern shores are more frequently affected than the western shores. Cuba is also in the path of hurricanes originating in the Gulf of Mexico. The season extends from June to November, peaking in September.

The three small Cayman Islands lying midway between the SW of Cuba and Jamaica enjoy a very similar climate to the latter. The prevailing wind is NE with a southerly component in summer. *Northers* do affect the island in winter, although Cuba does block some of their force. The Cayman Islands are in the hurricane zone.

East coast of Central America

This coast has several attractive cruising areas, particularly the Bay Islands off the Honduras coast. The winter months are characterised by pleasant NE trade winds, although these are interrupted periodically by *northers* blowing down from the Gulf of Mexico with squally winds and heavy rain. The *northers* gradually decrease in intensity further south and are not so strong below the islands off the Mosquito Coast. However, these *northers* combined with strong NE trade winds can result in very strong winds called *intensified* trades in the most southerly portion of the Caribbean towards Panama.

From November to March the wind off the coast of Central America tends to be more northerly than the NE which prevails at other times of the year. This coast is particularly affected by land and sea breezes. The sea breeze commences from the NE in mid-morning and gradually increases, drawing around to the E between mid-afternoon and sunset. The breeze carries on moving around clockwise until in the night it blows moderately from the SE. In the more southern coastal areas this land breeze can become W and SW.

The summer rainy season is characterised by squally weather, especially in the late afternoon. It is rarely calm and a similar pattern of land and sea breezes prevails to that in the winter. These summer months from June to November are the hurricane season, but although within the zone, most hurricanes turn north before entering the Gulf of Honduras. Nevertheless there are exceptions and hurricanes do strike the Central American coast from time to time.

The best time to cruise these areas is in the late winter and early spring from approximately April to June, when the *northers* have ended, the trades are reliable, and before the hurricane season commences.

Gulf of Mexico

This is an area more crossed over than cruised in, having no pleasant cruising season. In the winter months from December to April when the prevailing wind is from the NE, the whole area is subject to strong *northers*, which sweep across the Gulf at a rate of about one a week and sometimes more frequently. These *northers* last about two days, can gust up to 60 knots and are accompanied by dark weather. Their arrival can be quite sudden with little warning and during this season boats must be prepared for them. Small signs of the arrival of a *norther* can be the NE trade wind shifting to the SE, followed by a calm and heavy dark clouds on the NW horizon. After a *norther* the weather usually stays clear for 4 or 5 days.

In the summer the prevailing winds are from the SE and the weather is rainy with heavy squalls and calm periods. From April to July land and sea breezes alternate along the south coast of the USA. The Gulf is one of the

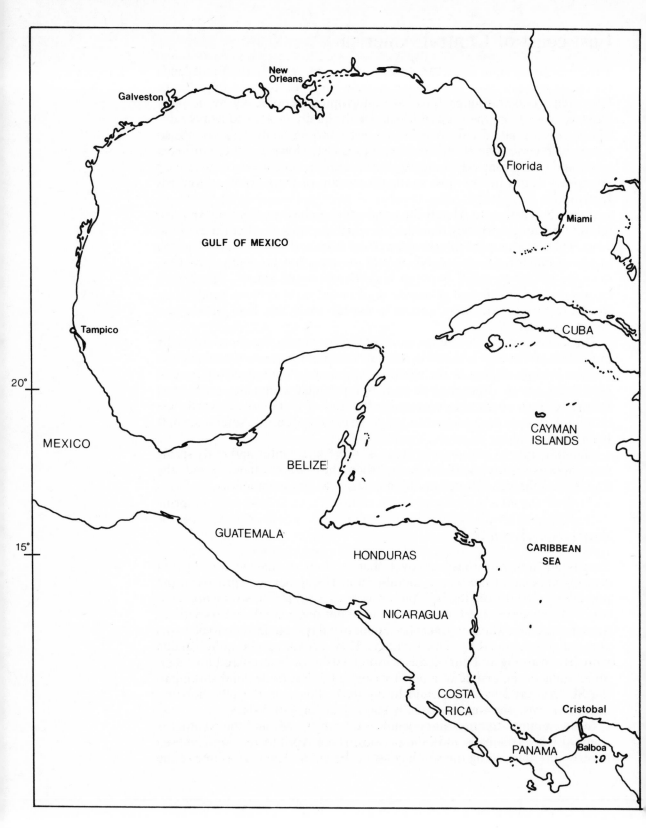

GULF OF MEXICO

New Orleans

Galveston

Florida

Miami

Tampico

20°

MEXICO

BELIZE

CUBA

CAYMAN
ISLANDS

GUATEMALA

15°

HONDURAS

CARIBBEAN
SEA

NICARAGUA

COSTA
RICA

Cristobal

PANAMA   Balboa

19. CENTRAL AMERICA AND THE GULF
        OF MEXICO

areas most affected by hurricanes in the season between June and November, being struck both by hurricanes that form in the Gulf itself and those travelling from other areas of the Caribbean. The usual pattern of hurricane movement in the Gulf is W, then NW, curving NE to strike the Gulf coast, although some do continue west and hit the north coast. From September to November hurricanes spawned in the western Caribbean are most likely to pass through the Yucatan Channel and then curve around north and east towards Cuba and Florida. Tornadoes, waterspouts and arched squalls are also a feature of the hurricane season.

In the southern part of the Gulf the winter trades are similarly interrupted by *northers* from October to March. From April to July the wind prevails from E and ESE and can be interrupted by calms and short strong squalls with thunder and heavy rain. At night a strong land breeze from S to SW blows off this coast for about 70 miles offshore until it meets the E and ESE trades.

Bahamas

These low lying islands and their associated banks and reef areas offer a wide choice of anchorages, especially to shallow drafted craft. Their popularity has declined of late due to reported cases of piracy and associated crimes connected to drug running, and yachts are advised to cruise in company in more remote areas.

The prevailing winds are from NE to SE with the most northern islands lying on the edge of the trade wind belt. As the islands are low there is no regular land breeze. *Northers* interrupt the NE trades throughout the winter and typically start with the wind veering to the S and SW. When the cold front arrives, the wind suddenly shifts to the NW, then N, and usually blows itself out in the NE. In mid-winter, the cycle can take several days, in spring only 24 hours. Most *northers* are dry, although on occasions they can be accompanied by rain and thundery squalls. However, they very rarely bring winds over 30 knots into the Bahamas. The more northerly Bahamas are the most affected by *northers*.

Summer weather starts around May after the last *norther* has blown itself out, and lasts until November. The trades are more SE in the summer and most winds during these months are from E or SE. During August and September there can be periods of calms, especially at night. The balmy summer weather can be interrupted occasionally by an *Easterly Wave*, a trough of low pressure found in the trade wind belt. This is usually accompanied by showers and high humidity. Sometimes *Easterly Waves* can degenerate into tropical depressions and even hurricanes. May to October are the wettest months and rainy squalls occur during this season.

The hurricane season is from June to November, although usually in June and July hurricanes pass to the south of the Bahamas. The most dangerous months are August to October, but hurricanes have been recorded as early

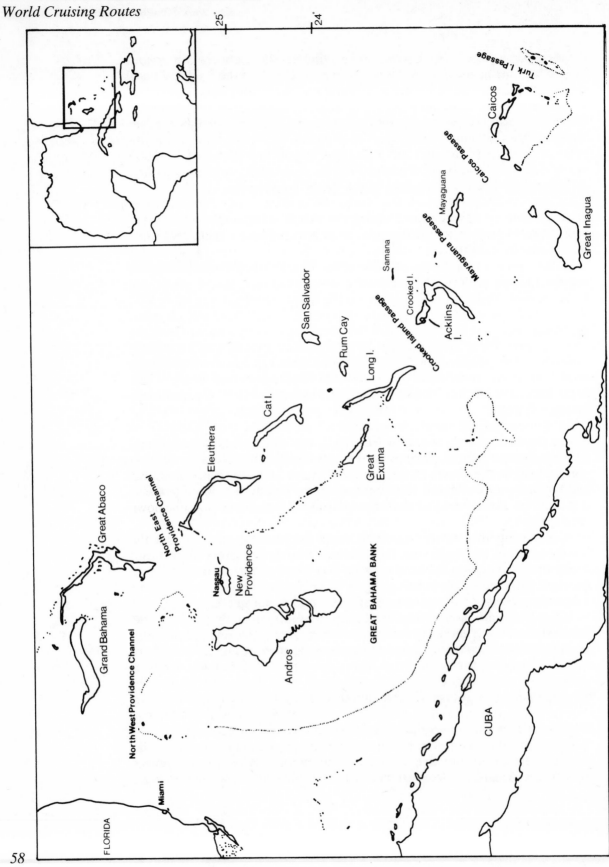

20 *BAHAMAS, TURKS AND CAICOS ISLANDS*

as May and as late as December. The Bahamas have one of the highest frequencies of hurricanes in the North Atlantic, as they are in the path of hurricanes generated in both the Atlantic and the Caribbean.

Temperatures vary little over the year, remaining in the region of 29–30°C in the day, although some winter nights can drop to 18°C and even lower when a *norther* blows.

US coast from Florida to Cape Hatteras

It is possible to sail this coast entirely within the Intracoastal Waterway system, but as only a limited mileage can be covered each day, many people still prefer to sail offshore.

In the summer months the position of the North Atlantic high affects this region. Florida, with its tropical climate, has prevailing E and SE winds, but these become more variable higher up the coast, tending to be more SW. Thunderstorms are more common in summer, although there are few gales. However, in this season hurricanes can affect the eastern seaboard over the whole region, those arising in the Atlantic usually approaching from the E and SE. Tropical storms generated in the Caribbean Sea come from the south and are more frequent in the months of September and October. The temperature is higher during these months, up to 30°C in the more southerly areas.

In winter the NE trade winds prevail in Florida from October to February, but further north the coast lies in the area of variable winds and gales can come from any direction. The whole area is affected by weather conditions on the North American land mass and the semi-permanent anticyclone stationed there. As the pressure rises, it develops into a *norther*, a N and NW flow of cold air that blows hard for several days at a time down this coast.

Also during the winter, gales occur as depressions move across the southern states eastward into the Atlantic. North of Florida these fronts bring strong SW gales, the wind veering W or NW behind the depression. In Florida, these depressions bring strong SE gales and colder temperatures. Cape Hatteras itself is particularly exposed and liable to NE storms.

When winds are lighter, land and sea breezes are felt along this coast and some coastal fog does occur from time to time. The seasonal variations in the weather are more pronounced in the north of the region.

Cape Hatteras to Cape Cod

This area is in the region of variable winds and is similarly affected by weather on the continental land mass, with winter *northers* and gales associated with fronts which move across to the east. Hurricanes can reach up to 40°N, which is the region of New York, and their tails may affect areas even further north from time to time, particularly in late summer and autumn.

Between Cape Hatteras and New York, summer weather is controlled very much by the North Atlantic high and although winds are variable, there is a high proportion of SW winds. Above New York, the coast falls into the prevailing westerly belt and the daily weather is influenced by the land mass more than the ocean, the weather systems moving generally in a west to east direction.

Rainy thunderstorms occur in June, July and August and often there is coastal fog, especially in the mornings. A lot of local variations occur in this area with sea breezes on some coasts and frequent wind shifts.

Cape Cod to Newfoundland

The prevailing winds over this area are SW or S, which veer to NW as depressions pass over. In summer there are few gales and the wind is lighter inshore than at sea. The area from Maine to Newfoundland and over the Grand Banks is affected by fog, particularly in the spring and summer. This is caused by a S or SW wind bringing warm moist air over the sea, which is kept cool by the Labrador Current. A careful lookout for the many fishing boats and lobster pots in this area must be kept under these conditions. A northerly wind tends to clear the fog. Also in spring and summer up to July, when the polar ice is breaking up, icebergs are sometimes carried south into the area off Newfoundland. The US coast and Nova Scotia are normally out of the iceberg zone.

Bermuda

This group of small islands linked by causeways, standing far out in the Atlantic Ocean, are a pleasant stopover for yachts on several routes. Bermuda is in the Horse Latitudes, the region of variables north of the trade wind zone and south of the westerlies. There is no prevailing wind and the weather on the island is affected by two main systems, the position of the Azores high and the flow of weather systems over the eastern seaboard of the United States into the Atlantic. In summer the Azores high is the dominating feature and produces SW winds of around 15 knots. The Gulf Stream also influences the climate, making the water around Bermuda warmer and keeping the winters mild. Even when cold air blows across from the North American continent, the temperature rarely drops below 15°C. The summer months can be hot and sultry with temperatures around 30°C.

Hurricanes cannot be ignored, although most of these tropical storms curve to pass to the west of Bermuda, very few storms passing directly over the island. The season is officially 1st June to 30th November, the greatest frequency occurring from August until October. In winter, although lacking

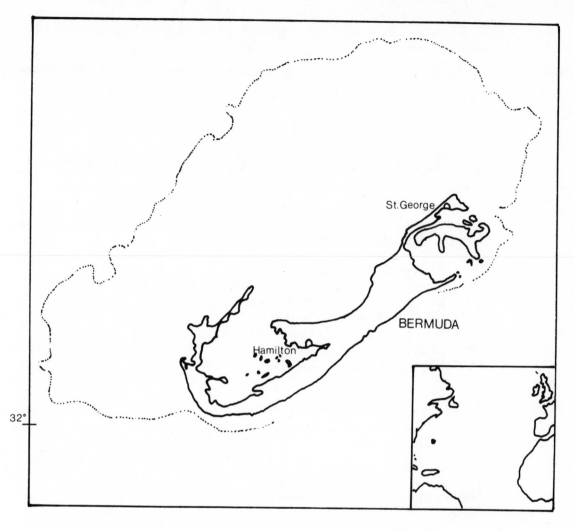

21. BERMUDA

the hurricanes, many high winds and gales do strike the island, February
being the worst month, with an average of eight gales.

6 Routes in the North Atlantic

AN10 Routes from North Europe

AN11 Europe to North America
AN12 Southbound from Northern Europe
AN13 Routes across the Bay of Biscay
AN14 Northern Europe to Madeira
AN15 Northern Europe to Canary Islands
AN16 Madeira to Canary Islands
AN17 Northern Europe to Azores

AN11 Europe to North America

| DIAGRAM 22 | Cape Wrath to Cape Cod 2560 miles |
| | Falmouth to Newport 2730 miles |

Best time:	May to August
Tropical storms:	June to November
Charts:	BA: 4011
	US: 121
Pilots:	BA: 27, 40, 59, 67, 68, 69
	US: 140, 142, 145

From the Vikings to the Pilgrim Fathers and singlehanders in the OSTAR race, the westbound transatlantic routes of high latitudes have been well sailed over the centuries. The great circle route from the English Channel (AN11A) is probably the most difficult as there is a battle with head winds all the way across. The alternatives are either to make a detour to the north, in the hope of finding more favourable winds (AN11C), a track closer to the great circle route from Scotland (AN11B), or to make a detour to the south, in search of warmer weather, either direct (AN11D) or via the Azores (AN11E). All of these routes, except the most southerly, are affected by fog and ice and their timing is therefore crucial. In July, the maximum

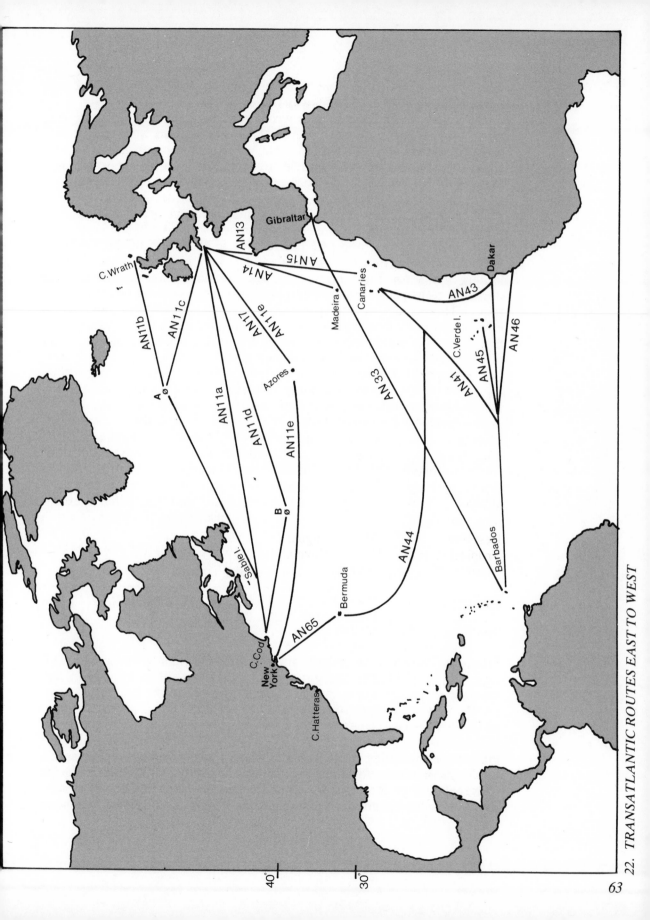

22. TRANSATLANTIC ROUTES EAST TO WEST

iceberg limit extends SE from Newfoundland to 39°N, 50°W (point B). In August the limit recedes to above latitude 41°N.

The object of the most northerly routes (AN11B and AN11C) is to stay north of the lows that move across the Atlantic from west to east and produce easterly winds in higher latitudes. These may attain gale force, but at least their direction is favourable. Between the lows the winds are most likely to be NW to SW. The routes converge at point A (55°N, 30°W), from where the great circle route is taken to the port of destination. As these routes pass through an area with a very high incidence of fog and ice, they should only be attempted later in the summer.

The intermediate route (AN11D) keeps to the south of the ice limit, which fluctuates from year to year and month to month. The average iceberg limits for July and August are mentioned above, but a more northerly course can be chanced if up-to-date ice reports can be obtained by radio. The winds on this route are mostly westerly with the added disadvantage of running against the Gulf Stream. It can be counterproductive to try to avoid the contrary current by moving south, as this brings the possibility of straying into the Azores high.

Route AN11E is a continuation of Route AN17 and although longer than the above routes, has the advantage of warmer weather and a mid-Atlantic stop for rest and reprovisioning. The course westward from the Azores will depend both on the final port of destination and the weather encountered. It should not move north of about latitude 37°N so as to avoid the southern limit of the Gulf Stream. South and south-westerly winds prevail along this route in summer. This route is the only one likely to be affected by tropical storms and this should be borne in mind if it is used after the middle of June. A stopover in Bermuda is not practical and not recommended, except in an emergency. Route AN65 should be consulted for details if a stop in Bermuda is envisaged.

AN12 *Southbound from Northern Europe*

DIAGRAM 22	Kiel Canal to Dover Straits 360 m

Best time:	May to August
Tropical storms:	None
Charts:	BA: 2182A, 2182B
	US: 37010, 126
Pilots:	BA: 1, 22, 27, 28, 54, 55, 67
	US: 191, 192

For routes originating in the Baltic, the Kiel Canal offers convenient access to the North Sea. All routes from Scandinavia and Northern Europe converge into the Straits of Dover on their way towards the Bay of Biscay. The early summer months are the best time for these southbound passages as weather conditions and winds are generally favourable both in the North Sea and the English Channel. The winds from May to July are mostly northerly and the frequency of gales in the North Sea is low. Good conditions can be relied upon to last until about the middle of August after which the risk of gales increases. September has some of the most violent storms, usually associated with the equinox. Although not ideal, October can be a reasonably good month for a southbound passage allowing those who have dallied too long to join the fleet heading south from Gibraltar and Madeira towards the Canary Islands.

AN13 Routes across the Bay of Biscay

DIAGRAM 22	
	Falmouth to La Coruña 430 m
	Falmouth to Lisbon 720 m
	Falmouth to Vilamoura 870 m

Best time:	May to mid-August
Tropical storms:	None
Charts:	BA: 4103
	US: 120, 126
Pilots:	BA: 22, 27, 28, 37, 40
	US: 143, 191

Whether starting off from an English harbour or some port in Northern Europe, it is advisable to make a last stop in Falmouth to wait for a good weather forecast before crossing the Bay of Biscay. A departure should not be attempted if SW winds are forecast, which are generated by depressions tracking across the North Atlantic. As soon as the depression has passed, NW winds can be expected and with a reasonable long-term forecast there is usually sufficient time to reach Cape Finisterre before a change in the weather. Regardless of the forecast and the actual direction of the wind, it is wise to try to make some westing and not follow a rhumb line across the Bay. As a rule, a SSE or SE tack should be avoided so as not to be embayed by a SW gale, which is the usual direction of the worst gales. Because of the relatively shallow water, seas can become extremely rough even in a moderate storm. The situation is sometimes exacerbated by a high swell generated by a hurricane blowing thousands of miles away.

   The best time to make this passage is in early summer, between May and July, when the weather is often settled and the winds favourable. Towards the end of the summer the frequency of gales increases and more attention to the forecasts should be paid from the middle of August to the end of September when some of the most violent storms have been recorded. Although called equinoctial gales, these violent storms can occur on either side of the autumn equinox and the seas generated by them in the Bay of Biscay can be extremely rough.

AN14 Northern Europe to Madeira

DIAGRAMS 22, 23		Falmouth to Funchal 1200 m
Best time:	May to July	
Tropical storms:	None	
Charts:	BA: 4011	
	US: 120	
Pilots:	BA: 1, 22, 27, 67	
	US: 143, 191	

As the direct course from the English Channel to Madeira passes close to Cape Finisterre, the same directions apply for the passage across the Bay of Biscay as for Route AN13. As the intention is not to stop in Northern Spain or continental Portugal, some westing should be made after leaving the English Channel so as to have sufficient sea room should a south-westerly blow up while crossing the Bay of Biscay. This would also avoid the shipping lanes that converge on Cape Finisterre.

During the summer, winds are mostly favourable with the Portuguese trade winds blowing off the Iberian peninsula and African coast. Also favourable is the Portugal Current which sets in a SSW direction.

In theory this passage can be made at any time of the year with the advantage on a winter passage that the weather usually improves as one moves south. If a late start is made as part of a transtlantic passage, particular attention should be paid to the weather forecasts during September and October, as West Indian hurricanes can influence weather conditions even on this side of the Atlantic. The worst weather on this route has been recorded in September when gale force south-westerlies are common.

AN15 Northern Europe to Canary Islands

DIAGRAM 22		Falmouth to Las Palmas 1400 m
Best time:	May to July	
Tropical storms:	None	
Charts:	BA: 4011	
	US: 120	
Pilots:	BA: 1, 22, 27, 28, 55, 67	
	US: 143, 191	

The direct course from the English Channel follows closely the route to Madeira and the same directions apply as for Routes AN13 and AN14. As such a non-stop passage from Northern Europe to the Canaries is usually attempted late in the season by boats hurrying to join the trade wind route to the Caribbean, the weather can be less favourable and the likelihood of gales much greater than in summer. This route is only recommended for those who wish to provision in the Canaries before a transatlantic passage to the Caribbean. If planning to sail on to Cape Town, Brazil or any other South Atlantic destination, it might be better to keep to the west of the Canaries so as to cross the equator on a meridian where the doldrums are narrower than in the proximity of the African coast. Transequatorial routes are discussed in Chapter 7.

AN16 *Madeira to Canary Islands*

DIAGRAM 23		Funchal to Las Palmas 285 m
Best time:	May to October	
Tropical storms:	None	
Charts:	BA: 4104	
	US: 120	
Pilots:	BA: 1	
	US: 143	

An easy down-wind run for most of the year. From November onwards winds tend to be strong at times and rough seas have been encountered between the two island groups.

AN17 *Northern Europe to Azores*

DIAGRAMS 22, 23		Falmouth to Horta 1230 m
Best time:	May to September	
Tropical storms:	None	
Charts:	BA: 4103	
	US: 120	
Pilots:	BA: 22, 27, 28, 55, 67	
	US: 140, 143	

The best time to make this passage is in June or July when favourable conditions can usually be expected. Although the likelihood of W and SW winds is quite high at the start of the voyage, the frequency of N winds increases further south during the summer. It pays to wait before leaving the English Channel until N winds are forecast, as they allow some westing to be made in the early stages of the passage. However, if W winds persist or strong SW winds are encountered en route and a direct course to the Azores does not seem practicable, it might be better to change plans and sail there via Spain or Portugal. On the subsequent leg from one of the ports on the Iberian peninsula one has the benefit of the Portuguese trades, although such a detour can add about 300 miles to the total distance.

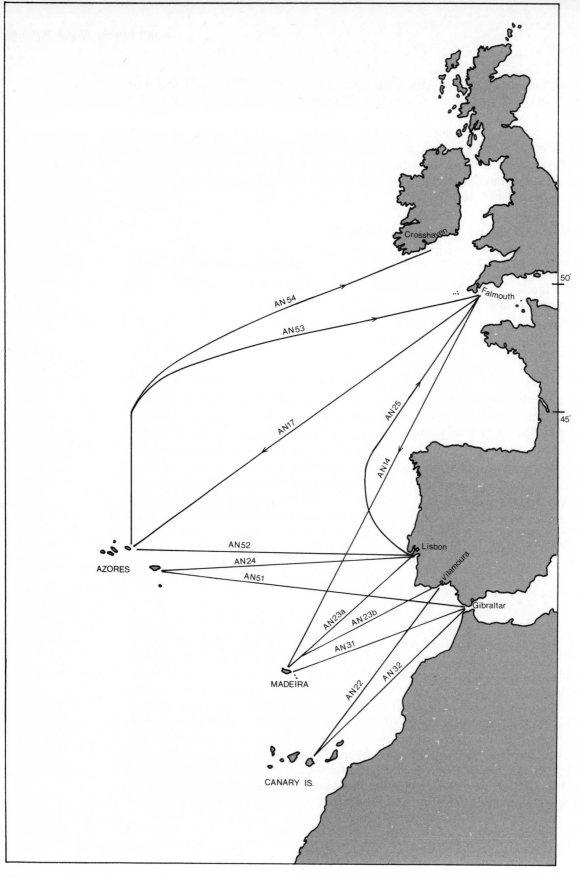

23. *ATLANTIC ROUTES FROM WESTERN EUROPE*

AN20 Routes from Portugal

AN21 Portugal to Gibraltar
AN22 Portugal to Canary Islands
AN23 Portugal to Madeira
AN24 Portugal to Azores
AN25 Portugal to Northern Europe

AN21 *Portugal to Gibraltar*

| DIAGRAM 23 | Lisbon to Gibraltar 290 m |
| | Vilamoura to Gibraltar 145 m |

Best time:	April to October
Tropical storms:	None
Charts:	BA: 92
	US: 51013
Pilots:	BA: 67
	US: 131, 143

Along the western coast of Portugal northerly winds can be expected, especially in summer, when the Portuguese trades are the prevailing winds. The winds become variable after Cape St Vincent and they usually blow either in or out of the Straits in the vicinity of Gibraltar. The current is favourable on this route as there is a constant flow of water from the Atlantic to the Mediterranean. The easterly *Levanter* wind produces a steep sea when blowing against the contrary current, which can make conditions difficult for a small boat when the wind is strong.

AN22 *Portugal to Canary Islands*

| DIAGRAM 23 | Vilamoura to Las Palmas 660 m |

Best time:	May to October
Tropical storms:	None
Charts:	BA: 4104
	US: 120
Pilots:	BA: 1, 67
	US: 143

Usually a pleasant passage, especially in summer time when the Portuguese trades blow consistently and the southward passage is further aided by the

Portugal Current. If leaving from Vilamoura a course should be shaped well off the African coast as steadier winds will be encountered further offshore.

AN23 Portugal to Madeira

DIAGRAM 23	Vilamoura to Funchal 510 m
	Lisbon to Funchal 530 m

Best time:	May to October
Tropical storms:	None
Charts:	BA: 4104
	US: 120
Pilots:	BA: 1, 67
	US: 143

Throughout the year the predominant winds on this route are from the northerly quarter, but best sailing conditions are usually experienced between June and August, when NE winds prevail. Although these Portuguese trades normally reach as far as Madeira, the likelihood of contrary winds increases during winter. The weather in the vicinity of Madeira is influenced by the position of the Azores high, light winds and calms occurring when this high moves south of its normal position.

AN24 Portugal to Azores

DIAGRAM 23	Vilamoura to Horta 980 m
	Lisbon to Horta 920 m

Best time:	June to September
Tropical storms:	None
Charts:	BA: 4103
	US: 120
Pilots:	BA: 67
	US: 143

This route between continental Portugal and its offlying archipelago has the benefit of the Portuguese trades during summer months when northerly winds predominate. If the passage is made in May, strong northerly winds will be encountered for the first days, being replaced by calms if a ridge of high pressure extending from the Azores high is crossed. The winds on the other side of the ridge normally blow from a SW direction and can be quite strong. At the beginning and end of summer the frequency of gales is higher, as are SW winds.

AN25 *Portugal to Northern Europe*

DIAGRAM 23	Lisbon to Falmouth 720 m
	Vilamoura to Falmouth 870 m

Best time:	April to August
Tropical storms:	None
Charts:	BA: 4103
	US: 126
Pilots:	BA: 22, 27, 28, 55, 67
	US: 142, 143, 191

The prevailing northerly winds of summer, the Portuguese trades, which provide excellent sailing conditions for southbound passages, make the task of reaching northern destinations very difficult throughout the summer months. The easiest solution is to sail up the coast in easy stages and set off across the Bay of Biscay only when conditions are favourable. The other alternative is to take an offshore tack and try to make as much northing as possible until more favourable winds are met. North of latitude 45°N westerly winds become increasingly predominant, but towards the end of summer the frequency of SW gales also increases, so it is better to plan this passage for the first half of summer. The time to avoid, if at all possible, is the period leading up to the autumn equinox as the equinoctial gales can produce hazardous conditions in the Bay of Biscay.

AN30 Routes from Gibraltar

AN31 Gibraltar to Madeira
AN32 Gibraltar to Canary Islands
AN33 Gibraltar to Lesser Antilles
AN34 Gibraltar to Northern Europe

AN31 *Gibraltar to Madeira*

DIAGRAM 23	Gibraltar to Funchal 610 m

Best time:	May to October
Tropical storms:	None
Charts:	BA: 4104
	US: 120
Pilots:	BA: 1, 67
	US: 131, 143

Gibraltar should not be left in a strong westerly wind as the wind reinforced by the permanent flow of water from the Atlantic into the Mediterranean makes it almost impossible to beat one's way out of the straits. An equally strong easterly wind does not improve matters much as it creates a short steep sea blowing against the current. Ideally Gibraltar should be left when the wind is light, but if this is not possible, it is better to keep to the North African shore where the current is weaker.

During the summer months the steady Portuguese trades usually ensure favourable sailing conditions for the rest of the trip to Madeira. At the beginning and end of summer, sailing conditions are less pleasant and both calms and SW winds can be encountered en route. Passages in May and November are particularly vulnerable to this kind of weather, but between June and early October the prevailing northerly winds should provide a fast sail for most of the way.

AN32 Gibraltar to Canary Islands

DIAGRAM 23	Gibraltar to Gran Canaria 730 m

Best time:	May to October
Tropical storms:	None
Charts:	BA: 4104
	US: 120
Pilots:	BA: 1, 67
	US: 131, 143

Sailing conditions to the Canaries are normally better than those encountered on the way to Madeira but this fact alone should not dissuade anyone from visiting green and lush Madeira. On leaving the Straits of Gibraltar, the same directions apply as for Route AN31. After Cape Espartel, the African coast should not be hugged too closely as steadier winds will be found further offshore. From June to September the Portuguese trades and a favourable current usually provide excellent sailing conditions along this route. In May and October the winds are less constant, although their direction continues to be predominantly northerly. November has a higher incidence of winds from other directions, but winds from the northern quarter are still in the majority.

AN33 Gibraltar to Lesser Antilles

DIAGRAM 22	Gibraltar to Barbados 3220 m
	Gibraltar to Antigua 3190 m

Best time:	November to April
Tropical storms:	June to November
Charts:	BA: 4012
	US: 120
Pilots:	BA: 1, 67, 71
	US: 131, 140, 143, 147

This long passage is only done without calling either at Madeira or one of the Canary Islands by those in a great hurry, as both these island groups lie close to the route. During the winter months, the prevailing winds on this route are NE, but one cannot be sure of finding the proper trade winds until south of latitude 25°N. The initial course leads between Madeira and the Canary Islands and one should continue in a SW direction until consistent NE winds are found. Only then should the course be altered for the port of destination.

If this passage is made during the summer months, which is the hurricane season in the West Indies, stations broadcasting early warnings of tropical depressions, such as WWV, should be listened to regularly. As the trade wind belt lies further north during the summer months, a more direct course can be sailed across the Atlantic than in winter. Between the end of May and July the frequency of hurricanes is quite low, but their frequency increases after August, reaching a peak in September.

More details about the transatlantic passage are given in Route AN41.

AN34 *Gibraltar to Northern Europe*

DIAGRAM 23	Gibraltar to Falmouth 1000 m

Best time:	April to August
Tropical storms:	None
Charts:	BA: 4011
	US: 126
Pilots:	BA: 1, 22, 27, 28, 55, 67
	US: 131, 142, 143, 191

The passage out of the Straits is particularly difficult when a strong easterly wind blows against the current, which always flows from the Atlantic into the Mediterranean. After the Straits have been cleared it is better to keep close to the northern shore where conditions are more likely to be favourable. From Cape St Vincent the course runs parallel to the coast, but this should not be hugged unless a stop is planned in one of the ports en route. During summer the prevailing winds are the Portuguese trades which make the task of reaching any northern destination extremely difficult. For those who are in a hurry it is better to head immediately offshore by sailing on the tack that makes most northing. Otherwise it might be easier to make short hops along the coast until better winds are met or Cape Finisterre is passed. Westerly winds may not be found until latitude 45°N is crossed. Often in late summer SW winds reach gale force in the Bay of

Biscay when conditions can be very rough so it is advisable to make this passage before the middle of August.

AN40 Routes from the Canary Islands and West Africa

AN41 Canary Islands to Lesser Antilles
AN42 Canary Islands to Cape Verde Islands
AN43 Canary Islands to West Africa
AN44 Canary Islands to Bermuda
AN45 Cape Verde Islands to Lesser Antilles
AN46 West Africa to Lesser Antilles

AN41 Canary Islands to Lesser Antilles

DIAGRAM 22	Gran Canaria to Barbados 2630 m
	Tenerife to Barbados 2590 m
	Gran Canaria to Antigua 2640 m
	Tenerife to Martinique 2620 m

Best time:	December to April
Tropical storms:	June to November
Charts:	BA: 4012
	US: 120
Pilots:	BA: 1, 71
	US: 140, 143, 147

This classic trade wind route has been plied by an enormous variety of vessels in the five hundred years since Christopher Columbus himself set sail from the Canary Islands to expand the limits of the known world. Although a lot has been learnt about prevailing winds and weather forecasting in the intervening years, the routeing suggestions made by Columbus as a result of his four voyages to the Caribbean are still valid and can hardly be improved upon. His two fastest passages took 21 days, an excellent time even by today's standards, following a track very close to the optimum route for the time of year. On both those voyages, a SW course was sailed by the fleet until steady trade winds were found in the vicinity of latitude 20°N and only then was the course changed to the west. This essential rule of not setting a course for the desired destination until well inside the trade wind belt has been followed to advantage by all navigators since.

The time of departure from the Canaries is crucial, both for the conditions to be encountered en route and the weather on the other side of the ocean. The hurricane season in the Caribbean lasts in theory about six months, although the really dangerous period is August to October, with September the peak month. Most people plan to cruise in the islands between December and April, which is not only the safest time of the year but also has the pleasantest weather, with trade winds blowing consistently throughout the winter months. Therefore a late November or early December departure from the Canaries suits most people's plans and this is the time when the majority of boats leave the Canaries for their transatlantic passage. An earlier departure is not recommended, mainly because of the risk of a late hurricane, but also because the winter trades are seldom established before the second half of November. From the second half of November until April the NE trade winds can be relied on to blow steadily along this route, their average strength gradually increasing during February and March. Although winds continue to be favourable, summer passages are not recommended for reasons of safety, the risk of hurricanes making such a timing hard to justify.

Every book that has been written on transatlantic voyaging has something to say about the optimum route for a trade wind crossing, although very little can be added to what Columbus found out himself. The first concern is to move out of the region of calms and variable winds which surround the Canary Islands as soon as possible. With a bit of luck a northerly wind may spring up, otherwise one must be prepared to wait, or motor. The old advice to make for a point at 25°N, 25°W needs some qualification as the winter trades seldom blow consistently as far north as latitude 25°N, so this suggestion should only be followed in summer-time. A more valid and often repeated suggestion is to sail SSW for 1,000 miles on leaving the Canaries, to pass between 100 and 200 miles north west of the Cape Verde Islands before turning west. The suggestion to pass close to the Cape Verdes has indeed a lot to recommend it as steadier winds are usually found in their latitude. Nevertheless the added mileage of such a detour must also be taken into account. A more direct route, which crosses latitude 20°N in about 30°W and latitude 15°N in about 40°W, will probably find the trade winds slightly later but has the advantage of being shorter. Unfortunately there is no hard and fast rule, as weather can vary from one year to another and in some years successful fast passages have been made by boats taking the shortest great circle route across.

The direction of the NE trade winds becomes more easterly as one moves west and they usually include a southern component as summer approaches. Their strength is not very consistent either and the average force 4 mentioned in some publications is simply an *average*, and nothing else. Although gale force winds are rarely experienced in winter, except in squalls, between December and March the trades can blow at force 6 for days on end, accompanied by a correspondingly high swell. The swell itself is only regular and steady in direction if the wind has been blowing from the same quarter over a long period, otherwise a cross swell is not uncommon on this route, with a wind swell being superimposed over another swell generated by some storm many thousands of miles away. In some years the uncomfortable swell has caused more complaints among transatlantic voyagers than the strength of wind, or the lack of it. It would appear that practically no voyage is spared at least one calm period on this run, such calms lasting from a few hours to several days. They are usually followed by a burst of trades heralded by a procession of squalls.

This route has the benefit of both the Canary Current and North Equatorial Current which set westward at an average rate of ½ knot. Their constancy, however, is not too reliable, although their direction is.

The above directions apply with small adjustments to all destinations in the Lesser Antilles, from Trinidad in the south to Antigua in the north. After the trade winds have been found the best course can be set for any particular island and the last few hundred miles will probably be sailed on its latitude. The route to the Virgin Islands passes so close to Antigua that it is advisable to make landfall there before proceeding. The same recommendation applies in the case of Anguilla and other islands to leeward of Antigua.

AN42 Canary Islands to Cape Verde Islands

DIAGRAM 30	Gran Canaria to São Vicente 870 m

Best time:	October to May
Tropical storms:	None
Charts:	BA: 4104
	US: 120
Pilots:	BA: 1
	US: 143

This route is taken by an increasing number of people using the Cape Verde Islands as an intermediate stage in their transatlantic voyage. One of the recommended sailing routes from the Canaries to the Lesser Antilles passes NW of these islands, so a detour is easily justified. Although provisioning in Mindelo on São Vicente, the main island of the group, cannot be compared to Las Palmas, the Cape Verde Islands make a good starting point for the transatlantic voyage mainly because they lie in the trade wind belt and fast passages have been made along their latitude.

During the winter months, from December to April, the NE trades blow strongly between the Canary and Cape Verde Islands. Fast passages are aided by the SW setting Canary Current which merges with the North Equatorial Current in the vicinity of the islands. The visibility near the islands is often poor, either because of haze or the dust laden *harmattan* which blows here in winter. In October and November, winds between the two island groups are less consistent in direction, although the NE trades gradually become more established as one approaches the latitude of the Cape Verde Islands. The area south of the Cape Verde Islands is subject to the SW monsoon from June to October, although the frequency of southerly winds is extremely low north of latitude 15°N, even at the height of the SW monsoon.

AN43 *Canary Islands to West Africa*

DIAGRAM 22	Las Palmas to Nouadhibou 450 m
	Las Palmas to Dakar 840 m
	Dakar to Banjul 95 m

Best time:	October to May
Tropical storms:	None
Charts:	BA: 4104
	US: 120
Pilots:	BA: 1
	US: 143

An increasing number of boats sail to West Africa, some of them en route to Brazil, others just making a detour before crossing the Atlantic to the Caribbean. The situation for cruising boats is gradually improving in this region which has a lot of attractions, as both officials and local people are getting used to the influx of foreign sailors.

The best time to make the passage south is in winter, when favourable winds will be found all along the coasts of Mauritania and Senegal. The NE trade winds blow consistently as far as the latitude of Dakar, but south of latitude 13°N they become increasingly light and after latitude 10°N are variable. The current along the African coast always sets to the south.

The ports along the coast where basic facilities are available are Nouadhibou in Mauritania, Dakar and Ziguinchor in Senegal and Banjul in the Gambia.

AN44 *Canary Islands to Bermuda*

| DIAGRAM 22 | Gran Canaria to Bermuda 2560 m |
| | |

Best time:	May to July
Tropical storms:	June to November
Charts:	BA: 2059
	US: 120
Pilots:	BA: 1, 70, 71
	US: 140, 143, 147

The number of boats sailing non-stop from the Canaries to Bermuda is relatively small, probably because the best sailing conditions on this route coincide with the start of the hurricane season in the Western Atlantic. The greatest frequency of hurricanes in Bermuda itself has been recorded from mid-August to mid-October, June and July being considered relatively safe months.

For anyone in a hurry to return to the United States, this direct route has much to recommend it and fast passages have been recorded. If the voyage is made during the safe season, from November to April, the winter trades are so far south that a detour to find them would take the track so close to the Lesser Antilles that it would be just as easy to make a stop there. As the sun changes its declination and starts moving north, the trade wind belt does the same and a passage to Bermuda can be done between latitudes 20°N and 25°N. Consistent NE and later E winds will be found around these latitudes for most of the transatlantic voyage. The temptation should be resisted to alter course for Bermuda too soon as this leads into an area of variables with a high frequency of strong SW winds, which are the prevailing winds in Bermuda during the summer. Ideally, latitude 25°N should not be recrossed until longitude 60°W has been reached, so that Bermuda is approached from the SSE.

AN45 Cape Verde Islands to Lesser Antilles

DIAGRAM 22	São Vicente to Barbados 2020 m
	São Vicente to Martinique 2090 m
	São Vicente to Antigua 2110 m

Best time:	December to April
Tropical storms:	June to November
Charts:	BA: 4012
	US: 120
Pilots:	BA: 1, 71
	US: 140, 143, 147

Columbus was first to see the attraction of these islands as a better springboard for a trade wind passage than the Canaries and he set off on his third voyage to the Caribbean from here. The advantage of this route is not only that the actual transatlantic passage is shorter but also that the Cape Verdes are situated for most of the year in the heart of the NE trades. Fast passages are usually logged by boats starting off from the Cape Verdes provided their course does not dip too far south into an area where the trade winds become less constant. More detailed directions for the transatlantic passage are given in Route AN41.

AN46 *West Africa to Lesser Antilles*

DIAGRAM 22	Dakar to Barbados 2460 m
	Dakar to Martinique 2530 m

Best time:	December to April
Tropical storms:	June to November
Charts:	BA: 4012
	US: 120
Pilots:	BA: 1, 71
	US: 140, 143, 147

Whether leaving from a port in Senegal or the Gambia, steady favourable winds will be encountered on this route, which has many similarities to Route AN45. As the Cape Verdes are so close to the direct route it may be convenient to stop there before proceeding west. If leaving from mainland Africa direct, especially from more southern ports, attention must be paid to the currents both in the vicinity of the coast and during the transatlantic passage. If sailing too close to the southern limit of the NE trades there is a danger of being pushed by a branch of the North Equatorial Current towards the doldrums and an area of less steady winds.

AN50 Routes from the Azores

AN51 Azores to Gibraltar
AN52 Azores to Portugal
AN53 Azores to English Channel
AN54 Azores to Ireland
AN55 West Africa to Azores

AN51 *Azores to Gibraltar*

DIAGRAMS 23, 24	Horta to Gibraltar 1120 m

Best time:	May to September
Tropical storms:	None
Charts:	BA: 4103
	US: 120
Pilots:	BA: 67
	US: 131, 140, 143

This passage is usually made at the beginning of summer when favourable winds can be expected for most of the way. The winds in the vicinity of the islands are variable, with a predominance of SW winds. In May and early June a belt of calms is usually crossed somewhere between the Azores and the mainland before entering the area of prevailing northerly winds. At times the calms can be quite extensive and one should be prepared to motor. Steadier winds can be expected towards the middle of summer; during July and August the strong Portuguese trades blowing at a steady 15–20 knots make this a fast and exhilarating trip. If a *Levanter* is blowing strongly when approaching Gibraltar, it might be better to seek shelter on the Algarve coast rather than put up with the uncomfortably steep seas produced by the easterly wind blowing against the current setting from the Atlantic into the Mediterranean.

AN52 *Azores to Portugal*

DIAGRAMS 23, 24	Horta to Lisbon 920 m
	Horta to Vilamoura 980 m

Best time:	May to September
Tropical storms:	None
Charts:	BA: 4103
	US: 120
Pilots:	BA: 67
	US: 140, 143

Similar directions apply as for the route to Gibraltar AN51, although ports lying further north on the Portuguese coast will be even more to windward at the height of the Portuguese trades than Gibraltar or Vilamoura. Allowance should be made both for the prevailing NE winds and the south setting Portugal Current earlier in the trip so as to approach the coast slightly to windward of the port of destination.

AN53 *Azores to English Channel*

DIAGRAMS 23, 24	Horta to Falmouth 1230 m

Best time:	June–July
Tropical storms:	None
Charts:	BA: 4103
	US: 120, 126
Pilots:	BA: 22, 27, 67
	US: 140, 142, 143, 191

The prevailing winds of summer are NE and therefore all northbound passages from the Azores are usually close hauled. A direct course for the English Channel is rarely possible, nor is it advisable as the westerly winds and east flowing current that prevail in higher latitudes will set the boat into the Bay of Biscay. The general advice for this route is to sail due north until steady westerly winds are encountered, but not to join the great circle route to the English Channel before latitude 45°N has been reached. North of the islands calms are frequent, their extent depending on the position of the Azores high and the ridges of high pressure that normally extend from it towards Europe during summer. If such calm spots are encountered one should be prepared to motor through them and make the desired northing. Even if there is no wind, the weather will be fine and sunny before it gives way to westerly winds, overcast skies and generally wet and cold weather. Summer weather for the English Channel is impossible to predict and the winds can come from any direction and at any strength. Visibility can become poor in the approaches to the Channel and both this fact and the presence of strong tidal currents, as well as the large amount of shipping, must all be borne in mind when making a landfall on the English coast.

AN54 Azores to Ireland

DIAGRAMS 23, 24		Horta to Crookhaven 1120 m

Best time:	June–July
Tropical storms:	None
Charts:	BA: 4011
	US: 126
Pilots:	BA: 22, 27, 40, 67
	US: 140, 142, 143

The same general directions apply as for Route AN53, but as destinations in Ireland are slightly more westerly than those in the Channel, it is even more important to sail north on leaving the Azores. Even if leeway is made to the west, this can be corrected later on with the help of the westerlies that normally prevail in higher latitudes. Calms are sometimes experienced in the vicinity of the Azores, particularly in July and August, when the Azores high reaches its maximum pressure of the year; calms and light variable winds might also be encountered en route.

With the exception of the odd sunny day at the start, the weather along this route is usually grey, wet and cold.

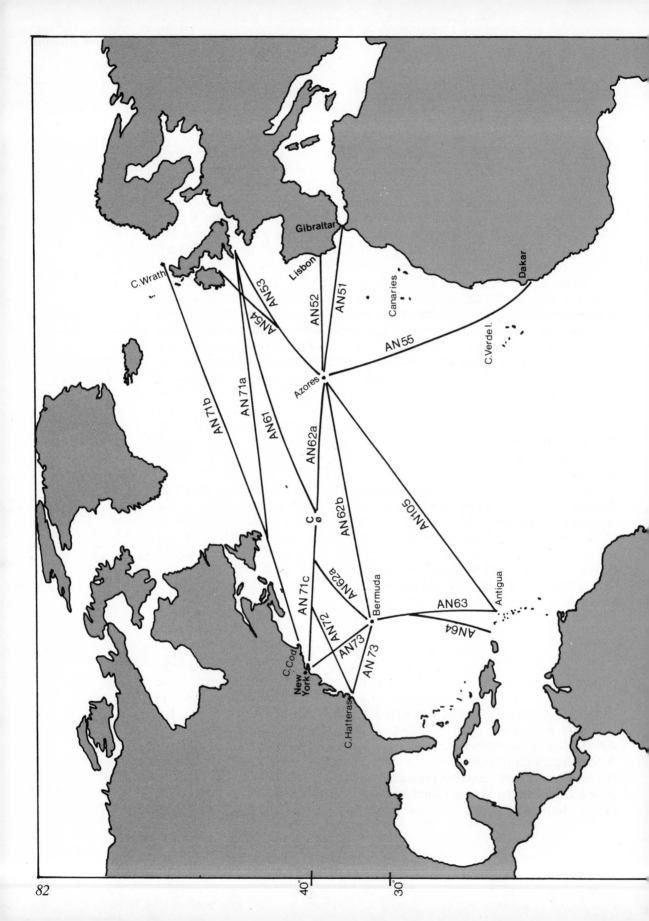

AN55 *West Africa to Azores*

DIAGRAM 24	Dakar to Horta 1560 m

Best time:	April to July
Tropical storms:	None
Charts:	BA: 4012
	US: 120
Pilots:	BA: 1, 67
	US: 140, 143

Both current and winds will probably be contrary on the first leg from Senegal to the Cape Verde Islands and strong to very strong NE winds can be expected, particularly during the winter months. The recommended route passes on the African side of the Cape Verde Islands, close to Sal, the most north easterly island of the group. From there a course should be laid for a point situated about 5 degrees south of the Azores, on the meridian of the port of destination. Generally it can be assumed that the trades will be lost somewhere between latitudes 25°N and 30°N, where the required northing will be easier to accomplish. Winds north of latitude 30°N depend greatly on the position of the Azores high. If this lies further south than its normal position, light winds or even calms can be expected in the run up to the Azores.

The time to make this passage depends on the destination after the Azores, for one does not wish to arrive too early in Europe. It is not advisable to attempt this passage before April, when the NE trades of winter start diminishing in strength. South of latitude 15°N they are replaced during the summer months by the SW monsoon, which blows between Senegal and the Cape Verde Islands from June to October. The start of the SW monsoon would therefore seem to be a better time to leave Senegal for the Azores as it would ensure better winds at least for the first part of the voyage.

AN60 Routes from Bermuda

AN61 Bermuda to Northern Europe
AN62 Bermuda to Azores
AN63 Bermuda to Lesser Antilles
AN64 Bermuda to Virgin Islands
AN65 Bermuda to USA

AN61 Bermuda to Northern Europe

DIAGRAM 24	Bermuda to Falmouth 2820 m

Best time:	May to July
Tropical storms:	June to November
Charts:	BA: 4011
	US: 120, 121
Pilots:	BA: 27, 40, 67, 70
	US: 140, 147, 191

Only used by sailors in a hurry to reach Northern Europe without a stop in the Azores, this route has the advantage over Route AN62 that once the prevailing westerly winds have been found they can usually be held for most of the crossing. On leaving Bermuda it is recommended to sail almost due north to latitude 40°N before joining the great circle route to the English Channel. The frequency of gales is lower to the south of this route, but the temptation to turn east too soon should be resisted because of the danger of losing the westerlies as one enters the Azores high which extends further north in summer. Ideally latitude 40°N should be crossed in 55°W, but if SW winds are picked up soon after leaving Bermuda, the point where latitude 40°N is crossed can be farther east. The great circle route should be joined from there for the rest of the passage. The Gulf Stream runs along most of this route and a favourable rate of at least ½ knot can be expected. Boats that have tried to follow the great circle route all the way from Bermuda to the Channel have experienced prolonged calms as the route crosses the area of high pressure.

Hurricanes rarely affect this route outside the immediate vicinity of Bermuda, but late summer passages are nevertheless discouraged because of the violent storms that often occur in the eastern Atlantic after the middle of August. Attention should be paid to the ice limit in the early part of the summer when the initial course should not go beyond 39°N in the area south of Newfoundland (see Route AN71).

AN62 Bermuda to Azores

DIAGRAM 24	Bermuda to Horta 1800 m

Best time:	May–June
Tropical storms:	June to November
Charts:	BA: 4011
	US: 120
Pilots:	BA: 67, 70
	US: 140, 143, 147

The Azores are situated in such a convenient position in mid-Atlantic that very few boats choose to sail non-stop to Europe. Because Bermuda lies to the south of the region of prevailing westerlies, the recommended strategy is to make as much northing as possible after leaving Bermuda in the hope of picking up favourable winds around latitude 40°N. The advantages of a route that goes north of 40°N (AN62A) are a greater certainty of SW winds and also a favourable current. The disadvantages are a higher frequency of gales and a colder and wetter passage than along a more southerly route which does not go beyond latitude 38°N. Opinions are divided as to which is the best course to follow and in fact some people go even further in their attempts to find the most pleasant alternative and follow a rhumb line to the Azores (AN62B), which at least has warmer weather, but is often bedevilled by calms and head winds. If the northern route is chosen, it is advisable not to sail beyond 40°N before point C (39°00'N, 50°00'W) is reached, because of the danger of ice in the early part of summer.

Looking at the records of passages made over a number of years, it would indeed appear that the slowest passages were made by those who were not prepared to go far enough north in search of westerlies. Most of those who stayed south of latitude 38°N encountered calms, as they entered the ridge of high pressure that extends between Bermuda and the Azores much earlier than if they had kept further north. Sooner or later the Azores high will slow down any boat making this passage, but by approaching the Azores from the north west rather than the west, the ridge of high pressure will be crossed at right angles and the time needed to cross it will be shorter. At such times the use of the engine is recommended and, particularly if taking a southern route, a good supply of fuel should be taken on board before leaving Bermuda.

May and June are the best months to make this passage, a later start being preferable if the northern route is chosen. If this decision is taken, it is best to commit oneself fully to that route and sail almost NNE on leaving Bermuda so as to enter the region of westerlies as soon as possible. After the beginning of July, the risk of hurricanes becomes increasingly higher in the area around Bermuda and this passage should only be made at such a time if absolutely necessary. The risk of hurricanes recedes as one moves east across the Atlantic, although the effects of a hurricane can be felt as far east as the Bay of Biscay.

AN63 *Bermuda to Lesser Antilles*

DIAGRAMS 24, 25		Bermuda to Antigua 940 m

Best time:	November to mid-December
Tropical storms:	June to November
Charts:	BA: 3273
	US: 124
Pilots:	BA: 70, 71
	US: 140, 147

The same directions apply as for Route AN64 until the area of trade winds has been reached. As the northern approaches to the Lesser Antilles are extremely dangerous and boats are lost every year on the many unlit reefs, as much easting as possible should be made in the early part of the passage so as to pass well to windward of all dangers and make a landfall on Barbuda. If this proves to be impossible, it is better to choose an easier landfall and continue to Antigua or any other island in shorter, daily stages.

Although a passage along this route during the hurricane season cannot be recommended, fair weather can be expected at the beginning of summer when the risk of hurricanes is not very high. If southerly winds are encountered on leaving Bermuda, which is very likely, these should be used to make some easting before the trades are found near latitude 25°N. Occasionally the summer trades do not have a southerly component and then it is possible to lay the Leeward Islands, Antigua being one of the easiest to approach. Otherwise it might be necessary to either tack or head for the Virgins.

AN64 Bermuda to Virgin Islands

DIAGRAMS 24, 25   Bermuda to St Thomas 850 m

Best time:	November to mid-December
Tropical storms:	June to November
Charts:	BA: 3273
	US: 124
Pilots:	BA: 70, 71
	US: 140, 147

It is difficult to suggest an optimum time for this passage as the summer carries the danger of tropical storms and the winter that of northerly gales. The best time to make this passage is at the change of seasons, when the risk of hurricanes has abated and the frequency of winter storms is acceptably low. The winds on leaving Bermuda could be from any direction and if they are light, it might be advisable to motor so as to make as much southing as possible. Having passed through the belt of variables, the NE trade winds should be found between latitudes 22°N and 25°N. Approaching the islands from the north presents serious difficulties as most dangers are unlit. It might be advisable to make a landfall on Sombrero Island, which has a light, and approach the Virgins from windward rather than try to make landfall directly on St Thomas.

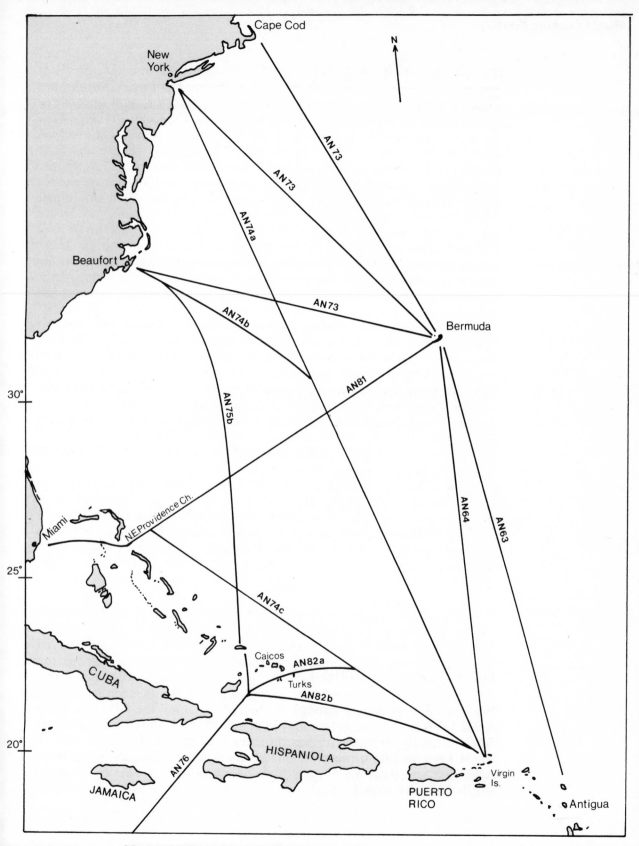

**25. ROUTES BETWEEN THE US EAST
COAST AND THE CARIBBEAN**

AN65 Bermuda to USA

DIAGRAMS 22, 26	Bermuda to Boston 680 m
	Bermuda to New York 670 m
	Bermuda to Beaufort 620 m

Best time:	May–June
Tropical storms:	June to November
Charts:	BA: 4403
	US: 124
Pilots:	BA: 69, 70
	US: 140, 147

The fact that the tracks of many hurricanes come so dangerously close to Bermuda limits the safe period when this passage can be made. The high frequency of SW winds in summer should provide good sailing conditions to most ports lying north of Cape Hatteras, but this is rarely the case. Even in May and June, the weather can often be extremely rough along this route and the worst conditions have been recorded in the vicinity of the Gulf Stream. The passage of cold fronts from continental America produces unsettled weather, which is often accompanied by violent rain squalls. Later in the summer unsettled weather is usually caused by tropical depressions that occasionally develop into hurricanes.

It is wise to try to obtain a long term forecast before leaving Bermuda, which would warn about the existence of any tropical depression threatening to come this way. Unfortunately the behaviour of NW fronts heading offshore is more difficult to predict and by the time a warning is received one could be in the midst of one. This can be particularly dangerous in the Gulf Stream, which should always be crossed at right angles.

AN70 Routes from USA

AN71 USA to Northern Europe
AN72 USA to Azores
AN73 USA to Bermuda
AN74 USA to Virgin Islands
AN75 USA to Bahamas
AN76 USA to Panama

AN71 USA to Northern Europe

DIAGRAM 24	Newport to Falmouth 2730 m
	Cape Cod to Cape Wrath 2560 m

Best time:	June to August
Tropical storms:	June to November
Charts:	BA: 4011
	US: 120, 121
Pilots:	BA: 27, 40, 59, 66, 68, 69
	US: 140, 141, 142, 191

A cold, wet and foggy route at the best of times, at least it has the advantage of both favourable winds and current. The great circle route is the obvious choice for a fast passage to Northern Europe, but for destinations south of the Bay of Biscay some of the alternatives should be considered. These are described in Routes AN61, AN62, AN72 and AN73.

Having chosen the great circle route, some of the problems which affect this northernmost route must be considered first. There are two main causes of concern for those who undertake this passage: fog and ice. Both of them are linked to the Labrador Current, a cold current that flows along the coasts of Newfoundland and Nova Scotia. Fog is caused by warm air blowing over the cold waters brought down from the Arctic by the Labrador Current, which also carries icebergs south during the summer. As the North Atlantic warms up with the advance of summer, fog becomes less frequent and the icebergs also start melting, although they sometimes drift as far south as latitude 40°N. Therefore the latter part of summer apears to be safer and the recommended time for this passage is August. This might be too late for those who intend to do some cruising in Northern Europe during the same summer and the alternative is either to leave earlier and brave the dangers or take a more southerly route (AN71C). The initial course of this route leads to point C (39°N, 50°W), from where the same directions apply as for Route AN61.

The great circle route passes south of Nova Scotia and Newfoundland from where it splits into a northern branch, going round the north of Scotland towards Scandinavia (AN71B), and a southern branch to the English Channel (AN71A). The most difficult part of the voyage is the first few hundred miles, until the concentration of fishing boats on the Grand Banks has been left behind, and also the area with the highest risk of fog and icebergs, close to Newfoundland.

The winds should be westerly around 15 knots. The frequency of gales in August is low for these latitudes and calms are rare. As the route passes well to the north of the Azores high, the weather should be outside of its direct influence, but there might be an effect if the high does move north. If the Azores high is stationary in its usual position, the weather is more likely to be affected by one of the lows tracking across the Atlantic from North

America to Europe. Such lows can produce gale force NE or E winds. The favourable effect of the Gulf Stream becomes less noticeable from about longitude 40°W where it changes its name to the North Atlantic Current.

AN72 USA to Azores

DIAGRAM 24		Newport to Horta 1960 m
		Norfolk to Horta 2230 m

Best time:	May to July
Tropical storms:	June to November
Charts:	BA: 4011
	US: 120
Pilots:	BA: 59, 67, 68, 69
	US: 140, 143

The advantage of this direct route to the Azores over Route AN62 which originates in Bermuda is that the latitudes of prevailing westerly winds can be reached sooner. The first objective after leaving the East Coast is to cross latitude 40°N in about longitude 60°W from where the same directions apply as for the route from Bermuda. Boats leaving from ports to the south of Cape Hatteras normally ride the Gulf Stream to this latitude before turning east once steady westerly winds have been found. Although latitude 38°N is sometimes mentioned as the recommended turning point, during the summer, when the Azores high extends farther north, consistent westerly winds will only be found in higher latitudes. For boats leaving from ports north of New York, the area of prevailing westerlies can be reached sooner, although one should sail south of the Nantucket Shoals before turning east.

From May to July, mostly S or SW winds can be expected for the first part of the passage. The danger of early season hurricanes should be borne in mind especially if leaving from southern ports, but up to the middle of July the risk is reasonably low. A rhumb line course along a southerly route is only recommended if one is prepared to motor through the calms associated with the area of high pressure.

AN73 USA to Bermuda

DIAGRAMS 24, 25		New York to Bermuda 670 m
		Beaufort to Bermuda 620 m

Best time:	May–June, November
	June to November
Tropical storms:	BA: 4403
Charts:	US: 124
Pilots:	BA: 69, 70
	US: 140, 147

This passage is usually made by those on their way to the Virgins, Lesser Antilles or the Azores, rarely to cruise solely in Bermuda itself. An early summer passage from any port on the East Coast should not be too difficult to accomplish. Prevailing winds in summer are from the SW and provided a favourable forecast has been obtained before leaving, the crossing of the Gulf Stream should present no problems. Rather than cross the Gulf Stream, boats leaving from Florida try to use it to speed them on their way to Bermuda. An increasing number of passages are made in May and June by boats leaving for Bermuda, the Azores and Europe, after having spent the winter in Florida. In the early summer the weather is usually pleasant and even if the winds are light, at least the weather is warm. The occasional depression forming over the Bahamas and then following a NE track can produce prolonged squalls and rough seas, but they are the exception rather than the rule. Later in the summer particular attention must be paid to hurricanes developing in the Caribbean as their tracks usually pass between Bermuda and the mainland. September and October are the months with the highest incidence of hurricanes. Although the danger of hurricanes diminishes after the end of October, there is an increasing risk of encountering an early winter *norther* which can produce extremely rough conditions when blowing against the Gulf Stream.

AN74 USA to Virgin Islands

DIAGRAM 25	New York to St Thomas 1420 m
	Beaufort to St Thomas 1170 m

Best time:	November (offshore)
	November to May (via Bahamas)
Tropical storms:	May to November
Charts:	BA: 4403
	US: 124
Pilots:	BA: 69, 70, 71
	US: 140, 147

This route has a lot of alternatives, which depend both on the type of boat and the experience of the crew. The most direct route leads well offshore and should be attempted only with a thoroughly tested boat and crew. If the voyage starts from any port east of New York, a stop in Bermuda can be contemplated as it does not greatly lengthen the distance. However, as the frequency of gales in November around Bermuda is higher than elsewhere, such a detour may not be the wisest course. One solution is to make the passage to Bermuda earlier in the summer, spending some time there and carrying on to the Virgins or Lesser Antilles later in the year. Directions for a passage via Bermuda can be found in Routes AN73, AN63 and AN64.

The timing for a direct passage to the Virgins (AN74A) is critical as a summer voyage carries the risk of hurricanes and a winter voyage that of northerly storms. Therefore the best time appears to be November, when the danger of hurricanes is low and winter gales are still rare. The winds down to about latitude 30°N are normally NW and especially when these are strong, the Gulf Stream should be crossed as quickly as possible. If the winds are SW, the course will arc to the east but this does not matter as any ground lost can easily be recuperated when the trades are found around latitude 24°N or 25°N. If this passage is made at the end of spring, easting should be made in the early part of the voyage to compensate for the SE slant of the trades. Easting is less important in November when the trades are NE.

The direct route to the Virgins can also be taken from ports south of New York. If the initial southbound voyage is made through the Intracoastal Waterway, it is not advisable to carry on south past Beaufort or Morehead City because of the windward work required later on. Leaving from Beaufort (AN74B) with a favourable forecast, an easterly course should be steered to cross the Gulf Stream as quickly as possible, after which a course can be set for the Virgins. To avoid beating against the trades it is best to set a course that crosses the meridian of the port of destination in about latitude 25°N. This means that the islands are approached from a better angle in relation to the prevailing wind.

The offshore route from Florida (AN74C) has the advantage that it can also be done in winter, although it has the disadvantage of strong contrary winds once the trades are met. The route from Florida leads through the NW and NE Providence Channels after which it stays to the north of all the islands. The recommended practice is to make one's easting along latitude 25°N and only turn south and east after meridian 65°N has been crossed. In November and December the trades are moderate NE, but become E and stronger after January, so even this route should not be used too late in winter.

Yet another alternative is to reach the Eastern Caribbean by the inter-island route that threads its way through the Bahamas, Turks and Caicos, Puerto Rico and beyond, an intricate and time-consuming route that still does not avoid the strong head winds which await one at the end. This alternative is discussed in some detail in Routes AN75 and AN82.

AN75 USA to Bahamas

| DIAGRAM 25 | Beaufort to San Salvador 660 m |
| | Beaufort to Mayaguana 770 m |

Best time:	November (direct)
	November to April (from Florida)
Tropical storms:	June to November
Charts:	BA: 4403
	US: 108, 124
Pilots:	BA: 69, 70
	US: 140, 147

A direct route to the Bahamas from ports north of Cape Hatteras is only worth considering if the destination is in the Southern Bahamas and even then the route has to swing well to the east to avoid the strength of the Gulf Stream. A more convenient offshore alternative is Route AN75B originating in Beaufort, Morehead City or Charleston, for which the best time is November. An earlier start carries the risk of hurricanes, which can in fact occur as late as the middle of December, whereas a later start runs the risk of the dreaded winter *northers* that produce dangerous conditions in the Gulf Stream. The frequency of hurricanes after the beginning of November is reasonably low and a good forecast obtained before departure would warn both of existing tropical depressions and of impending *northers*. The course on leaving the coast should lead in an ESE direction so as to cross the Gulf Stream at right angles and one should proceed for at least 100 miles in this direction before shaping a course for the Southern Bahamas. If the wind is light or calm, it is advisable to use the engine to move away quickly from the coast and the Gulf Stream. Variable winds can be expected for the entire run as calms are rare at this time of year. Suggested landfalls are on the islands of San Salvador and Mayaguana, but if this passage is made as part of a voyage to either Panama or the Eastern Caribbean, the latter is preferable. Extreme caution must be exercised if Caicos Passage is used, as currents are strong and unpredictable. This warning applies to all passages through the Bahamas where more boats are lost due to currents than weather.

The Bahamas can be reached by a multitude of routes from Florida, but as they cannot be regarded as offshore routes they fall outside the scope of this book. Such inshore routes can be used throughout the winter season. Offshore passages should either be undertaken in November, as stated above, or before the start of the hurricane season, between April and the middle of June.

AN76 USA to Panama

| DIAGRAM 25 | Beaufort to Windward Passage 930 m |
| | Windward Passage to Cristobal 720 m |

Best time:	May–June, November
Tropical storms:	June to November
Charts:	BA: 3273
	US: 108, 124
Pilots:	BA: 69, 70, 7A
	US: 147, 148

Whether one plans to stop in the Bahamas, Haiti or Jamaica or sail direct to Panama, this route should present few problems during the transitional periods from spring to summer or autumn to winter. Details about the best routes to the Bahamas are given in Route AN75. The difficult part of this passage is crossing the Bahamas, where shallow banks, extensive reefs and unpredictable currents call for accurate navigation. From ports north of

Cape Hatteras, but also from Beaufort or Morehead City, it is best to sail directly to the Southern Bahamas and make landfall on Mayaguana. The route from there to the Windward Passage, passing either side of Great Inagua, is easily accomplished, although particular attention must be paid to navigation when sailing through the Bahamas. The trades are usually lost in the lee of Hispaniola and winds are often light in the Windward Passage but they are picked up again as one moves south. Further directions will be found in Route AN83.

The best months are May–June and November, when favourable winds can be expected for most of the way and the danger of both hurricanes and winter *northers* is acceptably low. The second half of May and the first half of November are considered the best time for a non-stop passage to Panama, Beaufort in North Carolina probably being the best port to leave from. A favourable forecast is essential for the first leg across the Gulf Stream, after which winds should be E or SE for most of the way to the Bahamas. For the passage through the Caribbean Sea, favourable winds will also be found in winter, from December to April, although the strong trade winds can make sailing in the Western Caribbean uncomfortable. This passage should not be undertaken during the hurricane season from July to October.

After passing Jamaica allowance should be made for the strong current that sets towards the Pedro and New Banks.

AN80 Routes from the Bahamas and Virgin Islands

AN81 Bahamas to Bermuda
AN82 Bahamas to Virgin Islands
AN83 Bahamas to Panama
AN84 Puerto Rico and Virgin Islands to Bermuda
AN85 Virgin Islands to USA
AN86 Virgin Islands to Bahamas
AN87 Virgin Islands to Jamaica and the Gulf of Mexico
AN88 Virgin Islands to Panama

AN81 Bahamas to Bermuda

| DIAGRAMS 25, 27 | Caicos Passage to Bermuda 780 m |
| | NE Providence Channel to Bermuda 770 m |

Best time:	May to mid-June
Tropical storms:	June to November
Charts:	BA: 4403
	US: 108, 124
Pilots:	BA: 70
	US: 140, 147

Similar directions apply as for Route AN73 which is also used by boats coming up to Bermuda from Florida. The recommended time for this passage is late spring or early summer, when weather conditions on this route will be better than at any other time. If leaving from the Northern Bahamas a NNE course can easily be followed with the help of the prevailing easterly winds and the north setting Gulf Stream. As the trade winds of summer are often SE in direction, it is sometimes possible to lay a direct course from the Bahamas to Bermuda right through the Horse Latitudes. Light winds are sometimes experienced along this route and gales are very rare at this time of year. Although the hurricane season officially starts in Bermuda on 1st June, hurricanes rarely pass that way before the middle of August and even when they do, their path is to the west of Bermuda nearer to the American mainland.

AN82 *Bahamas to Virgin Islands*

DIAGRAM 25

Best time:	mid-April to June, November to mid-December
Tropical storms:	June to November
Charts:	BA: 3273
	US: 108, 124
Pilots:	BA: 70, 71
	US: 147

Having reached the Southern Bahamas either via one of the offshore routes or through the islands, the subsequent leg to the Virgins will be to windward for most of the year. The best time for the eastward passage is at the change of seasons, when the trades are lighter and the risk of hurricanes not so great. Another matter of concern, apart from the contrary winds, are the strong currents that occur in this area. These, combined with the numerous reefs, low islands and few lights, call for accurate navigation at all times.

An offshore passage from the Southern Bahamas to the Virgins, either direct (AN82A) or via Puerto Rico, can regain the ocean through the Crooked Island, Mayaguana, Caicos or Turks Passages. The initial course should lead well clear of all dangers, including the banks east of Grand Turk. Because of the contrary wind and current, this passage is often very difficult to accomplish and unless the winds are northerly or light, an alternative route (AN82B) might have to be considered. The obvious alternative is to stay south of Caicos and sail along the coasts of Hispaniola and Puerto Rico. Even when the trades are strong, these high islands provide some lee and lighter coastal breezes.

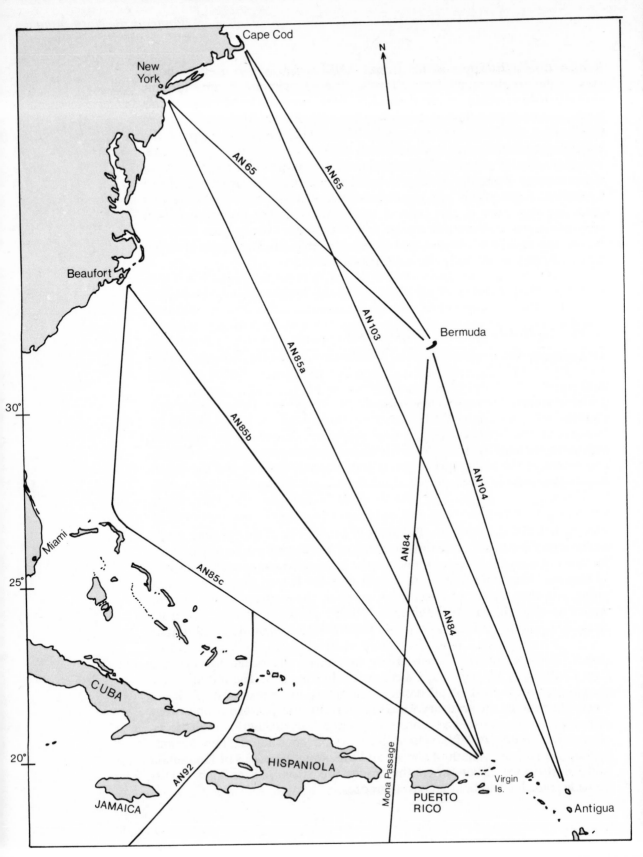

**26. ROUTES BETWEEN THE CARIBBEAN
AND THE US EAST COAST**

AN83 Bahamas to Panama

DIAGRAMS 27, 28	Windward Passage to Cristobal 720 m

Best time:	April–May, November–December
Tropical storms:	June to November
Charts:	BA: 3273
	US: 108, 124
Pilots:	BA: 7A, 70
	US: 147, 148

All routes from the Bahamas converge on the Windward Passage which can be approached either east or west of Great Inagua Island. From the Windward Passage the course south can pass on either side of Navassa Island, but its western side is to be preferred in strong winds as seas break on the shallows off the SW extremity of Hispaniola. If a stop in Jamaica is not intended, the course leads east of Morant Cays to the Panama Canal. Allowance should be made for leeway if passing close to Pedro and New Banks as the current sets towards them.

The winds are favourable along this route throughout the year, although both the hurricane season and the strong trade winds of winter should be avoided. In the latter case boisterous sailing conditions can be predicted with certainty from January to March when the trades are at their strongest. The extent of the hurricane season is less precisely defined and the actual months when there is no danger of hurricanes are the same winter months from January to April. The intermediate months have a much lower frequency of tropical storms, but hurricanes have been recorded even as late as Christmas, making passages through the Caribbean Sea more dangerous at the end than at the beginning of the season.

AN84 Puerto Rico and Virgin Islands to Bermuda

DIAGRAM 26	San Juan to Bermuda 840 m
	St Thomas to Bermuda 850 m
	Mona Passage to Bermuda 860 m

Best time:	Late April to June
Tropical storms:	June to November
Charts:	BA: 4403
	US: 108, 124
Pilots:	BA: 70, 71
	US: 140, 147

This is a clear run north for boats planning either to continue to Europe or the east coast of America. Best conditions on this route, which crosses the Horse Latitudes, will be found in late spring or early summer. At this time of year the trade winds are much more E or SE in direction than in winter, but even when they are from the NE, it does not matter too much if one is pushed slightly to the west of the desired course, because the further north one goes, the greater likelihood of a shift of wind to the SE or even S. The ground lost to the west can be regained in the doldrums if one is prepared to motor and approach Bermuda from a better angle. North of the zone of calms and legendary Sargasso Sea, the winds are variable in direction, with a predominance of S and SW and only rarely N winds. The danger of a blustery winter *norther* is minimal after the middle of April when most passages are made on this route. Generally, the best conditions are encountered in May. This route is not recommended after the end of June because of the increased frequency of hurricanes.

AN85 Virgin Islands to USA

DIAGRAMS 26, 27	St Thomas to New York 1420 m
	St Thomas to Beaufort 1170 m
	St Thomas to Charleston 1190 m

Best time:	Late April to June (direct)
	November to June (via Bahamas)
Tropical storms:	June to November
Charts:	BA: 4403
	US: 108, 124
Pilots:	BA: 69, 70, 71
	US: 140, 147

For boats bound for ports to the north of Cape Hatteras similar directions apply to those for Route AN84 and in fact many people prefer to break the voyage in Bermuda and reach the more distant ports on the East Coast that way. On the direct route (AN85A) favourable winds can be expected to the northern limit of the trades. Southerly winds occasionally last right through the zone of calms that extends between latitudes 25°N and 30°N. The temptation of a ride in the Gulf Stream should be resisted if this passage is made early in the season to avoid being caught by a late *norther*.

When bound for ports south of Cape Hatteras a detour via Bermuda is not justified and Diagram 26 shows the various alternatives. Although Route AN85B appears to be the shortest as it is the most direct, it may not be the quickest as it cuts diagonally across the zone of calms that will be found north of latitude 25°N. The suggested alternative (AN85C) is to follow a NW course on leaving St Thomas so as to pass to windward of both Turks and Caicos and the Bahamas. From Great Abaco the route turns

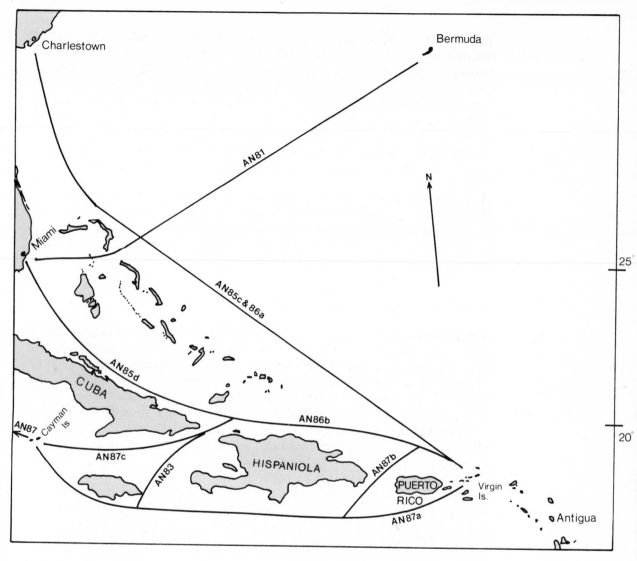

27. ROUTES TO AND FROM THE BAHAMAS

north and enters the Gulf Stream. Both winds and current are favourable along most of this route. Whichever alternative is chosen, the optimum time for leaving the Virgins also coincides with the end of the safe cruising season in the Eastern Caribbean.

A direct passage along any of the above routes should not be attempted during the winter months when a slower cruise through the Bahamas to Florida is to be preferred and the United States can be reached in a more leisurely way. For boats bound for Florida there are three alternatives. The most direct route between April and June is the same as AN85B as far as Great Abaco. From there it branches off through the NE and NW

Providence Channels and crosses the Gulf Stream to Florida. The other two alternatives can be used at any time between November and June, although they cannot be regarded as offshore passages because both consist of island hopping, either right through Turks and Caicos and the Bahamas, or along the northern shores of Puerto Rico, Hispaniola and Cuba (AN85D).

AN86 Virgin Islands to Bahamas

DIAGRAM 27

Best time:	November to May
Tropical storms:	June to November
Charts:	BA: 3273
	US: 108, 124
Pilots:	BA: 70, 71
	US: 147

The offshore route (AN86A) to the Northern Bahamas is similar to Route AN85C and follows a NW course parallel to the chain of islands as far as the NE Providence Channel. Whether taking the offshore route from St Thomas, or making an intermediate stop in San Juan, Puerto Rico, the course should pass well to windward of Silver and Mouchoir Banks, north of Hispaniola. The Southern Bahamas can be reached via any of four deep water passes – Turks, Caicos, Mayaguana or Crooked Island Passage. All of them are subject to strong currents as indeed is the entire area of the Bahamas.

The offshore passage can be made at any time outside of the hurricane season, when fair, if strong, winds can be expected as well as the favourable Antilles Current. An alternative inshore Route AN86B can be taken along the northern coasts of Puerto Rico, Hispaniola and Cuba that leads through the Old Bahama Channel, south of the Great Bahama Bank, to Florida.

AN87 Virgin Islands to Jamaica and the Gulf of Mexico

DIAGRAM 27		St Thomas to Kingston 690 m
		St Thomas to Galveston 1900 m

Best time:	April–May, November
Tropical storms:	June to November
Charts:	BA: 3273
	US: 400
Pilots:	BA: 69A, 70, 71
	US: 147

This is a convenient route for those wishing to sail to the southern states bordering on the Gulf of Mexico as it is more direct and less dangerous than a crossing of the Bahamas. The initial route (AN87A) from the Virgin Islands leads SW between St Croix and Puerto Rico and then direct to Jamaica keeping clear of the southern coast of Hispaniola. The alternative route keeps to the north of Puerto Rico (AN87B), and possibly Hispaniola as well (AN87C), and uses either Mona or Windward Passage to regain the Caribbean Sea. The advantage of the first route is the certainty of better winds, whereas by keeping to the north of the large islands, the trade winds are blocked and one has to rely on coastal breezes.

As with most trans-Caribbean passages, the best time is the transition months of April–May, before the hurricane season, or November, before the onset of winter *northers*. For the second leg from Jamaica to the Gulf, a convenient stop is Grand Cayman Island, less than 200 miles WNW of Jamaica. Favourable winds and currents can be expected along the entire passage.

AN88 *Virgin Islands to Panama*

| DIAGRAM 28 | St Thomas to Cristobal 1030 m |
| | St Croix to Cristobal 1020 m |

Best time:	April–May, November–December
Tropical storms:	June to November
Charts:	BA: 3273
	US: 400
Pilots:	BA: 7A, 71
	US: 147, 148

A downwind trip at all times, this passage should not be undertaken either during the peak months of the hurricane season, between July and October, or at the height of the winter trades, between January and the middle of March. Reference should be made to Route AN102 as directions are similar, with the exception that for those who start off from the Virgin Islands, the recommended stop in the ABC islands or Venezuela is not applicable unless one wishes to spend some time cruising there. The direct Route AN88A leaves Vieques Island to starboard, although some people prefer to call in first at San Juan, Puerto Rico, and lay a course for Panama only after having negotiated Mona Passage (AN88B). The detour around the north of Puerto Rico can be windless at the end of winter when the island blocks the trades.

Most boats leave the Virgins for Panama in winter and all those who have done this passage in February complain about the rough conditions in the Caribbean Sea. A later start, when the winter trades have lost some of their power, might be the solution, but such a timing clashes with the plans of those who intend to continue their cruise along the Pacific coast of Central America where the hurricane season starts towards the end of May. For those who intend to head for the islands of the South Pacific, an early start from the Virgins is not essential as the seasons there are the opposite to those in the Caribbean and a later passage to Panama in April or early May may be preferable.

AN90 Routes in the Caribbean Sea and from Panama

AN91 Panama to Central America and the Gulf of Mexico
AN92 Panama to the Windward Passage, Jamaica and Hispaniola
AN93 Panama to Hispaniola
AN94 Panama to Virgin Islands
AN95 Panama to Lesser Antilles
AN96 Panama to Venezuela and the ABC Islands

Most routes in the Caribbean Sea and Gulf of Mexico either start or end in Panama and because they have many features in common it is worth considering them together. Because of the multitude of destinations, the routes are difficult to define, although there are certain considerations that have to be taken into account whichever route is contemplated. Most of these considerations are closely related to weather and passages through the Caribbean are discouraged during the hurricane season, especially during the months of highest frequency, from August to October. Some of the later hurricanes actually form in the Caribbean and warnings are therefore shorter than when the depression has been tracked across the Atlantic. Rough weather can also be experienced in the Western Caribbean at the height of the winter trades, whereas in the Gulf of Mexico winter is associated with violent northerly storms. Another concern in the Gulf of Mexico is the unpredictability of the currents.

Besides the weather, there are concerns of a different nature that have to be taken into account by those planning to sail through the Caribbean, whether of politics or of piracy. The latter is mostly associated with drug running, the waters off Colombia having the worst reputation in this respect. Also dangerous can be some of the more isolated islands in the Bahamas, where crews of solitary yachts have been attacked by gangs needing a boat for some smuggling operation. It is therefore advisable to cruise in company when visiting out-of-the-way places.

Eastbound passages from Panama can be extremely difficult at all times of the year, because of the prevailing direction of the winds and current. Many people are tempted to make this passage late in the year so as to arrive in the Lesser Antilles during the hurricane-free season. In such a case, the eastward passage must be made before the onset of the strong

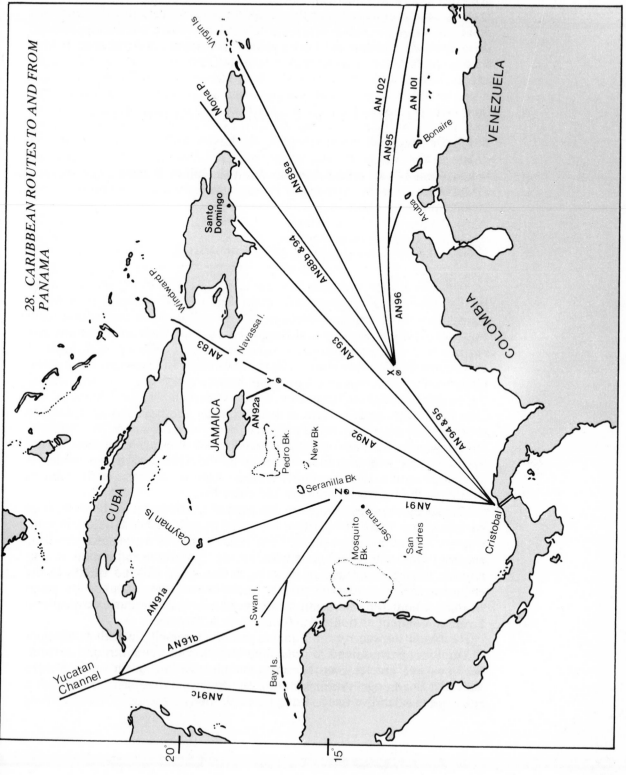

28. CARIBBEAN ROUTES TO AND FROM PANAMA

VENEZUELA

COLOMBIA

Bonaire

Aruba

AN 102

AN 101

AN95

AN96

AN88a

AN88b & 94

AN93

AN94 & 95

Virgin Is

Mona P.

Santo
Domingo

Windward P.

Navassa I.

AN83

JAMAICA

AN92a

Pedro Bk.

New Bk

AN92

Seranilla Bk

Serrana

San
Andres

Mosquito
Bk.

AN91

Cristobal

CUBA

Cayman Is

AN91a

Swan I.

AN91b

Bay Is.

AN91c

Yucatan
Channel

20°

15°

winter trades. Better and more comfortable passages have been made in late spring or early summer, although this has the disadvantage of arriving in the Lesser Antilles at the beginning of the hurricane season. In order to make this passage at the best time and also avoid the hurricane season, there are two options. If the Panama Canal cannot be transited before winter it is better to wait until April or May and then head for Venezuela and the islands to the north of it. As this area is outside the hurricane zone it is safe to cruise there until November when the voyage can be continued to the Lesser Antilles. If the Canal can be transited in late October or early November and the trade winds are already too strong to attempt a direct passage, it may be worth approaching the Lesser Antilles from the north, by sailing to the Virgin Islands via Puerto Rico. As the winter trades blow mostly from NE or ENE, a cruise down the chain of the Lesser Antilles would in fact benefit from more favourable winds than those encountered on a reciprocal course.

AN91 Panama to Central America and the Gulf of Mexico

DIAGRAM 28	Cristobal to Swan Island 600 m
	Cristobal to Grand Cayman 620 m

Best time:	November, mid-April to June
Tropical storms:	June to November
Charts:	BA: 3273
	US: 400
Pilots:	BA: 7A, 69A
	US: 148

On leaving the Panama Canal area there are two alternatives, either a direct route for those who wish to reach the Gulf of Mexico as soon as possible, or an indirect route for those who intend to cruise en route in Honduras, Belize or other parts of Central America. The more direct route requires careful navigation, especially at the beginning, because of the numerous banks and cays that lie off the coast of Central America. After leaving Cristobal Colon a course should be steered to pass west of Roncador Bank and between Sueno and Serrana Banks, all of which have lights. It is also possible to stop at either San Andrés or Providencia Island. If conditions are unfavourable or visibility poor, it might be better to pass to windward of all these islands and alter course for either Grand Cayman Island or the Yucatan Channel at point Z (14°30'N, 79°30'W).

The routes fan out from this point, with the possibility of either calling in at Grand Cayman Island (Route AN91A) or continuing directly towards the Yucatan Channel. Another alternative is to stop at Swan Island (Route AN91B). Going north from Swan Island, one can either make another stop at Cozumel Island or head straight for the Gulf.

Those who wish to make a detour towards the Bay Islands of Honduras or beyond should lay a course that passes outside of Gorda Cay (AN91C). As this course leads over some shallow spots it should only be taken if the weather is not too rough, otherwise the seas breaking over the banks can make conditions hazardous. The course from Gorda Cay passes north of Hobbies Cays after which it runs parallel to the coast of Honduras. The cruising grounds of Guatemala and Belize can also be explored before rejoining Route AN91C which continues to the Gulf of Mexico either direct or via Cozumel Island.

As in the case of all Caribbean passages, the timing for this route is crucial. Apart from the danger of being caught by a hurricane, especially from July to October, many boats get themselves into trouble when hit by a *norther* in the Gulf of Mexico. The whole area is affected by *northers* from November until the beginning of April and their effect can be felt as far south as Panama. The violent conditions produced by the northerly wind blowing against the strong currents in the Gulf have caused boats to capsize, break masts or even founder. It would appear that the best time to make this passage is either from late October to early December, or from the middle of April to the end of June. Both periods avoid the worst of the winter *northers* and fall outside the months with the highest frequency of hurricanes. The prevailing winds in the Western Caribbean are NE to E, with a southern component making itself felt north of Yucatan. The currents along this route set in a NW direction, attaining their strongest rate in the Yucatan Channel. The sets in the Gulf of Mexico are complex and difficult to predict, particularly in the area of the Dry Tortugas where extreme caution should be exercised.

Because of its complexity, this route via the Gulf of Mexico is only recommended for boats bound for ports in states bordering on the Gulf. Alternative routes should be considered for other destinations on the east coast of the USA.

AN92 *Panama to the Windward Passage, Jamaica and Hispaniola*

DIAGRAM 28	Cristobal to Windward Passage 720 m
	Cristobal to Kingston 560 m

Best time:	April–May, November
Tropical storms:	June to November
Charts:	BA: 762
	US: 400, 402
Pilots:	BA: 7A, 70
	US: 147, 148

This is a route favoured by those who wish to sail quickly to ports along the east coast of the USA, although the times when this route can be used safely are relatively short. The best periods are either between April and June, when the trades have lost their winter strength and winds have a southerly element in them, or November, before the onset of the strong winter trades. When sailing this route late in the year, there is also the danger of encountering a *norther*. During the hurricane season, it is advisable to tune in regularly to WWV radio which gives hurricane warnings for this area.

Navigation in the central Caribbean is made difficult by the large number of banks, reefs and shoals, aggravated by the strong west setting current. Because of this current, a direct course for Jamaica leads dangerously close to the New Bank (Bajo Nuevo) and Pedro Bank, and adequate leeway should be allowed for when setting a course. Both these banks can be very dangerous in heavy weather and their vicinity should be avoided.

If a stopover in Jamaica is not envisaged, the course from Panama should lead to point Y (16°45′N, 77°55′W), about 40 miles south of Morant Cays, SE of Jamaica. This course leads outside all dangers. From this point the course can pass either to the west of Navassa Island, or between this island and Cape Tiburon, the SW extremity of Hispaniola. In strong winds it is safer to take the westerly route to avoid the breaking seas on the shallow banks lying close to the Haitian coast.

Important Notice: Windward Passage is clear of dangers but attention is drawn to those continuing their voyage northwards through Caicos Passage, between Mayaguana Island and the Caicos Bank. Strong and unpredictable currents have been recorded in the Caicos Passage, which have caused many ships and yachts to be lost on the reefs surrounding Mayaguana Island, particularly the reef extending from its eastern extremity. The currents appear to be much stronger than stated and are difficult to detect, especially if one sails through the area by night, which should be avoided if at all possible.

AN93 Panama to Hispaniola

DIAGRAM 28	Cristobal to Santo Domingo 800 m
Best time:	May–June, November
Tropical storms:	June to November
Charts:	BA: 762
	US: 400, 402
Pilots:	BA: 7A, 70
	US: 147, 148

Because the prevailing winds in the Caribbean are NE or E, all destinations on this route are to windward of Panama for most of the year. Unless there is a shift of wind to the south, it would be better to follow directions as for Route AN92 and then work one's way eastward along the south coast of Hispaniola with the help of land breezes. Close inshore there is sometimes an east setting current.

AN94 Panama to Virgin Islands

DIAGRAM 28	Cristobal to St Croix 1020 m
	Cristobal to Mona Passage 910 m

Best time:	April–May, November
Tropical storms:	June to November
Charts:	BA: 762
	US: 400, 402
Pilots:	BA: 7A, 71
	US: 147, 148

This is a difficult route throughout the year on account of the prevailing winds and the west setting current. The direct route, either south of Puerto Rico, or via the Mona Passage and north of Puerto Rico, should only be attempted at the change of seasons, when the trades are usually lighter. Depending on the time of year, it might be better to sail Route AN92 through the Windward Passage and then along the north coasts of Hispaniola and Puerto Rico. Another possibility is to sail as close to the wind as possible to the south coast of Hispaniola (AN93) and then continue to the Virgins by either staying south of Puerto Rico or going north of the island through the Mona Passage.

As the northern routes should not be attempted during the hurricane season, a radical alternative is a southern route which can be sailed at almost any time of the year. This entails a detour to Venezuela and the islands off the Venezuelan coast and offers the possibility of spending the dangerous months in this safer area before heading north at the end of the hurricane season (see also AN96 and AN112).

AN95 Panama to the Lesser Antilles

DIAGRAM 28	Cristobal to Grenada 1120 m
	Cristobal to Martinique 1150 m
	Cristobal to Antigua 1160 m

Best time:	mid-April to May, November
Tropical storms:	June to November
Charts:	BA: 762
	US: 400, 402
Pilots:	BA: 7A, 71
	US: 147, 148

This can be a very rough trip as it is to windward all the way. It is a challenge that is faced by all those who intend to head east after transiting the Canal. Some people call in first at the San Blas Islands, for which the compulsory cruising permit can be obtained before leaving Cristobal. An additional permit must be obtained on arrival in Porvenir, which is an obligatory stop for those wishing to cruise the San Blas Islands (see Chapter 27).

Whether calling at the San Blas Islands or not, the waters of Colombia should be avoided after leaving Panama. This is best done by sailing in an arc via point X (13°N, 76°W) to Aruba, which is a convenient stop en route unless one is prepared to sail non-stop to the Lesser Antilles, a task which is not easily accomplished because of the contrary wind and current. A more logical alternative to an exhausting beat to windward is to take a more southerly route and sail in short stages along the coasts of Venezuela and offlying islands.

The best time for a southern passage is between June and August, when the trade winds are less consistent in both strength and direction than in winter. September and October, the other two months when one can expect lighter winds, are at the height of the hurricane season and although Venezuela and the offlying islands are outside the hurricane belt, conditions in the Western Caribbean can become extremely uncomfortable if a hurricane is passing farther to the east or north. The worst time to do this passage is at the height of the trades, from January to early April.

The eastbound passage through Venezuelan waters should be made as close inshore as possible to take advantage of both land and sea breezes and a favourable current that runs close to the coast. At night the trade winds usually die away and this is the time to sail inshore to use the land breeze. A boat which sails well to windward can take an offshore tack during the day and head for the shore before nightfall. In this way Grenada can be reached in short hops, and from there, any of the other islands.

AN96 *Panama to Venezuela and the ABC Islands*

DIAGRAM 28	Cristobal to Aruba 640 m
	Cristobal to Caracas 860 m

Best time:	mid-April to June, November
Tropical storms:	June to November
Charts:	BA: 762
	US: 400, 402
Pilots:	BA: 7A
	US: 148

In order to avoid the proximity of the Colombian coast, the initial course on leaving Panama should lead to point X (13°N, 76°W) and then in an arc to

Aruba. Such a course is difficult to hold against the prevailing NE or E winds of winter and this passage should preferably be attempted at the change of seasons. Light winds and even calms occur sometimes in November and if one is prepared to use the engine, maximum progress can be made while favourable conditions last.

There is unfortunately no alternative to a hard beat to windward and the undisputed difficulty of this route must be seriously considered before including it in one's overall cruising plans. A different way to reach Venezuela and the ABC Islands is to reserve them for the end of a Caribbean cruise and stop there on the return voyage to Panama. In such a case, it would be easier to sail north on leaving Panama by following the directions for one of the northbound routes and eventually reach Venezuela from the north east and Lesser Antilles.

AN100 Routes from the Lesser Antilles

AN101 Lesser Antilles to ABC Islands and Venezuela
AN102 Lesser Antilles to Panama
AN103 Lesser Antilles to USA and Canada
AN104 Lesser Antilles to Bermuda
AN105 Lesser Antilles to Azores

AN101 Lesser Antilles to ABC Islands and Venezuela

DIAGRAMS 28, 29	Grenada to Margarita 150 m Martinique to Bonaire 450 m Antigua to Aruba 550 m

Best time:	December to May
Tropical storms:	June to November
Charts:	BA: 762
	US: 400, 402
Pilots:	BA: 7A, 71
	US: 147, 148

This is a straightforward passage benefiting from favourable winds throughout the year. Sometimes in winter, during January to March, when the trades blow strongly, conditions can be rough but never really dangerous. Better sailing can be had at the change of seasons when winds continue to be favourable, but are usually light. Sailing conditions are just as good during the summer when the Lesser Antilles are under the threat of hurricanes. As the ABC Islands and Venezuela are just outside the hurricane belt, they provide a convenient haven to those who wish to

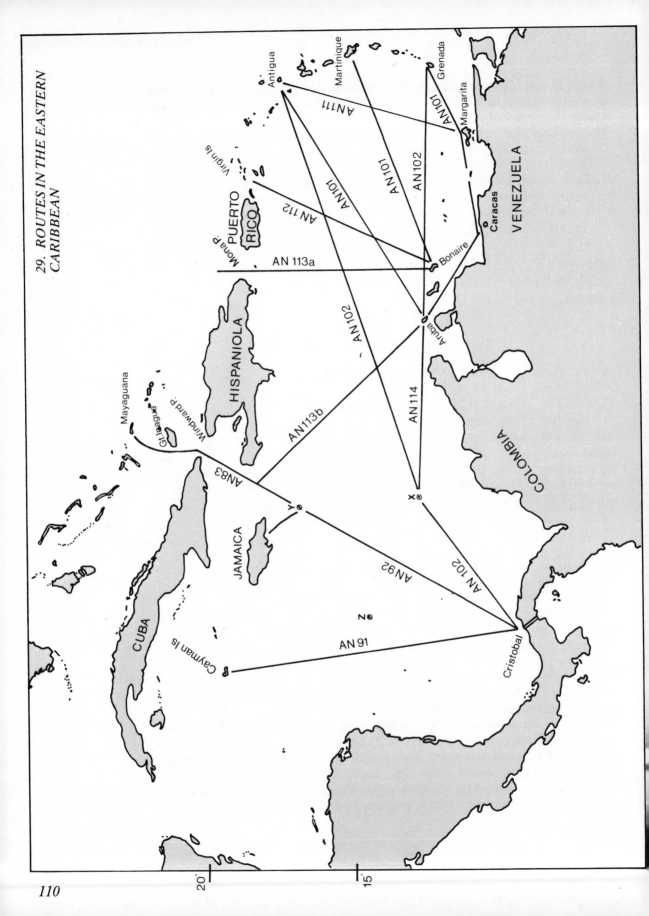

29. ROUTES IN THE EASTERN CARIBBEAN

remain in the Caribbean during the summer. On all southbound passages allowance should be made for the strong Equatorial Current which can set westward at rates of up to 2 knots.

AN102 Lesser Antilles to Panama

DIAGRAMS 28, 29	Grenada to Cristobal 1120 m
	Martinique to Cristobal 1150 m
	Antigua to Cristobal 1160 m

Best time:	April–May, November–December
Tropical storms:	June to November
Charts:	BA: 762
	US: 400, 402
Pilots:	BA: 7A, 71
	US: 147, 148

This can be a very rough passage, confirmed by the fact that many experienced sailors consider that their passage across the Caribbean Sea was the roughest part of their voyage around the world. At the height of the trade wind season, the constant easterly winds pile up the water in the western part of the Caribbean, making sea conditions hazardous. Many boats have been knocked down or pooped by the steep following seas, while others were lost on the coast of Colombia after having been set off course by the strong current. The coast of Colombia is also dangerous on account of the many reports of piracy. Most of these cases appear to be connected with drug running and a sailing boat with a small crew is extremely vulnerable if intercepted on the high seas. It is therefore recommended to keep at a distance of at least 100 miles off the Colombian coast and alter course for Panama only at point X (13°00′N, 76°00′W).

This passage should not be done between July and October when hurricanes are most frequent. The best times are either in November–December, when the trades are not yet blowing at full strength, or in April–May, when the strength of the trades starts to diminish. The months of January to March, although free of hurricanes, are also the period of the strongest trades, when conditions in the western part of the Caribbean can become uncomfortable for small boats.

When planning this passage through the Caribbean Sea it is well worth considering a stop in Venezuela or the offlying islands, which are situated outside the hurricane belt and can provide a welcome break. The advantage of such a stop is that the voyage towards Panama can be continued at any time of the year, even during the hurricane season, as the route from Aruba to Panama lies to the south of the area affected by tropical storms.

AN103 Lesser Antilles to USA and Canada

DIAGRAM 26	Antigua to New York 1560 m
	St Barts to Beaufort 1260 m
	Antigua to St John 1900 m

Best time:	Late April to mid-June
Tropical storms:	June to November
Charts:	BA: 4403
	US: 108
Pilots:	BA: 59, 68, 69, 70, 71
	US: 140, 145, 147

Similar directions apply to those for Route AN85 which gives details of various alternatives for a passage from the Virgin Islands to the East Coast. As the Lesser Antilles are to windward of the Virgins, a direct route to the East Coast will benefit from a better slant even if the trades are north-easterly, which they rarely are during the recommended time for this passage. For destinations east of New York as far as Nova Scotia, a stopover in Bermuda has certain attractions. Details for that route are given in AN104 which should be consulted together with Routes AN65, AN84 and AN85, as similar considerations apply for all these routes.

Passages along any of these routes are definitely discouraged during the hurricane season as the tracks of past hurricanes almost coincide with these routes, passing north of the Bahamas and running between the East Coast and Bermuda.

AN104 Lesser Antilles to Bermuda

DIAGRAM 26	Antigua to Bermuda 940 m

Best time:	Mid-April to mid-June
Tropical storms:	June to November
Charts:	BA: 3273
	US: 108, 124
Pilots:	BA: 70, 71
	US: 140, 147

The favoured point of departure for this route is English Harbour, Antigua, from where many boats take their leave of the Lesser Antilles and head north for Bermuda as part of a return trip either to Europe or North America. A departure from Antigua puts a boat more to windward than a departure from the Virgin Islands or even Puerto Rico, as described in Route AN84. The better slant allows boats to reach to the northern limit of the trades which at the optimum time for this passage can be carried as far as latitudes 26°N to 28°N. The winds in late April to the middle of June are mostly E to SE for the first half of this passage, becoming lighter farther north. Light southerly winds are sometimes carried right through the Horse Latitudes, but calms are the rule not the exception in the region of the Sargasso Sea. If constant SE winds are carried through, the weather remains clear, otherwise it becomes cloudy and overcast.

For those who are determined to make good time to Bermuda there is no alternative but to motor through the belt of calms and this is definitely advised later in the season because of the risk of hurricanes. Tropical depressions become more common after the middle of June and even if they do not generate strong winds, the weather in their vicinity is very unsettled, with heavy rain. If such a depression forms close to the northern extremity of the Lesser Antilles, contrary winds can be expected on the way to Bermuda.

This passage can also be done towards the end of the hurricane season, when the frequency of S and SW winds on the way to Bermuda is higher, but so also is the risk of a late hurricane. Fortunately the best time for this route is also the most convenient as it coincides with the end of the safe cruising season in the Caribbean, Antigua Week, and optimum weather for a subsequent passage to Europe.

AN105 *Lesser Antilles to Azores*

DIAGRAM 24	Antigua to Horta 2170 m

Best time:	May to July
Tropical storms:	June to November
Charts:	BA: 4011
	US: 120
Pilots:	BA: 67, 71
	US: 140, 143, 147

For many years yacht skippers were not prepared to challenge the accepted wisdom that a return voyage from the Caribbean to Europe should only be attempted along the classic route that passes through Bermuda and the Azores. What started as a devil-may-care route used mostly by delivery crews and skippers of charter boats in a hurry to return to the Mediterranean at the end of the season in the Caribbean, is now attracting cruising boats as well. As the route via Bermuda is at least 500 miles longer than the great circle route from Antigua to Horta, and one cannot even be sure of fair winds for half that voyage, many prefer to stay in warmer weather and hope for the best.

On leaving Antigua, or any other of the Lesser Antilles or Virgins, a NE course is set, which should be possible to achieve as the trade winds are mostly south of east when this passage is usually made, in May or June. The chances of SE winds increase as one moves north until the belt of calms and light winds is reached which separates the trade winds from the westerlies of higher latitudes. This is the time when a powerful engine and a good reserve of fuel make up for the lack of wind, and this is the tactic preferred by most of those who take this route. With a bit of luck, winds on the other side of the Horse Latitudes can be favourable. If this occurs, some people are tempted to bypass the Azores altogether and carry on non-stop to Gibraltar. A boat that goes well to windward is a great asset, as the Portuguese trades might have to be crossed at an acute angle.

The optimum time for this passage is between May and July, although most people probably prefer to make it earlier rather than later. April is a little too early as the frequency of gales in the Atlantic is still high. After July the frequency of hurricanes increases, making all passages to or from the Caribbean a risky business.

AN110 Routes from the ABC Islands

AN111 ABC Islands and Venezuela to Lesser Antilles
AN112 ABC Islands and Venezuela to Virgin Islands
AN113 Northward from Venezuela and the ABC Islands
AN114 ABC Islands and Venezuela to Panama

AN111 ABC Islands and Venezuela to Lesser Antilles

| DIAGRAM 29 | Margarita to Grenada 150 m |
| | Bonaire to Antigua 490 m |

Best time:	April–May, November–December
Tropical storms:	June to November
Charts:	BA: 762
	US: 400, 402
Pilots:	BA: 7A, 71
	US: 147, 148

Because of the direction of the prevailing wind it is usually better to work one's way east along the coast of Venezuela and the offlying islands before heading for the Lesser Antilles. The distance between the nearest islands, Margarita and Grenada, is only 140 miles, which makes a longer offshore route hard to justify, taking into account the strong NE winds of winter. Towards spring, with a better chance of SE winds, direct passages to more northerly islands in the Antilles are easier to accomplish, but even then it is better to start off from as far east as possible.

AN112 ABC Islands and Venezuela to Virgin Islands

| DIAGRAM 29 | Aruba to St Thomas 470 m |
| | Bonaire to St Croix 410 m |

Best time:	mid-April to May, November
Tropical storms:	June to November
Charts:	BA: 762
	US: 400, 402
Pilots:	BA: 7A, 71
	US: 147, 148

This is a difficult passage during the winter months when the trades have a lot of north in them. From December to April it is usually better to sail to the Virgins in shorter hops along the chain of Lesser Antilles. For a direct passage, it is advisable to wait until the second half of April, when there is a better chance of having the wind from a favourable direction. If it proves too difficult to lay a direct course for the Virgins, it is better to use the Mona Passage and approach the islands from the west (AN113A). However, should it be impossible to lay a course even for Mona Passage because of unfavourable winds, landfall can be made further west, along the coast of Hispaniola, from where it is possible to work one's way east along the coast with the help of a fair inshore current and land breezes. The same can be done along the south coast of Puerto Rico if a detour via Mona Passage is not attractive.

AN113 Northward from Venezuela and the ABC Islands

| DIAGRAM 29 | Bonaire to Mona Passage 390 m |
| | Aruba to Windward Passage 510 m |

Best time:	April–May, November
Tropical storms:	June to November
Charts:	BA: 762
	US: 400, 402
Pilots:	BA: 7A, 70, 71
	US: 147, 148

For those who have cruised in this area and do not plan to continue their voyage towards Panama and the Pacific Ocean, but intend to sail either to the USA or Europe, the best season for this passage is spring, when the winds usually start shifting to the SE. It is best to start from as far east as possible, although both Bonaire and Curaçao are good points of departure. If heading for the Mona Passage (AN113A), allowance should be made for the westerly current. If Mona Passage cannot be laid and one is swept to the west, it is possible to break the trip on the south coast of the Dominican Republic and then work one's way east with the help of an easterly current that sets close inshore.

As there is a good deal of north in the trades during the early part of winter, the passage should not be attempted too early in the year. The best time for crossing the Caribbean Sea is April or May, when there is little chance of the winds swinging to the north. If one plans to carry on towards Europe, a straight course for Bermuda can be set from Mona Passage (AN84). The other alternative after leaving Mona Passage for those making for ports on the east coast of the USA is to cross the Bahamas and then use the Intracoastal Waterway. If this latter is the intention it is hardly worth fighting against the wind on leaving Venezuela, and it would make more sense to head straight for the Windward Passage (AN113B) and approach the USA from that direction.

AN114 ABC Islands and Venezuela to Panama

DIAGRAM 29	Aruba to Cristobal 640 m

Best time:	April–May, November–December
Tropical storms:	June to November
Charts:	BA: 762
	US: 400, 402
Pilots:	BA: 7A
	US: 148

Although this route is just outside the region affected by hurricanes, it is better to plan this passage for the intermediate seasons when more pleasant conditions can be expected. Reference should also be made to Route AN102 where more detailed directions are given.

The best point of departure for Panama is Aruba, from where a course should be steered to pass well off the coast of Colombia. The initial course should lead in an arc to point X (13°00′N, 76°00′W), then direct to the Panama Canal. The recommended course is outside the 1,000 fathom line, which not only avoids the vicinity of Colombia, but also the rough seas that often occur in the relatively shallower waters closer to land.

7   Transequatorial routes in the Atlantic

AT10 Transequatorial Routes

AT11 Europe to Cape Town
AT12 Canary Islands to Cape Town
AT13 US east coast to Cape Town
AT14 Canary Islands to Brazil
AT15 Cape Verde Islands to Brazil
AT16 West Africa to Brazil
AT17 Brazil to Lesser Antilles
AT18 Brazil to Europe
AT19 Cape Town to the Azores
AT20 Cape Town to US east coast
AT21 Cape Town to Lesser Antilles
AT22 Cape Horn to Europe
AT23 Cape Horn to US east coast

The best way to sail from one hemisphere to the other has preoccupied mariners ever since early explorers discovered the belt of calms that separates the trade wind systems of the two oceans. 'The well known equatorial embarrassments' is how Alexander George Findlay refers to the doldrums in his *Memoir of the Northern Atlantic Ocean,* published last century, a comprehensive book in which he tries to bring together all that was known at the time about the wind systems of the North Atlantic. The best strategy for tackling the doldrums is discussed in great detail, because fast passages across the equator were still of utmost importance to the masters of sailing ships linking Europe and North America with the rest of the world before the opening of the two great canals and the proliferation of powered vessels.

The first meteorologist who tried to put wind and weather observations on a proper scientific basic was an officer in the US Navy, Captain Matthew Fontaine Maury, who started collecting weather information in a methodical way in the early part of the nineteenth century and originated the pilot charts. Although primarily concerned with the weather of the

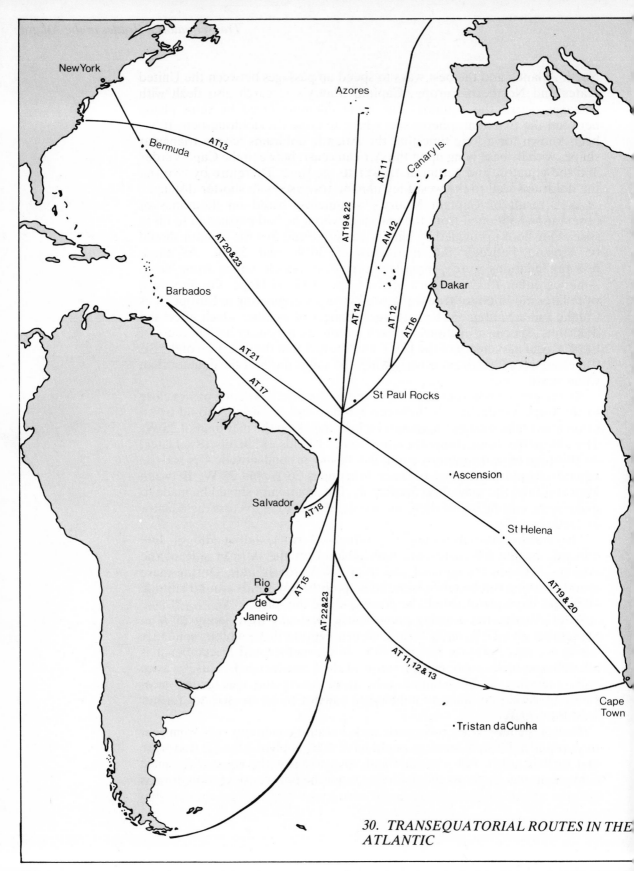

30. *TRANSEQUATORIAL ROUTES IN THE ATLANTIC*

North Atlantic and the best ways to speed up passages between the United States and Northern Europe, Captain Maury's research also dealt with passages across the equator. The main dilemma faced by ships plying between the two hemispheres was where to cross the doldrum belt. It has been known for a long time that the Atlantic doldrums have a triangular shape, with its base lying upon the African coast, between the Cape Verdes and the equator, and getting narrower to the west. Therefore by crossing the doldrums well to the west they may be traversed in a shorter distance.

As a result of Captain Maury's arguments, based on thousands of observations obtained from the mariners whom he had persuaded to fill in special log books provided by him, it was suggested that the equator should be crossed between the meridians of 30°W and 31°W. As these recommendations were primarily directed at vessels sailing from North America either to Cape Horn or the Cape of Good Hope, the directions were later modified for transequatorial voyages originating in Europe so as to take full advantage of the seasonal changes of weather which affect the doldrums. Specific directions for each month are necessary both because of the seasonal movement of the ITCZ and the fact that the direction of the SE trades tends to be more southerly when the sun is north of the equator than when south.

As the great circle route from Europe to the South Atlantic passes close to the Cape Verde Islands, between January and April one should try to pass close to the west of the islands by keeping along the meridian of 26°W. The alternative route inside the Cape Verde Islands will be discussed later. At this time of year southerly winds will be met around latitude 4°N and the equator should be crossed between longitudes 26°W and 28°W. Between May and July, the same directions apply, but an attempt should be made to make some easting below the Cape Verde Islands so as to cross the equator in 25°W or 26°W.

The transequatorial routes are influenced from the middle of July onwards by the SW monsoon, which blows on the African side of the Atlantic between the equator and the Cape Verde Islands. During these months easting can be made with the help of the SW winds around latitude 10°N and the equator should be crossed along meridian 23°W.

After August, the crossing points move gradually west, being 25°W in September and 27°W or 28°W in October. During these months southerly winds are met between 7°N and 8°N. In November and December it is advisable to make some easting south of the Cape Verde Islands, so as to cross meridian 25°W in about 6°N, from where the tack giving most southing should be taken to enable the equator to be crossed not further west than 29°W.

These instructions are only guidelines, because conditions vary from year to year and a different strategy might have to be applied if the SE trades are met further north. For a southbound voyage across the equator the most convenient place to cross the doldrums is not the only consideration, for it is also important to have sufficient easting in hand to be able to keep the SE trades on the port tack past the bulge of South America.

Another debate among masters of southbound sailing vessels was the best way to sail around the Cape Verde Islands, whether to westward or between the archipelago and the African coast. Taking up the challenge of Captain Maury's arguments in favour of a westerly crossing of the equator at all times of the year, the Royal Netherlands Meteorological Institute published a comparative study of the routes followed by a number of Dutch sailing ships, both inside and outside of the Cape Verde Islands. The passage times of the 455 Dutch vessels were then compared with the times taken by 144 American vessels, many of them clippers, which had also chosen either the inside or outside route on their voyages across the equator. The results of the combined experience of 599 vessels makes fascinating reading, even if the conclusions are not as clear cut as expected. Many more ships (340 Dutch, 111 American) decided to stay west of the islands than east (114 Dutch, 34 American), but the mean times showed only one day in favour of those that went outside. It does appear that the western track is to be preferred and the only months when the inside passage might be advantageous is between December and February, but the advantage is so small that the final decision as to which route to pursue should be determined by other considerations, which will be discussed in connection with the relevant routes.

The transequatorial strategy for northbound vessels is somewhat less daunting and the point where the equator should be crossed depends both on the port of departure and the destination. As most boats sailing north from Cape Town usually call at St Helena, the best course from there is to sail close to Ascension Island so as to cross the equator between longitudes 25°W and 30°W. In July and August, the equator should be crossed further east, between longitudes 20°W and 25°W, to ensure better winds north of the equator, as this is the time of the SW monsoon. The longitude of crossing depends greatly on the route that will be pursued in the North Atlantic, as a more easterly crossing will ensure a better slant in the NE trade winds on the subsequent leg to the Azores. However, for boats bound for the Caribbean, Bermuda and the east coast of the United States, a more westerly crossing of the equator might be advisable so as to take advantage of the favourable currents.

The controversies caused by the Atlantic doldrums continue to this day and the dilemma has still to be resolved. The optimum strategy for southbound transequatorial routes becomes a topical subject every four years during the run up to the Whitbread Round the World Race when the skippers of today's maxi boats rack their brains over which route would give them the best run to Cape Town, just as the masters of yesterday's clippers did before them. However, with ever improving satellite observations, the doldrums might finally give up their secrets and land-based weather routeing services might soon advise even small sailing boats on the best way to go. Much of the fun and excitement will be taken out of route planning, but at least the 'equatorial embarrassments' will cease to be a nuisance.

AT11 Europe to Cape Town

DIAGRAM 30	Falmouth to Cape Town 6500 m
	Gibraltar to Cape Town 5750 m

Best time:	October to January
Tropical storms:	None
Charts:	BA: 2127
	US: 22, 120
Pilots:	BA: 1, 2, 5, 22, 27, 67
	US: 121, 123, 140, 142, 143, 191

The optimum time to round the Cape of Good Hope limits the departure from Europe to one or two months. Most favourable conditions around the tip of Africa can be expected between December and February and therefore boats bound for Cape Town should plan to make this passage in November or December.

The routes from Southern Europe should follow directions as for AN22 and AN32 as far as the Canary Islands from where the same directions apply as for AT12. If a non-stop passage is preferred, the route from Gibraltar passes between Madeira and the Canaries and joins the route from Northern Europe in longitude 20°W.

Boats leaving from Northern Europe through the English Channel should make westing with a favourable wind at least as far as longitude 12°W. The object is to avoid being embayed in the Bay of Biscay by the prevailing westerly winds. Having reached longitude 12°W, the course should lead well past Cape Finisterre. The next change of course will aim to pass close to the west of Madeira. A decision will have to be taken at this point whether to go inside or outside the Cape Verde Islands and the various alternatives are described in AT10. Steadier winds are usually found on the west side of the Cape Verdes and if such a route is taken, some easting must be made south of the islands so as to arrive in the SE trades at a better angle. Normally the SE trades will have been found by the time the equator is crossed. In November–December the recommended longitude for crossing the equator is between longitudes 27°W and 29°W. Although such a crossing normally benefits both from better winds and a narrower belt of doldrums, some people prefer to make more easting north of the equator and carry this advantage through into the SE trades. The risk of such an action is the chance of meeting a wider band of doldrums.

South of the equator the object is to make as much easting as possible while still in the SE trades, which usually extend to 25°S. Beyond the southern limit of the trades the winds are variable and often strong. Down to the latitude of Cape Town the predominant direction of the winds during summer is northerly, so it should not be too difficult to make easting in these latitudes. Having lost the trades, the route loops towards the Cape of Good Hope crossing meridian 20°W in about 30°S, 10°W in 32°S and 0° in 35°S. The rest of the voyage will be made more or less on the latitude of Cape Town.

Occasionally the SE trades extend further south and make it difficult to make sufficient easting above latitude 30°S. In such a case the route might have to take a more southerly dip and pass close to Tristan da Cunha. A stop in this remote and wind-swept island is well worth a small detour and the warm welcome from its lonely inhabitants will make up for the rough anchorage. As the main anchorage is exposed, it must be left if the weather deteriorates. See also Routes AS15 and AS16.

On nearing the South African coast, care must be taken not to be swept northward by the strong current. Ideally Cape Town should be approached from the SW.

AT12 Canary Islands to Cape Town

DIAGRAM 30	Las Palmas to Cape Town 5100 m

Best time:	October to January
Tropical storms:	None
Charts:	BA:2127
	US: 22, 120
Pilots:	BA: 1, 2, 5
	US: 121, 123, 140, 143

As the route from Europe to Cape Town passes close to the west of the Canaries, some people plan to stop in these islands on their southbound voyage. Such a stop allows a departure from Europe during the summer and the subsequent passage to South Africa can be made when the time is right. For those who are already underway, a stop in the Canaries is not always justified, particularly in winter when it is better to cross the equator further west.

On leaving the Canaries the route runs SSW and passes NW of the Cape Verde Islands. This route to the west of the Cape Verdes is to be preferred between October and January, when steadier winds are found west of the islands. Directions concerning the longitudes in which the equator should be crossed are given in AT10. South of the equator the same directions apply as for Route AT11.

Although the route crosses a potential breeding ground for hurricanes to the west of the Cape Verde Islands, these storms rarely reach hurricane force while they are still developing.

AT13 US east coast to Cape Town

DIAGRAM 30	New York to Cape Town 6800 m

Best time:	November
Tropical storms:	June to November
Charts:	BA: 2127
	US: 22, 120
Pilots:	BA: 1, 2, 5, 69, 70
	US: 121, 123, 124, 140

The time of departure from the East Coast is dictated by the best time for rounding the Cape of Good Hope, which is between December and February. If the voyage is intended to terminate in Cape Town, the time of arrival is less crucial and the passage can be made at any time, although the winter months in the Cape area, from May to November, are best avoided.

A good departure time from anywhere on the East Coast is the beginning of November. Such a departure would hopefully avoid both the first of the winter *northers* and the risk of a late hurricane. As the NE trade wind belt will have to be traversed across its entire width, it is preferable to make as much easting as possible around latitude 35°N, where NW winds prevail in November. After meridian 45°W has been crossed, the route turns gradually SE to pass close to the west of the Cape Verde Islands. Some easting should be made south of the Cape Verdes so that latitude 5°N is reached in the vicinity of the 25°W meridian. The SE trades will be met close to this latitude and the recommended easting allows the equator to be crossed on the port tack. The point where the equator is crossed is governed by the width and position of the ITCZ, and AT10 describes the optimum longitudes in which the narrowest band of doldrums can be expected at different times of year. On a passage to Cape Town, however, the skipper may decide to carry his easting across the equator, even if a wider doldrum belt has to be crossed, and make use of the engine if necessary. Otherwise, for the recommended time of year, the equator should be crossed between longitudes 27°W and 29°W.

The SE trades are crossed at the best angle the windward-going qualities of the boat will permit. Their southern limit extends normally to a line joining the Cape of Good Hope to the Brazilian island of Trinidade. The route continues SE into an area of variables to a point in 30°S, 30°W and then along latitude 35°S to Cape Town. See also routes AT11, AS15 and AS16.

AT14 Canary Islands to Brazil

DIAGRAM 30	Las Palmas to Salvador 2820 m

Best time:	September to February
Tropical storms:	None
Charts:	BA: 4012, 4022
	US: 22, 120
Pilots:	BA: 1, 5
	US: 121, 124, 140, 143

The timing of this passage is dictated primarily by the preferred time of arrival in Brazil, rather than by sailing conditions expected en route. The majority of those who make this passage do so in order to be in Brazil for Carnival, which means arriving in Salvador (Bahia) or Rio de Janeiro before the beginning of February.

The passage across the doldrums presents a major dilemma, with opinions divided over the best place to cross the equator. The first decision, however, is whether to sail inside or outside the Cape Verde Islands after leaving the Canaries. If a stop in either the Cape Verde Islands or West Africa is not being considered, it is probably better to keep slightly to the west of the Cape Verde Islands. Depending on the time of year, the NE trades will be lost somewhere between 10°N (September) and 4°N (December). As the Atlantic doldrum belt narrows towards the west, it is more logical to try to cross it nearer the Brazilian coast. This assumption has been borne out by the fact that boats crossing the doldrums near the African coast have had to sail much farther in search of the SE trades than those who crossed further west. The width of the doldrums fluctuates greatly according to season and longitude, being anything from 100 to 400 miles wide. Southbound vessels normally find the SE trade winds between the equator (July) and latitude 3°S (January), although southerly winds can be encountered anywhere south of 10°N.

A convenient stop for boats en route to Brazil is Fernando de Noronha, a small island off the coast of Brazil. Between October and February NE winds prevail along the Brazilian coast between Cape São Roque and Cape Frio, making southbound passages easy, also helped by the SW setting current.

AT15 Cape Verde Islands to Brazil

DIAGRAM 30	São Vicente to Salvador 1970 m
	São Vicente to Rio de Janeiro 2620 m

Best time:	October to February
Tropical storms:	None
Charts:	BA: 4202, 4215
	US: 22, 106
Pilots:	BA: 1, 5
	US: 124, 143

Suggestions regarding the optimum point to cross the equator are given in AT10. If the destination in Brazil is between Cape São Roque and Cape Frio, the equator can be crossed further west than the recommended crossing points for routes which continue towards Cape Town. However, it should not be crossed further west than 30°W, as this might mean beating against the SE trades south of the equator. The rocks of St Peter and St Paul must be approached with extreme caution as they are often difficult to see until very close to them.

During the favourable season, the winds along the Brazilian coast are NE and the current sets SW, making it easy to reach any port along this stretch of coast. Between March and September the winds are predominantly SE and the current sets NE. This makes it necessary to make southing well off the coast and attempt to make landfall to windward of the port of destination. Coming from the north it is advisable to plan to arrive in the more southern ports between October and February, when the winds are NE, and sail up the coast during the rest of the year, when the SE trades take over.

AT16 West Africa to Brazil

DIAGRAM 30	Dakar to Salvador (Bahia) 2090 m
Best time:	October to February
Tropical storms:	None
Charts:	BA: 4202, 4215
	US: 22, 106
Pilots:	BA: 1, 5
	US: 124, 143

West Africa is becoming a more popular destination and most boats that cruise there continue their voyage to Brazil before sailing on to the Caribbean. The transequatorial passage requires careful planning as the doldrum belt in the proximity of the African coast can be 400–500 miles wide. Even if one is prepared to try to motor through, there can be difficulties in obtaining fuel in some countries in this region. A power-assisted passage through the doldrums can also be very uncomfortable because of the confused swell generated by the trade wind systems meeting at that point. It is therefore recommended to try to stay with the NE trades north of the equator and only cross it in longitude 29°W or 30°W. A more westerly crossing point is not advisable if making for Salvador because of the risk of head winds south of the equator. See also AT10 and AT15.

AT17 Brazil to Lesser Antilles

| DIAGRAM 30 | Rio de Janeiro to Barbados 3200 m |
| | Salvador to Tobago 2550 m |

Best time:	March to June
Tropical storms:	June to November
Charts:	BA: 4202, 4216
	US: 22, 108
Pilots:	BA: 5, 7A, 71
	US: 124, 147, 148

Northbound passages from southern ports in Brazil are hampered by the strong NE winds and SW current, which predominate between October and February. Passages during this time from ports south of Recife are best avoided as the only solution is to stand well offshore until the SE trades are found and then make northing with their help. Boats coming from ports south of Rio de Janeiro will find better conditions between March and September when the prevailing winds are the SE trades. If an inshore passage from southern ports is preferred, care must be taken when passing between the Abrolhos Islands and the mainland as the charts are inaccurate and the reefs more extensive than charted. If the islands are passed offshore, caution must also be exercised as the reefs extend about 35 miles offshore.

From ports north of Recife (Pernambuco), the passage to the West Indies can be made at any time of the year. Winds along the north coast of Brazil are always favourable and the current sets strongly to the north-west. The waters along this coast of Brazil are often very muddy from the Amazon and as depths are often shallow, a good distance offshore must be kept as the colour of the water gives no indication of its depth.

The extent of the doldrums varies with the time of year, being wider in the northern summer. An area of variable winds, calms and squalls normally extends from the equator in longitude 30°W to about latitude 3°N–5°N in longitude 38°W.

AT18 Brazil to Europe

DIAGRAM 30	Rio de Janeiro to Falmouth 4700 m
	Salvador to Gibraltar 3300 m
	Rio de Janeiro to Gibraltar 4000 m

Best time:	April to September
Tropical storms:	June to November
Charts:	BA: 2059, 4202
	US: 22, 120
Pilots:	BA: 1, 5, 22, 27, 67
	US: 124, 140, 142, 143, 191

Northbound passages from Brazilian ports south of Cape Frio should avoid the period October to February, when NE winds prevail along the coast. During this time, the normal practice is to take a long tack offshore until well inside the SE trades which makes it possible to weather Cape São Roque at the eastern extremity of Brazil. After sufficient easting has been made, the course can be altered to northward so that the equator is crossed between longitudes 28°W and 30°W.

From April to September northbound passages are much easier and the equator should be crossed as far east as possible so as to enter the NE trades at the most favourable slant. North of the equator the route runs close to the Azores, which should always be passed to the west if the vessel is bound for Northern Europe. Depending on the winds encountered in the vicinity of the islands, the recommended practice is to stay on the tack which gives most northing, as westerly winds will be found in higher latitudes and the course can then be altered to NE. For the rest of the passage to Northern Europe see Routes AN53 and AN54.

For vessels bound for Gibraltar, the route north of the equator should stay as far east as the trades will allow. If the Azores cannot be avoided, Horta offers a convenient stop from where Routes AN51 and AN52 give details for the continuation of the passage

AT19 Cape Town to the Azores

DIAGRAM 30	Cape Town to Horta 5540 m

Best time:	January to April
Tropical storms:	None
Charts:	BA: 4012, 4022
	US: 22, 120
Pilots:	BA: 1, 2, 67
	US: 121, 123, 140, 143

The great circle route from Cape Town to the Azores runs close to both St Helena (AS11) and Ascension (AS12) and few boats pass these islands without stopping briefly. If no stop is intended, the great circle route should be taken from Cape Town to one of the longitudes recommended in AT10. As most of the passage in the South Atlantic is made in the SE trades, steady winds can be expected almost all the way to the equator. From Ascension, the route continues in a NW direction towards the equator, which is crossed further west during the northern winter and further east in summer. The recommended longitudes are between 26°W and 28°W in December to February, 22°W to 25°W in June to September. The latter period coincides with the SW monsoon, when it may be better to cross the equator more to the east and take a route between the Cape Verde Islands and the African coast to take advantage of the SW winds. This would mean that the NE trades would be approached from a better angle north of the

Cape Verdes. Such an alternative route could also include a detour to West Africa.

The route inside of the Cape Verdes is not recommended in winter when the islands should be passed as closely as possible on their west side. This is usually possible if some easting is made while north of the equator and the doldrums are crossed at right angles, probably with help from the engine. A route close to the Cape Verdes is essential and enables the Azores to be laid on one tack. The rest of the route to the Azores is similar to AN55.

AT20 Cape Town to US east coast

DIAGRAM 30	Cape Town to New York 5800 m

Best time:	January to April
Tropical storms:	June to November
Charts:	BA: 2127
	US: 22, 120
Pilots:	BA: 2, 5, 69, 70, 71
	US: 121, 123, 140, 147

Similar directions apply as far as the equator to those for Route AT19, although a more westerly crossing of the equator is preferable for boats bound for the USA. A convenient stop south of the equator is the small Brazilian island Fernando de Noronha. Because the optimum departure time from Cape Town (January to March) brings boats too early into the North Atlantic, some people prefer to make a detour via the Caribbean, especially as the route runs quite close to the Lesser Antilles. Route AN103 describes the subsequent leg from the islands to the East Coast.

Having crossed the equator, the direct route runs NW through the NE trades to Bermuda. Route AN65 gives directions for a return to the USA. If a non-stop passage is planned from Cape Town, an arrival in Bermuda is not recommended before the middle of April. A departure from Cape Town at the end of February or beginning of March is not too late, as favourable sailing conditions still prevail in the South Atlantic.

AT21 Cape Town to Lesser Antilles

DIAGRAM 30	Cape Town to Barbados 5200 m
	Cape Town to Martinique 5300 m

Best time:	November to March
Tropical storms:	June to November
Charts:	BA: 3273, 4022
	US: 22, 124
Pilots:	BA: 2, 5, 71
	US: 121, 123, 124, 147

As an alternative to AN20, this route has the advantage that it can leave Cape Town earlier so as to arrive in the Caribbean after the middle of November and the start of the safe cruising season there. As the route passes close to St Helena, most boats make a brief call there before continuing towards the equator. Another favoured stop en route to the Caribbean is the island of Fernando de Noronha, off the coast of Brazil. The route crosses the equator in about longitude 32°30′W, where the doldrums are very narrow at this time of year (December to February). The SE trades are normally lost soon after the equator has been crossed and the NE trades are picked up 100 to 150 miles further on. The route continues parallel to the north coast of Brazil, where a very strong current setting NW at rates of 1½ to 2 knots gives an excellent boost.

The NE trades are normally found in about latitude 5°N and as their initial direction is sometimes NNE, boats that are bound for the Leeward or Virgin Islands are advised not to cross the equator too far west so as to have a better slant through the trades. In such a case, the recommended longitude for crossing the equator is between 30°W and 32°W. See also AT17.

Note: Holders of South African passports are advised that they are not welcomed in a number of Caribbean countries and if they arrive without a visa they risk being refused entry.

AT22 Cape Horn to Europe

| DIAGRAM 30 | Cape Horn to Falmouth 7100 m |
| | Cape Horn to Gibraltar 6360 m |

Best time:	December to March
Tropical storms:	None
Charts:	BA: 2127
	US: 20, 120
Pilots:	BA: 1, 5, 6, 22, 27, 67
	US: 121, 124, 140, 142, 143, 191

This busy route in the heyday of the clipper ships is only used nowadays by a few cruising boats, which choose this tough way of reaching Europe from New Zealand, or the participants in round the world races. After rounding Cape Horn, the route can pass either east or west of Staten Island. If the island is passed to seaward, a wide berth should be given to Cape St John, as a dangerous tide rip extends offshore for about six miles, making conditions hazardous when the wind blows against the tide. Alternatively, the route through Le Maire Strait can be taken, especially if the intention is to pass to the west of the Falkland Islands. These can be passed on either side, after which the route runs in a general NE direction through an area of prevailing westerly winds. It is advisable to make some easting in these latitudes before reaching the SE trades so that the subsequent route to the equator will intersect them at a better angle. From the Falklands the route crosses latitude 45°S in 48°W, 40°S in 42°W and 30°S in 34°W, so that the SE trades will be found somewhere along meridian 30°W.

The SE trades normally extend to latitude 25°S and near their southern limit their direction is more easterly. Once in the trades, the course becomes northerly so that the equator is crossed between longitudes 26°W and 30°W, depending on the time of year (see AT10). During the southern winter, from May to September, it is usually possible to stay closer to the Brazilian coast and sail between Cape Frio and the offlying islands. For the continuation of the passage to Europe see Routes AT18 and AT19.

AT23 Cape Horn to US east coast

| DIAGRAM 30 | Cape Horn to Bermuda 6600 m |
| | Cape Horn to New York 7240 m |

Best time:	December to February
Tropical storms:	June to November
Charts:	BA: 2127
	US: 20, 120
Pilots:	BA: 5, 6, 69, 70, 71
	US: 121, 124, 140, 147

This route follows the same track as Route AT22 until the SE trades are met, from where a more westerly route can be taken to the equator, passing close to Fernando de Noronha island. The equator is crossed in about longitude 30°W and the great circle route is taken from there either to Bermuda or direct to the port of destination. This route is not recommended during the hurricane season, but as Cape Horn will have been doubled probably during the most favourable months, which are the southern summer months of December to March, this passage will reach the North Atlantic at a convenient time.

Route AT20 describes some of the alternatives which avoid an arrival in the USA in the middle of winter. This can be accomplished by spending some time en route in Brazil, the Lesser Antilles or Bermuda.

The direct route north of the equator passes through the NE trades which normally last as far as latitude 25°N, from where the Horse Latitudes will have to be crossed.

8 Winds and currents of the South Atlantic

Maps 2 to 6

South-east trade winds

Because the Intertropical Convergence Zone is situated north of the equator throughout the year, it may be said that the South Atlantic Ocean does not have a doldrums zone. The SE trade winds are more constant than their North Atlantic counterpart, the NE trades. They form the equatorial side of the air circulation around the oceanic anticyclone, which is situated between latitudes 22°S and 30°S and has a direct bearing on the winds and weather of the entire tropical South Atlantic.

The SE trade winds extend as far as the equator during the southern winter and their northern limit retreats by a few degrees to the south in the summer after December. Occasionally these winds reach beyond the equator and southerly winds can be encountered as far north as 10°N. Their direction varies from being SE or SSE on the eastern side of the ocean to becoming almost easterly in the western part. The average strength of the SE trades is 15 knots, but they diminish in strength towards the equator.

Variables

A zone of light variable winds extends to the south of the SE trade wind belt and is similar to the Horse Latitudes of the North Atlantic. This region of variable winds coincides with the areas of oceanic high pressure which are located between latitudes 25°S and 32°S approximately. Their position is influenced by the seasonal movement of the sun, reaching their southern limit in January and their northern limit in July. To the east of the 0° meridian the winds tend to be mostly southerly and can be regarded as an extension of the trades. The summer winds in the western half of this region are mostly NE.

Westerlies

The winds in the higher latitudes of the South Atlantic are predominantly westerly. This is the region of the Roaring Forties where winds being generated by the continuous passage of depressions from west to east often blow with gale force. The strong westerlies are a normal feature of southern waters where they blow unhindered south of the three great capes.

Tropical storms

Tropical revolving storms do not occur in the South Atlantic Ocean.

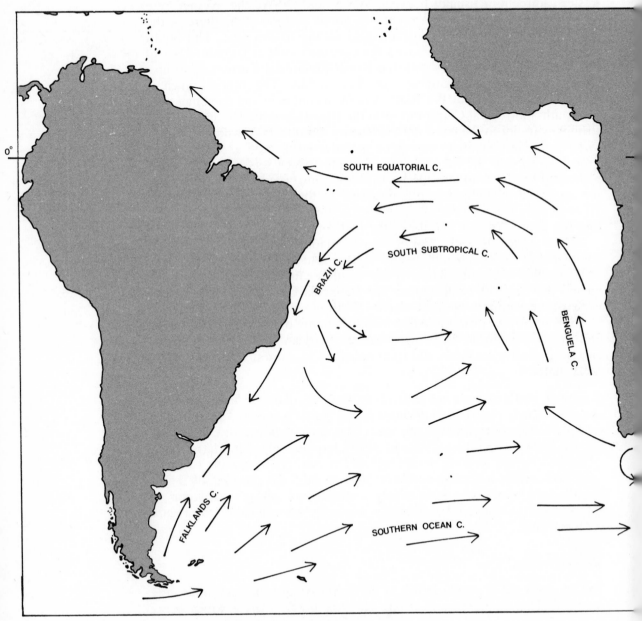

31. *SOUTH ATLANTIC CURRENTS*

Currents

The currents of the South Atlantic Ocean are part of a well defined anti-clockwise circulation. The South Equatorial Current flows in a broad belt from east to west with its axis roughly along latitude 6°S. The part of this current which is between the equator and latitude 6°S is reputed to be one of the most constant currents in the world. The set is always in a westerly direction, usually between WNW and WSW, the average rate being about 1 knot. Further south, to about latitude 20°S, there is the weaker South Subtropical Current, also setting to the west. The South Equatorial Current extends across the equator to about latitude 4°N and one branch of it combines with the North Equatorial Current to form a strong current setting towards the West Indies. The other branch is deflected to the south by the South American continent and combines with the South Subtropical Current to form the Brazil Current. This current sets strongly parallel to the coast until it reaches latitude 25°S, where part of it turns east. The remainder carries on as far as latitude 35°S, where it also turns east to join the the vast body of water which sets eastward and is generated by the Southern Ocean Current. This broad belt of cold water sets eastward in the southern hemisphere to the south of all continents. After passing Cape Horn, a branch of this current turns to the north east into the South Atlantic and forms the Falklands Current.

On the African side the main ocean circulation of the South Atlantic is completed by the Benguela Current. This current sets north along the coast of Africa and is a continuation of the Agulhas Current after the latter has passed the Cape of Good Hope. The Benguela Current is reinforced by some of the Southern Ocean Current. North of latitude 20°S the Benguela Current sets away from the African coast fanning out into the Subtropical and South Equatorial Currents. Near the African coast, the set of the current is always northerly and from February to April it reaches as far as the equator.

9 Regional weather in the South Atlantic

South Africa

This staging post for sailors on world voyages can be described as little else but tempestuous. With the hot mass of Africa to the north and the cold antarctic ice to the south, this high inhospitable coastline presents an obstacle to opposing air currents from these regions. The main feature of weather conditions in this area is the high proportion of gale force winds, which come from almost any direction and with little warning, quickly raising high and dangerous seas. The weather forecasts here rarely give a prognosis for longer than 12 hours. Often winds build up to gale force in the day and fall at night, but this is not a rule, nor can it be relied on.

It is not uncommon to have gales from different directions, say NE followed by SW on succeeding days. The strong currents in this area are part of the reason why seas build up so high and so rapidly, especially when the gales are opposing the current. A typical sequence of weather is for a NE gale to blow hard, followed by a lull and then SW winds setting in with gale force. In summer depressions come up from the south giving a cold change similar to the southerly *busters* experienced in south east Australia.

On the Atlantic side the SE trades prevail in the summer, although these can become SE gales, blowing stronger than the trades do in the open ocean. In winter these are often replaced by the NW anti-trades, which cross Africa north of the cape. The stormiest weather is usually encountered around the high and steep Cape of Storms, so aptly named by early voyagers. December to February are usually the best months for rounding the Cape.

Magellan Straits to Rio de la Plata

Not a destination for clement cruising, this area is visited only by a few boats that make the passage around the Horn or through the Magellan Straits. Although in the belt of prevailing westerly winds which bring clear weather, winds and gales do occur from other directions.

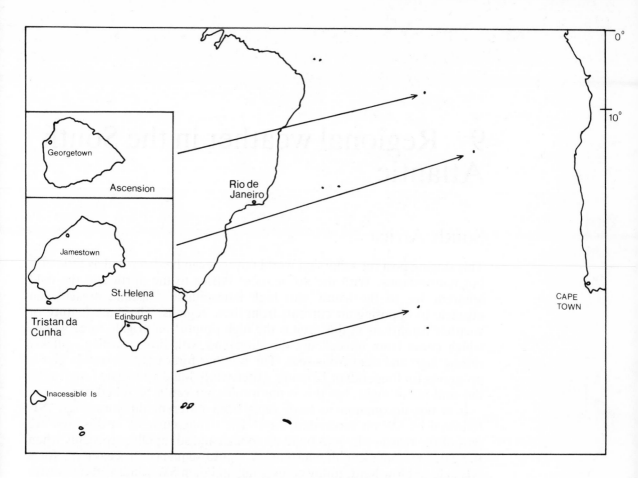

32. ISLANDS IN THE SOUTH ATLANTIC

From September through to June one can get SE gales coming with rain, bad weather and heavy seas. These winds can also bring fog. A very dense fog can also occur with NW winds along the southerly portions of this coast in the months from February to October. When the wind shifts more to the south of west the fog usually clears. In warmer weather thunder and lightning can occur with N and W winds.

Northerly gales are preceded by overcast skies, haze, lots of small cloud very high up and some lightning. The wind increases gradually to gale force. On the other hand, southerly winds increase to gale force much more suddenly and are more violent. A sign of impending bad weather from the south is large masses of heavy cloud on the southern horizon. If a very low barometer starts rising, this may also be a sign of a wind shift to the south. The old sailing ships considered it prudent to always furl sail when the barometer was very low and heavy clouds massed in the south. Squalls are not that frequent, but those from the cold wastes of the south can be extremely violent.

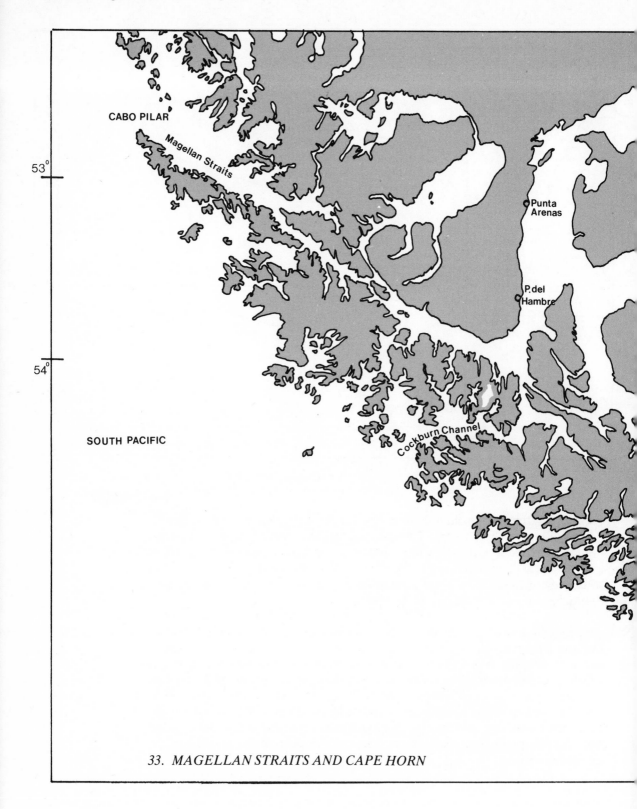

CABO PILAR

Magellan Straits

53°

Punta
Arenas

P. del
Hambre

54°

SOUTH PACIFIC

Cockburn Channel

33. MAGELLAN STRAITS AND CAPE HORN

ellan Straits

SOUTH ATLANTIC

ERRA DEL FUEGO

Le Maire Strait

Iª DE LOS
ESTADOS

Beagle Channel

CAPE HORN

Rio de la Plata

This large estuary of the rivers Paraná and Uruguay is sailed mainly by those wishing to call either at Montevideo, on the northern Uruguay shore, or Buenos Aires, on the southern Argentine shore. In the region of variable winds, the weather in the river estuary changes very frequently and very quickly.

In the summer months from September through to March, the prevailing wind is from an easterly direction, more north of east outside the river, becoming more easterly in the river entrance. The rest of the year a W to SW wind prevails in the entrance reaches, becoming more northerly in the river. The weather is usually fine only when the wind is settled in the north. Otherwise at this time of year variables, calms and squalls can occur, the wind shifting both clockwise and anticlockwise, blowing most strongly from either the east or the west.

During June to October, strong SW squalls called *pamperos* can occur with little warning. Named because they blow across the pampas, these squalls bring rain and cold temperatures that can even change the rain to hail. Most frequent in the winter months, the *pamperos* can last two or three days, occasionally longer. In other months they are less frequent and do not last so long, but may pack a more violent wind. Although centred on the Rio de la Plata, the *pamperos* affect the surrounding coastal area between latitudes 31°S and 40°S and as far out to sea as 48°W.

Dangerous conditions occur in the river when SE winds are blowing strongly as these pile up a heavy sea, making the northern coast a hazardous leeshore, and are usually accompanied by fog and rain. A forewarning is given by a steep rise of the barometer, cloudy skies and lightning.

Brazil

The attractions of cruising in Brazil are very varied, from the multicultural atmosphere of Rio de Janeiro in the south to the adventure of exploring the mighty Amazon in the north. It is a destination both for boats arriving from South Africa, the Canaries, Cape Verdes or the west coast of Africa as well as those coming from Cape Horn.

The southern coast of Brazil from Rio de Janeiro to Rio de la Plata has very variable winds with seasonal variations. From October through to April, winds from a NE direction predominate, which when strong are usually followed by calms and a SW wind. In April NW and SW winds blow in equal proportion to the north easterlies, which after a few SE to SW gales give way to SW winds in May. These SW winds prevail through until October. From July to September westerly winds bring bad weather on rare occasions. NW squalls lasting several hours also occur at this time near Rio de Janeiro.

Above Rio de Janeiro the lower east coast of Brazil enjoys NE winds, fine weather and a clear sky for most of the year, the winds being strongest close to the coast from December to February. Off the capes of Frio and São Tomé the combination of fresh NE winds and strong currents can create bad seas. The NE winds are not felt so strongly west of Cape Frio, as the mountains check their force.

Higher up the coast the SE trade wind is felt from March to August as far south as Salvador (Bahia), although the rest of the year it reaches only as far as Recife (Perambuco).

Both the SE and NE winds sometimes give way to squally SW weather lasting a few days and bringing clouds and rain. This SW weather occurs particularly from April to August when the winds are usually lighter and more variable. The barometer usually falls 24 hours before the onset of SW winds. Although there are land and sea breezes all along the coast, the land breeze is normally short lived and weak unless the sea breeze is strong.

On the north coast of Brazil towards the Amazon, the movement of the Intertropical Convergence Zone influences the weather, bringing the SE trade wind, accompanied by fine weather, from August to October and the NE trade from November to March. This latter period is the wet season along this coast. Both of these winds have a more easterly component tending to be ESE and ENE. Between April and the onset of the SE trades in August, the wind first moves into the ESE and then gives way to a couple of months of doldrum weather with calms, squalls and variables. Although more frequent in this season, the land and sea breezes are never very marked.

St Helena

This rather forbidding island, place of exile for Napolean, often stands out like a fortress, visible from 60 miles away, due to the excellent clear visibility that prevails in this region. The island is full in the flow of the SE trades, which rarely falter.

Ascension

A bustling military base, this outpost in mid-Atlantic is another welcome stop for those on long Atlantic voyages. The SE trades have often spent some of their force by the time they reach Ascension and can be as light as 5 knots. Heavy rollers and swell from the NW can be experienced when the NE trade is at its height in the North Atlantic, which can make landing difficult.

Falkland Islands

Lying in the South Atlantic, these islands are only just over 300 miles from Cape Horn and the weather has much in common with that of the dreaded Cape. However, the 200 islands that surround the two main islands of West and East Falkland have a lot to offer the intrepid sailor who is not daunted by their remoteness. Although navigation among the islands can be quite tricky, one is never too far from a safe anchorage.

The prevailing direction of wind is westerly and these truly windy islands have an average yearly wind speed of 17 knots with a slight rise in the summer months of December to March. These winds can drop to calm at

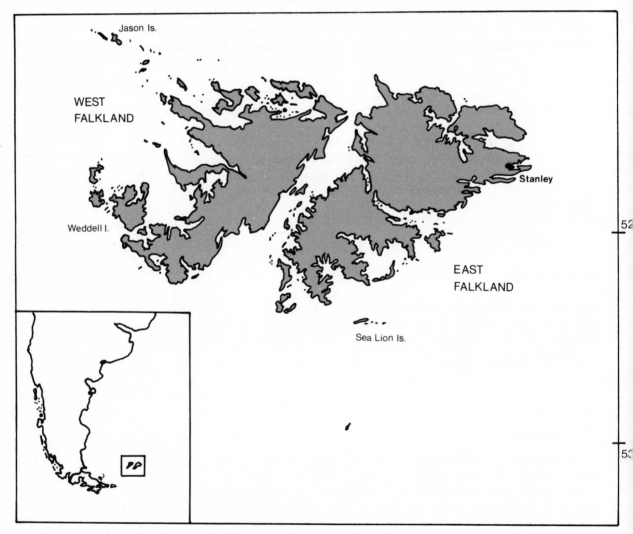

34. FALKLAND ISLANDS

sunset with a tendency to increase to 10–15 knots during the night, calming again at dawn. The winds tend to increase during the day and can reach gale force by the afternoon.

Gales usually begin in the NW and quickly draw around to the SW. The worst gales tend to be those from the N and NE, which are not easily predicted and often occur without warning. They are caused by depressions moving north between the islands and the Patagonian coast. Northerly winds, which are common in the summer months from December to April, often produce fog along the north coast. When strong westerlies are blowing, the islands are prone to *willywaws*, which can be extremely dangerous to small craft. These occur mostly in the lee of the islands and in some of the narrow passages between islands in the west.

Those who plan to cruise among the islands should obtain the 'mine maps' which are given free of charge by the Secretariat Building in Port Stanley and contain details of the areas which were mined during the 1982 war.

10   Routes in the South Atlantic

AS11 Cape Town to St Helena
AS12 St Helena to Ascension
AS13 St Helena to Brazil
AS14 Cape Town to Brazil

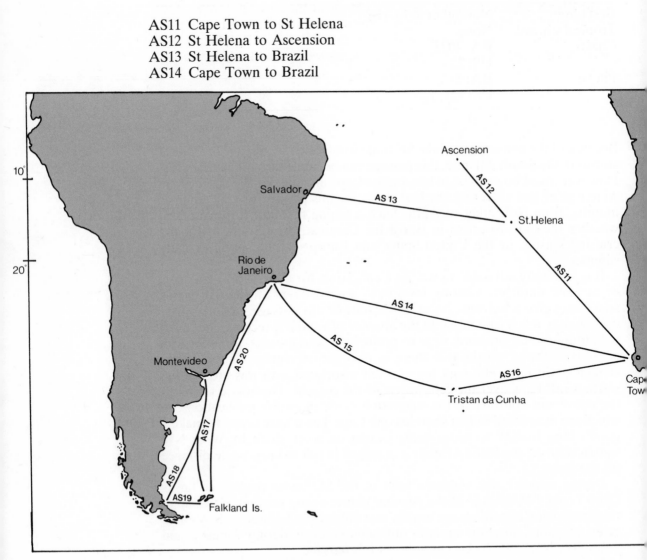

35. SOUTH ATLANTIC ROUTES

AS15 Brazil to Tristan da Cunha
AS16 Tristan da Cunha to Cape Town
AS17 South America to Falkland Islands
AS18 South America to Magellan Strait
AS19 Magellan Strait to Falkland Islands
AS20 Falkland Islands to South America

AS11 Cape Town to St Helena

DIAGRAM 35	Cape Town to St Helena 1680 m
Best time:	November to March
Tropical storms:	None
Charts:	BA: 4022
	US: 22
Pilots:	BA: 2
	US: 121, 123

Because of the consistency of the SE trade winds and the absence of tropical storms in the South Atlantic, this passage can be made throughout the year. However, most boats plan on leaving the Cape area before the onset of the winter gales and therefore the best times for this passage are the summer months, from November to April. Such a timing fits most forward plans, whether they are to arrive in Brazil for Carnival, the Caribbean for the cruising season, or the United States and Europe in late spring or early summer.

It is generally advisable to wait in Cape Town for a favourable forecast, or at least until any existing lows have passed over. Strong SW winds sometimes give a welcome boost at the start of this passage, although they occasionally reach gale force. In the absence of wind it is recommended not to venture too far offshore, so as to profit from land breezes. If the African coast is followed northward, there is also the advantage of the strong Benguela Current, although fog is often associated with this area, when warm winds blow over the cold waters of the current. The advice to follow the coast runs contrary to the suggestion made in earlier publications, in which the masters of sailing ships leaving Cape Town were urged to make a good offing to NW to avoid being caught on a lee shore by W or NW squalls. During unsettled weather it is indeed better to keep a safe distance off the coast.

During summer, the southern limit of the SE trades reaches as far as Cape Town, but because of the peculiar nature of the weather in this area, true trade wind conditions are usually met only above latitude 25°S. Violent gales of short duration are not uncommon even during January and February, which are the best months for this passage.

AS12 St Helena to Ascension

DIAGRAM 35	St Helena to Ascension 710 m

Best time:	All year
Tropical storms:	None
Charts:	BA: 4022
	US: 22
Pilots:	BA: 2
	US: 123

As a continuation of a northbound passage from Cape Town, the subsequent leg from St Helena to Ascension benefits from favourable winds throughout the year. The direction of the wind is predominantly SE, although its strength varies and can sometimes be light, especially in the summer months January to March.

AS13 St Helena to Brazil

DIAGRAM 35	St Helena to Salvador 1920 m
	St Helena to Fernando de Noronha 1740 m

Best time:	All year
Tropical storms:	None
Charts:	BA: 4022
	US: 22
Pilots:	BA: 2, 5
	US: 123, 124

Boats bound for the Caribbean find it more convenient to make a detour via the Brazilian coast before heading NW. One of the prime attractions on the north east coast is Salvador, formerly known as Bahia, whose annual Carnival is a keen rival of the more famous Carnival of Rio. The island of Fernando de Noronha, off Cape São Roque, is used as a convenient stepping stone by boats en route to the Caribbean. See also Route AT17.

The weather on this route is mostly pleasant, with consistent E and SE winds that very rarely reach gale force.

AS14 Cape Town to Brazil

DIAGRAM 35	Cape Town to Rio 3270 m
	Cape Town to Salvador 3330 m

Best time:	December to March
Tropical storms:	None
Charts:	BA: 4022
	US: 22
Pilots:	BA: 2, 5
	US: 123, 124

The great circle route to Rio de Janeiro and ports south of Cape Frio is well outside the southern limit of the SE trade winds, so it is advisable to make this passage between latitudes 20°S and 25°S where the chances of having favourable winds are much greater. The SE trade wind belt has its southern limit along a diagonal line that runs from Trinidade Island to the Cape of Good Hope. The initial route from Cape Town runs NW for about 1,200 miles until steady SE trades are found. It then goes west as far as longitude 30°W, from where a course is shaped for the coast. A similar route, taking full advantage of the SE trade winds, should also be followed for ports lying further south along the coast of South America.

A more direct route from Cape Town can be steered to ports lying north of Cape Frio. As the ports on the Brazilian coast between Cape São Roque and Cape Frio are under the influence of steady NE winds between October and February and the current along the coast also sets SW, a subsequent passage from Rio northward should be planned for the SE season, from March to September.

AS15 Brazil to Tristan da Cunha

DIAGRAM 35	Rio de Janeiro to Tristan da Cunha 1800 m
Best time:	November to March
Tropical storms:	None
Charts:	BA: 4022
	US: 22
Pilots:	BA: 2, 5
	US: 121, 123, 124

As the great circle route from Rio de Janeiro to Cape Town passes through an area of variable winds, it is advisable to steer a more SW course on leaving Rio so as to arrive sooner on latitude 35°S where prevailing winds are NW and W. From a point in 35°S, 30°W the route runs almost due east along parallel 35°S. If this passage is made at the beginning of summer, in October or November, westerly winds are usually found in latitude 33°S or 34°S and it may not be necessary to go further south in search of steady winds. As the summer progresses, the belt of variables moves south and in February or March it may be necessary to go to 37°S to fall in with steady westerlies. The winds in these latitudes are usually 20 to 25 knots, occasionally reaching 40 knots.

As the more southerly route passes so close to Tristan da Cunha, sailing by without stopping at this remote island would be hard to justify. The small harbour on the NE side of the island is only suitable for the small local boats, but an anchorage can usually be found in the lee of the island.

AS16 Tristan da Cunha to Cape Town

DIAGRAM 35	Tristan da Cunha to Cape Town 1510 m

Best time:	December to March
Tropical storms:	None
Charts:	BA: 4022
	US: 22
Pilots:	BA: 2
	US: 121, 123

The winds below latitude 35°S are much more favourable in direction for a passage to Cape Town than those blowing further north, and a more southerly course is therefore recommended. Near Tristan da Cunha the winds are mostly from between N and W in summer becoming more westerly as one moves east. After the prime meridian has been crossed, a more direct course can be shaped for Cape Town so that latitude 35°S is recrossed in longitude 10°E. As the prevailing summer winds in the Cape Town area are SE and gales from that direction are frequent, the coast should be approached from SW to avoid being set to leeward by the wind and current setting strongly northward.

AS17 South America to Falkland Islands

DIAGRAM 35	Rio de Janeiro to Stanley 1860 m
	Montevideo to Stanley 1020 m

Best time:	December to February
Tropical storms:	None
Charts:	BA: 4200, 4201
	US: 20
Pilots:	BA: 5, 6
	US: 121, 124

The route from Rio de Janeiro southward runs close to the coast, and if not calling at ports in the Rio de la Plata estuary, the direct offshore route is preferable. The winds between Rio de Janeiro and latitude 35°S are mostly NE in summer. South of latitude 35°S, the prevailing winds become increasingly westerly and it is advisable to stay well to the west of the direct route to the Falklands to avoid being blown off course by a westerly gale. The weather is generally better close inshore than offshore. Another reason why an inshore route is preferable is that it avoids the strong north setting Falklands Current which can reach as much as 2 knots offshore. The inshore route should be taken as far as latitude 47°S from where a direct course can be shaped for Stanley Harbour.

AS18 *South America to Magellan Strait*

DIAGRAM 35	Montevideo to Cape Virgins 1200 m

Best time:	November to February
Tropical storms:	None
Charts:	BA: 4200
	US: 20
Pilots:	BA: 5, 6
	US: 121, 124

The route from Rio de Janeiro follows the coast to Montevideo, where favourable winds and current are normally found in summer. Caution must be exercised if the route runs close to the land because of the danger of onshore currents. From Rio de la Plata southward, the route runs very close to the coast to stay in sheltered waters and also to avoid the strong north setting Falklands Current. The winds in this region are predominantly westerly so that the risk of being caught on a lee shore is remote. Gales from the east are extremely rare and when they occur, there is always sufficient warning.

The strait must be approached with extreme caution as the tidal range is great and the tidal streams set strongly towards Sarmiento Bank and the dangers extending from Cape Virgins.

The time of arrival at the strait depends on the tides and it must be remembered that the times of high and low water get later as one proceeds westward, until Royal Road is passed. This fact greatly assists passages from east to west and a vessel that catches the beginning of the west setting stream in the First Narrows has a good chance to ride the favourable tide for 9 hours, possibly as far as Punta Arenas. The tidal stream runs through the First Narrows from 5 to 7 knots and through the Second Narrows from 3 to 6 knots. The tidal range itself varies from about 40 feet at the east end of the strait to only 5 feet at its western end.

The usual route from the Atlantic runs through the following channels: Smyth, Sarmiento, Inocentes, Concepción, Largo, Messier and out through the Gulf of Peñas into the Pacific Ocean. A shorter route reaches the Pacific through Cockburn Channel.

AS19 *Magellan Strait to Falkland Islands*

DIAGRAM 35	Cape Virgins to Stanley 400 m

Best time:	December to March
Tropical storms:	None
Charts:	BA: 4200
	US: 20
Pilots:	BA: 6
	US: 124

The prevailing westerly winds make this a relatively easy passage, but caution must be exercised when leaving the strait as the strong tidal stream often sets towards the rocks extending offshore from Cape Virgins. The route rounds East Falkland Island from the south, passing between it and Sea Lion Island.

AS20 Falkland Islands to South America

DIAGRAM 35	Stanley to Montevideo 1020 m
	Stanley to Rio de Janeiro 1860 m

Best time:	December to May
Tropical storms:	None
Charts:	BA: 4200, 4201
	US: 20
Pilots:	BA: 5, 6
	US: 121, 124

The northbound passage as far as Rio de la Plata can be done throughout the summer months and the direct route benefits both from the strong north setting Falklands Current and the prevailing W winds. North from Rio de la Plata, the prevailing winds in summer are NE and therefore such a passage should not be attempted before April. Ideally the passage from the Falklands to Rio de la Plata should be done between December and February, with the subsequent leg to Rio de Janeiro and beyond only being undertaken later, between May and September, when favourable winds prevail along the entire Brazilian coast.

A passage from the Falklands to Europe or the east coast of the USA can either incorporate the above alternative or it can join the direct routes from Cape Horn to those destinations described in Routes AT22 and AT23.

11   Winds and currents of the North Pacific

Maps 2 to 6

North-east trade winds

These winds blow on the southern side of the area of high pressure, which is normally located around latitude 30°N. During the summer months this high is usually situated farther north than in winter and the NE trades can be found as far north as latitude 32°N. During the summer the trades are predominant to the east of the 150°E meridian, being replaced to the west of this meridian by the SW monsoon of the Western Pacific Ocean.

The NE trade winds of the North Pacific Ocean are particularly consistent in both direction and strength over large areas. Their direction is more N and even NW near the American coast, becoming increasingly E towards the west. Their strength is about 10–15 knots, although they can become fresher at times and at the height of the trade wind season stronger winds of 30 knots are not uncommon. The strongest trades likely to be encountered are in winter, between November and March, but they diminish in strength as one moves south towards the equator.

The entire trade wind belt moves north and south through the year in accordance with the declination of the sun. However, its northern and southern limits do not run in a straight line from east to west, but in a curve which reaches its highest point in summer in about latitude 35°N about 200 miles from the American coast, the corresponding southern limit being in latitude 8°N. The northern limit of the trades in winter is 29°N, in about longitude 150°W, with the southern limit for the same period being the equator.

Intertropical Convergence Zone

The NE trades are bound to the south by the ITCZ, which remains north of the equator throughout the year east of meridian 160°W. To the west of that longitude it moves south of the equator during the northern winter, from about December to April or early May. During the summer of the northern hemisphere, when the SE trade winds are at their strongest in the South Pacific, the ITCZ disappears altogether west of about 150°W, where the two trade wind systems almost run into each other and the belt of doldrums is virtually nonexistent. In the western part of the North Pacific, the ITCZ is only present during the changeover periods of the monsoons, either from mid-April to mid-May or from mid-September to mid-November.

The weather inside the zone is typical doldrums weather, with calms or very light winds alternating with squalls, heavy rain and thunderstorms. However, as one moves west, the frequency of calms and light variable winds becomes less and the prevailing winds, even inside the doldrums, are easterlies. This is a fact worth bearing in mind if planning transequatorial passages, especially west of the meridian of the Marquesas.

North-east monsoon

The intense cold of the winter months over the land mass of Asia creates an area of high pressure over parts of the Far East. The resulting wind circulation around this winter high produces a flow of NE winds which prevail during the winter months in the China Sea and adjacent waters. The NE monsoon of the Western North Pacific is particularly noticeable between latitudes 5°N and 30°N. Its eastern limits are more difficult to define as it merges with the NE trades of the North Pacific. Although the monsoons of the China Sea can be regarded as an extension of the monsoon system of the Indian Ocean, there is a certain difference between them. In the China Sea, it is the NE monsoon of the winter months which is the stronger and more consistent wind, whereas in the Indian Ocean, the SW monsoon of summer is the strong constant wind. At its height, the NE monsoon of the China Sea forms a continuous wind system with the NE trade wind of the North Pacific, so that in December and January particularly, there is a belt of strong NE winds right across the ocean from California to China.

The arrival of the monsoon depends on latitude and it starts earlier in the north and later further south. Although it commences around September at its northern limit, the NE monsoon is only fully established throughout the area by November, and lasts until March. During the changeover periods with the SW monsoon, in April–May and August–September, there are calms and variable winds.

The strength of the wind is also influenced by latitude, the monsoon being strongest in the north, where it blows an average 25 knots, decreasing to 15 knots and less among the islands of the Philippines and Northern Indonesia. However, at the height of winter, in December and January, the monsoon can blow with gale force for many days, the stormiest area being the open waters between the Philippines, Taiwan and Japan.

South-west monsoon

A reversal of the NE monsoon occurs during the summer when the heating up of Asia creates a large area of low pressure over the eastern part of the continent. As a result of this, the SE trade winds of the Indian and Pacific Oceans are drawn across the equator. Because of the rotation of the earth, the SE winds are deflected to the right, becoming the SW monsoon in the western part of the Pacific Ocean. In the China Sea the winds are predominantly S and SW, whereas towards Japan they are either S or SE. The area affected by the SW monsoon is generally situated west of the 140°E meridian and south of latitude 40°N.

Steady SW winds are experienced in the China Sea during July, but towards the NE, the monsoon is felt less and less and variable winds become increasingly common. The weather during the SW monsoon is often unsettled and there is a high frequency of squalls, in which the wind reaches gale force.

Variables

The two monsoons and the NE trade winds are replaced on the polar side of the North Pacific by a belt of variable winds. Although it corresponds to the Horse Latitudes of the Atlantic Ocean, the variable belt of the North Pacific is much narrower and rarely exceeds 300 miles in width. The variable zone is influenced by the position of the high pressure area, which moves north in summer, when light and variable winds can be expected between latitudes 35°N and 40°N. The high moves south in summer, when it stretches from about 25°N to 30°N. The movement of air around the North Pacific high has a direct bearing on the winds of the variable zone. In the eastern half of the ocean, winds tend to be northerly in summer and merge with the NE trades. In the western part of the ocean, the direction of the winds is more southerly so that they form an extension of the SW monsoon.

Westerlies

The zone of variable winds is gradually replaced by an area of prevailing westerlies north of about latitude 35°N. These are not so boisterous as the westerlies of the Southern Ocean and the northern limit of the variables is more difficult to define. Westerly winds are more reliable both in direction and strength during the winter months, but this is hardly the time when anyone would consider cruising in the higher latitudes of the North Pacific, where the weather is very rough. In summer the weather is more benign, when fewer depressions race across the North Pacific between Japan and Alaska. The best weather can be expected in July, when light to moderate westerly winds predominate north of latitude 40°N.

Tropical storms

There are two areas of the North Pacific Ocean that are subject to tropical revolving storms, the typhoons of the Far East and the hurricanes of the eastern part of the North Pacific.

The region affected by hurricanes lies in the vicinity of the American coast, south of latitude 30°N to about latitude 10°N and west to longitude 140°W. This area includes the Pacific coasts of Mexico and Central America and extends as far offshore as longitude 140°W, an aspect that must be borne in mind by those planning to cross this area during the dangerous season. Theoretically the hurricane season lasts from May to November, although most hurricanes have been recorded between June and October, the month with the highest frequency being September. The only four months considered to be safe are January to April, as hurricanes have occurred in December on a few occasions. As a general rule only the earlier hurricanes travel to the western limit, whereas later in the season hurricanes are more likely to hug the coast. Therefore if a passage through this area is undertaken towards the end of the hurricane season, it is advisable to move offshore as quickly as possible.

The region affected by typhoons covers a much larger area stretching all the way from the Caroline Islands to Japan. To the east the area is bounded by Guam and the Mariana Islands, to the west by the Philippines, Taiwan and the northern part of the South China Sea. The typhoon season is less well defined than the hurricanes of the eastern Pacific and no month can be regarded as completely safe. However, most typhoons occur between May and December and during this period over half the typhoons have been recorded between July and October. September is the most dangerous month, with an average of over four typhoons. The period with the least likelihood of typhoons is January to April. As no typhoons have been recorded from December to April in the area between the northern part of the China Sea and the western side of the Eastern Sea, this is considered to be the safest time for passages to and from Japan, although this coincides with the winter weather.

Currents

The surface circulation of the North Pacific Ocean resembles a huge merry-go-round in which various currents move in a clockwise direction around a cell located slightly off-centre in the northern hemisphere. The mainspring of this circular movement is the North Equatorial Current which flows westward with its axis at about latitude 12°N. To the south of this current is the eastward flowing Equatorial Countercurrent, which has its southern limits between latitudes 2°N and 4°N, where it is bounded by the South Equatorial Current.

The North Equatorial Current is fed mainly by the California Current and the northern branch of the Equatorial Countercurrent. Further west it is reinforced by the North Pacific Current and further still it divides in two, the southern branch reversing its direction to become the Equatorial Countercurrent, while the northern branch carries on towards Taiwan and Japan. This is the main source of the Kuro Shio, a flow of warm water similar to the Gulf Stream of the North Atlantic. The main difference is that the direction of the Kuro Shio is seasonal, setting to the NE during the SW monsoon, but reversing its direction in winter, at the height of the NE monsoon.

The main direction of the Kuro Shio is NE along the southern coast of Japan. It subsequently fans out in about latitude 35°N to form the North Pacific Current. This current, reinforced by the Aleutian Current, flows in a broad band across the North Pacific towards America. East of latitude 160°W this current starts fanning out, part of it turning south, while the main body continues eastwards towards the North American continent where it turns SE. This southerly drift changes its name to the California Current which flows into the North Equatorial Current, thus completing the clockwise circulation round the North Pacific basin.

The surface circulation along the Pacific coast of Central America and Gulf of Panama is more erratic, with great seasonal variations that make predictions impossible. The Equatorial Countercurrent flows into this area and is normally deflected to the north west along the coast of Central America to join the California Current and eventually the North Equatorial Current. In the first months of the year a branch of the Equatorial Countercurrent turns south and flows into the South Pacific. In the Gulf of Panama the movement of water is more complicated, with an inflow of water at both extremes and an outflow in the centre that finally joins the South Equatorial Current.

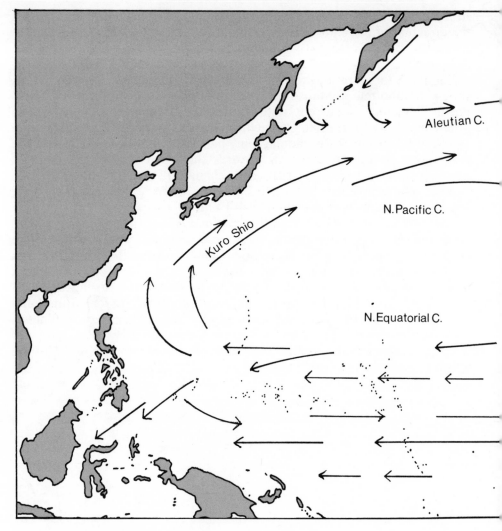

36. NORTH PACIFIC CURRENTS

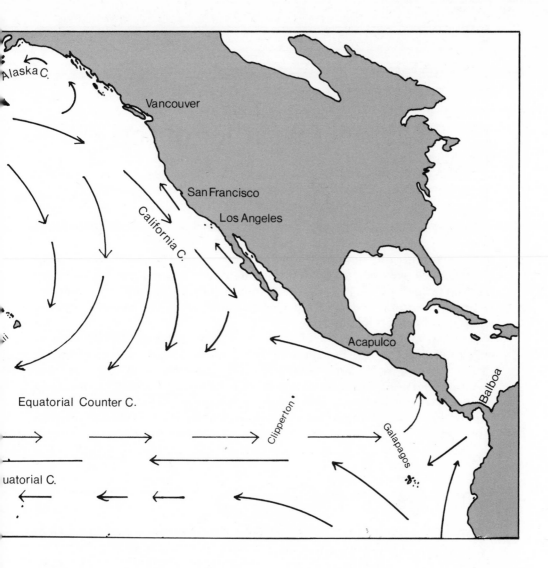

12 Regional weather of the North Pacific

Alaska

This beautiful but icy state has a very short cruising season and unpredictable weather. Even in the summer months some gales with heavy rain can occur and it is always cold at night when strong winds are blowing. Fog and drizzle are a common occurrence, mainly in the morning, the fog tending to burn off during the day.

One reason for making the effort to cruise here is the spectacular glaciers which fall into the sea, but these do bring the hazard of chunks of ice. A careful watch must be kept for bits of broken up iceberg and also for logs. Night sailing along the coast is thus best avoided. It is possible to cruise in sheltered waters anchoring every night, although careful attention has to be paid to the high tidal range, strong currents and wind accelerating down the mountains.

British Columbia

The summer months from May to September are the best season in which to explore this beautiful and dramatic coastline. Winds tend to be either from the SE or NW, these two directions accounting for about 65% of all winds. In the summer the NW winds are dominant, while in the stormy season from October to March, the SE winds are more common. Storms are less frequent in the summer months and also less violent. The strongest winds accompany depressions and the fronts associated with them. As a rule, when a front approaches the coast, winds back into the SE quadrant and increase in strength to gale force. As the storm passes, the winds shift into the NW quadrant and become more moderate. On rare occasions a cycle is not completed and winds blow from the SW. Both spring and autumn are transitional seasons with weather to match.

The climate is cloudy with abundant rainfall due to frequent depressions crossing over from the Pacific. There are prolonged spells of unsettled weather with few intervals of finer weather in winter, whereas fine spells are more common in summer. Sea fog occurs most frequently in summer, and August to October have the highest proportion of foggy days.

The majority of people cruising in British Columbia use the inside passages, where tide tables are essential to cope with the extreme tidal currents. The effect of the mountains often means that there is either no wind or it is blowing down the hills at gale force. Extreme weather occurs when a pressure gradient aligns itself with a geographical feature. Strong to gale force winds blow out of all coastal inlets during SE winds. If SE winds are predicted it is certain that there will be strong outflows both at the mouth of inlets and in the inlets themselves.

US west coast

The northern parts of this area have similar conditions to British Columbia. Weather in this region is affected by two main phenomena, the Pacific high and the California Current. In the spring as the expanding Pacific high takes over there is a gradual changeover from cold rainy days to mild sunny ones. The high brings fair weather with prevailing winds from W to N. In the spring there are still a few gales bringing SE to N winds on their passage up the coast but these become quite infrequent in summer months. The temperatures are kept from getting too hot by the cold California Current, which also brings fog over this area in summer and autumn for up to one third of the time. There is much less rain in the summer months.

Although there are still some mild sunny days, by the end of September the winter weather starts setting in with frequent gales, plenty of rain and cold weather. If a big storm is stationary in the Gulf of Alaska, bad weather can last for as long as a week.

Difficult conditions can prevail off the Columbia river, due to the amount of fresh water pouring over the bar and meeting the westerly swell. This creates confused and dangerous seas. It is better to stay further offshore in this area, especially in bad weather when a lot of shipping in the area waits for better conditions to cross the bar. Similar problems occur off Coos Bay in Oregon.

California

The winds blowing around the North Pacific high tend to blow parallel to the California coast for most of the year. In winter the NW wind does not blow so far north but prevails in the south, while in summer months SW or S winds occur in the south.

In the winter SE gales with heavy rain occur, although these affect central and northern California more, being rarer south of Los Angeles. Occasionally strong northerly gales blow out of a clear sky. NW storms in which winds of 50–60 knots can be experienced usually blow after a front has passed, mainly in the winter months. These storms last for 2–3 days and are often followed by a calm period.

In summer the occasional SE gale can disturb the normally good weather, the extreme south generally having lighter winds and calmer seas. During the summer months there can be long periods of calm weather, when those planning to make passages against the prevailing wind are advised to motor, especially at night and in the early hours. These calm periods are of great importance to those planning a cruise to windward, as the predictable afternoon westerlies can give a welcome boost in the desired direction. In the proximity of land, even in settled weather, local winds can sweep down the canyons on clear dry days. Although called *sundowners* due to their appearance as the sun sets, they can also blow at dawn.

There is a threat of tropical storms from June to November, which is the hurricane season in the eastern North Pacific. Only rarely do these strike above 30°N, August and September being the most likely months. Often tropical cyclones have spent most of their force by the time they reach southern California.

Apart from tropical cyclones, another strong wind that must be heeded, although infrequent, is the *Santa Ana*. This is an offshore desert wind of up to 50 knots, which can occur in the San Pedro Bay area, usually in late autumn or winter.

Fog is a perpetual problem along this coast, especially in the San Francisco to Los Angeles area, and is due to the warm moist winds blowing around the Pacific high meeting the cold California Current. Coastal areas are regularly afflicted with dense fog, which tends to lift as the earth heats up during the day.

In the Gulf of California, fine weather with NW winds prevails from November to May, while the rest of the year SE winds predominate. This is the rainy season and the SE winds can rise to gale force at times. In the upper part of the Gulf, NW gales can occur in December, January and February.

Mexico

As on the Californian coast, the prevailing winds tend to follow the coastline. Fine weather usually predominates from January to April with northerly winds as well as land and sea breezes near to the coast. The sea breeze usually sets in around noon from the SSW moving into the W. Late at night a less regular land breeze springs up.

The rainy season is April to September, when squally weather with thunder, lightning and heavy rain occurs. SE to SW gales occur during this period. The hurricane period almost coincides with this season, when on average 15 tropical cyclones a year originate off the west coast of Mexico. Normally only about half of these reach hurricane intensity.

The mountains of central Mexico cause a great local variety in winds and also interrupt the general air flow. In winter strong and violent winds blow down from the heights of Mexico across the coast and for several hundred miles to sea to the south and west. Sometimes these strong clear winds, called *papagayos* or *nortes*, can be felt almost to the equator and the Galapagos. These winds occur during the same period as the *northers* of the Gulf of Mexico.

Central America

The grand mountains of the Cordillera cause land and sea breezes to dominate the fine season, wherever these mountains are near to the coast. This fine season lasts from February until May, when variable winds usher in the rainy season, the rain often falling in squally showers. The hurricane season is coincident with this summer period from June through to September.

The changeover to winter is often marked in September and October by strong W and SW gales bringing heavy rain, especially around the September equinox. During the winter months, while the threat of hurricanes is absent, strong northerly gales can sweep down out of clear skies to affect the whole area down to Panama Bay. In the bay NNE winds prevail in winter months, and SW winds the rest of the time, it being wet and rainy almost all year.

Apart from the occasional *norther*, rare westerly gale or summer hurricane, the west coast of Central America could be described as having a truly Pacific weather with little wind and smooth seas. Local conditions along the coast do vary very much with the topography of the land.

Hawaii

The large rollers of the Pacific which make this a surfers' paradise are not so welcomed by yachtsmen and in strong weather some of the harbours here can be affected by large swells.

The NE trade wind prevails around Hawaii for most of the year. The wind tends to be northerly in March, becoming more easterly later on. The NE trades are stronger near these islands than anywhere else in the Pacific. Lighter winds and calms can be experienced in October, while in November and December, southerly winds can interrupt the trades. The worst months are January and February, when S and SW gales called *konas* strike, lasting from a few hours to 2–3 days, and bringing rain. The rainy season is from November to April.

The high volcanic islands do affect winds locally and gentle land and sea breezes flow on and off the land. The trades also divide and flow around the coast to the north and south of Molokai and Maui especially.

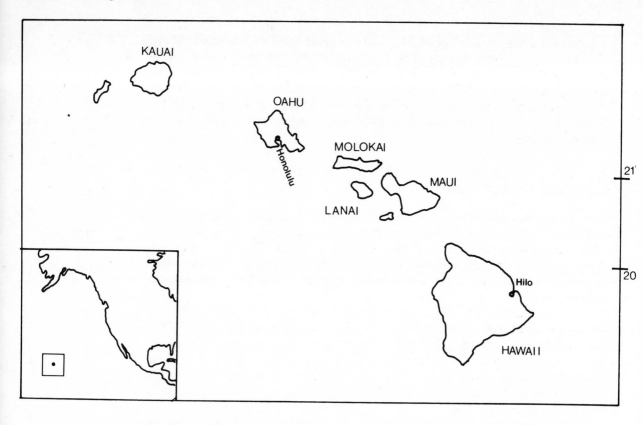

37. HAWAII

Line Islands

These small flat islands, rarely 20 feet high, straddle the equator, from whence cometh their name. There is no definite doldrum belt between the NE and SE trades in this area, the doldrums being replaced by an almost constant easterly air stream. The prevailing winds are between NE and SE from 10–20 knots and occasionally 25 knots. The temperature varies little around 29°C by day and 22°C by night with rainfall very variable from year to year and island to island. Rain falls mainly between January and July, usually during rain squalls at night. Although regarded as being outside of the cyclone zone, Caroline Island to the very south of the group has been struck by a cyclone once in the last century.

Marshall Islands

The weather of these small islands acquired notoriety when an unexpected shift in the prevailing wind blew the radioactive cloud from a nuclear test on

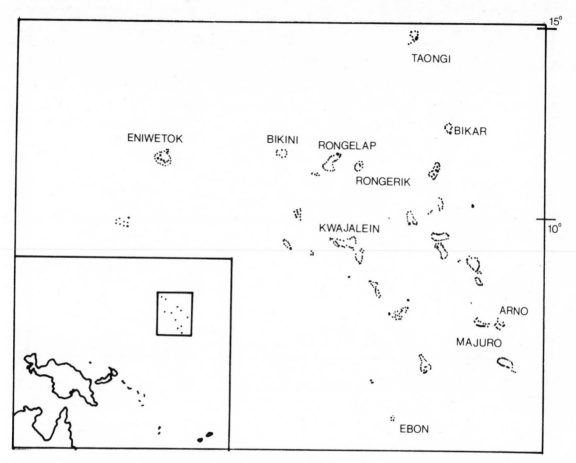

TAONGI

BIKAR

ENIWETOK

BIKINI

RONGELAP

RONGERIK

KWAJALEIN

ARNO

MAJURO

EBON

15°

10°

38. MARSHALL ISLANDS

Bikini atoll over the Marshall Islanders living on Rongelap and Rongerik. Under normal conditions from December to April the NE trade wind prevails over these islands. However, in some years the winds fail to appear or are very light and irregular. In such instances, they are often replaced by SE winds. From May to November, winds blow mainly from the east. Sometimes between August and November the easterly winds are interrupted by periods of calm or strong SW winds. During the NE season, the weather can be squally. When a squall arrives the wind usually shifts from NE to E, SE to S, returning to the NE when the squall has passed. No tropical storms have been reported in this area, the only violent storms coming from the SW. Several atolls in this group are contaminated by radioactive material.

Kiribati

Formerly known as the Gilbert Islands, the islands making up this now independent country lie both to the north and the south of the equator. This

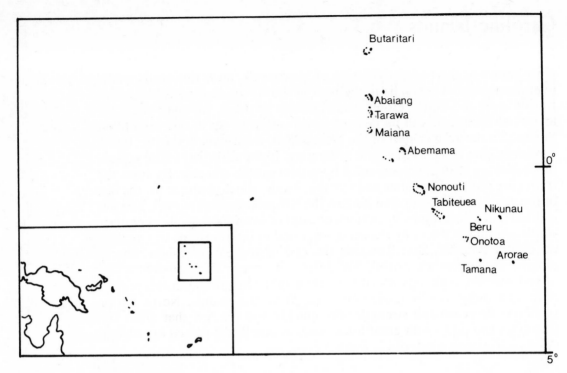

39. KIRIBATI

may be the reason why no uniform weather pattern emerges for this group, although winds do predominate from the easterly direction. The most pleasant season is from May to September, when the trades blow from ENE to ESE and rain is rare. From October through to April, the NE monsoon further to the west makes itself felt, and winds from the N and W are common, bringing much rain. This is also the season when violent gales can blow from the SW, shifting gradually to the north and lasting from 2–3 days. No cyclones have been reported in this region. The temperatures are normally high (30°C), as would be expected around the equator, and fall little during the night.

Caroline Islands

Now known as the Federated States of Micronesia, these tiny atolls spread over a vast area of ocean lie in the path of the NE trade wind, which blows freshly over the entire group from October to May. In some years the arrival of the trades can be delayed or advanced by up to one month. At Ponape, in the eastern part of the archipelago, the arrival of the NE trades can sometimes be delayed as late as January. In the early part of the season, the trades are strong, accompanied by violent squalls and rain. By June, the trades are replaced by calms and variable winds, which continue for the rest of the year. In June, July and August the SW monsoon takes over, and this is interrupted sometimes by periods of calm or even short spells of easterly winds. Although the rainy season is supposed to be from June to October, no month is totally dry. Towards the end of the SW monsoon, late in August or September, strong SW gales can occur. These appear to be linked with the typhoons which have their breeding ground in this region. Although these usually move NW away from the islands, North Pacific typhoons do reach full strength very quickly and the few that affect the Carolines can do so with great force, such as one which passed over Ulithi Atoll in 1960 with winds of 125 knots.

Palau

At the western edge of the Caroline Islands, the group of islands clustered around the large island of Palau are near to the limit of those areas affected by the Asian NE monsoon. These NE winds spread across gradually from the NW during October and by December are well established in Palau. From December to March NE winds blow steadily at about 10–15 knots. This is the relatively dry season. The few gales that do occur usually come from the NW during this season.

In April and May, although the NE or ENE winds still prevail, they gradually become weaker and more variable. The changeover to the SW monsoon takes place slowly and from June onwards winds from a southerly direction become more frequent. The SW monsoon prevails from July until September, even though at its height, in August, the winds are never too strong (5–10 knots). Winds can still occur from other directions during this

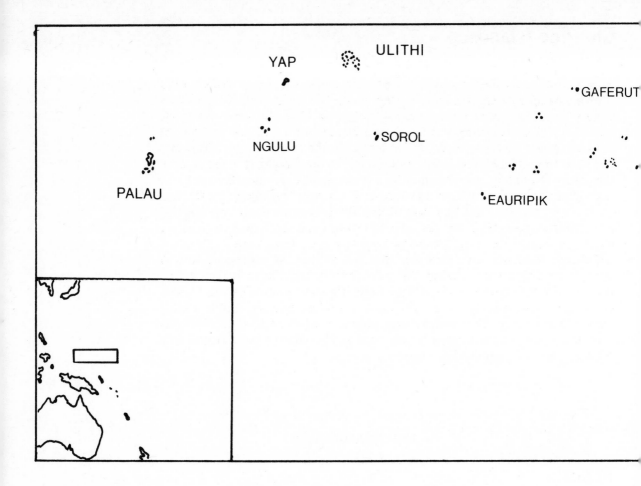

40. CAROLINE ISLANDS

period. In October as the monsoon changeover begins, winds are variable, often from SW or NW.

Palau is at the edge of the typhoon belt of the NW Pacific and although most typhoons either originate in higher latitudes or move more north and west away from Palau, their possibility cannot be completely ignored. The most likely months are between July and November.

Mariana Islands

The chain of the Northern Marianas follow a regular curve down to Guam, which is the largest island in Micronesia and is an incorporated territory of

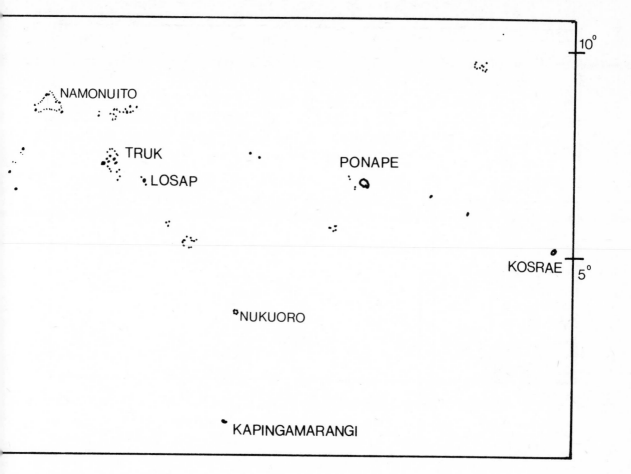

the USA. All these islands lie within the region of the NE winds and are under the influence of the NE monsoon blowing in the China Sea. From January to March, the prevailing winds are N to NE, while in April and May they gradually shift towards ESE and even SE. The influence of the SW monsoon is felt from June to October. In June and July, winds are usually from SE to SW, while from August to October they tend to blow between south and west. During November and December, the winds move slowly into the north and settle into the NE, which is the predominant direction for the first months of the year. During this NE season, rain squalls are most frequent. The most pleasant season is between April and June.

August to November is the wet period and these are the months when the

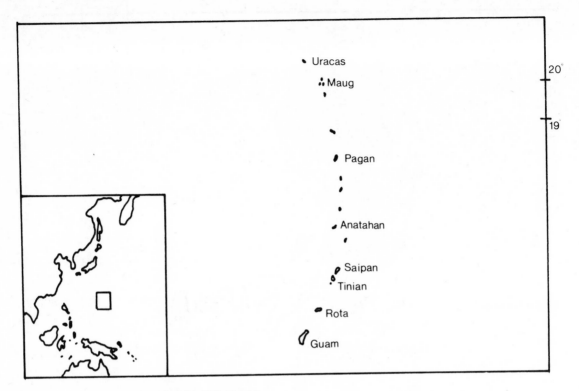

41. MARIANA ISLANDS

strongest winds are experienced, mostly from the west, with frequent thunderstorms. At this time typhoons are a possibility, curving west and north west from their breeding ground near to the Caroline Islands. There is considerable variation in the frequency of typhoons in any year, some islands being unaffected for many years and others being struck by several in one year, the overall average for Guam being one every other year. The most likely months are July to November, with August being the most dangerous month.

Philippine Islands

Over 7000 islands make up this large archipelago, of which Luzon to the north is the largest and on which is situated the capital, Manila. With so many islands over such a large area it is obvious that local conditions will vary considerably. The prevailing winds blowing over the islands are influenced mainly by the monsoons of the China Sea, the Philippines

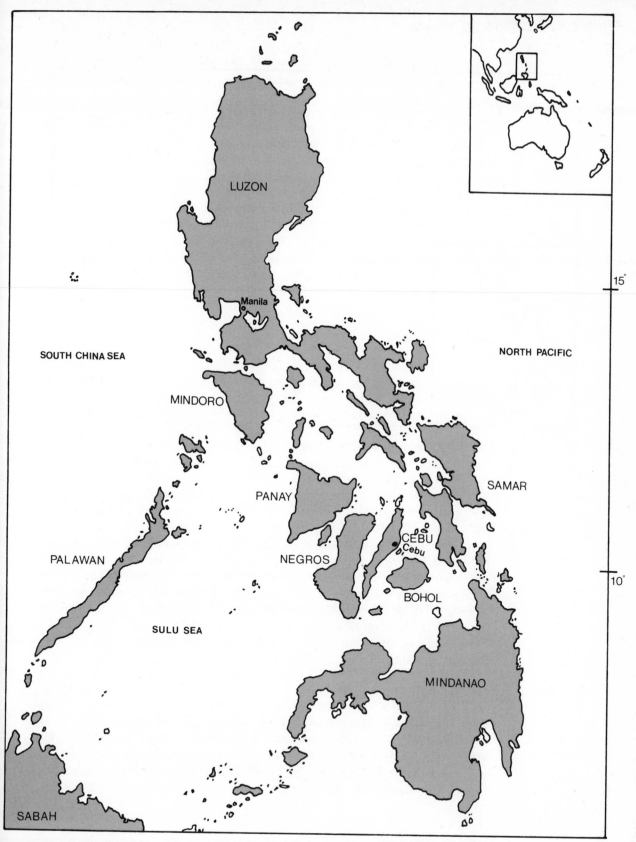

LUZON

Manila

SOUTH CHINA SEA

NORTH PACIFIC

MINDORO

SAMAR

PANAY

CEBU
Cebu

PALAWAN

NEGROS

BOHOL

SULU SEA

MINDANAO

SABAH

15°

10°

42. PHILIPPINES

forming a border between this sea and the Pacific Ocean. The NE monsoon blows from mid-October until mid-May and this is regarded as the fine season, with dry and clear weather.

The SW monsoon only becomes well established from July and lasts until October. During the latter part of this period the weather becomes squally with violent gales, which can last for several days. These gales usually begin from the N or NW and veer to SW or S, blowing strongly with heavy rain. September to November are the worst months for this kind of weather. This is also the period during which typhoons strike these waters. These storms usually originate to the SE of the islands and move across them into the China Sea, some reaching the China coast, while others curve up towards Japan. The Philippines have one of the highest incidences of typhoons and although the main season is from June to October they can occur at any time between May and November. Temperatures are high, about 30°C, with a high humidity all year round.

Hong Kong

The brightest jewel in the crown of the dwindling British Empire, this major trading and banking centre will revert back to China in 1997. On the edge of the tropics, Hong Kong has a seasonal climate with well marked seasons. The winter from November to April is the time of the NE monsoon, with cooler temperatures (15–18°C) and a lower humidity. The summer, from May to October, is hot and steamy (27–28°C) with plenty of rain. This is the time of the SW monsoon. During this period bad depressions from the SE and SSE affect Hong Kong and these can build up into typhoons. These storms usually start in the Pacific east of the Philippines and then move NW. Typhoons are most frequent between May and October, but they can occur at the beginning of the NE monsoon as well.

Because of the topography of the islands, its rivers and inlets, local conditions can vary enormously, both in wind direction and speed. For example, a front passing from the SE will produce SE winds at one point but N winds in other places. These SE lows occur at all times of the year, although they are more frequent in the summer.

Japan

The land of the rising sun does not offer the best cruising weather to visiting yachtsmen, who must sail here in search of other pleasures. It has a typical temperate climate and can be extremely stormy in winter months. Being situated in the belt of the variables the wind can blow from almost any direction in the summer. This summer period unfortunately bears the risk of typhoons from May through to October as these storms move NW out of their breeding grounds further south.

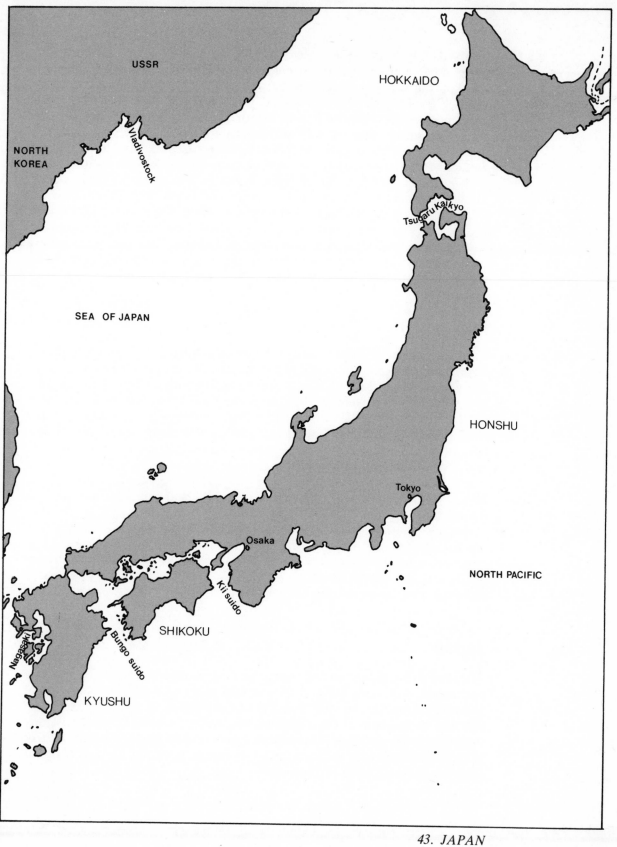

USSR

NORTH
KOREA

Vladivostock

HOKKAIDO

Tsugaru Kaikyo

SEA OF JAPAN

HONSHU

Tokyo

Osaka

NORTH PACIFIC

Kii suido

SHIKOKU

Bungo suido

Nagasaki

KYUSHU

43. JAPAN

Another hazard of sailing in Japanese waters is the high proportion of foggy days. This is due to the cold current coming down from the north meeting the warmer Kuro Shio current, producing a similar effect to the Grand Banks and Newfoundland area in the Atlantic. All these shortcomings are more than made up for by the warm hospitality extended to foreign sailors who venture to these shores.

13   Routes in the North Pacific

PN10 Routes from the west coast of North America

PN11 California to Hawaii
PN12 California to Panama
PN13 Northward from California
PN14 California to British Columbia
PN15 Alaska to British Columbia
PN16 British Columbia to California
PN17 British Columbia to Hawaii

Southward from California

Those who are heading south from California bound for some distant destination, be it Panama, Galapagos, Marquesas or Tahiti, are faced with two choices: either to head offshore and sail direct, or hug the coast and cruise in shorter stages. Both alternatives have certain advantages, but as this book deals with ocean routes only, the second alternative will not be detailed. Some people have successfully combined these two alternatives by cruising along the coast for some distance and then setting off for distant destinations either from Mexico or Costa Rica. This has the advantage of shaking down both boat and crew while still within a short distance of stateside facilities.

The advantage of an offshore passage south from California is that the prevailing NW winds will put the boat on a broad reach or run, as soon as the coast has been safely left behind. Because of the dependability of these prevailing winds, it is preferable to wait for a period of settled weather with a long-term forecast of N or NW winds before setting off on a long passage. Regardless of the final destination it is advisable to head offshore immediately on leaving the coast, as winds tend to be steadier about one hundred miles from the mainland.

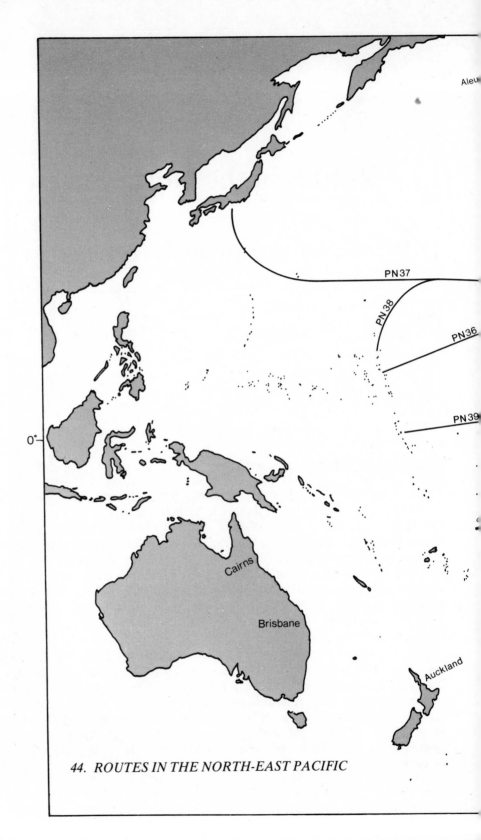

44. *ROUTES IN THE NORTH-EAST PACIFIC*

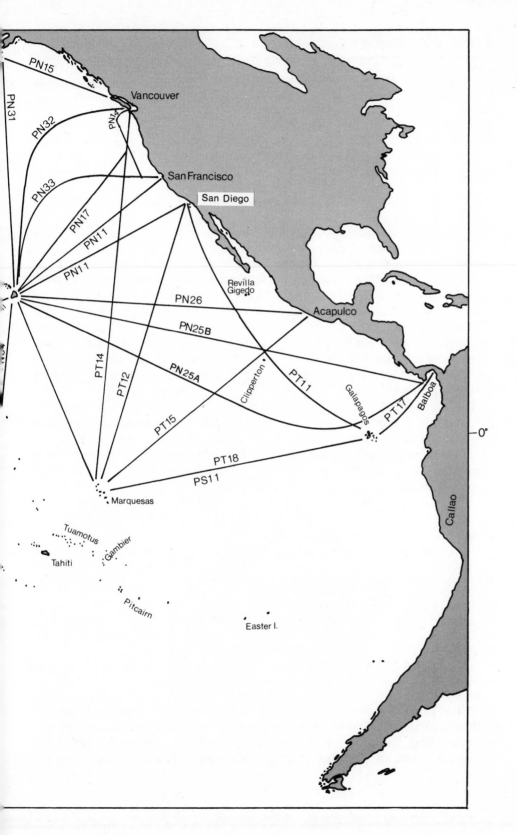

PN11 California to Hawaii

DIAGRAMS 44, 45	San Francisco to Hilo 2020 m
	San Diego to Hilo 2180 m

Best time:	May to September
Tropical storms:	June to October
Charts:	BA: 4807
	US: 51
Pilots:	BA: 8, 62
	US: 152

This route enjoys favourable winds throughout the year, although few boats attempt to make the passage in winter, on account of the cold and the high proportion of strong winds. On the other hand, summer months carry the risk of tropical storms, August and September being considered the most dangerous months. Between these two extremes there are some months when sailing conditions along this route can be perfect, May and November fulfilling most of the criteria. Good weather can also be had in April, although an early start is usually associated with colder temperatures. Even when the winds are fair, the sky is sometimes overcast, making life difficult for those who are keen to try their hand at celestial navigation on this long offshore passage.

The winds for the first few hundred miles are mostly N or NW, becoming NE and finally E closer to Hawaii. A great circle course should be sailed for the entire route as there is nothing to be gained from any other alternative. Because of increased wind strengths in channels separating the islands, it is sometimes better to gain the lee of the islands rather than approach them from windward.

PN12 California to Panama

	San Diego to Balboa 2900 m

Best time:	November to May
Tropical storms:	June to October
Charts:	BA: 587, 2323, 2324, 3273
	US: 51
Pilots:	BA: 7, 7A, 8
	US: 152, 153

The best time to make this passage is during the winter months, when the prevailing winds off the Mexican coast are northerly. There is a favourable current along the coast of Mexico, but a contrary current further south along the coast of Central America. The route should run at least 100 miles off the coast to avoid the influence of land breezes and also the many ships that ply the coast closer inshore. The route runs parallel to the coast of Central America and gradually curves in to enter the Gulf of Panama at Cabo Mala. The Las Perlas Islands can be passed on either side, although the pass on their west side is clearer.

This route is not recommended during the summer, when there is a risk of hurricanes in the area and the winds are less consistent, with long periods of calms.

PN13 Northward from California

Best time:	April
Tropical storms:	None
Charts:	BA: 4801
	US: 501, 520
Pilots:	BA: 8, 25, 26
	US: 152

Northbound passages from California are difficult to plan as it is very rare that one can be certain of a favourable wind. Therefore most people plan their cruise to include as many coastal stops as possible. In this way it is possible to take advantage of early morning breezes. One suggestion for an easier passage north is to leave in April with one of the last southerly gales. At this time of year they are usually milder than those of the winter months. Although it may be tempting to ride one of these storms, one should be very careful when running along the coast before one of them as most ports are on a dangerous lee shore.

During the summer one has to be prepared for a lot of beating, often into strong winds. If one is planning to motor it is usually better to do this at night when the winds are lighter.

PN14 California to British Columbia

DIAGRAM 44	San Francisco to Vancouver 760 m
Best time:	May–June
Tropical storms:	None
Charts:	BA: 4801
	US: 501
Pilots:	BA: 8, 25, 26
	US: 152, 154

Both in winter and summer NW winds predominate along the North American coast, which make a direct offshore passage virtually impossible. There are various ways of dealing with these head winds and the most radical suggestion is that the coast should be left immediately on a route heading offshore for about 200 miles before it turns north. The most favourable tack should be taken until the latitude of the port of destination is reached. A new course can then be set to approach the coast on the tack that would put the boat to windward of the destination. An inshore route can also be followed by taking shorter hops along the coast, while another alternative is to try and sail parallel to the coast about 30 miles offshore so as to be within range of VHF weather broadcasts and shelter if necessary.

PN15 Alaska to British Columbia

DIAGRAMS 44, 45	Kodiak to Prince Rupert 790 m

Best time:	June to August
Tropical storms:	None
Charts:	BA: 4810
	US: 531
Pilots:	BA: 4, 25, 26
	US: 152, 154

The winds in the Gulf of Alaska are variable in direction during the summer months, with a slight predominance of westerly winds. Fog can be a problem during the crossing of the Gulf, but gales are rare in summer. Prince Rupert harbour, where entry formalities into Canada can be completed, is reached through Dixon Strait, between Prince of Wales and Graham Islands. Because the sailing season in Alaska is so brief, most people are in a hurry when the time comes to move south. Although a faster passage can be made on an offshore route, few people choose to miss the unsurpassed beauty of the inshore route that threads its way past countless islets and inlets along British Columbia's fragmented coast.

PN16 British Columbia to California

	Vancouver to San Francisco 760 m

Best time:	May to October
Tropical storms:	None
Charts:	BA: 4801
	US: 501, 530
Pilots:	BA: 8, 25
	US: 152, 154

Winds along this route are always favourable, although they are sometimes too strong for comfort. Because of the big swell further offshore, it is advisable to stay as near the shore as caution permits. Several harbours have bars and are difficult or dangerous to enter when there is a heavy swell, especially if this breaks over the bar as it does in the entrance to the Columbia River. Another hazard along this coast is haze, which often reduces visibility drastically and can be extremely dangerous to small boats because of the high amount of shipping.

PN17 British Columbia to Hawaii

DIAGRAMS 44, 45	Vancouver to Hilo 2400 m

Best time:	June to September
Tropical storms:	None
Charts:	BA: 4806, 4807
	US: 50, 520
Pilots:	BA: 25, 62
	US: 152, 154

This route enjoys favourable winds throughout the year, although the high frequency of gales during winter makes a southbound passage less attractive between November and March. Most settled weather is usually encountered in June. Because of the heavy swell that is normally running off the coast, it is probably better to stay as close inshore as caution will permit for the first few hundred miles. From about latitude 40°N, the great circle route can be taken to Hawaii.

PN20 Routes from Panama

PN21 Panama to Central America
PN22 Panama to California
PN23 Panama to British Columbia
PN24 Panama to Alaska
PN25 Panama to Hawaii
PN26 Central America to Hawaii
PN27 Central America to Panama

After transiting the Panama Canal the choice of routes is quite limited. Basically, there are two options: either to stay in the North Pacific, where there is a narrow range of initial destinations, or to head towards the South Pacific, where the choices multiply constantly as one moves west.

There are only a handful of routes fanning out from Panama and the most popular is the route to the Galapagos Islands (Route PT17). Most boats bound for the South Pacific take advantage of the conveniently placed Galapagos Islands (Archipelago de Colon) to make at least a brief stop in these islands made famous by Charles Darwin. Throughout the 19th century the islands were used by sailing ships for reprovisioning. Unfortunately cruising is no longer allowed without a special permit (see Chapter 27) and because of these restrictions, some skippers prefer to avoid the Galapagos Islands altogether and head straight for the Marquesas and French Polynesia (PT18).

Those who intend to visit ports along the west coast of South America are faced with a tough voyage against wind and current (PT19). A few boats make this trip every year showing that, in spite of all difficulties, it can be done. In fact this route was used regularly in Spanish colonial times when sailing ships were not renowned for their windward-going capabilities. The other alternative is to postpone visiting this area until farther west across the Pacific when a course can be set for Chile with the help of favourable westerly winds of higher latitudes. However, this is a long and tough trip which is even less attractive than a beat against the Humboldt current. The major attraction of such a foray down the coast of South America is the opportunity to visit Ecuador and Peru as well as some rarely frequented islands such as Easter, Pitcairn or Gambier.

Sailing directly to the west coast of North America from Panama is just as hard to accomplish. An alternative preferred by many as the best way to reach California, and especially ports further north, is to sail first to Hawaii. As far as ports on the west coast of Central America are concerned, Panama is a good starting point and as the distances involved are relatively short, even if unfavourable conditions are encountered at least they do not have to be endured for too long. Because the hurricane season affects most of this area between June and October, sailing to Mexico or California during these months should be avoided. Therefore if heading north from Panama it is best to plan to transit the Canal between November and April, so as to avoid the danger of being caught by a hurricane off the coast of Central America.

Before sailing out of the Gulf of Panama, some people make a shorter or longer visit to the Las Perlas Islands, which have some excellent anchorages. They belong to Panama and one is not allowed to stop there after having cleared out in Balboa, without having obtained a cruising permit (see Chapter 27).

PN21 Panama to Central America

	Balboa to Puntarenas 460 m
	Balboa to Acapulco 1430 m

Best time:	February–May, November
Tropical storms:	June to October
Charts:	BA: 3273
	US: 51
Pilots:	BA: 7, 8
	US: 153

The passage to ports along the Pacific coast of Central America is always difficult, due either to contrary winds or prolonged periods of calms. Although a favourable current can be expected as far as the Gulf of Fonseca, from there onwards, the current is mostly contrary. One should be prepared to take advantage of every shift of wind and also to use the engine when necessary in order to counter the unfavourable current. The area is prone to thunderstorms with intense lightning.

For those sailing north, the best advice is to stand well offshore, especially after reaching Fonseca. If faced with a *norther* in the Gulf of Tehuantepec, it is better to sail off on the starboard tack rather than fight the weather. If the weather is particularly heavy and one is forced to heave to, one can expect a *norther* to last from two to four days. Usually the sky is clear, with only a red haze on the horizon.

PN22 Panama to California

DIAGRAM 45	Balboa to San Diego 2900 m

Best time:	February–May
Tropical storms:	June to October
Charts:	BA: 587, 2323, 2324
	US: 51
Pilots:	BA: 7, 8
	US: 152, 153

This can be a very long and arduous trip. For this reason it has been suggested that it is easier to sail to Hawaii and thence to the West Coast, rather than direct to California, especially for those who like long offshore passages and are not pressed for time (see Route PN25).

A non-stop passage to California should be undertaken well offshore where better winds can be expected, even if a longer distance has to be covered. From June to January, after leaving the Gulf of Panama the route runs between the Galapagos Islands and latitude 5°N as far as meridian 105°W (PN22A). At about this point, the course is altered to pass west of Clipperton Island. After picking up the NE trades and if the destination is San Francisco, the route crosses latitude 20°N in about 120°W and latitude 35°N in 135°W. For more southern Californian ports the most favourable tack should be taken after passing the point of 20°N, 120°W.

From February to May the recommended offshore route passes south of the Galapagos Islands after leaving the Gulf of Panama. It then heads west as far as 105°W before altering course to the NW into the NE trade wind zone. However, if winds are favourable after passing Cabo Mala, a route north of the Galapagos Islands can be taken, following a more direct course to California (PN22B). The initial course on the more direct route runs parallel to the coast of Central America as far as Costa Rica, keeping only about 20 miles off the coast. From northern Costa Rica, the route heads due west for about 1,000 miles to a point just north of Clipperton Island. The route then runs parallel to the coast in a NW direction, gradually curving in towards the port of destination. If taking.this route one must be prepared to motor sail when necessary, especially during the first leg from Panama northwards.

When sailing north from Panama one should plan to be north of Cabo San Lucas by 1st June, especially as some insurance companies make this provision in their policies, in view of the hurricane season in Central America. This consideration, coupled with weather conditions in the Caribbean, make it advisable to plan on transiting the Panama Canal early in the year, so as to have plenty of time either to reach the West Coast before the onset of the hurricane season or to make alternative arrangements.

PN23 Panama to British Columbia

DIAGRAM 45		Balboa to Vancouver 4400 m
Best time:	April–May, November	
Tropical storms:	June to October	
Charts:	BA: 587, 787	
	US: 51, 501	
Pilots:	BA: 7, 8, 25	
	US: 152, 153, 154	

Directions for this route are similar to those for Route PN22 and in fact skippers are faced with exactly the same dilemma whether they intend to sail from Panama to California or all the way to British Columbia. The choice is between a relatively direct route along the coast of Central America, an indirect offshore route close to the Galapagos Islands, or a grand detour via Hawaii. If the prospect of such a detour is not attractive, the choice is between the other two routes, both of which have advantages and disadvantages. The route that passes close to the Galapagos Islands offers a greater certainty of favourable winds, but is longer (PN22A). The route that follows the coast to Costa Rica is shorter but depends more on the use of the engine (PN22B). In both cases the final leg north of latitude 30°N will be the toughest because of the high proportion of northerly winds during the summer months. Whichever alternative is chosen, the route will finally run parallel to the coast probably as far as latitude 43°N, depending on the season (see also Route PN32), before turning in towards the coast of British Columbia.

PN24 Panama to Alaska

Balboa to Kodiak 5340 m

Best time:	May
Tropical storms:	June to October
Charts:	BA: 587, 787
	US: 51, 520
Pilots:	BA: 4, 7, 7A, 8
	US: 152, 153

A detour via Hawaii (see Route PN25) has certain advantages over a non-stop passage to Alaska, especially between September and March when it would be either too late or too early to head for Alaska. From April to August the more direct route should be considered, the best month for a northbound passage probably being May.

Directions as far as latitude 30°N are similar to those given for Routes PN22 and PN23. Having crossed latitude 30°N in about longitude 140°W, the route should arc northwards by trying to keep west of the North Pacific high. North of latitude 40°N the same directions apply as for Route PN31.

PN25 Panama to Hawaii

DIAGRAM 44

Balboa to Hilo 4550 m

Best time:	March to May, November
Tropical storms:	June to October
Charts:	BA: 2683
	US: 51
Pilots:	BA: 7, 62
	US: 152, 153

The painful dilemma faced by all those who plan to sail from Panama to Hawaii is whether to follow the traditional sailing route (PN25A) and make a detour of some 1,000 miles, or take the great circle route (PN25B) and hope for the best. The great circle route skirts an area of calms and light winds between longitudes 80°W and 110°W, which can be avoided by following the directions given to the masters of sailing ships who were advised to always try to make their westing with the help of the SE trades. This means staying south of latitude 5°N until meridian 110°W is crossed and then taking the great circle route from that point to Hawaii. This southerly route is recommended during the hurricane season, when the great circle route from Panama passes through the area of tropical storms. For the rest of the year, between November and April, the direct route from Panama is to be preferred as it takes less time to reach the NE trade wind belt, which extends further south in winter.

For those who prefer to break up this passage into shorter stages, it is possible to sail first to Costa Rica, either in one offshore leg, or in short hops along the coast. From there, similar directions apply for the rest of the voyage to those for Route PN26.

PN26 Central America to Hawaii

| DIAGRAM 44 | Manzanillo to Hilo 3120 m |
| | Puntarenas to Hilo 4100 m |

Best time:	March to May, November
Tropical storms:	June to October
Charts:	BA: 2863
	US: 51
Pilots:	BA: 8, 62
	US: 152, 153

Tropical storms affect this route throughout the summer, although boats leaving from Mexico are at greater risk than those setting off from Costa Rica, where the route can easily be shaped to stay south of the danger area. Mainly because of these storms, most passages are made either before June or after October. At all times it is essential to move offshore as quickly as possible to escape the influence of the land and find the prevailing NE trades. In April and early May, the weather in the vicinity of the coast is often unsettled, with thunderstorms and variable winds. The winds offshore are very steady during the early summer, especially west of longitude 120°W. In November and December the trades are much stronger and there is often a big swell, the result of gales further north.

PN27 Central America to Panama

	Acapulco to Balboa 1430 m
	Puntarenas to Balboa 460 m

Best time:	November to May
Tropical storms:	June to October
Charts:	BA: 587
	US: 51
Pilots:	BA: 7, 7A, 8
	US: 153

Because of the lack of protected harbours in Guatemala and the political situation in El Salvador and Nicaragua, most boats prefer to sail non-stop from Mexico to Costa Rica. The winds in the area are light variable and there are frequent calms. The strong NW setting current has caused problems for many people who have closed with the coast thinking that they were already in Costa Rican waters but were in fact still in Nicaragua. The topography along the south coast of Nicaragua is very similar to the north of Costa Rica, so it is easy to make a mistake. It is therefore advisable to keep well offshore on a southbound passage and only approach the coast when absolutely sure of the position (see also PN12).

PN30 Routes from Hawaii, Marshalls and Kiribati

PN31 Hawaii to Alaska
PN32 Hawaii to British Columbia
PN33 Hawaii to California
PN34 Hawaii to Line Islands
PN35 Line Islands to Hawaii
PN36 Hawaii to Marshall Islands
PN37 Hawaii to Japan
PN38 Marshall Islands to Hawaii
PN39 Kiribati to Hawaii

Routes from Hawaii

The main attraction of America's outpost in the North Pacific is the NE trade wind which ensures a fast downwind passage from any port on the West Coast. Hawaii's main disadvantage is the same trade wind, which makes a return voyage to those ports a very difficult undertaking. The logical solution for a return passage with fair winds is to make a big sweep to northward hoping to find in higher latitudes the favourable winds needed for the passage home. The prevailing NE winds also make a return to Hawaii very difficult from any of the Micronesian islands to the west and forward planning should be the main concern for anyone planning a voyage from Hawaii.

Only the route across the equator to Tahiti (PT24) offers a chance of good passages in both directions, although this is not the main reason for the popularity of this route. Ever since the South Pacific was put on the world cruising map in the early 30s, Hawaii has been used as a convenient stepping stone by boats on their way to other Polynesian destinations. Modern sailing boats have given back to Hawaii its important position at the apex of the triangle linking the far flung corners of Polynesia, from Aotearoa in the west to Rapa Nui in the east. For a foray into the South Seas, the islands of Hawaii offer an excellent starting point. For those who are not afraid of sailing a little farther in search of better winds, Hawaii is in

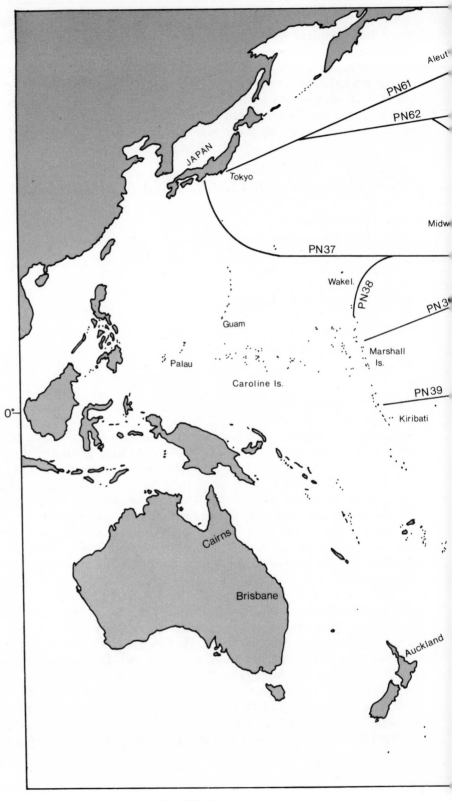

45. NORTH PACIFIC ROUTES

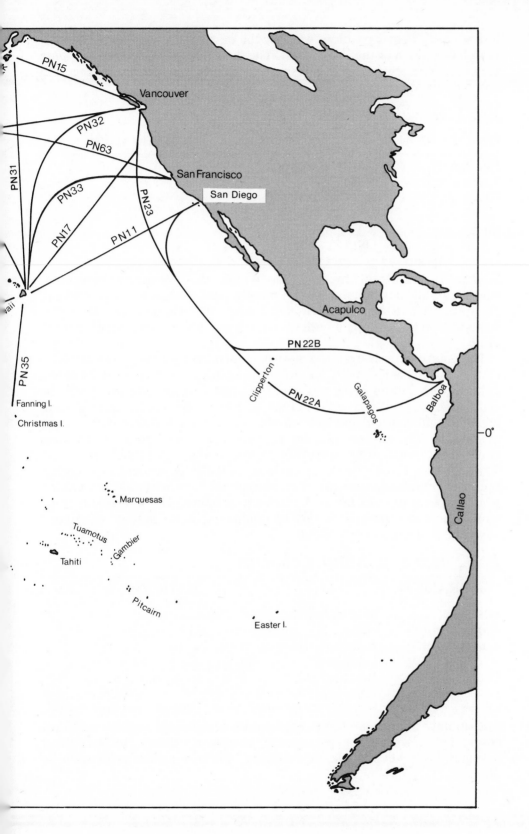

PN15

Vancouver

PN32

PN63

PN31

San Francisco

San Diego

PN33

PN23

PN17

PN11

Acapulco

PN35

PN22B

Clipperton

PN22A

Galápagos

Balboa

Fanning I.

Christmas I.

0°

Marquesas

Callao

Tuamotus

Gambier

Tahiti

Pitcairn

Easter I.

just as convenient a position, whether the destination is in Japan, Alaska, British Columbia or the West Coast. The distances indicated for each route are taken from a great circle course and therefore in reality the mileage will probably be longer.

PN31 Hawaii to Alaska

DIAGRAMS 44, 45		Hilo to Kodiak 2420 m
Best time:	mid-June to August	
Tropical storms:	None	
Charts:	BA: 782, 2460	
	US: 520	
Pilots:	BA: 4, 62	
	US: 152	

Summer is undoubtedly the best time to make this passage and most boats which take this northbound route normally leave Hawaii in the second half of June. Such a departure ensures longer and warmer days in higher latitudes and at least one month of cruising in Alaska before heading south again.

The course from Hawaii is almost due north and skirts the western edge of the North Pacific high. NE winds normally persist at least as far as latitude 40°N before being replaced by variable winds. In some years the shift to westerlies can be quite abrupt, in other years steady westerly winds are almost nonexistent and light variable winds and calms persist all the way to Alaska. The weather gets increasingly colder as higher latitudes are reached and north of latitude 40°N there is also a high proportion of fog. This can be a cause of concern because of the large amount of shipping, both cargo and fishing boats. Yet another problem is the overcast skies, which are a feature of higher latitudes in summer. The permanent cloud cover makes it impossible to take sun sights and in the absence of satellite navigation, one has to rely on DR.

PN32 Hawaii to British Columbia

DIAGRAMS 44, 45		Hilo to Vancouver 2400 m
Best time:	May to August	
Tropical storms:	None	
Charts:	BA: 4806, 4807	
	US: 520	
Pilots:	BA: 8, 25, 62	
	US: 152, 154	

The summer months are to be preferred for this passage, not because they ensure better winds, but because the weather is warmer. In fact, faster passages have been made in February, when a higher proportion of southerly winds have made it possible to sail almost a great circle course to Juan de Fuca. At all other times the directions are to sail due north on leaving Hawaii and only start turning east when steady westerly winds are met. This normally happens above latitude 40°N and the point where the route takes on that easterly curve is furthest north in August and furthest south in December. In summer it might be necessary to go as far north as 45°N before being able to turn east.

This route depends very much on the position of the North Pacific high, as at first it follows its western edge and then curves around its northern fringe trying to avoid the calms that are met if the area of high pressure is crossed. Undeterred by this prospect, some people who are prepared to use their engines try to steer the straightest course across and are occasionally rewarded by a faster, if windless, passage. For those who prefer to sail, there is less choice, and their reward for a longer and colder passage into higher latitudes is a fast reach in steady westerlies.

As the route skirts the fringes of the high, the skies are often overcast and celestial navigation is usually impossible. Arriving off the Canadian coast with only an estimated position is therefore almost unavoidable, the situation often being made worse by encountering one of the gales which in summer occur near to the coast.

PN33 Hawaii to California

DIAGRAMS 44, 45   Hilo to San Francisco 2020 m
                                        Hilo to San Diego 2180 m

Best time:	March to May, September to October
Tropical storms:	None
Charts:	BA: 4807
	US: 520
Pilots:	BA: 8, 62
	US: 152

Directions for this route are almost the same as for PN32 as laying a direct course from Hawaii to California is seldom possible due to the prevailing NE winds. The recommended sailing route from Hawaii runs almost due north before turning east once the area of steady westerly winds has been reached. The turning point varies in latitude throughout the year, being as far north as 40°N in summer and 32°N in winter. The recommended summer route turns quite sharply at the point where steady westerlies are met, whereas at other times the route follows a curve that turns gradually NE and then E towards the port of destination. If the passage is made at the end of winter, between February and April, the route should start turning NE at about latitude 25°N, pass through a point at 30°N, 150°W and then head directly for the destination. The NE turning point in May is 30°N, June 33°N and July 36°N, from where the route curves gradually north and crosses longitude 150°W in about latitude 38°N. The August turning point is the most northerly in latitude 40°N, whereas in September and October, the route can turn NE soon after latitude 32°N has been crossed. The subsequent route depends very much on the existing wind.

All these routes are greatly influenced by the position of the North Pacific high, as they attempt to follow the contour of this area of high pressure. Boats with good windward capabilities can often take a more direct route than the recommended one, as can those whose skippers are prepared to make their easting with help from the engine. Some fast passages have been made in May by boats taking the great circle route and motor sailing to windward in light winds. At other times, boats heading for southern California have tried to beat their way across by keeping south of the high, something that can be done especially if one is able to keep track of the weather. Otherwise it is better to follow the old practice and sail east with the westerlies of high latitudes. However, as the position of the North Pacific high has such a bearing on all routes to the mainland, it is worth obtaining a long-term forecast before leaving Hawaii so as to be able to plot the best course in relation to the existing weather conditions.

PN34 Hawaii to Line Islands

DIAGRAM 44	Hilo to Fanning 990 m
	Hilo to Christmas 1080 m

Best time:	November to May
Tropical storms:	None
Charts:	BA: 782
	US: 504
Pilots:	BA: 62
	US: 126, 152

The route running due south to these islands lying close to the equator has the benefit of NE trades throughout the year. The winds are particularly strong and steady in winter, but tend to get lighter as the islands are approached. The NE trades are usually lost in about latitude 8°N, with the doldrums rarely exceeding 2 degrees in width. South of latitude 8°N the proportion of southerly winds is always higher. The area is under the influence of all three equatorial currents, their direction, rate and steadiness varying through the year. Sometimes in winter a very strong west setting current makes itself felt between Christmas and Fanning Islands, whereas in summer the countercurrent can be just as strong in its easterly set.

The islands belong to Kiribati, but as there are no provisions for official entry procedures, the comings and goings of cruising boats are usually tolerated without formalities.

PN35 Line Islands to Hawaii

DIAGRAM 45	Fanning to Hilo 990 m
	Christmas to Hilo 1080 m

Best time:	June to October
Tropical storms:	None
Charts:	BA: 782
	US: 504
Pilots:	BA: 62
	US: 126, 152

The area separating these two island groups is always under the influence of the NE trades and particularly in winter, when the trades blow strongly, the northbound passage is to windward all the way. The winds are usually more easterly in summer and as they are also lighter, best passages are made at that time. The immediate vicinity of the islands is in the doldrum belt which extends to about latitude 8°N. The Equatorial Countercurrent normally sets strongly to the east close to the islands and can be used to advantage to make some easting before heading into the NE trades.

PN36 Hawaii to Marshall Islands

DIAGRAM 44, 45	Hilo to Majuro 2100 m

Best time:	All year
Tropical storms:	None
Charts:	BA: 781, 782
	US: 504
Pilots:	BA: 61, 62
	US: 126, 152

This is a downwind run all the way pushed along by the NE trades, which become more easterly in the proximity of the islands. Winds are less constant among the islands themselves and in summer the weather can be squally although the direction of the winds remains predominantly easterly. The unsettled summer weather is caused by the ITCZ moving north over the islands.

The North Equatorial and Equatorial Countercurrents set strongly through the archipelago producing a complex pattern. The set among the northerly islands is mostly west while in the southerly islands it is east. Because of the unpredictability of the currents and also because the islands are all low lying atolls, it is advisable to only day sail among them and avoid night passages.

PN37 Hawaii to Japan

DIAGRAM 44, 45	Hilo to Yokohama 3620 m

Best time:	April–May, November
Tropical storms:	May to December
Charts:	BA: 781, 782
	US: 53
Pilots:	BA: 42A, 42B, 61, 62
	US: 152, 158, 159

Favourable winds prevail along this route throughout the year, although the time of arrival in Japan must take into account the risk of typhoons. A passage in winter, when there is no danger of typhoons, is not recommended as the weather can be very cold in Japan. A better time is towards the end of the NE monsoon, before the start of the typhoon season. Another alternative is to make the passage just before the onset of winter, November being a good month in which both winds and current are favourable.

On leaving Hawaii the route runs due west along latitude 20°N if the passage is made between April and September. Later in the year and during winter, the NE trades are steadier further south and it may be necessary to go as far south as 16°N. The recommended route for November runs along latitude 18°N. The routes start curving NW after meridian 160°E has been crossed and pass to the east of Ogasawara Gunto. The North Equatorial Current sets west along this route throughout the year.

PN38 Marshall Islands to Hawaii

DIAGRAM 44, 45	Majuro to Hilo 2100 m
	Majuro to Tarawa 350 m

Best time:	June–September
Tropical storms:	None
Charts:	BA: 781, 782
	US: 504
Pilots:	BA: 61, 62
	US: 126, 152

An extremely difficult passage at all times, as the direct route is against the wind all the way. Very few boats can make it direct to Hawaii unless the skipper is prepared to power his way through the NE trades. In such a case the lighter winds at the beginning and end of summer would be preferable, but even then the trip would be upwind most of the way. The alternative to constant tacking is to make a detour, either to the north, possibly via Wake and Midway Islands, or south via Kiribati and possibly the Line Islands.

During summer, when the trades have more E and S in them, the northern alternative is preferable, although it must be stressed that if the idea of a non-stop passage to Hawaii is not attractive, both Wake and Midway are restricted islands used by the US military and only emergency stops are allowed. Even so, this does at least give the peace of mind that there is a place to get help in a real emergency. A feature of this northerly route at the beginning of summer are the northerly gales, some of which can be quite violent.

Whether calling in at Wake Island or not, the route from the Marshalls runs almost due north to latitude 20°N from where it curves NE, staying on the tack that makes most easting and trying not to go below the latitude of Hawaii. In reality, it might become necessary to go beyond latitude 25°N to be able to make the required easting. The route passes close to Laysan, the most north west of the Hawaiian islands, which is a bird sanctuary and has no safe anchorage. The only good anchorage close to this route is further south, at French Frigate Shoals, but permission to call there must also be obtained beforehand.

The southbound passage via Kiribati is best undertaken in winter when the trades are NE and E in direction and the weather is also more settled. In summer the winds have more S in them and the weather offshore can be squally. From Majuro the route passes between Jaluit and Mili atolls and enters northern Kiribati close to Little Makin, from where it continues through the archipelago to Tarawa, the capital of Kiribati. For the continuing route, Kiribati to Hawaii, see PN39.

PN39 *Kiribati to Hawaii*

DIAGRAM 44, 45		Tarawa to Hilo 2180 m
Best time:	October to April	
Tropical storms:	None	
Charts:	BA: 781, 782	
	US: 504	
Pilots:	BA: 61, 62	
	US: 126, 152	

This route is best taken in winter, and although some headwinds cannot be avoided, the weather is more settled and pleasant. The route runs east between latitudes 5°N and 8°N trying to take advantage of the east setting Equatorial Countercurrent. A stop can be made in the Line Islands, from where it should be possible to reach Hawaii on the other tack (Route PN35). If SE winds are encountered en route, the Line Islands should be bypassed altogether and an attempt made to reach Hawaii non-stop.

The difficulties associated with a return to Hawaii from either the Marshalls or Kiribati cannot be avoided and often the only way is to hope for a break in the trades, when the engine can be used to gain some ground to windward.

Routes in the Far East

Compared to other parts of the world, cruising routes in the Far East do not fall into a logical pattern. This is caused both by the fact that the area is off the beaten track and by the unpredictability of the weather. The western part of the North Pacific does not lie near any of the major cruising routes and including the countries of the Far East in a world cruise is no easy matter, as they can only be reached by a lengthy detour. For some people this remoteness is the main attraction and many more cruising boats might venture that way were it not for the appalling weather. Virtually the entire area is subject to violent typhoons, which limit the safe sailing season to only a few months per year. As most distances involved are very long, it usually means that one must be prepared to remain there between seasons and spend the typhoon season in or near a safe anchorage, of which fortunately there are many. Although tropical storms have been recorded in every month of the year, May to December is regarded as the typhoon season because the frequency of typhoons during these months is much higher than in winter.

The three main cruising areas are the Philippines, Japan and Micronesia. The main attractions of the Philippines are the generally pleasant climate and the great number of inlets and bays to explore. Although typhoons strike the archipelago with regularity, there are many good anchorages where shelter can be sought. The Inland Sea of Japan and the great number of small fishing harbours make Japan a very attractive cruising destination, although the safe sailing season is very short. The scattered islands of Micronesia are much closer in character to the islands of the South Pacific and are in fact a convenient stepping stone between the South Pacific and the Far East.

The main drawback of the Far East remains, however, the difficulty of getting there. In spite of the favourable NE trade winds that blow across the North Pacific ensuring a fast and pleasant sail from the west coast of America, the number of North American yachts that embark on such a transpacific voyage is surprisingly small. They are much more likely to be tempted by the lure of the South Seas and sail to the South Pacific instead, although some venture into the North West Pacific at a later stage, most reaching the Far East via Papua New Guinea. Another route that used to bring cruising boats to the Philippines and Hong Kong in the past was the route from Singapore. The reported cases of piracy in the South China Sea have made most people avoid this route and it is advisable to make enquiries in Singapore about the latest situation before leaving for either

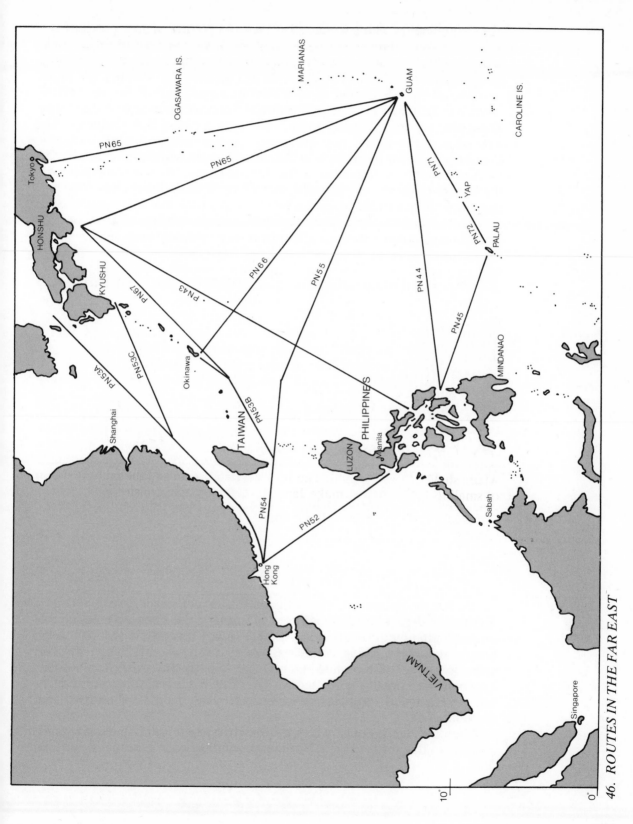

46. ROUTES IN THE FAR EAST

the Philippines or Hong Kong. Obstacles of a political nature preclude the use of the more direct route to Hong Kong across the Gulf of Siam, while the need for a cruising permit makes a detour through the Indonesian archipelago impossible. For the time being, the best solution for boats starting off from Singapore is to follow the north coast of Borneo, where stops can be made in the small states of Sarawak, Brunei or Sabah. The other alternative is to arrive in the Far East via Papua New Guinea at the end of a cruise in the South Pacific. Yet another possibility is to sail non-stop to Japan from the West Coast or Hawaii and either continue the voyage towards Singapore and the Indian Ocean, or sail south through Papua New Guinea to Australia, across to New Zealand and along the southern route to Tahiti.

There are countless variations for a cruise in the Far East but unfortunately there is no logical way of getting there and back again.

PN40 Routes from the Philippines and Singapore

PN41 Philippines to Singapore
PN42 Philippines to Hong Kong
PN43 Philippines to Japan
PN44 Philippines to Guam
PN45 Philippines to Palau
PN46 Singapore to Philippines
PN47 Singapore to Hong Kong

PN41 Philippines to Singapore

DIAGRAM 76	Balabac Strait to Singapore 870 m

Best time:	January to March
Tropical storms:	May to December
Charts:	BA: 1263
	US: 522
Pilots:	BA: 30, 31, 33, 44
	US: 160, 163, 166

Because of the low incidence of tropical storms in the areas traversed by this route, southbound passages can be made at any time of the year, although more favourable sailing conditions occur during months when the NE monsoon is well established. During the summer and the SW monsoon, typhoons occasionally pass through the Philippines and offshore passages are best avoided, particularly during the peak months of August and September.

After leaving the Sulu Sea through Balabac Strait, the offshore route runs parallel to the north coast of Borneo, passing between Luconia Shoals and

Cape Baram, north of Subi Kechil and through the southern Natuna islands. Few boats sail this route without stopping in one of the three small states in North Borneo, all of which have excellent harbours, Kota Kinabalu in Sabah, Muara in Brunei and Kuchin in Sarawak. A stop in any of these ports is particularly welcome during the SW monsoon when contrary winds and currents make this passage slow and tedious.

PN42 Philippines to Hong Kong

DIAGRAM 76	Manila to Hong Kong 620 m

Best time:	mid-December to mid-March
Tropical storms:	May to December
Charts:	BA: 2661B
	US: 508, 550
Pilots:	BA: 30, 31, 33
	US: 161, 160, 165

This passage is usually made either direct from Manila Bay or from some port further north along the west coast of Luzon. Whichever point of departure is chosen, the passage presents no problems during the NE monsoon, when favourable conditions can be expected for the entire passage, although the winds can be quite strong. The best time to do this passage is from mid-December to mid-March. During the remainder of the year, particular attention must be paid to tropical depressions forming in the South China Sea or even further afield, as these can develop into fully fledged typhoons before a safe harbour can be reached.

Pratas Reef should be given a wide berth and unless the weather is clear and settled, it should not be passed on its windward side. During the NE monsoon, when strong winds and overcast skies are sometimes prevalent for several days, vessels approaching Pratas Reef from the S or SE should check their position frequently, as many vessels have been lost on this reef due to a doubtful position.

PN43 Philippines to Japan

DIAGRAM 46	Luzon Strait to Okinawa 560 m
	Okinawa to Bungo Strait 460 m
	Bernardino Strait to Yokohama 1620 m

Best time:	May
Tropical storms:	May to December
Charts:	BA: 4509
	US: 522
Pilots:	BA: 33, 42A, 42B
	US: 158, 159, 160, 165

The best time to make this passage is in May, at the beginning of the SW monsoon, when the danger of being overtaken by an early typhoon is minimal. The winds are generally favourable for most of the passage, although calms can be expected when approaching the Japanese coast. The offshore route follows the Kuro Shio current, which sets NE at a considerable rate. Occasionally the weather can be quite rough as one passes from one wind system to the next and attention should be paid to the movement of frontal systems. An equally alert watch must be kept for the large amount of shipping in this area, both commercial and fishing.

If one is forced to make this passage during the NE monsoon, head winds can be expected for the best part of the passage. Early in the year, in February or March, an alternative to beating into the wind on an offshore route is to head for Okinawa and commence cruising among the Japanese islands from there. Starting from the SW extremity of the Japanese archipelago, it is easier to move NE along the chain of islands.

PN44 Philippines to Guam

DIAGRAMS 46, 47		San Bernardino to Guam 1200 m
Best time:	July to September	
Tropical storms:	May to December	
Charts:	BA: 781	
	US: 522	
Pilots:	BA: 33, 60	
	US: 126, 166	

The steadiness of the NE trades during winter, when the risk of typhoons is very low, makes this a tough windward passage during the safe season. The only time when fair winds can be expected is during the SW monsoon when, although the direction of the wind is favourable, the risk of typhoons is very real. If this passage is considered during the NE monsoon, a better slant would be obtained by rounding Luzon from the north and joining Route PN55.

PN45 Philippines to Palau

DIAGRAMS 46, 47		San Bernardino to Palau 680 m
Best time:	January to March	
Tropical storms:	May to December	
Charts:	BA: 781	
	US: 522	
Pilots:	BA: 33, 60	
	US: 126, 166	

This route is usually the first leg of a longer trip to the South Pacific. As in the reverse direction (see Route PT28) the best time for making this passage is during the winter months when there is little danger of being caught out by a typhoon. The first part of the passage benefits from the NE trades, which from December to March can blow quite strongly, although these winds gradually become lighter in the vicinity of Palau. The North Equatorial Current has a strong westerly set in this region and this should be taken into account.

PN46 *Singapore to Philippines*

DIAGRAM 76	Singapore to Balabac Strait 870 m
Best time:	May to July
Tropical storms:	May to December
Charts:	BA: 1263
	US: 508
Pilots:	BA: 30, 31, 33, 44
	US: 160, 163, 166, 174

This is a difficult route because of the various dangers that lurk in the South China Sea, both natural and man-made. A passage during the SW monsoon offers the chance of favourable winds, but also the risk of typhoons when approaching the Philippines, although tropical storms are rarer in the southern half of the archipelago. The passage can be made with less danger from typhoons during the NE monsoon, but winds will be mostly contrary. As the route runs along the coast of Borneo, the voyage can be interrupted in any one of the three states bordering on the South China Sea and there are several good ports in Sarawak, Brunei and Sabah where yachts have found shelter.

Two routes can be taken on leaving Singapore. The first leads between South Natuna and Subi Kechil islands, the second through Api Passage, NW of Borneo. In all these passes attention must be paid to the currents, which can be very strong at times. The two routes join south of Luconia Shoals from where a straight course can be steered for Balabac Strait, passing north of Mangalum island. The alternative is to call in at Kota Kinabalu, the capital of Sabah, one of the states belonging to the Federation of Malaysia. From Balabac Strait the route crosses the Sulu Sea where conditions can be quite rough during the NE monsoon. The inside route through the Sulu Sea is not necessarily the best if bound for Luzon and Manila, which can be reached by the Palawan Passage (see Route PN47).

PN47 *Singapore to Hong Kong*

DIAGRAM 76	Singapore to Hong Kong 1800 m

Best time:	May–June
Tropical storms:	May to December
Charts:	BA: 1263
	US: 508
Pilots:	BA: 30, 31, 44
	US: 160, 161, 163, 166, 174

Similar directions apply to those for Route PN46 as far as Balabac Strait, from where this route continues through Palawan Passage. The narrowest part of this passage is 28 miles wide, where it is bound on the west by Captain Royal Shoal and on the east by Balabac island. As the currents set strongly eastward through the Balabac Strait, the island should not be approached in bad weather. In the area between Borneo and Palawan, the currents often behave erratically and many vessels have come to grief on either side of the passage when going through in poor visibility. North of Palawan Passage the route passes east of Macclesfield Bank and then direct to Hong Kong.

Most favourable winds on this route will be found at the start of the SW monsoon and although more consistent winds can be expected in July and August, the increased likelihood of typhoons in the area around Hong Kong make a later date less attractive. The passage would be very difficult to accomplish during the NE monsoon when strong NE winds and an equally strong south flowing current occur north of Borneo.

PN50 Routes from Hong Kong

PN51 Hong Kong to Singapore
PN52 Hong Kong to Philippines
PN53 Hong Kong to Japan
PN54 Hong Kong to Guam
PN55 Taiwan to Guam

PN51 *Hong Kong to Singapore*

DIAGRAM 76	Hong Kong to Singapore 1800 m

Best time:	January to March
Tropical storms:	May to December
Charts:	BA: 1263
	US: 508
Pilots:	BA: 30, 31 44
	US: 160, 161, 163, 166, 174

Most favourable conditions on this route occur at the height of the NE monsoon, when steady winds and a south flowing current ensure a fast passage. The route can be taken for the entire duration of the NE monsoon, from October to April, although less consistent winds and squally weather can be expected during the transitional period. During the winter months the risk of typhoons in the Hong Kong area is remote, whereas in the southern part of the South China Sea, the Gulf of Siam and all of Northern Indonesia, tropical storms are extremely rare in all seasons.

Because of political considerations, the more direct route passing close to Vietnam is not recommended unless permission has been obtained from the Vietnamese authorities to sail through their waters, which is very unlikely. The two alternative routes pass either east of Macclesfield Bank, or between this bank and the Paracel Islands, before joining the main channel through Palawan Passage. Throughout this area extreme caution is necessary when sailing close to the various dangers which are difficult to see in poor visibility, the situation being compounded by the unpredictability of the currents. The most dangerous area is in the southern part of Palawan Passage, close to Balabac Strait, where strong currents make navigation extremely hazardous. An alternative route branches off to the Philippines before Palawan Passage and rejoins the main route north of Borneo.

The route continues parallel to the north coast of Borneo, where the voyage can be interrupted in Sabah, Brunei or Sarawak, all of which have good harbours. The route then passes south of Luconia Shoals, through the southern group of Natuna Islands and on to Singapore.

PN52 Hong Kong to Philippines

DIAGRAM 46	Hong Kong to Manila 620 m

Best time:	February to April
Tropical storms:	May to December
Charts:	BA: 2661B
	US: 508
Pilots:	BA: 30, 31, 33
	US: 160, 161, 165

Best passages on this route are made in the spring months towards the end of the NE monsoon, which lasts from early November until April or sometimes early May. Earlier passages in the NE monsoon can be unpleasant, as in early December the South China Sea can be quite rough, especially when a cold front passes through from the north. A good time to leave is soon after one of these fronts has passed. Good weather forecasts can be obtained from the Royal Observatory, which also gives advance warnings of the movement of any tropical storms within 400 miles of Hong Kong. In some years the arrival of the NE monsoon is accompanied by gale force winds in the northern part of the South China Sea, resulting in very rough passages in either direction. As an additional discomfort lower temperatures are usually associated with this kind of weather.

Southbound passages during the typhoon season, between June and October, can be quite risky, although reliable long-term forecasts can guarantee a safe start to a passage. The peak of the typhoon season coincides with the SW monsoon, when light winds can be expected during settled weather.

PN53 Hong Kong to Japan

DIAGRAM 46	Hong Kong to Nagasaki 1020 m

Best time:	May
Tropical storms:	May to December
Charts:	BA: 1263
	US: 523
Pilots:	BA: 30, 32, 42, 42B
	US: 157, 158, 159, 160, 161

If this passage is undertaken in May, at the beginning of the SW monsoon, it is possible both to have favourable winds and avoid the worst of the typhoon season. If one intends to sail towards Nagasaki and the NW coast of Japan, it is better to sail through the Taiwan Straits and then follow the coast of China (PN53A). A recommended place to cross to the south coast of Japan is through Tokara Gunto. During the NE monsoon this passage is much more difficult. By sailing parallel to the Chinese coast it might be possible to profit from the fact that the wind shifts slightly to the N at night and the E by day. The course should be altered to cross the China Sea only when the northern extremity of Taiwan can be weathered on the port tack. With the help of the favourable current it is possible to make progress to the NNE by keeping to the west of the Nansei Shoto Islands (PN53C). The south coast of Japan can then be reached through one of the channels south of Osumi Kaikyo.

An alternative route on leaving Hong Kong is to head E through the Bashi Channel, south of Taiwan, and then sail NE with a favourable wind and the help of the Kuro Shio Current (PN53B). However, the danger of being caught by a typhoon or even a depression in the Bashi Channel makes this alternative rather hazardous unless the weather is perfectly settled. The only time when this alternative should be undertaken by a small boat is towards the end of the NE monsoon, when it is easier to cross the China Sea without tacking, as the winds near the coast of Luzon tend to be E or even SE. If this passage is made in April, the weather in Japan starts to be warmer and cruising is more comfortable than during the cold winter months.

PN54 Hong Kong to Guam

DIAGRAM 46		Hong Kong to Guam 1850 m
Best time:	January to March	
Tropical storms:	May to December	
Charts:	BA: 781, 2661B	
	US: 522	
Pilots:	BA: 30, 32, 60	
	US: 126, 160, 161	

The direct route runs north of Luzon through Luzon Strait into the Philippines Sea from where the same directions apply as for Route PN55. This passage is best made in winter, when the risk of typhoons is low, the disadvantage being the strong NE trades. As winds tend to become more easterly in lower latitudes, it is advisable to make some easting while still on the latitude of Luzon Strait, which would also compensate for the west setting current that will be experienced further south.

If the passage is undertaken either at the start of or during the SW monsoon, a more sheltered course can be taken through the Philippine archipelago and out through the San Bernadino Channel. This alternative may be more attractive, although typhoons are not uncommon near Guam in April.

PN55 Taiwan to Guam

DIAGRAMS 46, 47		Bashi Channel to Guam 1400 m
Best time:	December to March	
Tropical storms:	May to December	
Charts:	BA: 781	
	US: 522	
Pilots:	BA: 32, 60	
	US: 126, 157	

December to March are the safest months to undertake this passage as the danger of being hit by a typhoon is quite remote. The only problem is the strength of the NE trades, which can make the entire trip hard on the wind. It is therefore advisable to make as much easting as possible after leaving Taiwan before laying a direct course for Guam. The route leaves through the Bashi Channel, south of Taiwan, and heads east to a point about 22°N, 125°E, from where a direct course is taken to Guam.

Although this passage can also be made during the summer months, it is not recommended to cross the Philippine Sea in the middle of the typhoon season. Even if there is no typhoon, the weather in July and August is often stormy with overcast skies and rough seas.

PN60 Routes from Japan

PN61 Japan to Alaska
PN62 Japan to British Columbia
PN63 Japan to California
PN64 Japan to Hawaii
PN65 Japan to Guam
PN66 Guam to Japan
PN67 Japan to Hong Kong

PN61 Japan to Alaska

DIAGRAM 45	Yokohama to Kodiak 3000 m

Best time:	July
Tropical storms:	May to December
Charts:	BA: 2459, 2460
	US: 523
Pilots:	BA: 4, 23, 41, 42A
	US: 152, 158

The few boats which take this route across the top of the North Pacific often break the passage in the Aleutian Islands. The only reasonable time to make this passage is in the middle of summer, in July or possibly August, when the weather is warmer and the days are long. During the summer months there are sometimes prolonged periods of calms or light winds when it may be necessary to motor. Equally one can be just as unlucky and experience rough weather all the way. The timing for this passage is influenced by future plans as September is the latest time for heading south from Alaska. However, if one intends to spend the winter in Alaska, an earlier arrival time is not so crucial.

PN62 Japan to British Columbia

DIAGRAM 45	Yokohama to Vancouver 4200 m

Best time:	June to August
Tropical storms:	May to December
Charts:	BA: 2683
	US: 520, 523
Pilots:	BA: 25, 42A, 62
	US: 152, 154, 158

Fair winds can be expected right across the North Pacific on this long passage. The most favourable conditions are in the summer months, from

June to August, when winds are mostly between S and W and some help can also be expected from the Aleutian Current. The percentage of gales in the summer months is low, although the occasional depression can pass over bringing stronger winds. Fog is quite frequent during these summer months and a careful watch should be kept when visibility is poor, as some of the fishing boats that work in this area are often left on automatic pilot with no one on watch.

The recommended summer route, if leaving from one of the ports in central Japan, is to make most of the crossing between latitudes 42°N and 45°N, where there are better chances of finding favourable winds. After leaving Japan, latitude 42°N should be reached on meridian 170°E, from where the route passes through a point 45°N, 160°W. A direct course can be taken from there to Juan de Fuca Strait.

PN63 *Japan to California*

DIAGRAM 45	Yokohama to San Francisco 4500 m

Best time:	June to August
Tropical storms:	May to December
Charts:	BA: 2683
	US: 520, 523
Pilots:	BA: 8, 42A, 62
	US: 152, 158

Directions are similar to those given for Route PN62 and a direct course for California should be shaped only after meridian 150°W has been crossed. If this passage is made either earlier or later in the year, the route should follow a more southerly course as it may not be necessary to go above 40°N in search of favourable winds.

PN64 *Japan to Hawaii*

DIAGRAM 45	Yokohama to Hilo 3550 m

Best time:	June to September
Tropical storms:	April to December
Charts:	BA: 2683
	US: 523
Pilots:	BA: 42A, 62
	US: 152, 158

The Kuro Shio will give a considerable boost at the start of this passage which should also benefit from SW winds which are common in summer. A course for higher latitudes has to be set in search of westerly winds and easting will most likely be made between latitudes 40°N and 44°N. The northern limit of the track depends on the winds encountered up to the point where meridian 180°W is crossed. From that point onward, the route starts curving ESE so that latitude 40°N is recrossed in longitude 170°W and 35°N in 160°W. Having reached meridian 160°W it is usually possible to lay a direct course for Hawaii through the prevailing NE trade winds which are more easterly in summer.

Although the passage is made during the typhoon season, as the route moves away from Japan the risk of being overtaken by one of these storms decreases.

PN65 Japan to Guam

DIAGRAM 46		Yokohama to Guam 1350 m
Best time:	November, April	
Tropical storms:	May to December	
Charts:	BA: 781	
	US: 522	
Pilots:	BA: 42A, 60	
	US: 126, 158	

This passage is best made either late in November, when the worst of the typhoon season is over, or in April, before the onset of the new typhoon season and after the worst winter gales. While in the region of the westerlies, some easting should be made, so that from about 22°N the NE trades can give a good reach all the way to Guam. Depending on the direction of the wind after leaving Japan, one can pass either to the west or east of the Mariana Islands.

A popular alternative is to break the trip by stopping in Chichi Jima in the Ogasawara Gunto group, which is also recommended as a place to seek shelter if a typhoon does threaten during the passage to Guam.

PN66 Guam to Japan

DIAGRAM 46		Guam to Yokohama 1350 m
Best time:	March to April	
Tropical storms:	May to December	
Charts:	BA: 781	
	US: 522	
Pilots:	BA: 42A, 60	
	US: 126, 158	

The best time to do this passage is in March or April, when the weather starts to become warmer further up north and the typhoon season has not started in earnest. However, typhoons can form just north of the equator at any time of the year in the Western Pacific, although with a good forecast from the US Navy's Typhoon Warning Center in Apra Harbour, it is possible to depart from Guam knowing that good weather can be expected for at least the first few days. Up to latitude 25°N the prevailing wind is the NE trade, which can be quite boisterous in the late winter months. If the trades have too much N in them, instead of beating, one can ease the sheets and head for Okinawa, from where it is just as easy to start cruising the many islands of the Japanese archipelago. The trades will be lost in about latitude 25°N and an area of changeable weather is entered, usually squally with the wind blowing in gusts. W or SW winds will be found farther north.

PN67 Japan to Hong Kong

DIAGRAM 46	Yokohama to Hong Kong 1700 m
Best time:	February to March, November
Tropical storms:	May to December
Charts:	BA: 1263
	US: 522
Pilots:	BA: 30, 32, 42A
	US: 157, 158, 159, 160, 161

The best time to do this passage is either towards the beginning of the NE monsoon in late November or at its end in February and March. From ports on the north coast of Japan and in the Korea Straits a SW course should be followed parallel to the Chinese coast leading through the Taiwan Straits and on to Hong Kong. Leaving from any of the ports along the south coast of Japan, there are two alternatives – either to stay close inshore and pass into the Eastern Sea through one of the channels south of Kyushu, or to stand offshore and cross the Kuro Shio in about 28°N, 135°E. In the former case directions are similar to those for boats leaving from the north coast. In the latter case, after having crossed the Kuro Shio, the Eastern Sea is reached through one of the channels that separate the islands in the Nansei Shoto group.

During the SW monsoon (April to September) this route is not recommended. However, if one is forced to make this passage in summer a SE course should be taken to 30°N, 145°E. From there the route passes east of Ogasawara Gunto and south of Kazan Reto. A direct course is then shaped to pass north of Luzon and straight to Hong Kong, making allowance for the NE setting current in the China Sea.

The majority of those who cruise in Japan choose to sail from there to another destination, such as Guam, which is easier to reach, rather than beat their way back to the Philippines or Hong Kong. However, if one is determined to return to either of these destinations, the passage should be planned during the NE monsoon.

PN70 Routes in Micronesia

PN71 Guam to Palau
PN72 Palau to Guam

PN71 Guam to Palau

DIAGRAM 47		Guam to Palau 720 m
Best time:	December to March	
Tropical storms:	All year	
Charts:	BA: 781	
	US: 522	
Pilots:	BA: 60	
	US: 126	

Unfortunately no month is completely free of tropical storms and one or more of these have passed through the area crossed by this route in every month of the year in recent history. This does not necessarily mean that typhoons occur in every month, only that such a possibility cannot be discounted. During the NE trade wind season NE and E winds make this a fast downwind passage. Visiting boats are not allowed to enter the Republic of Palau without a cruising permit, which must be obtained in advance, as well as entry visas for all crew members, including the skipper. The vessel's ETA must also be brought to the attention of the authorities by radio.

PN72 Palau to Guam

DIAGRAM 47		Palau to Guam 720 m
Best time:	July to October	
Tropical storms:	All year	
Charts:	BA: 781	
	US: 522	
Pilots:	BA: 60	
	US: 126	

As stated in directions for the reciprocal route, the risk of typhoons cannot be ignored in any month, although their highest frequency is during August and September. Unfortunately this is also the time when favourable winds

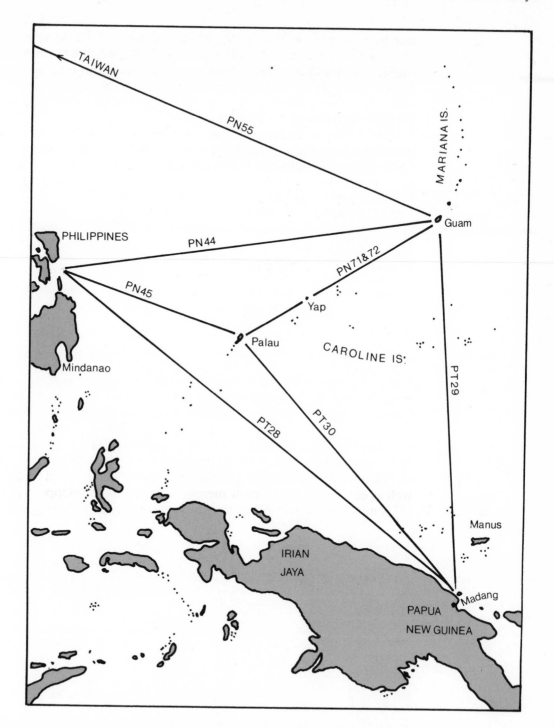

47. ROUTES BETWEEN PAPUA NEW GUINEA AND MICRONESIA

can be expected on this route, which for most of the year is under the influence of the NE trades. The prevailing NE winds are reversed during the summer months by the SW monsoon, although this is never as steady as its NE counterpart and easterly winds can never be discounted on this route. If contrary winds persist, the voyage can be broken in Yap, which lies on the direct route to Guam.

North of Palau the North Equatorial Current sets to the west, although its direction is normally deflected to the south by the SW monsoon. If NE winds are encountered on leaving Palau, it is better to make easting in the latitude of Palau, where at least there is the chance of getting some help from the east setting Equatorial Countercurrent.

14 Transequatorial routes in the Pacific

PT11 California to Galapagos
PT12 California to Marquesas
PT13 California to Tahiti
PT14 British Columbia to Marquesas
PT15 Central America to Marquesas
PT16 Central America to Easter Island
PT17 Panama to Galapagos
PT18 Panama to Marquesas
PT19 Southbound from Panama
PT20 Marquesas to Hawaii
PT21 Tahiti to Hawaii
PT22 Tahiti to Panama
PT23 Cook Islands to Hawaii
PT24 Hawaii to Tahiti
PT25 Hawaii to Marquesas
PT26 Tuvalu to Kiribati
PT27 Kiribati to Tuvalu
PT28 New Guinea to Philippines
PT29 New Guinea to Guam
PT30 Palau to New Guinea

Unlike the Atlantic, where most cruising routes keep to the northern hemisphere and only a minority cross the equator, the equatorial region of the Pacific is crisscrossed by a multitude of routes. The busiest area is in the east, where boats starting off from Panama or the West Coast have to cross the equator to reach their destinations in the South Pacific. Although the Intertropical Convergence Zone is widest at its eastern end, the crossing of the doldrums is seldom a major problem and the zone itself is usually transited in a relatively short time. The doldrums only become a problem when their position and extent have not been assessed accurately and the course remains in the doldrums too long. The main object is to intersect the ITCZ at right angles and the course should be always altered to achieve this whenever a route crosses the doldrums.

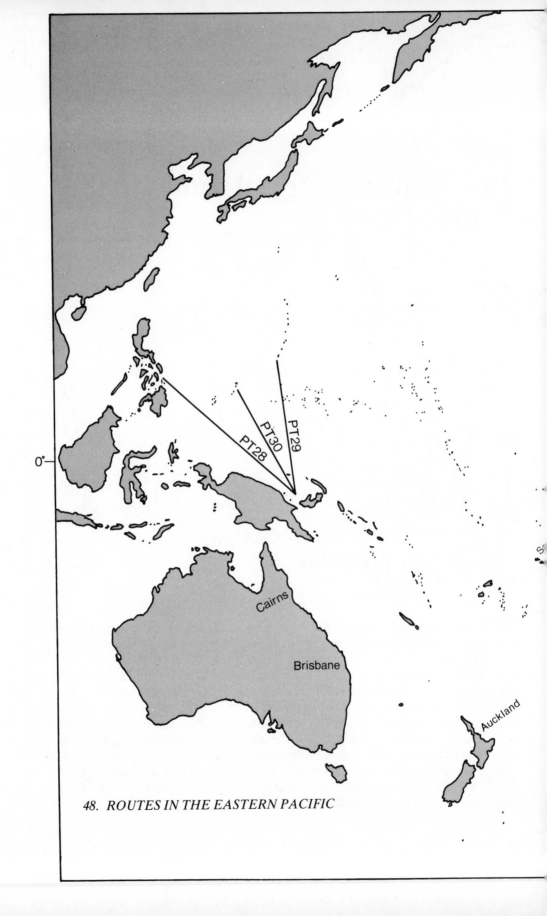

0°

PT29

PT30

PT28

Cairns

Brisbane

Auckland

48. ROUTES IN THE EASTERN PACIFIC

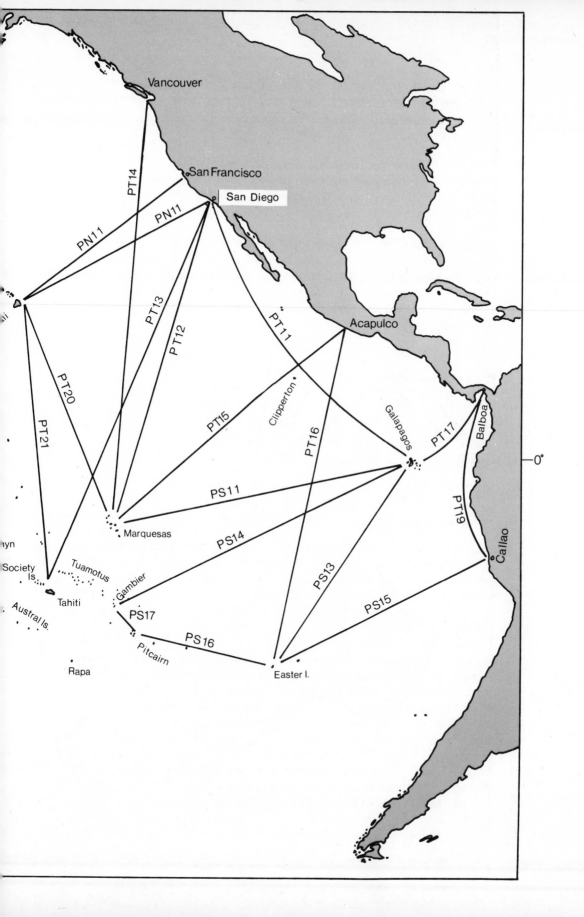

Vancouver

San Francisco

San Diego

PT14

PN11

PN11

PT13

PT12

PT11

Acapulco

PT20

PT15

Clipperton

Galapagos

PT17

Balboa

PT21

PT16

0°

PS11

PT19

Marquesas

PS14

Callao

Penrhyn

Society Is.

Tuamotus

Gambier

PS13

PS15

Australs Is.

Tahiti

PS17

Rapa

Pitcairn

PS16

Easter I.

West of about longitude 150°W, which is the longitude of Tahiti, the doldrums are very narrow and it is sometimes possible to sail from one trade wind into the next almost without interruption. Further west, transequatorial routes linking the two hemispheres seldom encounter true doldrum conditions, although the weather is sometimes squally and unsettled in the area where the two trade wind systems meet. Doldrum weather is also associated with the changeover period between monsoons, especially in Papua New Guinea, where the arrival of the NW monsoon is always heralded by this kind of weather, particularly evident on routes to Micronesia.

Another feature of the equatorial region of the Pacific, which can have an important bearing on the routes that cross it, is the complexity and unpredictability of the three main currents. All transequatorial routes are affected by them to a greater or lesser extent and even if their behaviour cannot be predicted with accuracy, being aware of their existence can avoid unpleasant surprises.

PT11 California to Galapagos

DIAGRAM 44		San Diego to Wreck Bay 2560 m
Best time:	March to April	
Tropical storms:	June to October	
Charts:	BA: 2683	
	US: 51	
Pilots:	BA: 7, 8	
	US: 125, 153	

Depending on the time of year when this passage is undertaken, one may have to sail through both the NE and SE trades to reach the destination, which requires making good some 30 degrees of easting. As the winds in the vicinity of the Galapagos Islands blow from the southerly quarter for most of the year, it is advisable to try to make as much easting as possible further north.

Leaving the Californian coast, the route passes to seaward of the various islands off the coast of Baja California. After passing the Revilla Gigedo Islands, a course is laid to pass as far to the east of Clipperton Island as the winds will permit. From Clipperton onwards one can expect to lose the NE trades and enter an area of variable winds. The doldrums lying further to the south will bring squally weather interspersed by calms. The Equatorial Countercurrent may give a welcome boost if not enough easting was made earlier in the passage, although it should be borne in mind that the west setting South Equatorial Current encountered later is likely to be much stronger. As this route crosses the hurricane zone off the coast of Mexico, this passage should not be made between June and October.

PT12 California to Marquesas

DIAGRAMS 44, 48	San Francisco to Hiva Oa 3000 m
	San Diego to Hiva Oa 2560 m

Best time:	March to May
Tropical storms:	June to October (N)
	December to March (S)
Charts:	BA: 783, 787
	US: 51
Pilots:	BA: 8, 62
	US: 122, 126, 152

The majority of people undertaking this passage prefer to call at ports in Baja California or even further south before setting off on this long ocean passage, although this tactic does not ensure better sailing conditions. Therefore, unless one wishes to cruise along the Mexican coast, it is better to make straight for the Marquesas. The time of arrival in the Marquesas should be considered before leaving, as a departure in November means an arrival in the Marquesas in the middle of summer, which can be very hot and is also the cyclone season. A better time of departure is between March and May, which ensures a winter arrival in the Marquesas at the most pleasant time of the year. These factors have to be weighed up against the advantages of a November departure, when the trades are at their strongest almost as far as the equator. From any point of departure, it pays to move offshore quickly as steadier NE winds are more likely to be encountered.

The great circle route crosses the doldrums at a slant and the course should be altered as soon as the doldrums are encountered in order to cut across at right angles. If the NE trades are steady, it might be better to stay with them and make as much westing as possible before crossing the equator towards the Marquesas rather than stick to the great circle route.

PT13 California to Tahiti

DIAGRAM 48	San Diego to Papeete 3550 m

Best time:	November to May
Tropical storms:	June to October (N)
	December to March (S)
Charts:	BA: 783, 787
	US: 51
Pilots:	BA: 8, 62
	US: 122, 126, 152

This is a rather uncommon route taken by those who are in a hurry to get to Tahiti and are prepared to sail non-stop rather than call at the Marquesas or sail the longer route via Hawaii. The direct route avoids all dangers and crosses the equator in about 140°W, where the doldrums are narrower than farther east. The width of the doldrums varies from year to year and there are times when no doldrums are encountered, the NE trades giving way to the SE trades almost without a break.

PT14 British Columbia to Marquesas

DIAGRAMS 44, 48		Vancouver to Hiva Oa 3700 m
Best time:	May to June	
Tropical storms:	June to October (N)	
	December to March (S)	
Charts:	BA: 783, 787	
	US: 520, 526	
Pilots:	BA: 8, 25, 62	
	US: 122, 126, 152, 154	

For those who intend to cruise in the Marquesas and the Tuamotus, a direct route from British Columbia is the most convenient. A detour via Hawaii can mean a lot of windward work to reach the Marquesas.

The best time to leave is in May or early June, when the winter storms are usually over off the coasts of Washington and Oregon and there is enough time to get south of 10°N before the start of the hurricane season. An earlier start is also possible, if the long-term weather forecast is good. A later start is more risky as most of the hurricanes that form off the coast of Mexico follow a track that intersects this route.

On leaving the coast it is essential to sail off shore as quickly as possible, as the seas are always rougher on the continental shelf. From a point about 200 miles SW of Juan de Fuca, a course can be shaped for the Marquesas. If one follows the great circle track, it is a good idea to try to keep east of 135°W until south of the equator, to avoid having to beat into the SE trades. During the first part of the passage the winds are likely to be NW or W from 5 to 20 knots and the current is also favourable. In May and June, the NE trades extend to latitude 25°N, although in some years they may only be found a few degrees further south. The doldrums are not too wide at this time of year, but if one motors through them, it is recommended to head slightly east of south, both to counteract the westerly set of the South Equatorial Current and also to be in a better positon when the SE trades are met.

PT15 Central America to Marquesas

DIAGRAMS 44, 48	Acapulco to Hiva Oa 2820 m
	Puntarenas to Hiva Oa 3460 m

Best time:	March to May
Tropical storms:	June to October (N)
	December to March (S)
Charts:	BA: 587, 783
	US: 51
Pilots:	BA: 8, 62
	US: 122, 126, 153

The length of this passage, which on average takes about four weeks, depends very much on the extent of the doldrums. As mentioned in Route PT12, it is advisable to try to stay with the NE trades as long as possible and only cross the equator in about longitude 132°W. This tactic is particularly recommended in the early part of the year, before the SE trades are fully established. In other months, a great circle route should be followed until in the doldrums when the course should be altered so as to pass through them as quickly as possible. If the departure is made after the beginning of June, it is best to head immediately offshore to avoid the *chabascos*. A summer passage is usually associated with thunderstorms, light and variable winds north of the equator, but consistent trades south of it. However, in 1983, which was a year of unusual weather conditions in the South Pacific, strong westerly winds were encountered south of the equator and the SE trades were virtually non-existent.

PT16 Central America to Easter Island

DIAGRAM 48	Costa Rica to Easter Island 2700 m

Best time:	December to February
Tropical storms:	June to October (N)
Charts:	BA: 4023
	US: 62
Pilots:	BA: 8, 62
	US: 122, 125, 153

This is a long haul southward for those who do not wish to make the detour via the Galapagos Islands (see also Route PT11). The initial course runs due south so that the equator is crossed around longitude 100°W. This gives an acceptable slant across the SE trades which become more easterly further south.

PT17 Panama to Galapagos

DIAGRAMS 44, 48, 63		Balboa to Wreck Bay 850 m
Best time:	February to June	
Tropical storms:	None	
Charts:	BA: 4023	
	US: 51	
Pilots:	BA: 7	
	US: 125, 153	

Weather conditions on this route are very varied and regardless of the time of year when the passage is made, it can take anything from six days to three weeks. Most boats have to contend with either long periods of calms, when a good reserve of fuel can be useful, or head winds, for S or SW winds are common between the mainland and the Galapagos Islands.

In the Gulf of Panama the winds blow mostly from the north between October and April. From May to September, the winds are either westerly or variable. If SW winds are encountered after Cabo Mala, it is preferable to stay on the starboard tack and pass east of Malpelo Island. By heading south parallel to the mainland coast, possibly as far south as latitude 3°S, the chances of finding favourable winds are better.

The N or NW setting current can be very strong in this area and this should be borne in mind when closing with the Galapagos Islands, as poor visibility in their vicinity and stronger currents than anticipated have caused the loss of several yachts. Those planning to make their landfall on Tower Island should exercise due care when approaching this low island, especially in squally weather. If the weather is particularly bad with poor visibility when approaching the Galapagos Islands, care must be taken if heaving to for the night in the proximity of the islands, both on account of the unpredictable currents and the absence of reliable lights.

On arrival in the Galapagos Islands, visiting yachts must clear in either Academy Bay on Santa Cruz Island or Wreck Bay on San Cristobal Island, where permission for a short stop is usually granted by the Port Captain (see Chapter 27).

PT18 Panama to Marquesas

DIAGRAM 48		Balboa to Nuku Hiva 3800 m
Best time:	February to June	
Tropical storms:	December to March	
Charts:	BA: 783, 4023	
	US: 51	
Pilots:	BA: 7, 62	
	US: 122, 125, 126, 153	

The difficulty of obtaining a cruising permit for the Galapagos Islands is the main reason why people make this passage non-stop. When sailing to the Marquesas direct, on leaving the Gulf of Panama (Route PT17), the decision has to be made whether to pass north or south of the Galapagos Islands. From June to January it is advisable to pass north of them, so as to avoid beating into the S winds which can be expected after leaving the Gulf of Panama. This route also takes advantage of the W set of the North Equatorial Current, which can be considerable. By crossing the equator in longitude 100°W, the route passes clear of all dangers. If unfavourable winds are encountered after the longitude of the Galapagos Islands has been passed, it is better to continue to make westing with favourable wind and current and only cross the equator when the winds have the desired slant.

From February to May it is better to pass south of the Galapagos Islands and once this group has been left safely behind, a direct course for the Marquesas can be laid. Whichever way the Galapagos are passed, they should be given a wide berth as poor visibility and very strong currents make navigation in their vicinity hazardous. An area to be avoided if passing south of the islands is between longitudes 90°W and 95°W and latitudes 3°S and 8°S, where several yachts have reported unpleasant weather conditions. The area appears to be an extension of the doldrums with little or no wind, thundery squalls and a heavy swell which make conditions very uncomfortable. Most of this area can be avoided if, after having passed the SE extremity of the Galapagos, the new course crosses longitude 100°W in 3°S latitude. Further west the same directions apply as for Route PS11.

PT19 Southbound from Panama

| DIAGRAMS 48, 63 | Balboa to Guayaquil 700 m |
| | Balboa to Callao 1270 m |

Best time:	November to March
Tropical storms:	None
Charts:	BA: 4023
	US: 62
Pilots:	BA: 7
	US: 125, 153

All passages southward from Panama, along the west coast of South America, are very difficult because of the persistent southerly winds and the contrary Peru or Humboldt Current, which sets north throughout the year. Sailing ships which did not have the advantage of an auxiliary engine were advised to only try to beat along the coast if bound for ports as far south as Callao, in Peru. Otherwise it was better to work their way offshore into the

SE trades and then reach the coast with the help of the prevailing westerlies which are to be found in about latitude 30°S. As far as Chilean ports are concerned, this suggestion continues to be valid for modern yachts. However, ports lying to the north of Callao can be reached from Panama without a lengthy detour, provided one is prepared to make the most of every shift of wind and use the engine when necessary.

After Cabo Mala a course should be laid to pass at least 50 miles to the west of Punta Galera, at the southern extremity of the Gulf of Panama. The currents are very complex and variable in this region, a combination of the Humboldt and Equatorial Countercurrent, which can reach up to 2½ knots at times, setting eastward into the bay. It is therefore very easy to be swept into the bay while crossing it, which is avoided by giving Punta Galera a wide berth.

South of the Gulf of Panama, the winds blow from between S and SW for most of the year, so it is a matter of always choosing the best tack to make as much southing as possible. As far as the Gulf of Guayaquil, it does not matter if the course is well offshore, as the doldrums in this area are not very wide. Southward from Guayaquil it is better to keep in with the coast to take advantage of the daily land and sea breezes. During periods of calm or light winds, it is necessary to motor to counteract the strong north setting current.

It is not uncommon to have favourable winds when crossing the Gulf of Panama, and during the northern winter, especially between February and April, the NE trades are sometimes felt as far south as the equator. From December to March, the doldrum belt is furthest south and extends west of Ecuador as far as the Galapagos Islands. Further south, along the Peruvian coast, the SE trades prevail for most of the year, although close to the coast, the wind has more S than E in it. Gales are very rare in Peruvian waters and cyclones unheard of. The one danger for small boats is the unusually big swell that sometimes occurs without warning along this coast. Its origin is probably submarine seismic activity, a known phenomenon in the region. The high swell can cause considerable damage to boats moored alongside wharves or docks.

PT20 Marquesas to Hawaii

DIAGRAMS 48, 64		Nuka Hiva to Hilo 1950 m
Best time:	April to October	
Tropical storms:	December to March	
Charts:	BA: 782, 783	
	US: 526	
Pilots:	BA: 62	
	US: 126, 152	

On leaving the Marquesas it is best to head due north and cross the equator in the vicinity of meridian 140°W. The same northerly course should be held until the NE trades are found around latitude 10°N. From there a direct course can be steered for Hawaii.

PT21 *Tahiti to Hawaii*

DIAGRAM 64	Papeete to Hilo 2270 m

Best time:	April to November
Tropical storms:	December to March
Charts:	BA: 782, 783
	US: 526, 541
Pilots:	BA: 62
	US: 126, 152

This passage is best made during the winter months of the South Pacific, when there is no danger of cyclones in the vicinity of the Tuamotus. During most of this period consistent trade winds are found south of the equator. The optimum time to leave Tahiti, or any other port in the Society Islands, is between April and July, when favourable conditions are usually encountered on both sides of the equator.

On leaving Tahiti a northerly course should be steered to pass to the west of all islands in the Tuamotus. From a position in 15°S, 149° 30'W, a new course should be laid to cross the equator between longitudes 145°W and 147°W. Any easting made at this stage will be an advantage later on. From Tahiti to about latitude 10°S the SE trades often blow from E or even NE, but after latitude 10°S is crossed, the trade winds are SE, so that it becomes possible to choose the best point for crossing the equator. In these longitudes the SE trades extend beyond the equator for most of the year and the doldrum belt rarely exceeds a width of 100 miles. Sometimes the doldrums are virtually nonexistent, the transit from one trade wind system to the next being quite sudden. The NE trades are normally found around latitude 10°N. The course should continue to be slightly to the east of the desired destination, both to allow for a west setting current and to arrive to windward of the Hawaiian Islands.

However tempting it might be to break the voyage in one of the Line Islands, as suggested on the reciprocal route from Hawaii to Tahiti, doing so on the way north might be a mistake as the subsequent leg to Hawaii would most probably be hard on the wind.

PT22 Tahiti to Panama

DIAGRAM 63	Papeete to Balboa 4450 m

Best time:	October–November
Tropical storms:	December to March
Charts:	BA: 783, 4023
	US: 62, 621
Pilots:	BA: 7, 62
	US: 122, 125, 126, 153

This rarely used route is taken by those who do not wish to reach the Atlantic either via Cape Horn or the westbound trade wind route. Depending on the time of year, those who wish to reach Panama from Tahiti have to either make their easting with the help of westerly winds of higher latitudes, or cut diagonally across the SE trade winds on a more direct but more difficult route.

The roundabout route with the help of westerly winds can be taken at all times of the year. From Tahiti the course leads SSE through the Austral Islands until the area of prevailing W winds is reached. During the winter months, when the limit of the SE trade winds is furthest north, easting should be made between latitudes 28°S and 32°S. During the summer months it might be necessary to go as far as latitude 35°S to find consistent W winds. On reaching the meridian of 100°W, the course becomes gradually NE until the SE trades are found again. The route then runs parallel to the South American coast taking advantage of the north setting Humboldt Current.

The more direct route can be taken when the SE trades are not so fully established, the best time being the southern summer from mid-October to mid-March. A SE course should be steered on leaving Tahiti so as to pass to the south of the Tuamotu Archipelago. Having passed the Gambier Islands the route leads past Pitcairn Island, from where the great circle route is taken to Panama. Having closed with the South American coast, both wind and current become favourable.

PT23 Cook Islands to Hawaii

DIAGRAM 64	Penrhyn to Hilo 1740 m

Best time:	April to November
Tropical storms:	December to March
Charts:	BA: 782, 783
	US: 541
Pilots:	BA: 62
	US: 126, 152

Most people who take this route through the Northern Cooks (Pukapuka, Manihiki, Penrhyn and Rakahanga) stop at one of these islands before heading north across the equator. As the Line Islands lie on the direct route to Hawaii, it is convenient to stop there too, Fanning and Palmyra having the best anchorages. The passage can be made in any month outside of the cyclone season, which should be avoided as the Northern Cooks have been hit by cyclones in the past. Weather conditions encountered to the north of the Cook Islands are often squally, with thunderstorms followed by calms. The last leg, from the Line Islands to Hawaii, is mostly hard on the wind, especially north of latitude 10°N where the NE trades are usually found.

PT24 Hawaii to Tahiti

DIAGRAM 64		Hilo to Papeete 2270 m
Best time:	April to November	
Tropical storms:	December to March	
Charts:	BA: 782, 783	
	US: 541	
Pilots:	BA: 62	
	US: 122, 126, 152	

The direct route passes close to the Line Islands where it may be convenient to break the journey (see PN34). Although NE trades will ensure fair winds possibly as far as latitude 5°N, once the SE trades are encountered, head winds are almost a certainty. This can be avoided by taking a more SE course after leaving Hawaii. An alternative is to possibly sail to the Marquesas first. As much easting as possible should be made at the beginning of the passage and, if going to Tahiti direct, the equator should be crossed between longitudes 148°W and 150°W.

The first part of the passage can be unpleasant, particularly in winter, with strong E winds and high seas. The width of the doldrums depends on the time of year, some boats having crossed them in a matter of hours, while others have had to battle with light winds and squalls for several days. Although the passage can be done at any time of the year, it is advisable to plan the arrival in Tahiti outside the cyclone season. April or May are considered to be the best months, as the SE trades are not yet fully established and the favourable season in the Society Islands is just beginning.

PT25 *Hawaii to Marquesas*

DIAGRAM 64	Hilo to Nuku Hiva 1950 m
Best time:	April to September
Tropical storms:	December to March
Charts:	BA: 782, 783
	US: 526
Pilots:	BA: 62
	US: 122, 126, 152

Similar directions apply to those for Route PT24, although an even more SE course will have to be steered after leaving Hawaii so as to cross the equator more or less on the meridian of the Marquesas. The route crosses all three equatorial currents and their combined sets will probably have a westerly resultant, which can make it even more difficult to make it to the equator in longitude 140°W. Therefore it is essential to make as much easting as possible while still in the NE trades. One way to overcome this difficulty is to use the Equatorial Countercurrent to make the required easting and only head south after the meridian of Nuku Hiva has been crossed.

PT26 *Tuvalu to Kiribati*

DIAGRAM 67	Funafuti to Tarawa 780 m
Best time:	March to October
Tropical storms:	None
Charts:	BA: 780, 781
	US: 526
Pilots:	BA: 61, 62
	US: 126

The passage between these two former partners in the Gilbert and Ellice Islands colony can be made throughout the year, although the best sailing conditions can be expected from March to October, when winds are mostly from the easterly quarter. November to February is the rainy season in the islands, when strong westerly gales are common. Especially during the westerly season, the currents among the islands are very irregular and their set impossible to predict. The currents among the islands of both Tuvalu and Kiribati behave in an erratic way throughout the year and this should be borne in mind when sailing in these waters.

The direct course from Funafuti to Tarawa passes close to several islands and crosses the equator in longitude 173°30′E. Although boats are supposed to clear first at Tarawa, in an emergency it is possible to stop briefly at one of the southern islands, the safest anchorages being found in the lagoons of Onotoa, Tabiteua and Abemama. When approaching Tarawa from the south, the island of Maiana should be treated with caution as it is wrongly depicted on the charts and the reef extending to the south west is more extensive than indicated.

PT27 Kiribati to Tuvalu

DIAGRAM 67	Tarawa to Funafuti 780 m
Best time:	March to October
Tropical storms:	None
Charts:	BA: 780, 781
	US: 526
Pilots:	BA: 61
	US: 126

The directions for this route are similar to those for the opposite route. If planning to call in at any of the southern islands of Kiribati, permission to do so should be obtained before leaving Tarawa.

The period October–March should be avoided if one intends to stop in Tuvalu for any length of time as most anchorages there are unsafe in strong westerly winds, which are common during this time. Although Tuvalu is normally considered to lie outside the cyclone zone, on very rare occasions tropical storms have tracked north from their breeding ground and hit the islands. The worst of these occurred in October 1952 and devastated Funafuti.

PT28 New Guinea to Philippines

DIAGRAM 47, 48	Madang to San Bernardino 1680 m
	Madang to Palau 1020 m
Best time:	December to March
Tropical storms:	April to December
Charts:	BA: 780, 781
	US: 524
Pilots:	BA: 33, 60
	US: 126, 164, 166

This is a favourite route for those who are looking for a change of scenery from the islands of the South Pacific, especially for those who intend to sail on to Hong Kong and Japan. The majority of boats make this passage during the NW monsoon, from November to March, so as to arrive in the Philippines before the onset of the typhoon season. Although this season is less well defined than the tropical storm seasons in other parts of the world, the most dangerous months are considered to be the summer months, from July to November, with the highest frequency of typhoons in August.

Boats leaving from Rabaul on the island of New Britain should follow a route to pass east of the Admiralty Islands, whereas for those leaving from Madang or other ports on the main island of New Guinea a NW course passing west of the Admiralty group is more logical. Although this westerly route also allows a stop at the Hermit Islands, at the height of the NW monsoon the wind can blow strongly from the north in the slot between New Guinea and the Admiralty Islands, making it a difficult and rough passage. The monsoon loses its strength as the equator is approached and the doldrum region entered. The width of the doldrums varies with the time of year, but it is seldom wider than 100 miles, and can be crossed quickly by motoring through, especially as currents in this area have a very complex pattern. The South Equatorial Current sets westward in a wide belt south of latitudes 4°N to 5°N. At the northern limit of this belt there is an abrupt reversal in the direction of the current. The east setting current is the Equatorial Countercurrent which is relatively narrow and gives way to the North Equatorial Current, which sets to the west and can extend from latitude 7°N or 8°N to 15°N to 20°N, depending on the season. The strength of these currents is about 1 to 1½ knots, so when sailing along this route particular attention should be paid to the complex character of these phenomena.

North of the doldrums light northerly winds can be expected until about latitude 5°N where the NE trades are encountered. During the winter months, from December to March, the trades are strongest and most consistent, becoming lighter and more variable with the approach of summer.

Most boats en route to the Philippines stop in Palau, which has several protected harbours. A cruising permit is required for Palau (see Route PN71). The weather forecasts broadcast from Guam cover this entire region and can be very helpful during the typhoon season.

PT29 New Guinea to Guam

DIAGRAM 47, 48		Madang to Guam 1130 m
Best time:	December to March	
Tropical storms:	April to December	
Charts:	BA: 780, 781	
	US: 524	
Pilots:	BA: 60	
	US: 126, 164	

Because of the high incidence of typhoons that either hit Guam or form between the island and the equator, most boats try to make their way to Guam during the northern winter. This is the time of the NW monsoon in

New Guinea when the weather in the Bismarck Sea and northern islands of Papua New Guinea is less settled than during the rest of the year. Few boats attempt to sail this passage non-stop and there are various islands which can be visited en route. If the passage is made at the change of monsoons, in November or early December, calms will be frequent south of the equator. By the middle of December steady NE winds become prevalent north of the equator and rather than beat all the way to Guam, some people prefer to break the trip in Truk, where it is also possible to refuel.

PT30 Palau to New Guinea

| DIAGRAM 47, 48 | Palau to Manus 960 m |
| | Palau to Madang 1020 m |

Best time:	October to March
Tropical storms:	April to December
Charts:	BA: 780, 781
	US: 524
Pilots:	BA: 60
	US: 126, 164

The best time to make this passage is from October to March, so as to arrive in New Guinea either after or before the SE monsoon (April to mid-October), thus avoiding contrary winds and the strong current which sets NW along the coast of New Guinea. During October and November little wind can be expected in the Bismarck Sea as the monsoon shifts from SE to NW, so one should be prepared to motor. From December to March one can expect favourable winds and current in the vicinity of New Guinea and the passage should present no problems.

After leaving Palau, stand to the SE to cross the equator in about longitude 140°E if wishing to call at ports on the main island of New Guinea or further east if bound for islands in the Bismarck Sea. Attention should be paid to the complex character of the currents in this region (see PT28).

If one has no choice but to make this passage after the onset of the SE monsoon south of the equator, it is recommended to make as much easting as possible while still north of the equator, taking advantage of the easterly set of the Equatorial Countercurrent. The equator should be crossed only in about longitude 150°E, allowing for the west going set of the South Equatorial Current, so as to enter the Bismarck Sea to the east of the Admiralty Islands.

The passage has been made in mid-September, when SW winds were encountered from Palau as far as latitude 5°N. From there it was necessary to motor through the doldrums, which extended to 1°S. As SE winds are still strong further south at this time, the change of seasons can be awaited either in the Ninigo or Hermit Islands, a convenient stopping point for boats making this passage in either direction.

15   Winds and currents of the South Pacific

Maps 2 to 6

South-east trade winds

The majority of cruising routes in the South Pacific are dependent on these winds which blow over a large area of this ocean. The SE trades blow on the equatorial side of the high pressure area situated in about 30°S. In the vicinity of the coast of South America, the trades blow from between S and SE, but their direction becomes increasingly E towards the west of the ocean. In the vicinity of Australia, the winds become SE again, especially during the winter months. During the summer months, from November to April, the trade wind is less steady over large parts of the ocean. West of about 140°W, there are frequently winds from other directions, although the prevailing direction remains between NE and SE.

The average strength of the SE trade wind is 15 knots, although sometimes it can increase to 20–25 knots over large areas. The strongest trades are experienced in the Coral Sea, where they reach 30 knots on occasions. However, the SE trade winds of the South Pacific are neither as steady nor as constant as the trades of other oceans. A continuous belt of SE wind blowing steadily across the entire ocean exists only during the months of June, July and August. During the rest of the year there is an area 600 miles wide, in which the force of the trade wind is not so constant. In this large area, stretching diagonally across the trade wind belt, extending SE from the Phoenix Islands through the Tuamotus as far as Easter Island, the direction of the wind often changes to the NE to be succeeded by calms. After a while the winds usually revert to blowing strongly from the SE and are frequently accompanied by heavy rain squalls.

The belt of trade winds moves considerably during the year, the southern limit moving almost 300 hundred miles, while the upper limit moves less, about 150 miles, and is situated north of the equator throughout the year except in the eastern part of the ocean. The northern limit of the SE trades forms a gentle curve with its highest point reaching 5°N in January and as far as 9°N in July. The southern boundary curves similarly in July with its higher limit being about 18°S, whereas in January the trade winds deepen closer to the South American coast reaching as far south as 30°S.

Intertropical Convergence Zone

The northern limit of the SE trade winds is determined by the position of the Intertropical Convergence Zone, which stays north of the equator throughout the year east of about longitude 160°W. In the western half of the ocean, it moves to the southern hemisphere from about November to April, reaching furthest south in February, at the peak of the southern summer. The movement of the ITCZ is most pronounced in the vicinity of Australia and Papua New Guinea, where the width of the doldrum belt can be greatest. On average it has a width of about 150 miles, but in some places it can be twice as wide, whereas in other areas it can be more or less nonexistent. Weather conditions inside the zone are typical of doldrums everywhere, with calms or light variable winds alternating with rain squalls and thunderstorms. These conditions are more extreme in the doldrums of the Western Pacific than elsewhere because of the wide angle at which the SE trades and NW monsoon meet in that area.

North-west monsoon

During the summer months, west of the meridian 180° and between the equator and the ITCZ, which is situated over Northern Australia, a prevailing NW wind blows over the western part of the South Pacific. The season of the NW monsoon depends on the latitude, but it normally lasts from December to March. The areas mostly affected by the NW monsoon are the Solomon Islands, Papua New Guinea and Northern Australia. The direction of the wind is mainly N or NE near the equator, becoming NW or even W in more southerly latitudes. The NW monsoon is not very consistent either in strength or in direction, but in spite of that, at the height of the season, winds from between S and E are quite rare. The strength of the monsoon is light or moderate, although it can reach gale force in squalls, which are quite frequent. The weather is generally cloudy and overcast, with heavy rainfall. In the vicinity of land, the direction of the wind can be greatly affected by local conditions.

Variables

Between the southern limit of the SE trades and the northern limit of the westerlies, there is an area of variable winds of moderate strength. This belt of variable winds extends from 25°S to 40°S during the summer months and from 20°S to 30°S during winter. The belt does not extend across the entire ocean and its position also varies from year to year. East of about 85°W, the prevailing winds are S or SE, being an extension of the SE trades. The strength and direction of these variable winds can vary considerably, although they tend to become stronger in higher latitudes.

Westerlies

The prevailing westerly winds or Roaring Forties predominate south of the South Pacific high, which is situated in about latitude 30°S. In the west, these winds are influenced by the movement of anticyclones tracking east from the vicinity of Australia. The almost continuous passage of depressions from west to east causes the wind to vary greatly in both direction and strength. The westerlies are most consistent between latitudes 40°S and 50°S. Gales are common in winter, although strong winds can be experienced at any time of the year.

Tropical storms

A large area of the South Pacific is affected by cyclones between December and April. The greatest frequency has been recorded from January to March. The area mainly affected lies to the south of about 8°S to 10°S, and to the west of 140°W, in a wide belt stretching all the way from the Marquesas in the east to Torres Strait in the west. In some areas, such as the Coral Sea, tropical storms have occurred on rare occasions at other times outside of the accepted cyclone season. A recent example is cyclone Namu which struck the Solomon Islands on 18 and 19 May 1986 with winds of over 100 knots causing extensive damage. The most dangerous months are December to March, when tropical depressions which develop over the Coral Sea or Gulf of Carpentaria can turn into a cyclone.

The number of tropical storms varies greatly from year to year as do their paths, although the central area of the South Pacific does experience more cyclones than the fringe areas. In some areas within the cyclone belt, such as Tahiti, cyclones may not occur for many years, which has lulled people into erroneously regarding these areas as cyclone-free.

Currents

The main surface circulation of the South Pacific Ocean is anticlockwise, although less is known about these currents than those of other oceans. Around the edges of the South Pacific, the four components of this anticlockwise movement are the west setting South Equatorial Current, the south setting East Australia Current, the east setting Southern Ocean Current, and finally the north setting Peru or Humboldt Current.

Many cruising routes are affected by the South Equatorial Current which has its northern limit from 1°N to 4°N or even 5°N depending both on season and longitude. The axis of this current lies furthest north of the equator in the southern summer and just north of the equator in winter. The South Equatorial Current decreases in strength south of latitude 6°S, although it maintains its westerly direction. Between latitudes 6°S and 20°S, this weaker current is known as the South Subtropical Current.

In the western part of the South Pacific, the direction of the current varies seasonally. Between June and August the current follows the coast of New Guinea in a NW direction. In September to November and also in March to May, there is a reversal of the Equatorial Countercurrent, which during those periods flows along the coast of New Guinea in a SE direction.

There is a SW flow from the South Subtropical Current past the islands of Tuvalu, Vanuatu and New Caledonia, but the currents in this region show considerable variation. The same can be said about currents among the islands of the Tuamotu archipelago and also between Tonga and Fiji, as well as among the islands of Fiji's Lau Group. When sailing in any of these areas utmost attention should be paid to the unpredictability of local currents.

The currents of the Coral Sea are also little known, except that in the northern part the current sets strongly towards Torres Strait, whereas in the southern part the current is S or SW. This current eventually joins the stronger East Australia Current which flows south along the coast of Australia and can be of great help to those bound for ports in New South Wales. In the Tasman Sea, between Australia and New Zealand, the current is mostly variable, although it tends to set east.

The Southern Ocean Current sets E or NE in higher latitudes. Most of this current flows into the Atlantic Ocean south of Cape Horn, but one part of it turns north along the west coast of South America to become the Peru or Humboldt Current. This cold current flows north towards the equator and eventually feeds into the South Equatorial Current. The flow of the Humboldt Current is sometimes reversed by the Equatorial Countercurrent, which extends further south during the southern hemisphere summer than at other times. A branch of this current sometimes turns south along the coast of Ecuador and on rare occasions can reach as far south as the latitude of Callao. Because this warm south going current appears around Christmas, it has been called El Niño, or the Holy Child Current. In years when it is fully established this warm current can greatly influence weather conditions in the eastern half of the South Pacific. The freak conditions of 1983 have been attributed to El Niño, which raised the surface temperature of the sea by several degrees, causing an unprecedented weather pattern.

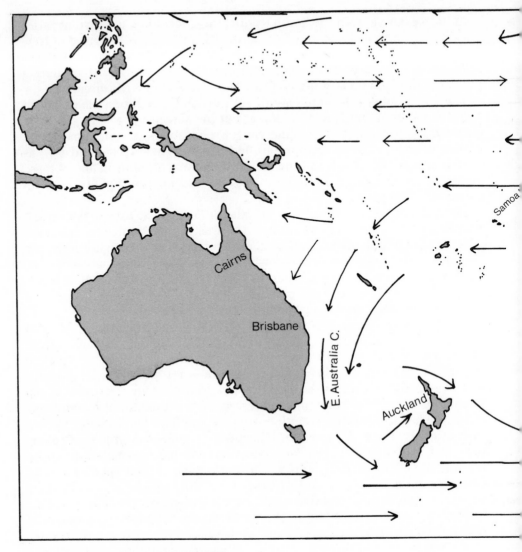

49. *SOUTH PACIFIC CURRENTS*

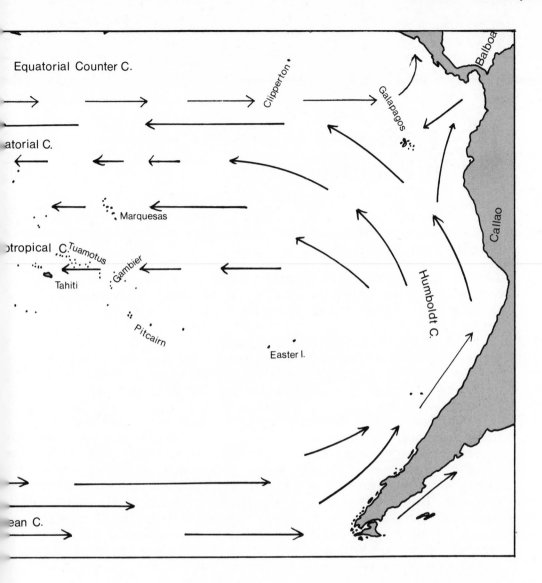

Equatorial Counter C.

Clipperton

Balboa

Galapagos

Callao

Humboldt C.

atorial C.

Marquesas

otropical C. *Tuamotus*

Gambier

Tahiti

Pitcairn

Easter I.

ean C.

16   Regional weather of the South Pacific

South American coast

The high Andes running down this continent like a backbone, interrupt the easterly flow of wind and most of this coast is dry and sterile compared to the lush steaming jungles to the east of the Andes where all the moisture is deposited.

The coastline of Colombia and Ecuador has consistent Pacific weather all year round with few strong winds and calm seas. The prevailing wind tends to follow the shore and blow between S and W, being more westerly north of the equator and more southerly to the south of the equator. There are frequent thunderstorms.

In Peru the prevailing winds tend to be SE to S, although rarely are they strong. In summer it is often calm for several days. There are some land and sea breezes down this coast, but they do tend to be quite light. Occasionally in winter, from April to August, light northerly winds can occur. For a tropical area, the Peruvian coast rarely gets very hot and can be quite cold in winter. This is due to the cooling effect of the Humboldt Current. Although it rarely rains, the sky is often cloudy and damp, thick fog being prevalent between April and August, but also occurring at other times. In some coastal areas of Peru it never rains at all, which has led to the preservation of desiccated mummified bodies and textiles for thousands of years.

In Chile September to May is the fine season with little rain and S to SE winds, which prevail for nine months of the year. At times there can be strong northerly gales which bring rain. As the coast tends south the bad weather becomes more frequent. In the southern parts of Chile, the westerlies of the southern ocean make their presence felt and winds blow more strongly here. The prevailing wind tends to be southerly, but gales from the SW to NW regularly bring rain onto this coast. In autumn and winter it is common for the wind to move in an anticlockwise direction from NW to SW clearing the sky, followed by a SE wind which dies away to nothing. Later a NE wind will spring up, freshening in the north and moving back to the NW, where the cycle begins again.

Juan Fernandez

Of these small islands belonging to Chile, the largest is also known as Robinson Crusoe Island, in honour of its most famous castaway inhabitant, Alexander Selkirk, who provided the model for the book by Defoe. Outside of the tropics and the trade wind belt, these islands are far enough off the Chilean coast not to be influenced by coastal weather. The winds here are variable, but often SE or S, mostly under 18 knots, stronger winds being rare. There are many calm periods.

Galapagos

The islands of the Galapagos are known best for their unique flora and fauna, being declared a National Park by the Ecuadorian government, to which they belong. A permit is needed to cruise among these islands, about which more information is given in Chapter 27.

Volcanic formations, these islands touch the equator and the climate is hot. Vegetation and trees tend to be more prolific on the windward side of the islands, the lee side being more arid. At the edge of the SE trade wind area, the prevailing wind is easterly. The warm current from the Gulf of

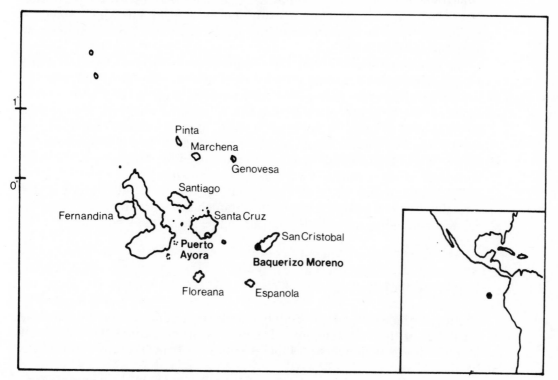

50. GALAPAGOS ISLANDS

Panama meets the cool Humboldt Current at these islands and joining together the currents flow west. This can result in the odd result of sea temperatures being 26°C on the north side and 16°C on the south side of the same island. The meeting of the currents frequently causes poor visibility and some fog. Often it is grey and misty. A strange local phenomenon known as the *garua* can result in the island disappearing from view after it was plainly visible. This phenomenon occurs mostly during the cool season from May to November. Surprisingly for islands so close to the equator, it can get quite cool at night because of the cold current. Some squalls do occur and the *northers* blowing from Central America can reach here on rare occasions. Even when they do not, a heavy northern swell indicates their distant path. In a similar fashion sometimes a strong southerly swell is also felt from distant southerly gales.

Easter Island

This dependency of Chile lies in the great empty expanse of ocean between the coast of South America and Pitcairn Island, its nearest inhabited neighbour. The Polynesian inhabitants call their island Rapa Nui, while the official Spanish name is Isla de Pascua. The island was discovered on Easter Day 1722 by the Dutch navigator Jacob Roggeveen who named it accordingly. Its main attraction are the giant statues which lie abandoned all over the island.

The prevailing winds during the summer months from October to April are SE, although occasionally they can blow from the NE. From May to September, when the trade wind belt has moved to the north, the prevailing winds are westerly and often it rains heavily. As the island is the only land for thousands of miles, it tends to generate its own weather conditions. In squally weather winds change direction rapidly and can put a boat on a lee shore. When anchoring at Easter Island one must be prepared to shift anchorage at short notice. Cyclones are unknown.

The only settlement is at Hangaroa, on the west side, where entry formalities can be completed ashore, although boats are sometimes cleared at anchor. Landing in the little harbour can be hazardous when there is a big swell running.

Pitcairn Island

The former hideaway of the *Bounty* mutineers continues to be inhabited by a handful of their descendants. Together with the uninhabited islands of Oeno, Ducie and Henderson, Pitcairn is the last British colony in the South Pacific.

Although lying on the verge of the SE trade wind belt, the winds blowing over Pitcairn are seldom steady from that direction. Both in winter and

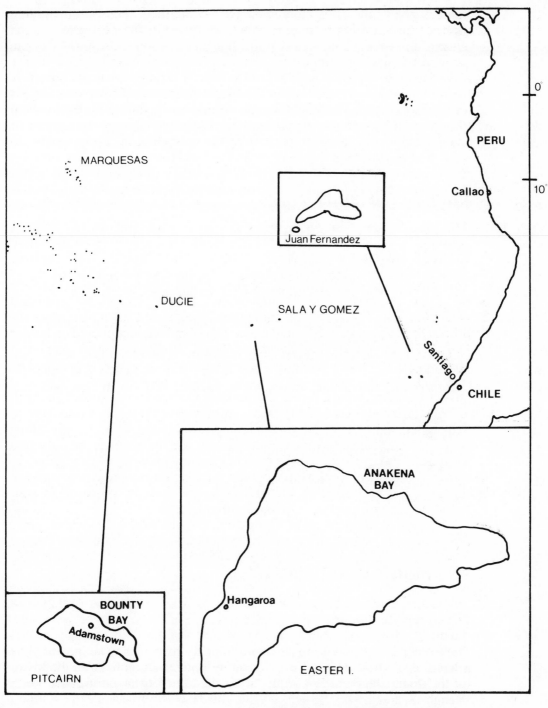

51. *ISLANDS IN THE SOUTH-EAST PACIFIC*

summer the winds often have an easterly component, but as in the case of Easter Island, those planning to stop at Pitcairn must be prepared to weigh anchor instantly should the wind change direction, which can happen without too much warning.

The most convenient anchorage is in Bounty Bay, on the north side of the island, close to the main settlement of Adamstown. Because of the difficulty in landing through the surf, visitors are usually collected in one of the islanders' boats. Entry formalities consist of having one's passport stamped by the Magistrate, probably the simplest entry procedure anywhere in the world.

Gambier Islands

This French dependency lying in the SE corner of the Tuamotu Archipelago is sometimes referred to as the Mangareva Islands after the principal island of the group. They are a volcanic cluster within a large lagoon, with three passes through the reef giving access to the main settlement of Rikitea on Mangareva. The largest islands in the group are Mangareva, Taravai, Aukena and Akamaru.

There are two distinct seasons in these islands: a hot season from January to June, and a cooler, rainy season, from July to December. The first three months of the year are accompanied by calms or light variable winds. The SE trade wind starts to blow towards the end of March and gradually increases in strength and consistency, reaching its peak in June and July. Gales sometimes occur in August, with winds shifting to W and NW. The trades gradually decrease in strength until they disappear altogether towards the end of the year. Cyclones very rarely reach these islands.

Although not officially a port of entry, boats arriving from abroad are sometimes allowed to call at the Gambier Islands en route to Tahiti. Formalities should be completed at the gendarmerie in Rikitea, from where permission to stay can be requested by radio from the authorities in Tahiti. Proper entry formalities into French Polynesia can be delayed until the arrival in Papeete.

Tuamotu Archipelago

Also known sometimes as the Paumotu, Low or Dangerous Archipelago, few of its islands were visited in the past by yachts because of the hazards involved. However, satellite navigation and a better knowledge of the area have recently opened up these islands to cruising and they are visited by an increasing number of boats every year. With a few exceptions all the islands of the archipelago are low lying coral atolls, the largest among them being Rangiroa, Fakarava, Makemo, Ahe and Hao. Mururoa, in the southern part of the archipelago, is the site of the French nuclear tests and the area around it is usually closed to navigation.

The climate of the archipelago is hot, with the period from May to October being slightly cooler than the rest of the year. The SE trade wind blows fairly regularly over the islands throughout the year. Its main direction is E, having a southerly component from June to October and a northerly component from November to May. The wind is steadiest during the winter months from May to October, when it can be quite strong on occasions. During the summer months, from November to April, light breezes are frequent, with the wind sometimes shifting to W or N and lasting for several days.

SE gales occur from May to September at the height of the trade wind season. The worst month is August, when these gales can last for several days. The gales are usually accompanied by a slight rise in the barometer. During the gale the sky is overcast, but clears towards the evenings. The end of the gale is preceded by a fall in the barometer, but if the barometer remains unusually high, the gale is likely to last for several days.

Gales from N through to SW occur during the summer months, from November to April, and are usually accompanied by a fall in the barometer. The cyclone season is from December to March, although the frequency of tropical storms is quite low in this part of the Pacific. Several years can go by without a cyclone occurring, to be followed by a particularly bad year, with more than one cyclone hitting the islands.

Entry formalities into French Polynesia should be completed either in the Marquesas or Tahiti before sailing to the Tuamotus. Ship's papers are sometimes checked in the islands by the resident gendarme.

Marquesas

These high, lush islands have attracted many Europeans to spend time here, from Herman Melville and Gauguin to Thor Heyerdahl, but probably the best description of the Marquesas is in R.L.Stevenson's *In the South Seas*. Although lying within the belt of the SE trades, these high islands do interfere with these steady winds and local variations occur. The commonest are winds from the SW or W, which squall down the hills into the anchorages despite the steady SE winds blowing outside. The trades are not always SE, but can also blow from an E or NE direction.

The South Pacific cyclone season does affect the Marquesas from December to March. Although it is rare for a fully fledged cyclone to hit the Marquesas, some tropical storms do reach the area and cannot be discounted.

Society Islands

The first European to put these islands on the world map was Captain Samuel Wallis who visited Tahiti in 1767, yet it was Captain Cook, two years

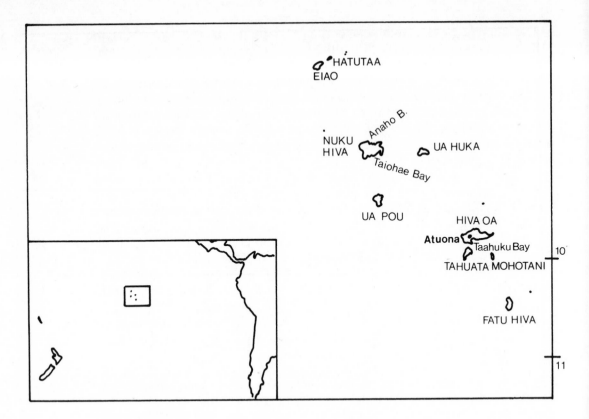

52. MARQUESAS

later, who gave the islands their present name, in gratitude to the Royal Society who had financed his voyage. Cook came to Tahiti to observe the transit of the planet Venus, with the object of simplifying the determination of longitude at sea. He made his observations in Matavai Bay, near Papeete, on a point of land since known as Point Venus.

The Society Islands are made up of two groups: the Windward Islands (Iles du Vent) and the Leeward Islands (Iles sous le Vent). The main islands in the Windward group are Tahiti and Moorea. The Leewards comprise Raiatea and Tahaa, which share the same lagoon, Huahine, Bora Bora, Maupiti and a few smaller atolls.

Both groups are within the SE trade wind belt and throughout the year the main direction of the wind is from the E. From May to August the trades blow at their strongest, the direction of the wind varying from SE to ENE. When it blows from the SE, the wind is strong and often accompanied by squalls. It becomes lighter as it shifts to the ENE before returning to the SE after a period of calm. Such shifts occur every one or two weeks and it is very seldom that the wind would blow from any other direction during the winter season. During the summer months, from

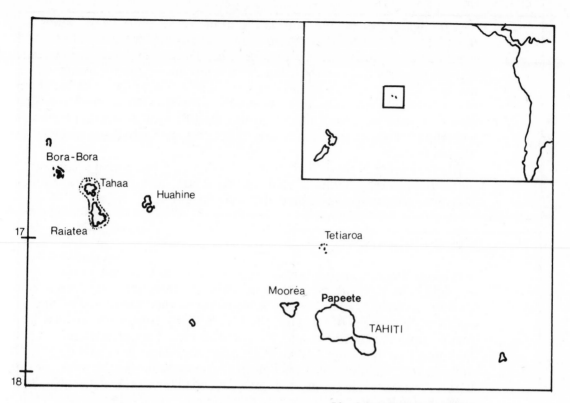

Bora-Bora

Tahaa

Huahine

Raiatea

17

Tetiaroa

Mooréa

Papeete

TAHITI

18

53. SOCIETY ISLANDS

December to April, the trades become weaker and are frequently interrupted by calms, variable or westerly winds, which can blow strongly.

The Society Islands are sometimes visited by tropical storms, the cyclone season extending from December to the end of March. Tahiti and Moorea are more likely to be hit than the Leeward Islands and although cyclones do not occur every year, when they do arrive, such as happened in February and March 1983, they can be devastating.

The main port of entry is Papeete, the capital of French Polynesia, although entry formalities can be carried out in any of the larger islands. However, because of the requirement of depositing a bond, it is preferable to make these arrangements in Papeete itself. (Further details are given in Chapter 27.)

Austral Islands

Also known as the Tubuai Islands, this group lying some 300 miles south of Tahiti is part of French Polynesia. It comprises the five inhabited islands of Tubuai, Rurutu, Raivavae, Rimatara and Rapa, as well as a number of smaller uninhabited islands.

Although lying near the southern limit of the SE trades, ESE winds are most frequent and steady in these islands throughout the year. N and NW winds occur mostly from October to December and are usually accompanied by fine weather, but are often followed by SW winds, which can be sudden and violent, veering to S and SE. With light NW winds, if clouds are observed rising from the south, a sudden shift of wind from that quarter can be expected, often accompanied by violent squalls. Cyclones sometimes reach these islands during the summer months, especially in March.

Boats arriving in the islands from a foreign port can obtain a temporary entry permit on condition that proper entry formalities into French Polynesia are completed on arrival at a port of entry.

Cook Islands

The Cook Islands are an autonomous state in free asociation with New Zealand. The ties with New Zealand are very strong and there are in fact slightly more Cook Islanders living there than in their own country. Spread over fifteen degrees of latitude, the fifteen Cook Islands are divided into two groups, the Southern and Northern Cooks. The main islands in the Southern Group are the capital, Rarotonga, and Aitutaki. The only port of entry in the Northern Cooks is Penrhyn. Among today's sailors one of the best known islands in the group is Suvorov, erstwhile home of Tom Neale, a modern-day Robinson Crusoe who lived for many years alone on that atoll.

As the islands of this group are spread out over so many degrees of latitude, only some of them are under the influence of the SE trade wind throughout the year. During the winter months, from May to October, SE winds prevail in all the islands. During the remainder of the year, SW and W winds, which can blow for several days in succession with gale force, are more frequent and cause a heavy surf on the west side of the islands. In January and February gale force winds from NE or E can also occur. The summer months, from December to March, is the cyclone season. Although tropical storms are quite rare, when they do occur, they usually arrive from NW or N and move away to the SE.

A newly built harbour at Avatiu, on the north side of Rarotonga, offers much better protection to visiting yachts. Those wishing to stop at Aitutaki can enter the lagoon through a pass on the west side of the island. The uninhabited atoll of Suvorov has been designated a nature conservation area by the Cook Islands government and those wishing to stop there should obtain permission from the authorities in Rarotonga.

Samoan Islands

Two administrative groups make up this Polynesian nation separated by the 171°W meridian. To the west of this imaginary line lies Western Samoa,

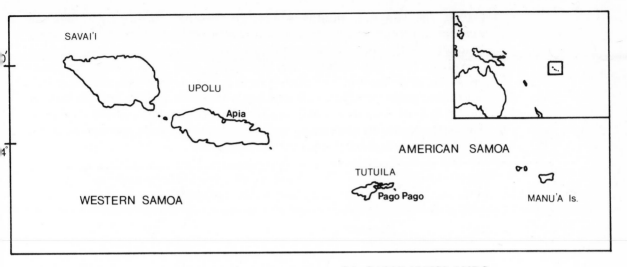

54. SAMOAN ISLANDS

an independent state consisting of the two large islands of Savai'i and Upolu and a few islets. To the east is American Samoa, an unincorporated territory of the United States, its main island being Tutuila.

From the middle or end of April until November fresh SE trade winds blow over these islands and are only rarely interrupted by calms or SW winds. The months of July, August and up to the middle of September are distinguished by cool SE winds, which frequently blow in violent squalls. After the middle of September, the trade wind is not so strong and is often interrupted by calms and light W winds in the vicinity of the islands. Further offshore the winds are constant in strength and only get lighter at night. As some of the Samoan Islands are several thousand feet high, local weather conditions can be quite varied, with alternating land and sea breezes. During the summer months, from November to April, the winds are light easterlies often interrupted by calms. During this period W winds are also experienced, sometimes being accompanied by rainy squalls and occasional storms.

Cyclones occur mainly between January and March or early April. They are preceded by a violent NE wind, which passes through N, W and SW. Although cyclones do not occur very often over the islands themselves, they are more frequent in the area of ocean between Samoa and Tonga.

Wallis and Futuna

Wallis and Futuna, an overseas territory of France, consists of two main island groups nearly 100 miles apart. The SE trade winds blow over the islands fairly constantly during the winter months from April to November. The trades are occasionally interrupted by squalls, some of them violent.

During the summer months winds are variable, mostly light, and the weather can sometimes be sultry. Severe westerly gales can occur during the summer months, but cyclones are rare.

Wallis is the more visited of the two islands, as it offers a safer anchorage inside the large lagoon. The port of entry on Wallis is the capital Mata Utu, but during unfavourable conditions boats normally anchor in Gahi Bay, on the SE side of the main island, and complete entry formalities from there. The only acceptable anchorage on Futuna is at Sigave Bay, on the west side of the island, which has some port facilities.

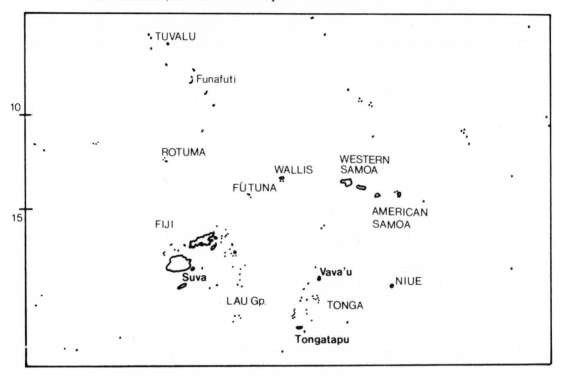

55. ISLANDS IN THE CENTRAL PACIFIC

Tuvalu

The former Ellice Islands are a cluster of nine low lying islands spread over a large area of ocean to the south of the equator. From May to September the islands are under the influence of the trade winds which blow from between ESE and ENE. These winds are rarely stronger than 15 knots and often die away at night in the vicinity of the islands. In some years the trade winds can be very light. During the summer months from October to April, the NW monsoon makes itself felt among these islands with variable winds from N or W and lots of rain. Strong gales are sometimes experienced during this period. They usually start from the SW, gradually shifting to the north and lasting two or three days. Cyclones occur on very rare occasions, but when they do little warning can be expected as Tuvalu lies near to one of the breeding grounds.

Tonga

The independent kingdom of Tonga consists of three main island groups and many smaller islands. The most southerly is the Tongatapu group, with the capital Nuku'alofa on the main island of Tongatapu (Sacred Tonga), which is also the largest island in the kingdom. The other two island groups are Ha'apai, in the centre of the archipelago, and Vava'u in the north. The islands of Niuatoputapu and Niuafoou, lying between Samoa and Tonga, also belong to Tonga.

The SE trade wind blows steadily over the islands of the Tongan archipelago from May to December, its strength varying from light to moderate. During the remainder of the year the wind is frequently

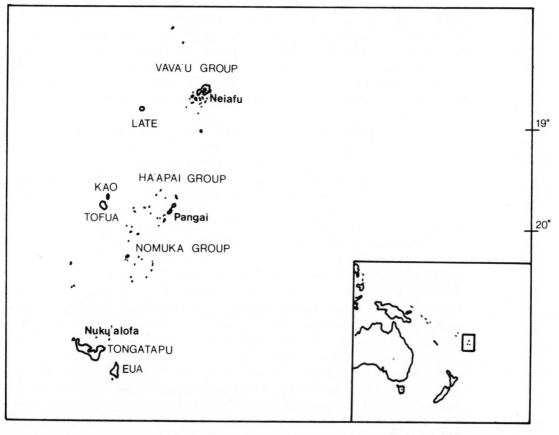

56. *TONGA*

interrupted by squalls and breezes from the W and NW, accompanied by rain and sometimes gales. Even at the height of the SE trade wind season, the wind can sometimes shift unexpectedly to the SW or W, especially during the night, putting boats at anchor on a lee shore.

The Tongan islands, particularly the more southern ones, are prone to be hit by about one cyclone per year, with devastating effects. The worst months are January, February and March. The safest anchorage during the cyclone season is at Neiafu in Vava'u. Nuku'alofa, on the north side of Tongatapu, has a small boat harbour, but it tends to get overcrowded with local boats seeking shelter when a cyclone threatens.

Although Tonga lies to the east of the 180th meridian, local time is 13 hours ahead of GMT.

Fiji

Over three hundred islands make up the Fijian archipelago which offers some of the best cruising in the South Pacific. The SE trade wind prevails throughout the archipelago from April to early November. In certain areas, the trend of the coast and the proximity of high land cause an alteration in the general direction of the wind. The trades are strongest in August and September, when they can reach moderate gale force. During the summer, from December to March, the weather is often unsettled, with northerly winds accompanied by heavy rain and squalls. Periods of fine weather with light winds can sometimes occur during the summer, and even a brief return to SE winds.

In the Lau or Eastern group, the trade wind is particularly strong during September and October, reaching 25–30 knots. During this time the skies are often overcast and hazy, making navigation difficult, and the islands should be approached with caution. The SE winds prevail longest in the centre of the archipelago, where they usually start in April and last until November or even early December. Among the islands to the NW of the main island of Viti Levu, the SE wind is deflected by the high hills into a NE and sometimes S wind. Violent gusts off the high land are sometimes experienced at night.

Cyclones occur during the hot months from December to March. They generally approach the islands either from the NW or the NE, curve around the western part of the archipelago and continue in a SE direction. Several cyclones have caused tremendous damage among the Fijian islands in recent years, making them a risky place to cruise in summer, especially between January and March.

The island of Rotuma, lying 250 miles NNW of the main group, also belongs to Fiji and can be visited without prior permission from the authorities in Suva. In contrast, islands in the Lau group can only be visited with a cruising permit and yachts are discouraged from stopping there before clearing in at one of the official ports of entry.

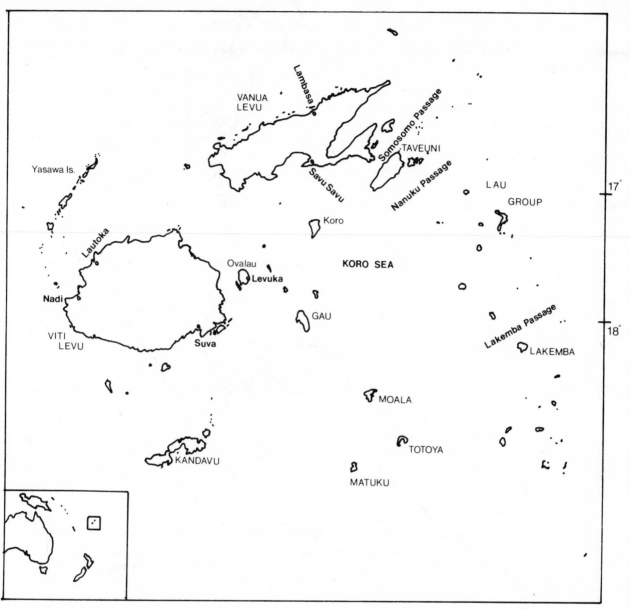

57. FIJI

New Zealand

This favourite destination for yachtsmen escaping from the cyclone season in the South Pacific has many boating facilities and a climate varying from the subtropical to snowy mountains.

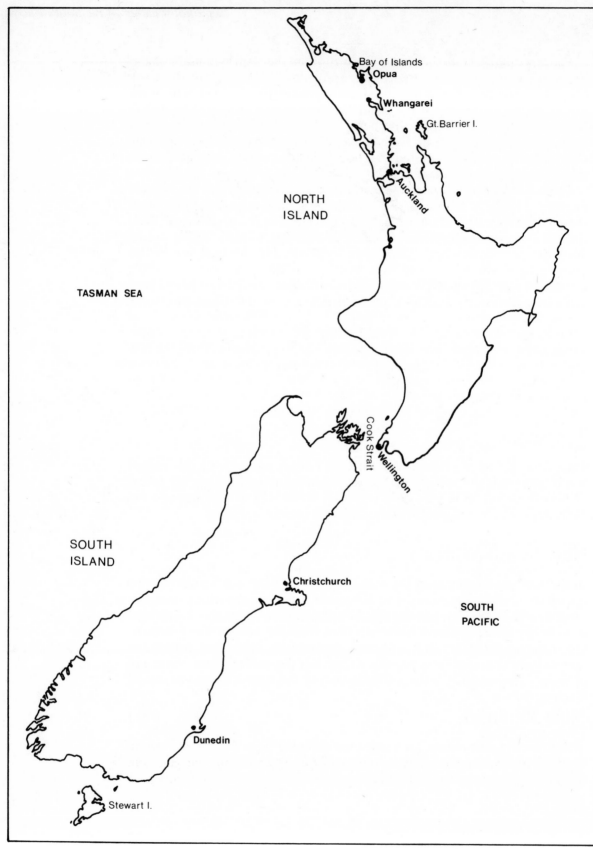

Bay of Islands
Opua

Whangarei

Gt. Barrier I.

NORTH
ISLAND

Auckland

TASMAN SEA

Cook Strait

Wellington

SOUTH
ISLAND

Christchurch

SOUTH
PACIFIC

Dunedin

Stewart I.

The prevailing wind should be westerly, but the high mountain chains deflect this and the wind often blows up or down the coast. In the Cook Strait between North and South Island the wind blows either NW or SE following the alignment of the strait. In the summer months, October to March, when most people cruise here, land and sea breezes greatly affect the coastal areas. The North Island has the pleasantest conditions, although occasionally in summer the tail of a South Pacific cyclone does stray down to hit the more northern areas.

South Island is not so hospitable and gales can occur even in the summer months. Although the scenery is spectacular, winds are accelerated down these grand mountains to reach gale force in many of the anchorages. Wind funnels and wind traps abound and few anchorages in the south can be described as 'all weather'. December to March are the best months for cruising in South Island and fine weather on the west coast is usually associated with SW or WSW winds. Foveaux Strait and Stewart Island have gales from a westerly direction almost all year round and in summer strong SE winds can occur.

In the winter, from April to September, there are variable winds over the whole of New Zealand and frequent gales, the worst coming from the NW and shifting to the SW. SE gales are also common. As the winter weather is so inclement, the first winter gale is usually the signal for most sailors to head back for the tropics.

Tasmania

The strong westerly winds of the Roaring Forties prevail over this rugged beautiful island, which has a windy, wet climate similar to the South Island of New Zealand. It is very cold in winter from May to October and the pleasantest weather is usually at the end of the summer season.

New South Wales

In the temperate climate of the variables, most of the bad weather in this region comes from the south. The dangerous winds are the strong *southerly busters*, which are often accompanied by line squalls. This area of Australia is fairly dry and sometimes hot winds blow from the interior like a *sirocco*. On occasion these are met with and replaced by cold polar winds, the temperature changing very rapidly. Generally the summers are warm and pleasant. The weather in the northern part of the state is similar to that of Queensland.

Queensland

Tropical Australia is attracting an increasing number of world voyagers who come to cruise along the Great Barrier Reef and also to take advantage of the various repair and servicing facilities that are available in many Queensland ports. As the state covers some 20 degrees of latitude, it would be virtually impossible to present a uniform weather picture and local variations can be expected, both in summer and winter.

All winter months are dominated by the SE trade winds that blow along the entire coast from the end of April or early May until the end of October. The trades are at their strongest and most regular from May to September and at their height they can blow for several days at 30 knots and even more in gusts. At the southern extremity of the area, the SE winds can be interrupted by spells of winds from the SW or W. In the northern half, calms and variable winds are very rare as the SE trades maintain their direction, if not strength, throughout the winter months. October to December are the spring months, a period of transition when SE winds persist in the northern part, although blowing with less force. In the southern part, the SE winds can be interrupted by a spell of N winds, a local phenomenon which can be very useful to those making a southbound passage.

The summer is greatly influenced by the NW monsoon, which usually arrives late in December or early January. During this season, N or NE winds predominate in the northern part of the state, being rarely interrupted by calms, whereas in the southern half calms are more frequent, although replaced increasingly by SE rain squalls as the season progresses. The NW monsoon is the wet season, when it usually rains more than in winter, which is regarded as the dry season. The summer winds are mostly light and they often die out at sunset to return in the morning or later in the day. Autumn is a transitional period similar to spring, and during April and early May there is a slow return of the SE trade winds, which establish themselves first in the northern part of the area.

December to April is also the cyclone season, a period during which low pressure systems in the Coral Sea or Gulf of Carpentaria can develop into tropical storms. Those that are born in the Coral Sea normally move in a southerly direction before curving away to the east, although sometimes they reach the Australian coast and cause a lot of destruction. Cyclones which develop in the Gulf of Carpentaria sometimes cross the Cape York Peninsula and either carry on in an ESE direction or follow the coast of Queensland. There are a few good hurricane holes on the north east coast of Australia, Cairns being one of the best. Cyclones can occur, at least in theory, at any time of year, although they are extremely rare during winter. They are most frequent from January to March, but have also been recorded in November, December and April.

New Caledonia

Although the name New Caledonia was given by Captain Cook only to the largest island in the group, it now refers to the entire country. New

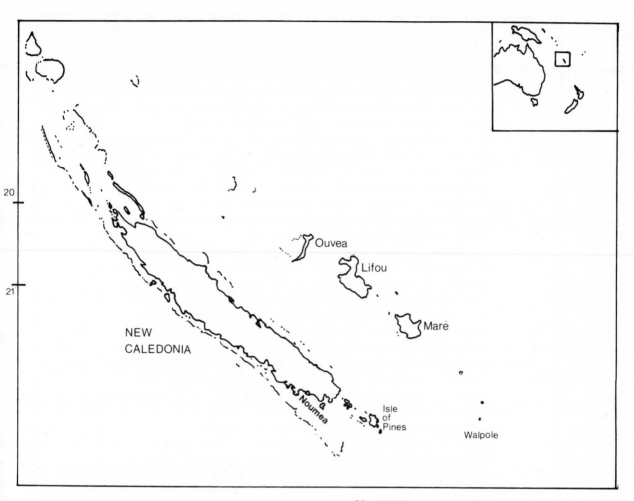

Ouvea

Lifou

Maré

NEW
CALEDONIA

Noumea

Isle
of
Pines

Walpole

59. NEW CALEDONIA

Caledonia and its islands are a French overseas territory. It consists of one
large and one small island, plus the Loyalty and Huon groups.

The islands are under the general influence of the SE trade winds,
although in the proximity of high land, the predominant SE or ESE winds
are sometimes deflected to blow from other directions. The best months are
July and August when the SE trades are at their height. On the south-west
side of the main island, the fine weather continues into September and
October, whereas in other parts gales do occur during this time. These
violent gales are often preceded by calms and misty weather charged with
electricity. From November onwards the weather becomes squally herald-
ing the start of summer, regarded as the bad season. In the first four months
of the year, the winds are irregular and often strong.

November to May is the wet season and this is also the time when New
Caledonia is exposed to cyclones, although most of these occur in January

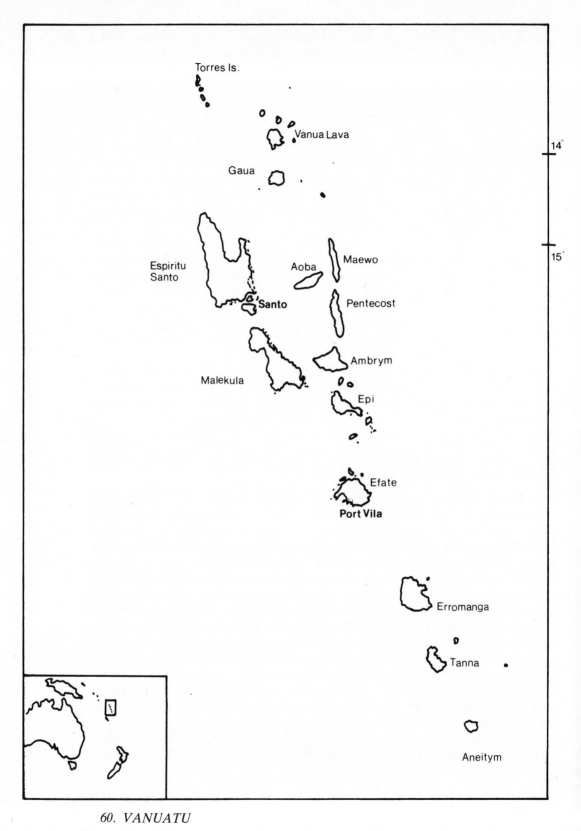

Torres Is.

Vanua Lava

Gaua

14°

15°

Espiritu
Santo

Aoba

Maewo

Santo

Pentecost

Malekula

Ambrym

Epi

Efate

Port Vila

Erromanga

Tanna

Aneitym

60. *VANUATU*

and February. The path of some of these storms is quite narrow, which means that some of their worst effects can be avoided if early warnings are heeded.

Although a French territory, formalities are simpler than in Tahiti and a bond is not required.

Vanuatu

The former condominium of the New Hebrides, administered jointly by Britain and France, has adopted the name of Vanuatu since achieving independence. It consists of about eighty islands spread out in a double chain on the east side of the Coral Sea.

The islands lie within the SE trade wind belt and between April and October the trade winds blow steadily, their direction varying from SSE to ENE. The most frequent direction is ESE and winds blowing from this direction are also the strongest. Yet even during the winter months, which are regarded as the fine weather season, the trades are sometimes interrupted by several days of calms or light NW winds.

The rainy season is from November to March, which is also the cyclone season. Although less frequent than in Fiji, cyclones do strike Vanuatu once every few years, particularly the more southerly islands of the group. Sailing boats are no longer allowed to spend the cyclone season in the water in Port Vila and arrangements must be made to have them hauled out on dry land.

Solomon Islands

The Spaniards gave the islands their present name after their discovery by the explorer Alvaro de Mendana, who had set out from Peru to discover the elusive islands of King Solomon reputed to have been visited by the Incas. Although the legendary riches were never found the name stuck and was kept even after independence in 1978. Also kept were the various Spanish names of the islands which stretch out in a double chain of six large islands and many smaller ones. The major island is Guadalcanal, the scene of some of the fiercest battles during the Second World War, and where the advance of the Japanese forces was finally halted. The other large islands are Santa Isabel, San Cristobal, Malaita, New Georgia and Choiseul.

From May to October is the SE trade wind season, which in most islands is also the dry season. The usual direction of the trades is ESE, but the stronger winds are from SE and such a blow is usually preceded by calms. It is said that a period of calms can be expected whenever the wind shifts to the E or NE. As some of the islands are quite high, the prevailing trade winds can be interrupted, to be replaced by calms or winds from other directions. Occasionally the wind shifts to the N or even W and when this

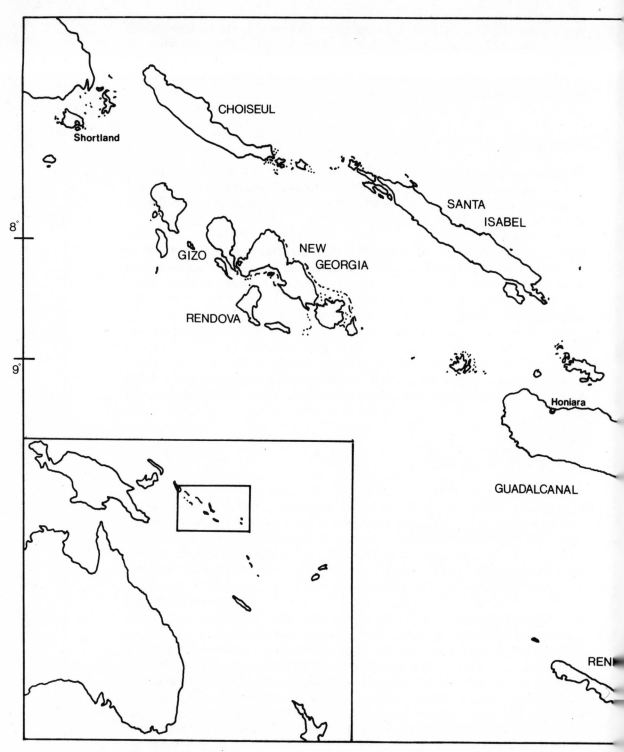

61. SOLOMON ISLANDS

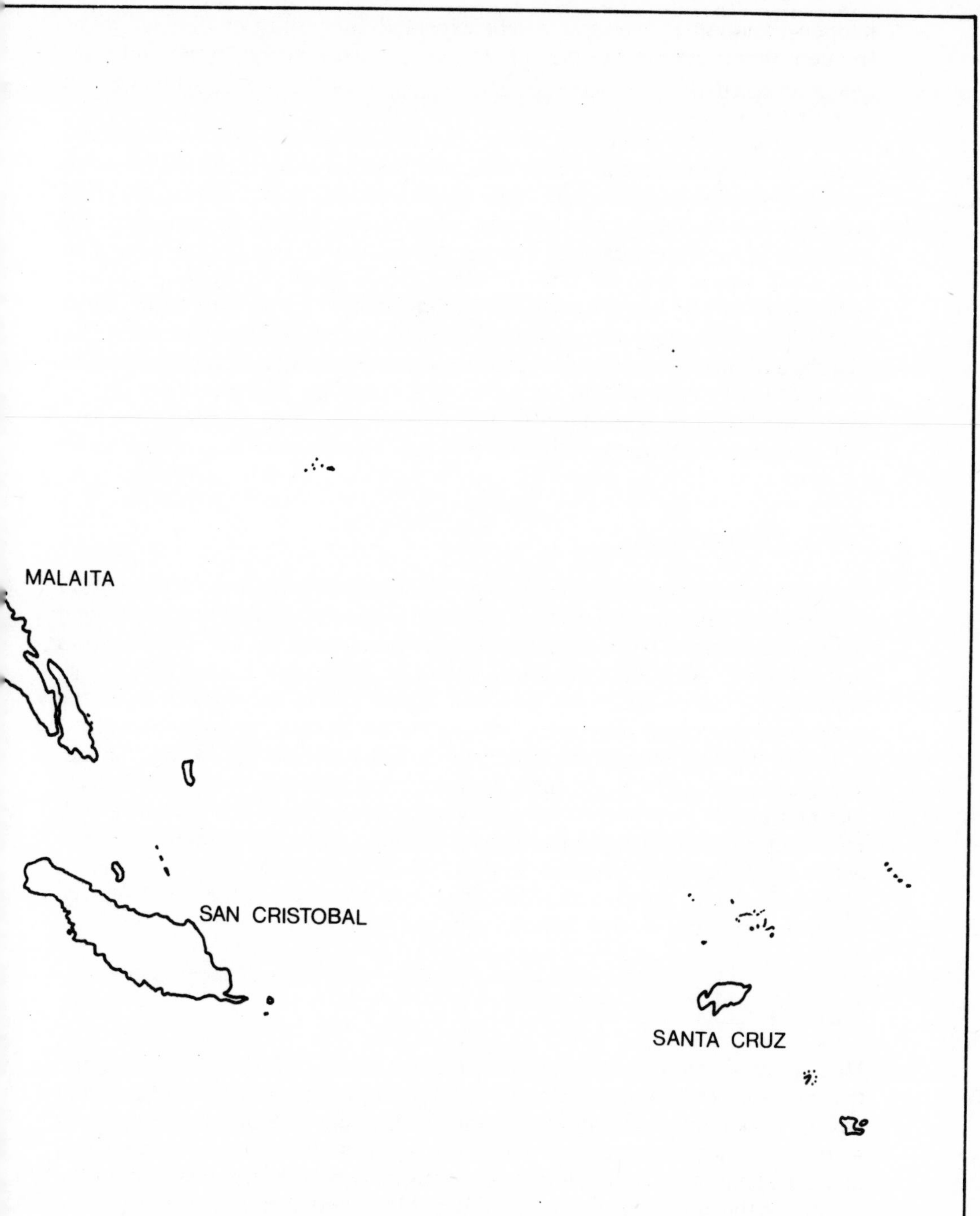

MALAITA

SAN CRISTOBAL

SANTA CRUZ

happens, a squall or even gale can be expected. Such shifts of wind are more frequent in the changeover period to the wet season, in November and early December, when anchorages should be chosen very carefully as winds can turn by as much as 180 degrees, often at night.

During the NW monsoon, which can set in at any time between the middle of November and Christmas, the weather is rainy, with calms or variable winds. Occasionally gale force winds arrive from the NW accompanied by heavy rain. In the western part of the group, the NW monsoon is rarely established before the middle of December, when the prevailing winds become NW or SW. This is also the cyclone season, although it is the more southern islands in the group which are most vulnerable. Although the accepted cyclone season is from December to March, cyclone Namu, which swept through the central group with winds of over 100 knots in May 1986, was a terrible reminder that no month can be regarded as entirely cyclone free in countries bordering on the Coral Sea.

All visiting vessels are required to pay light dues amounting to about $100.

New Guinea

The name of the largest island in the Pacific was coined in the 16th century by a Spanish captain who thought the local people reminded him of those of Guinea in Africa. The name was already mentioned on Mercator's world map of 1569. Although the name refers to the entire island, which also includes Papua on its south side and Irian Jaya in its western half, the conditions described here refer only to the north coast of New Guinea.

The prevailing wind from about May to November is the SE trade wind, which at times can blow strongly, reaching moderate gale force. During late October and November, in the changeover period from the SE to the NW monsoon, there are frequent calms or variable winds. By January, the NW winds are well established and they last until March, when they are replaced by calms or light winds until May. The NW monsoon is the rainy season, when occasionally severe storms occur over the area.

Papua

Huge *lakatoi* canoes used to trade along the coast of Papua, following the two monsoons as the Arab dhows did in other areas. The last Hiri trading voyage took place in the 1930s, the men setting sail as soon as the SE trades started blowing, taking clay pots to trade in more fertile areas for foodstuffs and especially sago, returning home with the onset of the NW monsoon.

The southern Papuan coast SE of Port Moresby lies in a rain shadow and this coast receives little rain. The dry SE trade winds start arriving in March, spreading into the Torres Strait area and south Papuan coast by April. In May the SE winds are established throughout Papua and blow

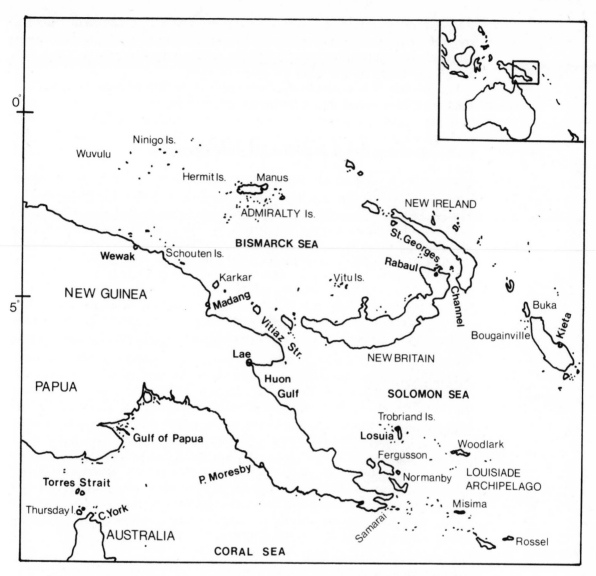

62. PAPUA NEW GUINEA

through until November. The SE trades can be fresh at times, but tend to die down at night and gales are rare. From October onwards the winds become a little more variable and the NW monsoon spreads progressively from the NW, reaching most areas by December and blowing until March when it starts to withdraw. The NW monsoon winds are generally light, but severe NW squalls called *guba* occur along the Papuan coast during the NW monsoon. These extended squalls usually come at night and can gust up to 50 knots.

Very rarely during the season (December to March) cyclones do migrate into this area from their spawning ground in the Coral Sea. The more southerly parts are most likely to be hit, although such cyclones have not usually reached full strength.

The climate is hot and humid with little variation around the 28–29°C mark, the SE season being drier than the NW season.

Louisiade and Trobriand Islands

These islands lying to the north of the Coral Sea belong to Papua New Guinea. Like surrounding island groups, they have two distinct seasons. The SE trade winds blow at their strongest during the winter months from July to September, when they often reach 25 knots. The best sailing conditions are either at the beginning of the season, between April and June, or at the end, in October. Towards the changeover period to the NW monsoon, the winds gradually shift to E and NE. In December, light winds from the NW are sometimes followed by periods of calm. The effects of the NW monsoon are fully felt from January to March, when local weather conditions can also be influenced by tropical storms forming in the vicinity of the islands. However, they are very rarely hit by a fully fledged cyclone.

Bismarck Archipelago

The islands of this group belong to Papua New Guinea and they are all under the influence of the SE trades, including the larger islands of New Britain and New Ireland. The trades blow with tolerable regularity from April until October, which is also the dry season when gales are very rare and the weather is pleasant. The changeover to the NW monsoon is accompanied by calms or variable winds. The NW monsoon takes some time to establish itself, but when it finally arrives, it blows strongly, at times in violent gales accompanied by heavy rain. The weather starts improving by the middle of February. Periods of calm precede the SE trades which as a rule reappear by mid-April.

In the vicinity of the higher islands, the SE trade wind is deflected by the mountains and generally blows along the coasts. During both seasons a land breeze is felt at night near the islands. Tropical revolving storms are generally unknown, although some of the storms which occur during the NW monsoon can be extremely violent.

Manus Islands

The islands grouped under this name belong to Papua New Guinea and comprise several smaller island groups scattered between the equator and the main island of New Guinea. The largest island is Manus, in the

Admiralty group. The other groups are the Hermit, Ninigo and Nauma Islands.

The entire area is under the influence of the SE trade winds, which are steadiest between June and September. During the SE season, the wind sometimes dies at night, but recommences after sunrise and blows strongest by mid-afternoon. During the period preceding the NW monsoon, the area is subject to calms which are sometimes interrupted by squalls. Those from the NW are as a rule more violent than those from the NE. The NW monsoon generally sets in by the middle of December and lasts until March.

17   Routes in the South Pacific

No other region of the world exerts such a lasting fascination on sailors and non-sailors alike, as the South Pacific. From the *Bounty* mutineers to Bernard Moitessier, many a sailor has succumbed to the irresistible temptation of the South Seas. This phenomenon is by no means limited to the past, as every year other people fall in love with the South Pacific. Although jet travel and better inter-island communications have brought much of the South Pacific within reach of the outside world, there are still countless places which can only be reached by boat. For those travelling in this way, the South Pacific offers an unspoilt face, especially to those who are prepared to deviate from the well trodden track. This vast expanse of water covering one third of the earth's surface is dotted with a myriad of tiny islands on which live some of the most remote and isolated communities in the world. Communications between most of the islands are usually by boat, although only in a few places are traditional sailing craft still in use. The small boat voyager is therefore at a great advantage and one of the greatest satisfactions experienced while sailing in the South Pacific is the warm welcome extended by islanders to those arriving from the sea.

Sailing conditions in the South Pacific are unfortunately not always as idyllic as people expect and the vagaries of the weather must be treated with as much caution as elsewhere in the world. Although the seasons are fairly well defined and there are few storms apart from tropical cyclones, which only occur in certain months and certain areas, the wind systems are less consistent than in other parts of the world. The SE trade winds which affect most of the cruising routes across the South Pacific are renowned for their fickleness and are often disappointing, especially to those who come from the Caribbean. There are years when the trades blow with surprising consistency, just as there are years when they come in spurts, either blowing at near gale force for weeks on end or being accompanied by prolonged calms and squally weather. Such a freak year was 1983 when the unusual weather conditions throughout the South Pacific were attributed to the El Niño Current. This warm water current is a branch of the Equatorial Countercurrent and the increased amount of warm water reaching the South Pacific has a detrimental effect on the weather pattern throughout the region, causing increased cyclone activity and other freak weather conditions.

Nevertheless the weather encountered by the majority of those who cruise in the South Pacific is usually pleasant and only rarely uncomfortable or outright dangerous. The worst conditions are often encountered not on passage, but in port, usually by those who have either picked an unsafe anchorage or have decided to spend the cyclone season in the tropics. Both these dangers can be avoided as there are sufficient safe anchorages available and the cyclone season can easily be spent outside the area affected by tropical storms.

Unfortunately weather is not the only hazard faced by those who sail in the South Pacific and in fact a much higher proportion of boats are lost every year because of other causes. The most obvious danger are the coral reefs which extend to windward of many low, unlit islands, making navigation throughout the South Pacific a very delicate operation. This problem is often compounded by the presence of strong unpredictable currents among some island groups and also by long periods of overcast skies, when traditional methods of navigation cannot be used. Every year the reefs of various archipelagos exert a heavy toll on boats, as do the cyclones that sweep through some of the same areas. Modern navigational equipment, a good dose of common sense, and some advance planning can reduce such risks to an acceptable minimum, making a cruise in the South Pacific as safe as anywhere else.

The main cruising route across the South Pacific runs in a gigantic arc linking Panama with the Torres Strait. It has been affectionately nicknamed the 'Milk Run', an apt description especially in the case of those who stick to it and avoid the cyclone seasons. The Germans call it more prosaically the 'Barefoot Route' underlining one of its greatest attractions for those who are used to sailing in colder climes. There are countless variations to this trunk route, with secondary routes branching off and rejoining it along its entire length. At its eastern end, the route is fed by a substantial influx of American and Canadian boats, most arriving directly in the Marquesas from the west coast of the USA or British Columbia. At its western end, the route is joined by boats from New Zealand or Australia setting off on their world voyages. This truly international trunk road of the oceans continues then into the Indian Ocean where it splits into two branches, one leading towards the Red Sea and Mediterranean, the other towards the Cape of Good Hope and the Atlantic Ocean.

The prime destination for practically any boat arriving in the South Pacific is French Polynesia and its main island, Tahiti. Most people take the direct route there by way of the Marquesas, especially those who have reached the Pacific Ocean through the Panama Canal or whose home ports are on the west coast of North America. Some of the latter arrive in Tahiti via Hawaii. There is also the possibility of getting there by a more roundabout way, via Peru and Easter Island, a route which offers the chance to visit some of the remotest communities in the eastern South

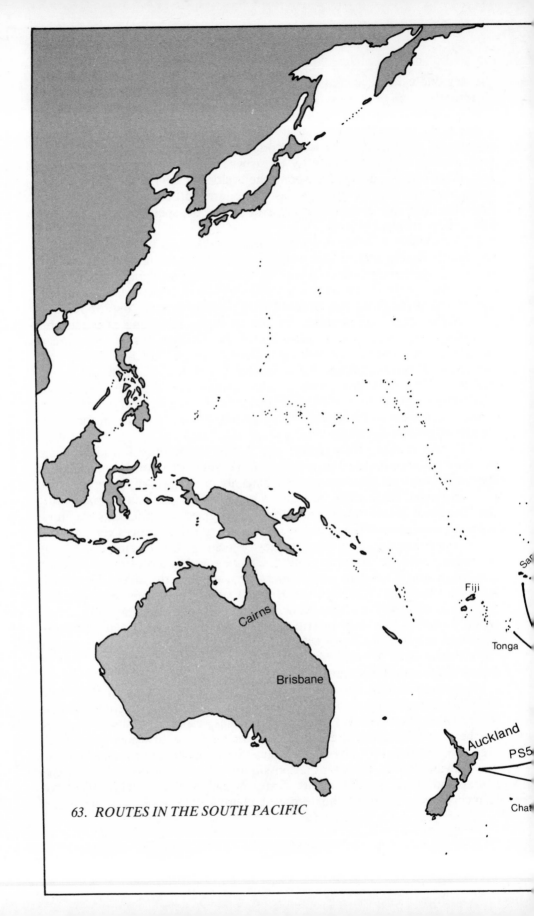

63. ROUTES IN THE SOUTH PACIFIC

Cairns

Brisbane

Fiji

Tonga

Sa

Auckland

PS5

Chat

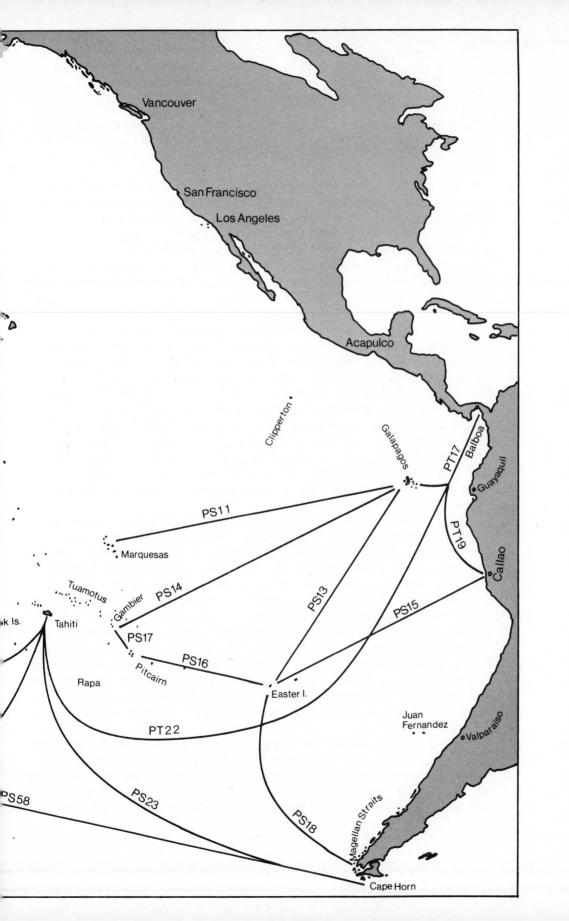

Pacific, Pitcairn Island being perhaps the most famous among them. By this southern route it is also possible to visit some of the outer islands of French Polynesia before rejoining the main route in Tahiti. Finally, an increasing number of boats make their way to Tahiti from New Zealand, their skippers undaunted by the tougher conditions associated with sailing in higher latitudes.

Lying at the centre of a network of routes, Tahiti offers several possibilities for the continuation of the voyage, although most people prefer to stick to the main route. A secondary route leaves from Tahiti across the equator to Hawaii, which is also the route taken by some of the boats returning to the West Coast. Several secondary routes branch off later on, the northbound routes leading mostly across the equator towards Micronesia. Having passed through the Cooks, Tonga or Samoa, the main route finally reaches Fiji, another major cruising centre. Fiji is at the centre of a number of routes, the pattern in the SW Pacific becoming more complex. This area offers a great choice of destinations, with the added advantage of shorter distances between them. Undoubtedly the most popular destination in the SW Pacific is New Zealand, where an increasing number of cruising boats spend the cyclone season in the safety of North Island's protected harbours. At the same time, many put their prolonged stay to good use by carrying out essential repair and maintenance work on their boats and taking advantage of the excellent facilities offered by the various boatyards, sailmakers and engineering shops that exist in the Whangarei and Bay of Islands area. Such a stop, whether in New Zealand or in Australia, where facilities are equally good, should be included in their plans by all those who intend to spend longer than a year in the South Pacific.

Many people seem to reach a turning point in their voyages during their cruise in the South Pacific. A decision has to be made about the future and the solutions are not always obvious. North American and European yachts now sail the South Pacific in almost equal numbers, but when a return home has to be considered, the choice for the Europeans is fairly simple. The obvious way is to carry on westabout around the world, taking advantage of favourable weather systems. This is probably also the most logical solution for those whose home ports are on the east coast of the USA. However, for those who hail from the West Coast and wish to restrict their cruising to the Pacific, the choices are less obvious and the sooner they are considered the better. Every year boats arrive in the Western Pacific with their skippers at a loss as to the best way of getting back home. Some of these alternatives are described in Voyage E in Chapter 2 and also in PS50, Routes from New Zealand.

These are only some of the aspects that should be considered before planning a cruise among the islands of the South Pacific. Apart from wind and weather, the human side should also be considered. Since the arrival of the first Europeans two centuries ago, Pacific islanders have often been subjected to cruel treatment by outsiders, from blackbirding to nuclear testing and dumping. That they still receive us with open arms is a sign of their generosity and forgiveness. The South Pacific continues to be one of the most peaceful, non-polluted regions of the world and it is in our best interests to help keep it that way.

PS10 Routes in the Eastern South Pacific

PS11 Galapagos to Marquesas
PS12 Marquesas to Tahiti
PS13 Galapagos to Easter Island
PS14 Galapagos to Gambier Islands
PS15 South America to Easter Island
PS16 Easter Island to Pitcairn
PS17 Pitcairn to Gambier Islands
PS18 Easter Island to Magellan Straits or Cape Horn

PS11 Galapagos to Marquesas

DIAGRAMS 48, 63		Wreck Bay to Nuku Hiva 3060 m
Best time:	April to November	
Tropical storms:	December to March	
Charts:	BA: 4023, 783	
	US: 51	
Pilots:	BA: 7, 62	
	US: 122, 125, 126	

For many cruising boats the passage from the Galapagos Islands to the Marquesas is their longest offshore passage and, if one is lucky with the weather, it can also be one of the most pleasant. Although the area lies under the influence of the SE trades for the best part of the year, weather conditions can differ drastically from one year to the next and the presence or absence of the El Niño Current can exert a great influence on weather conditions in the eastern half of the South Pacific.

Good passages have been made at all times of the year, but the most favourable period appears to be from April to August when the trade winds usually blow steadily from E or SE and the favourable west setting current is at its strongest (1–1½ knots). However, some people are tempted to make this passage early in the year in order to make a good start to their sailing season in the South Pacific. In some years this can be a mistake as a cyclone can either be met on the way or after arrival in the Marquesas. In February 1983 cyclone William reached a point nearly 1,000 miles to the east of the Marquesas, its effects being felt by several boats sailing along this route at that time. Two cyclones were recorded in the islands in that year, although the frequency of cyclones in the Marquesas is relatively low and years can go by without the islands being hit by a fully fledged cyclone. On such occasions however, trees and other debris washed out to sea create additional hazards to small craft and caution should be exercised, especially at night. This route runs through an area where collisions with whales have also been reported, so it pays to treat whales with suspicion.

The average length of this passage is about 30 days, although some boats have taken longer and even up to twice that time, mainly those who are not prepared to motor in calm or light weather conditions. In the vicinity of both the Galapagos Islands and the Marquesas the winds can turn light even at the height of the trade wind season. On average, the slowest passages appear to be those made in the early part of the year, when light winds and calms were encountered. In some years no real trade wind conditions are experienced until May, although throughout the year the currents along this route are favourable. Winds are stronger and steadier in the later part of the year and for those making this passage in October or November it may be worth laying a course to the north of the rhumb line, as both winds and current can be more favourable nearer to the equator.

PS12 Marquesas to Tahiti

DIAGRAM 64	Nuku Hiva to Papeete 760 m

Best time:	May to October
Tropical storms:	December to March
Charts:	BA: 783
	US: 526, 607
Pilots:	BA: 62
	US: 122, 126

The direct route leads right through the Tuamotu Archipelago, also known in the past as the Dangerous Archipelago on account of its reefs, low lying islands and very strong currents. Until recently many yachts preferred to bypass this area altogether rather than risk its many dangers. However, the advent of satellite navigation and the increased use of radar by small boats have made it possible for many more to cruise among these delightful atolls. For those who do not intend to stop en route to Tahiti, it is still recommended to lay a safe course outside all dangers. The recommended practice in the past has been to wait and leave the Marquesas with a full moon, both for improved visibility at night and to be able to use a wider selection of celestial bodies in navigation.

From May to November the SE trades are normally in full force in these latitudes, although occasionally they can be interrupted by squalls and short periods of light winds and calms. During the summer months, from December to April, which is the cyclone season, winds are less predictable and the weather can be hot and sultry. The Tuamotus should be avoided during the cyclone season as no anchorage can be regarded as really safe. Because of the revolving nature of these storms, even a relatively protected anchorage can quickly turn into a lee shore and the long fetch in most lagoons can create hellish conditions for boats at anchor.

PS13 Galapagos to Easter Island

DIAGRAMS 48, 63	Wreck Bay to Hangaroa 1950 m

Best time:	November to March
Tropical storms:	None
Charts:	BA: 4023
	US: 62
Pilots:	BA: 7, 62
	US: 122, 125

The few boats that take this rather unusual route to the island of giant statues are usually rewarded by a fast passage with the SE trades on the beam. The best period is between December and May when the trades extend furthest to the south, although the weather around Easter Island is more settled in the earlier months of the year. If sailing direct to Easter Island from Panama or other ports in Central America, the same directions apply for the first part of the voyage as for the routes to the Galapagos Islands.

PS14 Galapagos to Gambier Islands

DIAGRAMS 48, 63	Wreck Bay to Mangareva 3460 m

Best time:	April to October
Tropical storms:	None
Charts:	BA: 783, 4023
	US: 51, 607
Pilots:	BA: 7, 62
	US: 122, 125, 126

This route allows one to reach French Polynesia from the SE rather than the NE and the well-trodden route to the Marquesas. Directions are similar to those for the route from Galapagos to Easter Island, with the added advantage that as the Gambier Islands lie so much further to the west, the SE trades provide an even better slant for this route which crosses one of the most deserted areas of the world. Entry formalities can be completed at Rikitea, on Mangareva, the main island of the group.

PS15 South America to Easter Island

DIAGRAMS 48, 63		Callao to Hangaroa 2030 m
		Valparaiso to Hangaroa 1940 m

Best time:	November to March
Tropical storms:	None
Charts:	BA: 4023
	US: 62
Pilots:	BA: 7, 62
	US: 122, 125

Whichever point of departure is chosen, a passage to Easter Island from any port along the west coast of South America should present no problem. From ports lying to the north of Callao, a direct course can be steered immediately on leaving as favourable winds can be expected during most of the year. Although according to the pilot charts, Easter Island lies slightly outside the SE trade wind belt, the winds between the island and the continent tend to blow between E and S most of the time. A direct course can also be steered from ports lying further south, but if westerly winds are encountered, a NW course should be laid until the SE trades are found. Those sailing along the coast of Chile with a favourable wind and current should not lay a course for Easter Island before the latitude of Valparaiso has been crossed. Heading west from there, one can call in first at Juan Fernandez Island.

PS16 Easter Island to Pitcairn

DIAGRAMS 48, 63		Hangaroa to Pitcairn 1120 m

Best time:	November to March
Tropical storms:	None
Charts:	BA: 783
	US: 621
Pilots:	BA: 62
	US: 122, 125, 126

Fair winds can be expected along this route during the best part of the year. The most settled weather is in summer, from December to May, when the SE trades extend furthest south. However, even during these months the trade wind pattern can be interrupted by spells of squally weather, rain and variable winds. A direct course from Easter to Pitcairn Island leads well to the south of Ducie and Henderson Islands, both of which are uninhabited.

PS17 Pitcairn to Gambier Islands

DIAGRAMS 48, 63		Pitcairn to Mangareva 300 m
Best time:	March to June	
Tropical storms:	December to March	
Charts:	BA: 783	
	US: 607	
Pilots:	BA: 62	
	US: 122, 126	

This passage can be done at all times of the year as both Pitcairn and the Gambier group are very rarely threatened by cyclones. However, the first months of the year should be avoided so as not to arrive in French Polynesia during the cyclone season. Best sailing conditions can be expected either at the beginning or the end of winter. As this route skirts the southern extremity of the SE trades, weather conditions can be variable during winter months and westerly gales are not uncommon. The islands should be approached with caution in thick weather as they can be hidden by low cloud and currents in their vicinity can be strong at times. There are several passes leading into the lagoon, the Western Pass, between the islands of Taravai and Mangareva, having the best markings as it is normally used by the supply ship from Tahiti.

PS18 Easter Island to Magellan Straits or Cape Horn

DIAGRAM 63		Hangaroa to Cape Pillar 2180 m
		Hangaroa to Cape Horn 2500 m
Best time:	December to February	
Tropical storms:	None	
Charts:	BA: 4023	
	US: 62	
Pilots:	BA: 6, 62	
	US: 124, 125	

Only a handful of people have made Easter Island the starting point for a voyage to the stormy Southern Ocean. After leaving Easter Island the region of prevailing westerly winds should be reached as quickly as possible. By taking advantage of every shift of wind it ought to be possible to make some easting even before the Roaring Forties are reached, from where fair, if strong, winds can be expected. The proportion of gale force winds is highest in the vicinity of the southern tip of the American continent, the worst period being the winter months of June, July and August. The Magellan Straits are entered at Cape Pillar where landfall should be avoided in heavy weather, when currents create rough seas at the entrance to the Straits.

PS20 Routes from the Society and Cook Islands

PS21 Society to Cook Islands
PS22 Tahiti to Austral Islands
PS23 Tahiti to Cape Horn
PS24 Cook Islands to Samoa
PS25 Cook Islands to Tonga
PS26 Cook Islands to New Zealand

Tahiti and the Society Islands are one of the most enticing cruising destinations in the world and their continuing popularity is assured in spite of several shortcomings. The most obvious among these are the compulsory bond for all visiting yachts (see Chapter 27), the high cost of living, Papeete's worsening pollution, and the fact that most of French Polynesia's islands are in the cyclone belt. While the first three aspects are virtually unavoidable, the same cannot be said about the last point. The cyclone season in this part of the world lasts from December to March, with the worst months being February and March. It coincides with the southern summer, when the SE trades are absent and the weather is often muggy and overcast. It is therefore hardly the kind of weather to entice anyone to stay, when one could easily be somewhere else. It is all a matter of timing and a little bit of advance planning can make it possible to be in Tahiti at the best of times.

Ideally one should plan to arrive in French Polynesia in late March or early April, when the cyclone season is on the wane and the SE trade wind season is just about to begin. Whether arriving from the N (Hawaii), NE (California or Panama), E (Easter or Pitcairn Island), or SW (New Zealand), such a timing will ensure several months of carefree cruising before the onset of the next cyclone season. Those with only a limited amount of time can stay for two or three months before continuing their voyage. If one leaves the Society Islands only after the 14th July celebrations, a unique event which few visitors would like to miss, the safe cruising season in the rest of the tropics is well advanced and one has to be prepared to push on and probably spend the coming cyclone season in New Zealand. The other alternative is to remain in the tropics during the summer, either by delaying one's departure from French Polynesia until the

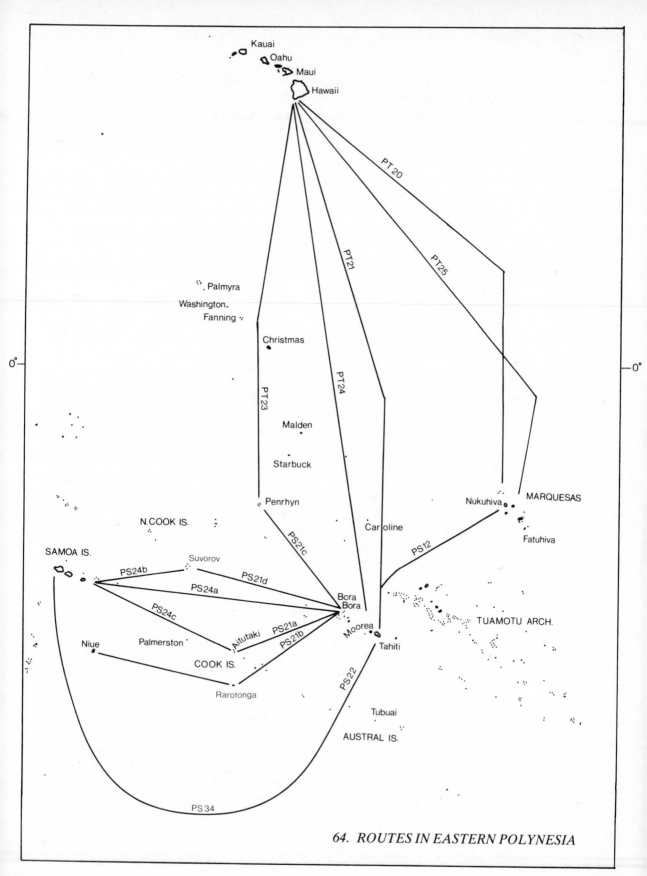

64. *ROUTES IN EASTERN POLYNESIA*

following year, or by making for one of the relatively safe harbours downwind from Tahiti, such as Pago Pago (American Samoa), Vava'u (Tonga) or Suva (Fiji). For those who decide to stay in the Society Islands, there are several harbours, both in the Windward and the Leeward Islands, that are reputed to be safe in a cyclone, although the best places tend to be very crowded, which can be a danger in itself.

Many boats continue to spend the cyclone season here, not heeding the lessons of 1983, when several cyclones swept through French Polynesia. It is true that several years can go by without a cyclone hitting these islands, but when a cyclone comes this way, great havoc can be wrought. Those prepared to take this risk and stay in French Polynesia between December and March, should try to be near one of the recommended ports and tune in to the weather forecasts several times a day, both local and those broadcast by WWVH.

In spite of several routes terminating in Tahiti, the number of routes originating from there is quite limited. The main one is PS21, the trunk route to the west, the 'milk run', which name is something of a misnomer, as ideal trade wind conditions are seldom present along the entire length of this route. Although it is possible to leave on this passage at any time from April to October, when reasonable sailing conditions can be expected, it would be wrong to set off without some idea of where to spend the following cyclone season. This would then dictate both the timing of one's departure from French Polynesia and the amount of time that could be spent visiting the islands en route. A favourite stop on the main route west is Suvorov, a typical South Seas atoll made famous by the New Zealander Tom Neale who exiled himself on Suvorov in the early 1950s and whose book *An Island to Oneself*, has caught the imagination of potential castaways all over the world. Although Tom Neale is no more, his hut still stands on Suvorov and has been taken care of by successive visitors on yachts, for whom it has become a kind of a shrine.

For those for whom Tahiti is a point of return, either to the west coast of North America, or to Europe and the East Coast, there are a limited number of alternatives to choose from. The usual route taken by those who plan to return to the Atlantic is to continue westabout around the world along the trade wind routes of the three oceans. The alternative to this is to take what Bernard Moitessier called 'the logical route' and reach the Atlantic via Cape Horn (Route PS23). Although shorter than the trade wind route, the Cape Horn route offers the prospect of a much tougher voyage. Another possibility is to reach the Atlantic via the Panama Canal (PT22). The coast of South America can be reached from Tahiti with the help of W winds in higher latitudes. From there, the SE trades and N setting Humboldt Current make the rest of the trip to Panama fairly easy.

A return from Tahiti to the Pacific coast of North America is more straightforward. The most convenient route leads from Tahiti to Hawaii (PT21) and this route should also be followed by those who hail from other parts of the world and wish to visit Alaska, British Columbia or California.

PS21 Society to Cook Islands

DIAGRAM 64	Bora Bora to Rarotonga 550 m
	Bora Bora to Aitutaki 500 m
	Bora Bora to Penrhyn 580 m
	Bora Bora to Suvorov 690 m

Best time:	April to October
Tropical storms:	December to March
Charts:	BA: 783
	US: 606
Pilots:	BA: 62
	US: 122, 126

Most westbound boats take their leave from the Society Islands in Bora Bora, where all departure formalities can be completed and a small selection of stores is available to provision the boat for the passage.

A choice of destinations is available as the boats fan out to visit islands either in the Southern or Northern Cooks, the two groups being separated by some 500 miles of ocean. Most boats head for Aitutaki (PS21A) or the capital Rarotonga (PS21B), with only a few using Penrhyn (Tongareva) (PS21C) in the Northern Cooks as a port of entry. Both Aitutaki and Penrhyn have good anchorages inside their lagoons, while Avatiu harbour, on the north coast of Rarotonga, has greatly improved after the building of new wharves and the provision of additional docking facilities for visiting yachts.

However, many boats make straight for Suvorov (PS21D), lying on the direct route to Samoa, which offers a good anchorage in settled weather. The anchorage becomes untenable in squally weather and because of the large fetch, the lagoon can become very rough. Yachts have been lost after breaking free from their anchors and being driven onto the reef, so that in threatening weather it is safer to put to sea immediately. It must also be stressed that Suvorov belongs to the Cook Islands, whose government does not approve of unauthorised visits. The atoll is occasionally inspected by a government vessel from Rarotonga and yachts found anchored there risk being either fined or asked to leave.

Depending on which course is chosen after leaving Bora Bora, attention should be paid to the various reefs and islands lying en route, such as Maupiti, Maupelia, Scilly or Bellinghausen, as they are all low and show no lights. During the SE trade wind season, from April to October, the passage between the two groups of Polynesian islands is straightforward. However, during July and August the trades reach their peak and sailing conditions can be boisterous, with large seas. During the summer months, from November to the end of March, the greater proportion of winds are still from the SE or E, but W and NW winds are not uncommon and are usually accompanied by squally weather.

PS22 Tahiti to Austral Islands

DIAGRAM 64	Tahiti to Tubuai 360 m
	Tahiti to Raivavae 400 m
	Tahiti to Rapa 670 m

Best time:	April–May, October–November
Tropical storms:	December to March
Charts:	BA: 783
	US: 607
Pilots:	BA: 62
	US: 126

This group of islands of which the nearest, Rurutu, lies 300 miles south of Tahiti, attracts only a few visitors every year. During the winter months, from May to September, when the SE trades blow strongly between Tahiti and the islands, it is sometimes difficult to reach some of the windward ones. When the wind has too much south in it, it is probably better to call in first at Tubuai, which has a pass into the lagoon, and then work one's way gradually to the other islands. Both Raivavae and Rapa have good anchorages.

PS23 Tahiti to Cape Horn

DIAGRAM 63	Tahiti to Cape Horn 4280 m

Best time:	November to December
Tropical storms:	December to March
Charts:	BA: 783, 788, 789
	US: 62, 621
Pilots:	BA: 6, 62
	US: 122, 125, 126

The time of departure on this passage is crucial so as to pass Cape Horn at the height of the southern summer, which is the optimum time. The recommended time to leave Tahiti is during November or December as such a departure would ensure a rounding of the Cape between January and March. The course on leaving Tahiti leads south through the Austral Islands. Depending on the direction and strength of the SE trade winds, the course should be slightly to the east of south. There is a south going current setting strongly through this area. Latitude 30°S should be crossed in about longitude 150°W and latitude 40°S in longitude 140°W. When the area of prevailing westerly winds is reached, the course becomes more easterly, so that latitude 50°S is only crossed in about longitude 115°W. A course is then laid to pass about 60 miles south of Cape Horn.

PS24 *Cook Islands to Samoa*

DIAGRAM 64	Rarotonga to Pago Pago 750 m
	Aitutaki to Pago Pago 690 m
	Suvorov to Pago Pago 450 m

Best time:	April to October
Tropical storms:	December to March
Charts:	BA: 780, 783
	US: 541
Pilots:	BA: 61, 62
	US: 122, 126

Most boats heading for the Samoan islands do so in order to reprovision in Pago Pago, in American Samoa, where a good selection of US goods is available. If bound for Western Samoa, the port of entry is the capital Apia, on the north coast of Upolu.

This passage is straightforward, whether sailing direct from the Society Islands, or stopping en route at one or more of the Cook Islands. During the SE trade wind season favourable winds can be expected for most of this passage, although there are occasions when the trades do not blow with the hoped for consistency. On the stretch between the Society Islands and Samoa, the trade winds follow a cyclic pattern, with several days of consistent winds followed by a short period of calms or variable winds, followed in turn by another spell of steady E or SE winds.

In some years the SE trades do not establish themselves until late in the season and boats making this passage in April and even May can have a mixed weather pattern, with calms at night and squally weather during the day. The fastest passages are usually made in July and August, although during these months the trades are too strong for some people's taste.

PS25 *Cook Islands to Tonga*

DIAGRAM 66	Rarotonga to Tongatapu 870 m
	Rarotonga to Vava'u 820 m
	Rarotonga to Niue 590 m
	Aitutaki to Tongatapu 880 m
	Aitutaki to Vava'u 810 m
	Aitutaki to Niue 580 m

Best time:	April to October
Tropical storms:	December to March
Charts:	BA: 780, 783
	US: 606
Pilots:	BA: 61, 62
	US: 126

At first sight a simple passage in the trade wind belt, but there are some problems associated with this route. In the winter months, from June to August, when most passages are made, the southern limit of the SE trades is slightly to the north of this area and, especially from Rarotonga to Tongatapu, one cannot speak of trade wind sailing conditions. Although the majority of winds still blow from an easterly direction, periods of settled weather never last long and it is usual to encounter rough weather somewhere along this route.

A hazard on this route are various reefs, the most dangerous being Beveridge Reef (20°02'S, 167°55'W), which has already claimed at least one yacht. It lies only slightly to the south of the rhumb line between Rarotonga and Tongatapu and as the charts are not entirely accurate and there have been reports of unpredictable currents in the area, both this reef and all others should be given a wide berth. The breakers marked on the charts in position 21°05'S, 164°05'W, first reported in 1945, should be taken seriously as a yacht was swamped by two abnormally large waves in exactly this area during a gale in 1984.

Westbound boats sometimes call at Palmerston Island, where yachts are welcome, especially if the skipper has had the foresight to bring the islanders' mail from Rarotonga. Another stop on the route to Tonga is at Niue, where a mooring buoy has been laid on for visiting boats off Alofi, the main settlement on the island.

This westbound passage from the Cooks calls for some advance planning, which can make life easier later on. If intending to sail on to Fiji after stopping in Tonga, it is probably better to sail first to Vava'u, in Tonga's northern group, where Neiafu is an official port of entry. The main island of Tongatapu can be visited afterwards. The subsequent passage from Tonga to Fiji is simpler along the southern route from Tongatapu to Suva, with fewer reefs to worry about and navigation made easier by the presence of lights on most dangers. Because of the prevailing winds it is easier to sail from Vava'u to Tongatapu than vice versa. Thus, by taking the northern route from the Cooks to Tonga, one can expect both better sailing conditions on that leg and fewer complications later on.

Although this route crosses an area subject to cyclones, these are quite rare. Caution must be exercised during January to March, especially in Tonga, where the incidence of cyclones during these months is much higher than in the Cook Islands.

PS26 Cook Islands to New Zealand

DIAGRAM 66	Rarotonga to Opua 1610 m

Best time:	mid-October to mid-November
Tropical storms:	December to March
Charts:	BA: 780, 783
	US: 622
Pilots:	BA: 51, 62
	US: 126, 127

Because of the risk of encountering a late winter gale if leaving too early, or an early hurricane if leaving too late, the optimum time for this passage is rather limited. Although the great circle route leads east of the Kermadec Islands, if this passage is made before November it is advisable to make some westing while still in the SE trades and pass to the west of the Kermadecs. This means that North Island is approached from the north, which is the accepted practice for this time of year to ensure a better slant in case a gale springs up from the west. After the middle of December the likelihood of SW gales is more remote, so that a more direct route can be taken and the Kermadecs passed to the east.

PS30 and PS40 Routes in the Central Pacific

The central area of the South Pacific offers some of the best cruising in the world, although navigation among the various island groups can be very difficult on account of reefs and strong currents. The triangular stretch of water between Samoa, Tonga and Fiji can be quite stormy at times and some boats have reported their worst South Pacific weather in this area. Although the area appears to be right in the path of the SE trades, these are sometimes absent and cannot be relied upon.

Passages between Tonga and Fiji have the reputation of being the most hazardous in the South Pacific and the number of cruising boats lost in these waters confirms this assumption. The route passes through an area infested with reefs and few of the dangers are marked by lights. The 180-mile wide stretch of water between Tonga and Fiji has strong unpredictable currents and because of the distance involved it is impossible to pass all dangers in daylight. Added to this, the sky is often overcast, making celestial navigation impossible. This can mean that the most dangerous area is reached with an unreliable DR position and the loss of most boats has been attributed to an inaccurate position.

These navigational difficulties are also compounded by Tonga's decision to keep the same date as Fiji, although lying well to the east of the 180th meridian. As a result of this decision, local time in Tonga is GMT +13, rather than GMT −11 as it should be. This means that the date in Tonga is one day ahead of the GMT day. Arriving from the east, most people change their time and date to the local standard after their first visit ashore and often do not give the matter another thought. The real problem starts on the next leg of the voyage when some navigators forget to set back their time by 24 hours. Working out a sight by using the wrong day entry in the *Nautical Almanac* can result in an error serious enough to have grave consequences in an area strewn with reefs, where passes between islands are only a few miles wide.

Another hazard to be borne in mind when sailing in Tongan waters is submarine volcanic activity, which has resulted recently in the formation of new islands. Another effect of this volcanic activity is the presence of floating pumice stones which can obstruct the engine water intake.

Another major disadvantage of the Central South Pacific is that the entire area is subject to cyclones which occur mostly in the first three months of the year. Although the majority of boats leave the area during the dangerous season, every year a number of boats spend the summer in or near one of the ports where shelter can be sought should a cyclone come that way. One of the safest places is Pago Pago, in American Samoa, while another favourite hurricane anchorage is Neiafu, in Tonga's Vava'u group, although boats did suffer damage here during a recent cyclone. In Fiji most boats remain in the vicinity of Suva, where the Tradewinds anchorage and surrounding inlets offer the best shelter. The decision to spend the summer in the tropics is a matter of personal choice, but the number of boats lost or damaged in recent years has persuaded most skippers to plan their South Pacific cruise so as to leave the area before the start of the cyclone season.

A great exodus takes place every year as cruising boats head out of the tropics to spend the summer in a safer area, New Zealand being the favourite destination. The best time to make this passage is on the eve of the cyclone season, late in October or early in November. Such a timing allows a stay in the tropics to the end of the safe season and a passage to New Zealand without much danger of encountering a late winter gale. The chance of a gale does not seem to worry the skippers of New Zealand boats returning home, who often make this passage earlier than others.

Although passages to New Zealand have been made at all times of year, it would be dangerous to set off during the cyclone season without a reliable forecast, as the tracks of some storms that have hit Fiji in the past almost coincide with the route to New Zealand. Official ports of entry for boats arriving from the north are Opua, Whangarei and Auckland. Opua, in the Bay of Islands, where most boats make their entry into New Zealand, has no permanent Customs and Immigration offices and officers come up from Whangarei to clear boats. During the peak arrival time from mid-November to mid-December officials are available in Opua during office hours.

PS30 Routes from Samoa and Tonga

PS31 Samoa to Tonga
PS32 Samoa to Fiji
PS33 Samoa to Wallis
PS34 Samoa to Society Islands
PS35 Tonga to Society Islands
PS36 Tonga to Samoa
PS37 Tonga to Fiji
PS38 Tonga to New Zealand

PS31 Samoa to Tonga

DIAGRAM 65	Apia to Niuatoputapu 230 m
	Apia to Neiafu 380 m
	Pago Pago to Neiafu 330 m

Best time:	April to October
Tropical storms:	December to March
Charts:	BA: 780
	US: 605, 606
Pilots:	BA: 61
	US: 126

For this passage similar directions apply to those for the reciprocal Route PS36. Southbound boats can now clear in at Niuatoputapu, but a stop-over at this island, conveniently placed half-way between Samoa and Tonga, should only be attempted in settled weather. Otherwise it is safer to proceed direct to Neiafu, on Vava'u, which can be entered under most conditions. Passages during the cyclone season should be avoided as the area is sometimes crossed by tropical storms.

PS32 Samoa to Fiji

DIAGRAM 65	Pago Pago to Suva 700 m
	Apia to Suva 670 m

Best time:	April to October
Tropical storms:	December to March
Charts:	BA: 780
	US: 605
Pilots:	BA: 61
	US: 126

Boats leaving Pago Pago bound for Fiji should lay a course for Nanuku Passage, on the NE side of the Fijian archipelago, which leads well clear of Curaçao Reef. In settled weather it is possible to stop briefly at Niua Foou, a high volcanic island belonging to Tonga. There is an anchorage in an open roadstead off the main settlement on the north side of the island. Great care should be exercised when approaching Nanuku Passage as the currents in this area can be very strong and the light on Wailangi Lala, marking the entrance to the passage, is not always operational. The route then leads through the Koro Sea, where one has the choice of two ports of entry, at Savusavu, on the south side of Vanua Levu, or at Levuka on Ovalau. Alternatively one can carry on as far as Suva, on the SE coast of Viti Levu.

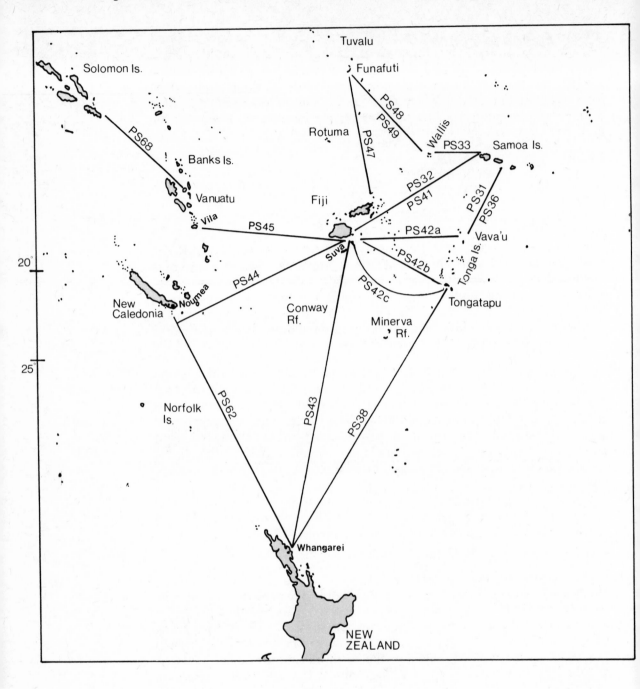

65. ROUTES IN THE CENTRAL PACIFIC

Boats leaving Apia bound for Fiji can either sail through Manono Passage, between the Samoan islands of Upolu and Savai'i, and then head for Nanuku Passage, or cruise along the north side of Savai'i before making for Fiji. In the latter case it is possible to arrive in the Fijian archipelago from the north and enter the Koro Sea via the Somosomo Strait separating Taveuni and Vanua Levu islands. Alternatively one can sail to Fiji via the French territories of Wallis and Futuna.

PS33 Samoa to Wallis

DIAGRAM 65	Apia to Mata Utu 280 m

Best time:	April to October
Tropical storms:	December to March
Charts:	BA: 780
	US: 605
Pilots:	BA: 61
	US: 126

After leaving Apia, on the island of Upolu, the route follows the north side of Savai'i before a course is set for Wallis. This route lies within the SE trade wind belt and for the best part of the year winds tend to have an easterly component. Altough both Wallis and Samoa are in the cyclone area, these are not frequent. Care should be exercised when approaching Wallis from the east as the reef surrounding the lagoon is sometimes difficult to see. The entrance into the lagoon is on the south side and is well marked by beacons. The port of entry is at Mata Utu, the main settlement on Uvea. If conditions at this anchorage are uncomfortable, visiting yachts are allowed to anchor in Gahi Bay, in the SE corner of the main island of Uvea.

Although lying to the east of the 180th meridian, both Wallis and Futuna have decided to keep the same date as New Caledonia, the nearest French territory. This means that Wallis is one day ahead of Samoa.

Warning: Check your GMT time and date on leaving Wallis.

PS34 Samoa to Society Islands

DIAGRAM 64	Pago Pago to Tahiti (a) via Cooks 1350 m (b) southerly route 1800 m

Best time:	November, April
Tropical storms:	December to March
Charts:	BA: 780, 783
	US: 541, 606
Pilots:	BA: 61, 62
	US: 122, 126

Only a few boats attempt to make this passage and the advice is to avoid it if at all possible. The only months when there is a chance of at least some favourable winds are the summer months, November to early April. This is the time when the SE trades are at their weakest and least consistent, but unfortunately it is also the cyclone season, with February and March being the most likely months for cyclones. If a direct course can be laid, a useful stop is at Suvorov or another of the Cook Islands.

During the winter months, from May to October, it is better to sail south in search of W winds (see Route PS57) and make easting between latitudes 30°S and 35°S, before turning north for Tahiti. If the southerly route is taken after leaving Samoa, it is possible to stop in Niue for a break or fresh provisions.

PS35 *Tonga to Society Islands*

DIAGRAM 63	Nuku'alofa to Tahiti 1480 m

Best time:	April to June
Tropical storms:	December to March
Charts:	BA: 780, 783
	US: 606
Pilots:	BA: 61, 62
	US: 122, 126

Although people have attempted to sail this route along the rhumb line by calling in at the Cook Islands, the passage can be very difficult even at the best of times. It is therefore better to follow the same instructions as those given for Route PS34 from Samoa to Tahiti and make this passage in higher latitudes with the help of westerly winds (see also Route PS57).

PS36 *Tonga to Samoa*

DIAGRAM 65	Neiafu to Pago Pago 340 m
	Neiafu to Apia 380 m

Best time:	April to November
Tropical storms:	December to March
Charts:	BA: 780
	US: 605, 606
Pilots:	BA: 61
	US: 126

Most boats take their leave from Tonga in Vava'u from where there is a relatively clear run to both Samoas. After leaving Vava'u a course should be steered to pass to the east of both Toku and Fonualei islands. The same course leads well to the east of Niuatoputapu and its surrounding dangers. If bound for Apia, the island of Upolu should be rounded from the east.

The weather on this route can be very variable and even at the height of the SE trade wind season one can never be sure what conditions to expect. Violent squalls are sometimes experienced in this area and also electric storms with tremendous sheets of lightning and thunder. These conditions can occur throughout the year. The cyclone-prone months of January to March should be avoided as cyclones have crossed this area in the past without hitting either Samoa or Tonga.

PS37 Tonga to Fiji

DIAGRAM 65

Nuku'alofa to Suva 420 m
Lifuka (Ha'apai) to Suva 440 m
Neiafu (Vava'u) to Suva 450 m

Best time:	April to October
Tropical storms:	December to March
Charts:	BA: 780
	US: 605
Pilots:	BA: 61
	US: 126

The route leaving from Tongatapu can pass either to the south or north of Vatua Island and then lay a course which leads halfway between Totoya and Matuku islands, both of which have lights. Having passed these two islands, a direct course can be laid for Suva. If passing to the south of Vatua it is easier to also keep south of Matuku and shape a course for Suva when the latter island has been safely passed.

Boats leaving from either Vava'u or Ha'apai should make for the 18 miles wide pass between Ongea Levu and Vatua. When Fulanga Island is abeam a course should be laid to pass between Totoya and Matuku islands. A more direct route from Vava'u leads through Oneata Passage, but neither this nor the Lakemba Passage to the north are recommended unless the intention is to clear in at Savusavu, on the south coast of Vanua Levu.

Regardless of the port of departure from Tonga, the most convenient port of entry for Fiji is the capital, Suva. Its approaches are well buoyed and lit and there are clear range markers making it easy to enter even at night if necessary.

The passage between Tonga and Fiji can be made at any time of the year, although the cyclone season should be avoided, especially the period January to March, when these routes are crossed by cyclones. During July and August, when the SE trade are at their strongest, the passage can be rough. At the beginning and end of the winter season the winds are lighter, but the weather in the area is often overcast which makes navigation by traditional means difficult.

There are four ports of entry in Fiji, at Suva and Lautoka, on Viti Levu, Savusavu on Vanua Levu and Levuka on Ovalau. Stopping and going ashore in any of the islands before clearing in first at one of the ports of entry is strictly prohibited. Special permission is necessary to cruise in the Lau Group and can be obtained from the Customs office in one of the ports of entry.

Warning: Check your GMT date on leaving Tonga.

PS38 *Tonga to New Zealand*

DIAGRAM 65	Nuku'alofa to Opua 1030 m
	Nuku'alofa to Whangarei 1080 m
	Nuku'alofa to Auckland 1130 m

Best time:	October–November
Tropical storms:	November to March
Charts:	BA: 780
	US: 605
Pilots:	BA: 51, 61
	US: 126, 127

This is a passage normally made just before the onset of the cyclone season, which officially starts at the beginning of November. Those who are tempted to leave on this passage too early risk encountering wintry weather further south. The direct course from Tongatapu leads close to Minerva Reef, which can be visited in settled weather. Some boats have anchored inside North Minerva Reef which can be reached through a pass on its NW side and offers adequate protection, especially at low tide, when the reef dries. However, if one does not intend to stop at Minerva it is wiser to give it a wide berth as many vessels have come to grief on this dangerous reef lurking in mid-ocean.

Depending on the direction of the wind after having passed Minerva Reef it is advisable to steer a course which would intersect the meridian of New Zealand's North Cape well to the north of it. Ideally this should be at least 300 miles to the north of North Cape. The idea of making sufficient westing early on in the passage is to counteract the possibility of SW gales later on. This precaution is worth taking if this passage is made during the winter months (May to October), but from November onwards it is probably just as well to steer the shortest course for the desired destination. See also PS30.

PS40 Routes from Fiji, Tuvalu and Wallis

PS41 Fiji to Samoa
PS42 Fiji to Tonga

PS43 Fiji to New Zealand
PS44 Fiji to New Caledonia
PS45 Fiji to Vanuatu
PS46 Wallis to Fiji
PS47 Tuvalu to Fiji
PS48 Tuvalu to Wallis
PS49 Wallis to Tuvalu

PS41 Fiji to Samoa

DIAGRAM 65	Suva to Apia 660 m
	Suva to Pago Pago 680 m

Best time:	April to October
Tropical storms:	mid-November to March
Charts:	BA: 780
	US: 605
Pilots:	BA: 61
	US: 126

For this passage it is best to leave Fiji through the Nanuku Pass. At the height of the SE trades, in July and August, this can be a rough windward passage. However, there are times when the trades betray their name and are less consistent than expected, which makes for easier sailing conditions. The weather between Fiji and Samoa can be quite stormy at times, as pointed out in directions for Route PS36.

If bound for Pago Pago, but unable to lay that port on account of the weather, it is better to make for the lee of Savai'i and then sail eastwards under the protection of the high islands of Savai'i and Upolu. The gap between Upolu and Tutuila can be crossed in settled weather. In strong winds the route can continue around the north side of Tutuila and reach Pago Pago from the east.

PS42 Fiji to Tonga

DIAGRAM 65	Suva to Nuku'alofa 420 m
	Suva to Neiafu 440 m

Best time:	April, October–November
Tropical storms:	mid-November to March
Charts:	BA: 780
	US: 605
Pilots:	BA: 61
	US: 126

Regardless of whether one is heading for Tongatapu (PS42B), at the southern extremity of the Tongan archipelago, or Vava'u (PS42A), at its northern end, this passage will be mostly hard on the wind. Most of those who make this passage do so either at the end or before the onset of the cyclone season. If Fiji is left before the start of the SE trades in April, the chances of encountering a late cyclone are remote and sailing conditions are less strenuous than later in the year. Similarly, for a departure in late October or early November the chance of an early cyclone is minimal. By this time, the SE winds would also be less strong and consistent than earlier.

After having cleared out of either Suva or Levuka the route threads its way through the islands of the Lau Group before heading for the open sea through the Lakemba or Oneata passes (PS42A). Alternatively, if the winds are favourable when leaving Suva, a SE course can be steered to pass between Matuku and Totoya islands (PS42B). A new course is laid from there to pass safely through the gap separating Vatoa and Ongea Levu islands. Another possibility is to leave Suva on a SSE course, leave all islands to port (PS42C) and arrive in Tongatapu from the SW.

Note: Although the 180th meridian will be crossed on this passage, the official date in Tonga is the same as in Fiji.

PS43 Fiji to New Zealand

DIAGRAM 65	Suva to Opua 1070 m
	Suva to Whangarei 1110 m
	Suva to Auckland 1160 m

Best time:	mid-October to mid-November
Tropical storms:	mid-November to March
Charts:	BA: 780
	US: 605
Pilots:	BA: 51, 61
	US: 126, 127

Favourable winds can be expected for at least the first half of this passage, but south of latitude 30°S it is very much a matter of luck, regardless of the time of year (see PS30). The conditions on this route can be extremely variable and the descriptions supplied by several people who have made this passage in recent years show that one can expect anything, from motoring in a flat calm for several days, to gale force winds on the nose, or a pleasant reach all the way. As the greatest risk on this passage is encountering a SW gale when approaching New Zealand, a suggested tactic is to make some westing soon after leaving Fiji. Ideally the meridian of New Zealand's Cape North should be intersected about 500 miles north of that Cape and this meridian followed south before altering course for the destination. This course of action is particularly recommended if the passage is made between June and September, when the probability of encountering a SW gale is much higher than later in the year. Receiving information about weather conditions over the Tasman Sea can be a great help, as this allows the best course to be planned. For those who do not have weather facsimile on board, but are amateur radio operators, there is a local maritime network, which provides the necessary information to those who wish to draw up their own weather chart.

PS44 Fiji to New Caledonia

DIAGRAM 65	Suva to Noumea 740 m
	Lautoka to Noumea 700 m

Best time:	mid-April to October
Tropical storms:	mid-November to March
Charts:	BA: 780
	US: 622
Pilots:	BA: 61
	US: 126

During the SE trade wind season, winds along this route are mostly fair and there is also a favourable current. Boats leaving from Suva should keep close to the south coast of Viti Levu to avoid the reefs surrounding Beqa (Mbenga) Island. After passing Vatu Lele Island a course can be set for the NE extremity of New Caledonia island if the intention is to sail direct to Noumea. Leaving from Lautoka it is best to reach the open sea through Malolo Passage before laying a course for New Caledonia. Some people take advantage of the fact that this route passes close to Aneityum, the southernmost island of Vanuatu, to make a brief stop there.

Boats arriving in New Caledonia from the NE use the Havannah Pass, which must be negotiated on a flood tide. Due to the prevailing SE winds the tide sets very strongly through the pass, creating large waves when the ebb tide runs against a strong wind.

Although New Caledonia is a French territory, a bond is not required from cruising boats as in the case of French Polynesia.

PS45 Fiji to Vanuatu

DIAGRAM 65	Suva to Vila 590 m
	Lautoka to Vila 530 m

Best time:	mid-April to October
Tropical storms:	mid-November to March
Charts:	BA: 780
	US: 604, 622
Pilots:	BA: 61
	US: 126

The route leaving from Suva follows the south coast of Viti Levu closely to avoid the reefs surrounding Mbenga (Beqa) Island. Having passed Thakau Lakalaka Reef, a direct course is steered for the southern extremity of Efate Island. From Lautoka the Malolo Pass is used to reach the open sea.

Favourable winds can be expected on this route during the SE trade wind season. The currents in this area set to the SW and this should be allowed for. The visibility in the vicinity of Efate is sometimes very poor and although a high island, it can remain obscured until close to.

Vila, on the SW side of Efate Island, is the capital of Vanuatu (formerly the New Hebrides). People who intend to spend the cyclone season in Port Vila must make arrangements to have their boats hauled out as the authorities do not allow cruising boats to stay in the water from December until March.

PS46 *Wallis to Fiji*

DIAGRAM 65	Wallis to Futuna 130 m
	Wallis to Suva 460 m

Best time:	April to October
Tropical storms:	mid-November to March
Charts:	BA: 780
	US: 605
Pilots:	BA: 61
	US: 126

Favourable winds are most likely on this route during the SE trade wind season. The journey can be broken at Futuna, the sister territory of Wallis, administered also by the French. There is an anchorage at Singave Bay on the west coast of Futuna. Continuing towards Fiji, one can gain access to the islands either through Nanuku Passage, on the NE side of the archipelago, or through Somosomo Strait. Both lead into the Koro Sea, where there are two ports of entry, at Savusavu on the south side of Vanua Levu and at Levuka, on Ovalau Island. All dangers in the Koro Sea are well buoyed and lit and it is not difficult to carry on as far as Suva, even at night.

PS47 *Tuvalu to Fiji*

DIAGRAMS 65, 67	Funafuti to Suva 630 m

Best time:	April to October
Tropical storms:	mid-November to March
Charts:	BA: 780
	US: 604
Pilots:	BA: 61
	US: 126

During the SE trade wind season the winds on this route are generally favourable, calms are quite rare and usually occur at night. At the change of seasons, in October, W winds become more frequent and are accompanied by squalls. Although the islands of Tuvalu are very rarely visited by tropical storms, a cyclone devastated the main island of Funafuti in October 1952, its earliness taking everybody by surprise. As Tuvalu lies close to the breeding ground of the cyclones, it is very unlikely that adequate warning would be given if one were heading in this direction.

The southbound route towards the Fijian archipelago can either pass through the Somosomo Strait and continue to Suva through the Koro Sea, or leave the entire archipelago to port and arrive in Suva from the west. If the first alternative is chosen, some easting should be made early even if it means going over the banks SSE of Niurakita Island.

Both alternatives have advantages and disadvantages, although often the decision will be influenced by the wind, because with a strong SE wind it may be too difficult to lay Cape Undu, the NE extremity of Vanua Levu Island, in the approaches to the Somosomo Straits. In this case either one of the passes into Bligh's Water can be used, or a course taken to stay to seaward of the Yasawa Group and make for Lautoka, which is a port of entry. The westabout route avoids the reefs and islets to the west of Viti Levu and continues along its south coast to Suva. The disadvantage of this course is the certainty of encountering headwinds after turning the SW corner of Viti Levu.

The course through Somosomo Straits and the Koro Sea has the advantage of two ports of entry more conveniently placed than Suva. These are Savusavu, on the south coast of Vanua Levu, and Levuka, on the east coast of Ovalau.

PS48 *Tuvalu to Wallis*

DIAGRAM 65	Funafuti to Mata Utu 360 m

Best time:	November, April
Tropical storms:	mid-November to March
Charts:	BA: 780
	US: 622
Pilots:	BA: 61
	US: 126

This passage is difficult to accomplish during the SE trade wind season from April to October, when the probability of encountering strong winds is very high. The alternative to beating all the way to Wallis, coupled with the disadvantage of a contrary current, is to make this passage at the change of seasons when W winds are more common. The passage can also be made during summer months, from December to March, although the danger of sailing in the cyclone season must be realised when making this decision.

If this passage is made at the height of the winter trades, from June to September, the winds at Funafuti are sometimes NE. If this is the case, as much easting as possible should be made on leaving Funafuti because the trades are bound to become more SE further south.

Although meridian 180 will be crossed on this passage, the date should not be changed, as Wallis keeps the same date as its neighbours to the west.

PS49 *Wallis to Tuvalu*

DIAGRAM 65	Mata Utu to Funafuti 360 m

Best time:	April to October
Tropical storms:	December to March
Charts:	BA: 780
	US: 622
Pilots:	BA: 61
	US: 126

During the SE trade wind season the winds along this route are mostly favourable. The direct course for Funafuti passes over several banks, but these present no danger to yachts as there is sufficient depth over them. They should only be avoided during strong winds when seas break, but in fair weather it is worth sailing over them as fishing is excellent. On a direct course to Funafuti, the first island to be passed will be Nukulaelae. There is no pass into its lagoon, but in settled weather it is possible to anchor outside the reef off the main settlement on the west side of the atoll.

The official port of entry for Tuvalu is at Funafuti, the capital of this small nation. There are several passes into Funafuti lagoon, but none of them should be attempted at night or when the visibility is not good.

PS50 Routes from New Zealand

PS51 New Zealand to New South Wales
PS52 New Zealand to Queensland
PS53 New Zealand to New Caledonia
PS54 New Zealand to Fiji
PS55 New Zealand to Tonga
PS56 New Zealand to Cook Islands
PS57 New Zealand to Tahiti
PS58 New Zealand to Cape Horn

There are several cruising routes which start from New Zealand, fanning out in all directions like the fingers of an outstretched hand. Although the number of local boats that go cruising in foreign waters is impressively high for a small nation, many of the boats that set sail from New Zealand fly the flags of distant nations. In recent years New Zealand has become a major cruising destination and few yachts sail through the South Pacific without making a detour to New Zealand. The majority come to New Zealand to spend the cyclone season in the safety of North Island's protected harbours.

This stay in New Zealand is often a time of decision making about the future direction of a voyage, as the many routes leaving from New Zealand offer a wide choice. For those with time on their hands, a return to cruising in the tropics is a possibility, either by sailing back to Tahiti or by making one of the easier passages to Fiji or Tonga (PS54 and PS55). Those for whom time is a commodity in short supply are probably mulling over the most pleasant way of getting back home.

For voyagers from Europe or the east coast of North America the choice is quite simple, as the logical way is to carry on around the world and reach the Atlantic either via the Cape of Good Hope or the Red Sea and Mediterranean. The other possibility is to make the return voyage using the prevailing westerly winds of higher latitudes and reach the Atlantic via Cape Horn (PS58), an alternative shunned by most blue water sailors, few of whom are concerned about joining the elite rank of Cape Horners.

The most difficult decision is faced by those hailing from the west coast of North America, both American and Canadian, who do not fancy the prospect of a complete circumnavigation, with a hard leg from Panama to their home port at the very end of it. Unfortunately there is no easy solution and the prospect of a return voyage of several thousands of miles, most of it to windward, is a matter of great concern. There are several routes that can be taken from New Zealand back to the West Coast and probably the simplest is the route via Tahiti and Hawaii (PS57). Those who are in a great hurry can complete this voyage in about four months, provided the boat goes reasonably well to windward. The course resembles a gigantic letter 'Z', with the horizontal bars representing the two legs in the westerlies of higher latitudes and the diagonal bar the slant across the SE and NE trade wind systems.

Although the route from New Zealand to Hawaii via Tahiti is the logical one, there are a number of other routes using different intermediate ports. All of them would probably take more time than the Tahiti route, although they do offer, by way of compensation, the chance to visit less frequented places in the Pacific. The first of these alternative routes leads from New Zealand to Rarotonga or Aitutaki in the Southern Cooks (PS56). It then passes through the Line Islands after having touched some of the Northern Cooks. This route to Hawaii has the advantage of less windward work after leaving New Zealand, a good enough reason perhaps to give Tahiti a miss. Unfortunately as this route approaches Hawaii from the south, the last leg will be against the prevailing NE winds. It must also be remembered that unlike Tahiti, there are few repair or servicing facilities in the Cooks, which might make them less attractive as an intermediate port on such a long passage.

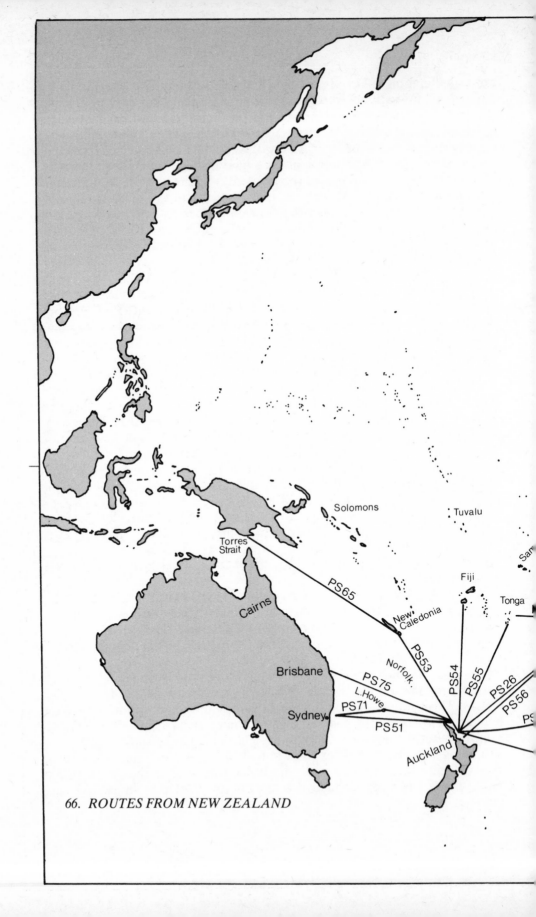

66. ROUTES FROM NEW ZEALAND

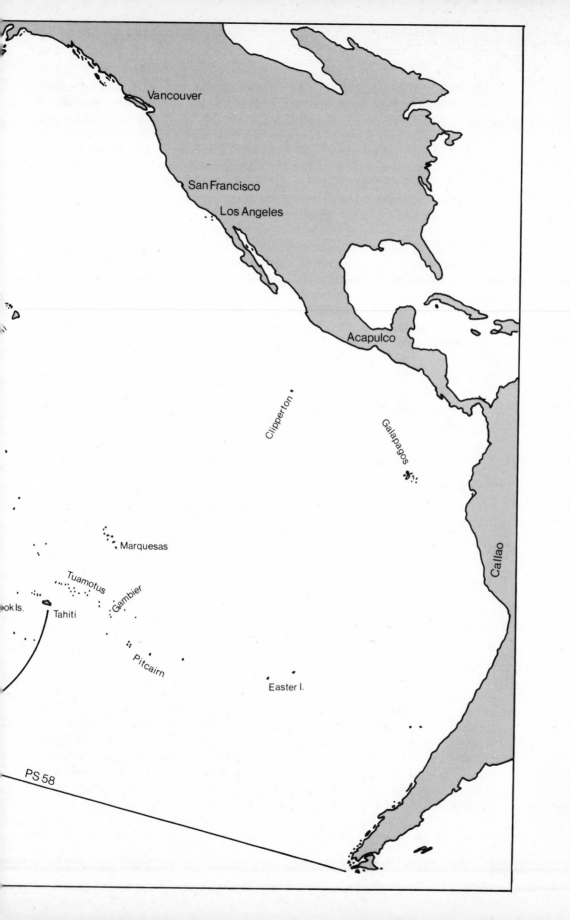

Vancouver

San Francisco

Los Angeles

Acapulco

Clipperton

Galapagos

Callao

Marquesas

Tuamotus

Gambier

ok Is.

Tahiti

Pitcairn

Easter I.

PS 58

All other alternative routes lie further to the west and although they might make the first leg from New Zealand to the tropics less tiresome, it must be remembered that the more west one moves, the more contrary will be the NE trades on the leg to Hawaii. The last acceptable alternative to the Tahiti route is the one that leads from New Zealand to Tonga, Samoa and the Phoenix Islands and on to the Line Islands and Hawaii. Taking an even more westerly track via Fiji, Tuvalu, Kiribati and possibly the Marshalls, cannot be recommended as it carries the guarantee of a prolonged and tough windward leg north of the equator.

The other main route from New Zealand leads across the Coral Sea towards the Torres Strait and beyond. Depending on the amount of time available, the choice is between a route via New Caledonia (PS53) or one via Australia and the Great Barrier Reef (PS52). The timing for the start of this passage is essential, not only for the first part of the voyage but also for later on. For those who wish to cruise en route but do not wish to be caught by the cyclone season in the South Indian Ocean (November to March), an early April departure from New Zealand is imperative. The more southerly route across the Tasman Sea to ports in New South Wales (PS51) is generally taken by people who wish to cruise along the east coast of Australia and do not mind the time it takes. There are also some who take a look at Australia and return to New Zealand for another quiet summer and an inexhaustible choice of cruising destinations.

PS51 New Zealand to New South Wales

DIAGRAM 66	Cape North to Lord Howe 740 m Cape North to Sydney 1090 m Wellington to Sydney 1210 m

Best time:	April-May
Tropical storms:	December to March
Charts:	BA: 780, 4601
	US: 601
Pilots:	BA: 14, 51
	US: 127

Most people prefer to make this passage either before or after the cyclone season, although the Tasman Sea is only marginally affected by these storms which originate in the tropics. Conditions encountered across the Tasman Sea can be extremely varied, from flat calms to violent SW gales. The general consensus is that May offers the best chance of decent weather, although prolonged periods of calms can be expected during this month. Several days of calm or light variable winds often occur after a SW gale has passed.

Good sailing conditions occur when a stationary high over the southern part of the Tasman Sea generates E winds further north. Such conditions can last up to a week and are sometimes followed by another high creating similar weather conditions. These are most common during the summer, which is also the cyclone season in the South West Pacific, although only a few of these tropical storms find their way into the Tasman Sea and usually by the time they get there, most of their fury is spent. Provided a favourable long-term forecast has been obtained, it is possible to leave New Zealand during the cyclone season, as cyclones generated further north would take several days to reach this route.

During the winter months both lows and highs move to the north, reducing the chances of E winds in the Tasman Sea. Lows are usually accompanied by strong SW winds and it is very rare that a winter passage can be made without encountering at least one gale.

When sailing around the top of North Island, Cape North and Cape Reinga should be given a wide berth so as to avoid not only the confused currents that set around the two capes, but also the dangerous area in the vicinity of the Three Kings, a group of rocky islets to the NW of Cape Reinga.

Although the majority of boats setting off across the Tasman take the route around North Cape, for those leaving from further south it might be more advantageous to reach the Tasman Sea via Cook Strait. Some boats break the trip across the Tasman by calling at Lord Howe Island, which is an official port of entry for Australia. The anchorage is not well protected and can become dangerous in strong westerly winds, especially at high tide.

PS52 New Zealand to Queensland

DIAGRAM 66	Cape North to Brisbane 1110 m

Best time:	mid-April to September
Tropical storms:	December to March
Charts:	BA: 780
	US: 602
Pilots:	BA: 15, 51
	US: 127

As all ports of destination on this route lie within the cyclone belt, an early departure during the summer months is not recommended. The best time to leave New Zealand is either in the second half of April or in May before the frequency of winter gales increases in the Tasman Sea. However, not all boats that have made this passage in later months have encountered totally unfavourable conditions. Although this route lies further to the north than the route to ports in New South Wales, weather conditions up to latitude 30°S and even beyond are influenced by the highs and lows lying over the

Tasman Sea. With a favourable weather forecast from New Zealand it is therefore possible to make a good start on this route which offers several options. A NW course can be taken after leaving New Zealand and a stop made in Norfolk Island. Another alternative is to take a more W course and stop at Lord Howe Island, Australia's lonely outpost in the Tasman Sea. As Elizabeth and Middleton Reefs lie virtually on the rhumb line from North Cape to Brisbane,some people cannot resist the temptation of anchoring behind a reef in mid-ocean. In unsettled weather the temptation should be resisted and the reefs given a wide berth.

Whichever route is chosen across the Tasman Sea, it should not reach the Australian coast too far south of the desired port because of the strong current setting south along the coast. The prevailing winds south of Sandy Cape are W from May to September. From October to April the winds are mostly NE. The area north of Sandy Cape is under the influence of the SE trade winds and during the winter months, from May to October, the winds are either SE or E.

In the case of boats bound for ports to the north of Sandy Cape, these may best be reached by going inside the Great Barrier Reef. Although there is also an offshore route, for small boats the inner route is more convenient. Those who are in a hurry and wish to get to the Torres Strait as soon as possible should sail from New Zealand to New Caledonia direct and from there take the recommended route across the Coral Sea (PS65).

PS53 New Zealand to New Caledonia

DIAGRAM 66		Whangarei to Noumea 930 m
		Opua to Noumea 880 m

Best time:	April to June
Tropical storms:	December to March
Charts:	BA: 780
	US: 602
Pilots:	BA: 51, 61
	US: 126, 127

The end of summer is the best time to make this passage, when favourable sailing conditions can be expected. A departure in April or early May reduces the chance of encountering winter gales in the first half of the passage, although if a gale is encountered, it only speeds progress to the north. The incidence of gales after June is higher and the weather colder, two factors which dissuade most people from making this passage too late in the season. For some boats the passage to New Caledonia is the first leg of a longer voyage to the Torres Strait and beyond, which makes an early start from New Zealand essential if the intention is to cross the Indian Ocean during the best season.

Having passed Cape North a direct course can be set for New Caledonia. The islands should be approached with care both on account of the reefs extending to the south of the main island and the currents reported in this area. If strong W winds are encountered below latitude 25°S it does not matter if only a northerly course can be steered. The lost ground can be made up later in an area where SE and E winds are prevalent, usually N of latitude 25°S. Some boats stop en route at Norfolk Island, but the anchorage there is not safe and should be left in impending bad weather.

Either Boulari or Dumbea Pass on the SW side of New Caledonia can be used to reach Noumea, the capital of New Caledonia.

PS54 New Zealand to Fiji

DIAGRAM 66	Auckland to Suva 1160 m
	Whangarei to Suva 1110 m
	Opua to Lautoka 1090 m

Best time:	April to July
Tropical storms:	December to March
Charts:	BA: 780
	US: 605
Pilots:	BA: 51, 61
	US: 126, 127

As for all other passages from New Zealand to the tropics, this route is not recommended during the cyclone prone months from December to the end of March. Even at the beginning of April the weather should be carefully watched, because the direct course from New Zealand to Fiji intersects the tracks followed by some of the cyclones recorded in the past.

Most boats make this passage after the first week in April, when the cyclone season further north has drawn to a close, as has the summer season in New Zealand. For those who have spent this season in New Zealand such a timing is perfect as it offers the prospect of at least six months of carefree cruising in the tropics. A later departure has the disadvantage of colder weather and a higher probability of SW gales. Regardless of the time of departure, a direct course leads clear of all dangers. Should strong W winds be encountered in the early part of the passage, it does not matter if one is pushed to the east of the rhumb line as the loss can be made up later with the help of the SE trades which blow north of latitude 25°S. If sailing to the east of the rhumb line, the route should avoid passing too close to the two Minerva Reefs, which have claimed many boats in the past.

Boats bound for Suva should approach the port from the south passing to the east of Kandavu Island and giving Astrolabe Reef a wide berth. Those intending to sail to Lautoka should pass to the west of Kandavu and Vatu Lele islands and reach Lautoka through Navula or Malolo Pass.

PS55 New Zealand to Tonga

DIAGRAM 66		Whangarei to Nuku'alofa 1080 m Auckland to Nuku'alofa 1120 m
Best time:	April-May	
Tropical storms:	December to March	
Charts:	BA: 780	
	US: 605	
Pilots:	BA: 51, 61	
	US: 126, 127	

With the exception of the cyclone season, this passage can be made in any month. The best time to leave New Zealand is between the beginning of April and the middle of May when winter has not yet established itself in southern latitudes and the danger of encountering a cyclone either en route or on arrival is minimal. A later departure would probably run the risk of strong W or SW winds at the beginning and also colder weather. Regardless of the time of year when this passage is made, it will be a close hauled affair most of the way.

A rhumb line from North Island to Tongatapu leads well to the west of the Kermadec Islands and also misses the two Minerva Reefs by a safe margin. The same course passes close to Ata Island, a high island lying some 90 miles SW of Tongatapu. The next Tongan island to be seen will probably be Eua, which is much higher than Tongatapu, the main island of the kingdom, lying close to the north-west of Eua. There are passes into Tongatapu's lagoon both from the east and the west. In strong SE winds it is better to gain the lee of Eua Island and enter the lagoon from the east.

PS56 New Zealand to Cook Islands

DIAGRAM 66		Auckland to Rarotonga 1630 m Whangarei to Rarotonga 1620 m
Best time:	April to July	
Tropical storms:	December to March	
Charts:	BA: 780, 783	
	US: 622, 526	
Pilots:	BA: 51, 62	
	US: 126, 127	

As a return passage to the tropics, this route is easier and more pleasant than the route via Tahiti. However, on no account should this route be taken as a first leg to Tahiti, as the subsequent beat from the Cooks to Tahiti has put off most of those who have tried to sail it direct. If for whatever reason the voyage has to continue from the Cooks to the Society Islands, the best way is to sail south into the area of prevailing westerlies and curve north through the Austral Islands. (See also Route PS57.)

Those who take the direct route from New Zealand to the Cooks have the choice of an early start, with the advantage of warmer weather when leaving New Zealand, or a later start, when the probability of W winds is higher. If an early departure date is chosen, this should not be before the middle of March as the cyclone season has not come to an end in the tropics and it would not be wise to arrive in the Cooks before the end of March, or preferably in early April. For a passage in April, easting should be made in the latitude of the port of departure and a course laid north only near meridian 160°E. In the case of a later departure, from May to July, easting should be made between latitudes 35°S and 30°S. Latitude 30°S should not be crossed before reaching longitude 170°W after which, depending on the wind, a direct course can be set for the desired destination. The same directions also apply for the remaining winter months when the SE trade wind belt lies furthest north and better winds can be expected to make the required easting, although the weather on leaving New Zealand would be very cold.

Ports of entry for the Southern Cooks are Avatiu, on the north side of the main island of Rarotonga, and Aitutaki, where a narrow pass through the reef leads to the main settlement on the west side of the island.

PS57 New Zealand to Tahiti

| DIAGRAMS 63, 66 | Whangarei to Papeete 2220 m |
| | Auckland to Papeete 2280 m |

Best time:	mid-March to May
Tropical storms:	December to March
Charts:	BA: 783, 788
	US: 621, 622
Pilots:	BA: 51, 62
	US: 122, 126, 127

The recommended procedure is to stay south of latitude 40°S in order to take full advantage of W winds prevailing in higher latitudes, although this means rather cold weather, especially if New Zealand is left after April. Most people prefer to compromise and attempt to make their easting between latitudes 35°S and 30°S, where the weather is indeed warmer. This is an area of variable winds that lie between the trade winds and prevailing westerlies, although the conditions differ from year to year and in some winter months consistent W winds have been encountered as far north as 32°S. Similarly there are years when even keeping south of latitude 40°S is no guarantee of consistent westerlies. This passage to Tahiti is usually a tough windward passage with a high proportion of SE winds. From the reports of those who have taken this route in recent years, at least one gale has been encountered en route. Very often the gales are from E and the best solution is to heave to and wait for them to blow over. In spite of the temptation to head NE earlier on, this should not be done before meridian 155°W is crossed. Meridian 150°W should be crossed in latitude 30°S, from where a course is shaped to pass through the Austral (Tubuai) Islands. In April the SE trades are normally found around latitude 25°S.

Some people stop in the Austral Islands as they are exactly on the route to Tahiti and there are some good anchorages. Entry formalities into French Polynesia can be completed later, on arrival in Tahiti.

This passage can also be done at the end of winter, in October–November, when the winds are often light and it can be a slow journey. As this is a windward passage at the best of times, it is better to do it when the weather is warm. The disadvantage of a summer passage from New Zealand is the risk of arriving in Tahiti in the midst of the cyclone season.

Whatever time is chosen for this passage, on no account should it be attempted to reach Tahiti via Rarotonga as the subsequent leg from the Cooks to Tahiti against the full force of the trades will be very rough, if not impossible to accomplish.

PS58 New Zealand to Cape Horn

DIAGRAMS 63, 66	Auckland to Cape Horn 4410 m

Best time:	January to March
Tropical storms:	None
Charts:	BA: 788, 789
	US: 621, 622, 625
Pilots:	BA: 6, 51
	US: 122, 125, 127

Only a handful of cruising boats attempt nowadays to take this classic route across the Southern Ocean. Most of this passage is made in the Roaring Forties where usually there is a high proportion of westerly winds. On leaving New Zealand the route heads SE so as to reach the area of W winds as soon as possible. However, as mentioned in Route PS57, there is no guarantee of encountering consistent W winds even in latitude 40°S and therefore it may be necessary to continue into higher latitudes. During the summer months, when the limit of the ice lies furthest to the south, the route runs between latitudes 47°S and 50°S. From longitude 120°W the course becomes gradually more southerly and passes about 60 miles south of Cape Horn.

A more southerly course is recommended for the summer months from December to February when the passage should be made in about latitude

55°S. Westerly winds in this latitude are more consistent, although the danger of encountering ice discourages most skippers from sailing in such high latitudes. But even in higher latitudes W winds can be absent in summer as happened in March 1986 during the Whitbread Round the World Race. Even on the great circle route which dips down to 62°S, there was an unusually high proportion of NE winds. Icebergs were sighted as far north as latitude 54°S showing that an extreme southerly route is both risky and hard to justify.

PS60 Routes from New Caledonia, Vanuatu and Solomon Islands

PS61 New Caledonia to Fiji
PS62 New Caledonia to New Zealand
PS63 New Caledonia to New South Wales
PS64 New Caledonia to Queensland
PS65 New Caledonia to Torres Strait
PS66 Vanuatu to New Caledonia
PS67 Vanuatu to Torres Strait
PS68 Vanautu to Solomon Islands
PS69 Solomon Islands to Papua New Guinea

PS61 New Caledonia to Fiji

| DIAGRAM 67 | Noumea to Suva 740 m |
| | Noumea to Lautoka 700 m |

Best time:	April
Tropical storms:	December to March
Charts:	BA: 780
	US: 622
Pilots:	BA: 61
	US: 126

Because of prevailing E and SE winds this passage is mostly on the wind. Leaving either from the main island of New Caledonia or from one of the Loyalty Islands, as much easting as possible should be made at the beginning of the passage. Keeping to the north of Matthew Island and Conway Reef a course is shaped for Kandavu Passage, if bound for Suva, or for Navula or Malolo Passage, if bound for Lautoka.

A good time to do this passage is early in April, when the danger of a late cyclone is not great and the SE trades are not yet fully established.

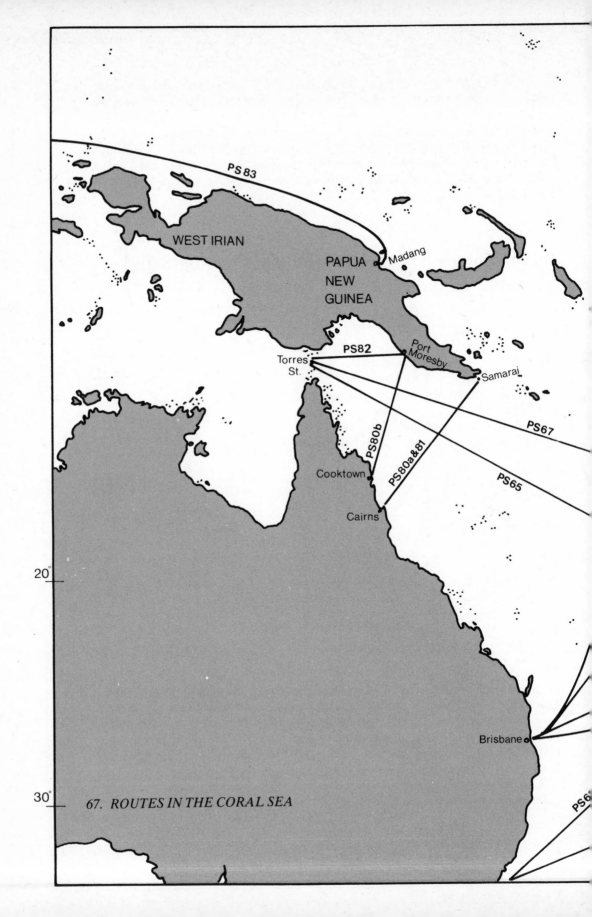

PS 83

WEST IRIAN

PAPUA
NEW
GUINEA

Madang

PS82

Port
Moresby

Torres
St.

Samarai

PS67

PS80b

PS80a&81

Cooktown

PS65

Cairns

20°

Brisbane

30°

67. *ROUTES IN THE CORAL SEA*

PS6

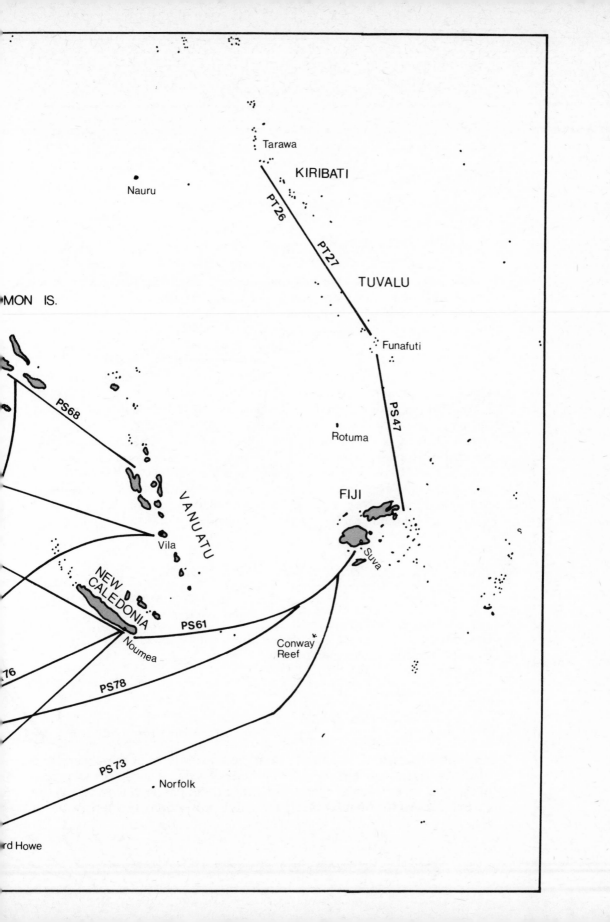

Tarawa

KIRIBATI

Nauru

PT26

PT27

TUVALU

MON IS.

PS68

Funafuti

PS47

Rotuma

VANUATU

FIJI

Vila

NEW
CALEDONIA

Suva

PS61

76

Noumea

Conway
Reef

PS78

PS73

Norfolk

rd Howe

PS62 New Caledonia to New Zealand

DIAGRAM 65	Noumea to Whangarei 930 m
	Noumea to Opua 880 m

Best time:	October–November
Tropical storms:	December to March
Charts:	BA: 780
	US: 602, 622
Pilots:	BA: 51, 61
	US: 126, 127

Similar directions apply for this route to those given for Route PS43 from Fiji to New Zealand. Boats starting off from New Caledonia have a better chance of encountering favourable winds as they are more to the west. Yet from the reports of boats which have made this passage in recent years it does appear that the proportion of headwinds were just as high as, if not higher than, those encountered by boats sailing direct from Fiji. This is usually caused by the SE trades reaching further south than their seasonal limits. Although this passage has been made at all times of the year, November is considered to be the safest month as the danger of an early hurricane is not too great, nor is that of a late winter gale.

After leaving Noumea through the Dumbea Pass a course is set to pass to the east of Norfolk Island. In SE winds it is better to stay on the port tack until Norfolk Island has been passed rather than head east too early.

Some people stop briefly at Norfolk Island, which lies almost halfway along the route to New Zealand, but the anchorage is only safe in settled weather and should be left if conditions deteriorate.

PS63 New Caledonia to New South Wales

DIAGRAM 67	Noumea to Sydney 1070 m
	Noumea to Coffs Harbour 870 m

Best time:	April-May, September to mid-November
Tropical storms:	December to March
Charts:	BA: 780
	US: 602
Pilots:	BA: 14, 15, 61
	US: 126, 127

The only conclusion to be drawn from the observations of those who have made this passage at various times of the year is that one can never be sure of the kind of weather to expect along this route. Favourable winds can be expected down to about latitude 30°S, as the proportion of easterly winds is generally higher, especially during the SE trade winds of winter. The transitional months between summer and winter are preferable in order to avoid the SW winds of winter months.

If a direct course for the desired port cannot be steered because of consistent headwinds, it is better to try to reach the Australian coast by the shortest route and use the south setting current to reach ports further south. South of Sandy Cape the prevailing winds off the coast are W from May to September and NE from October to April. The south going current is generally strongest around the 100 fathom line.

Boats taking the direct route from New Caledonia to Sydney should pass Middleton and Elizabeth Reefs at a safe distance. Boats on this route often call in at Lord Howe Island, which is a port of entry for Australia.

PS64 New Caledonia to Queensland

DIAGRAM 67	Noumea to Brisbane 800 m
	Noumea to Bundaberg 820 m

Best time:	April to mid-November
Tropical storms:	December to March
Charts:	BA: 780
	US: 602
Pilots:	BA: 15, 61
	US: 126, 127

Favourable winds can be expected along these routes throughout the SE trade wind season, although W winds can sometimes be encountered on routes that lead to ports in South Queensland, mainly in winter. If persistent headwinds make it difficult to lay a direct course for ports lying south of Sandy Cape, it is better to head for the coast and use the strong south setting current. Because of the large number of reefs dotted about the southern half of the Coral Sea, for ports lying north of Sandy Cape it is advisable to sail inside the Great Barrier Reef which can be entered through several passes. Curtis Channel should be used for Bundaberg and Gladstone, while Capricorn Channel is convenient for ports lying further north.

PS65 New Caledonia to Torres Strait

DIAGRAM 67	Noumea to Bramble Cay 1530 m

Best time:	May to October
Tropical storms:	December to April
Charts:	BA: 780
	US: 622
Pilots:	BA: 15, 61
	US: 126, 127, 164

After leaving Noumea a parallel course to the coast is steered to pass between the main island and the various dangers lying to the west of New Caledonia.

This route across the Coral Sea lies within the SE trade wind belt and favourable winds can be expected throughout the winter months. However, cyclones can occur in the Coral Sea during both the summer and autumn months and although in most years this passage can be made at any time after the middle of April, it is safer not to attempt it too early.

For directions on the approaches to the Torres Strait, see Route PS82.

PS66 *Vanuatu to New Caledonia*

DIAGRAM 67	Vila to Noumea 330 m

Best time:	April to November
Tropical storms:	December to March
Charts:	BA: 780
	US: 602
Pilots:	BA: 61
	US: 126

This passage is rarely made non-stop as most of those who take this route try to visit some of the southern islands of Vanuatu on the way. Permission to do this should be sought before leaving Vila. It is also possible to stop at some of New Caledonia's Loyalty Islands before continuing to Noumea via Havannah Pass. The other alternative, that of sailing west from Vila and reaching New Caledonia through Grand Passage, is not recommended because of the near certainty of encountering SE winds when sailing along the south-west coast of New Caledonia.

PS67 *Vanuatu to Torres Strait*

DIAGRAM 67	Vila to Bramble Cay 1520 m

Best time:	May to October
Tropical storms:	December to April
Charts:	BA: 780
	US: 622
Pilots:	BA: 15, 61
	US: 126, 127, 164

This is a long passage across the breadth of the Coral Sea but good winds can be expected throughout the SE trade wind season. During the winter months the SE trade winds blow strongly and consistently along this route and fast passages are accomplished, especially between July and

September. Although December to March are the months with the highest incidence of cyclones in the Coral Sea, it must be stressed that these can occur as late as June and this should be borne in mind when planning a passage across the Coral Sea.

The recommended procedure for routes passing through Torres Strait is to make a landfall on Bramble Cay, a low island with a light, lying in the eastern approaches to Torres Strait. For further directions see Route PS82.

PS68 *Vanuatu to Solomon Islands*

DIAGRAMS 65, 67	Vila to Honiara 720 m
	Santo to Honiara 560 m

Best time:	May to October
Tropical storms:	December to March
Charts:	BA: 780
	US: 604
Pilots:	BA: 60, 61
	US: 126

Having sailed through the island chain of Vanuatu, the 300 mile passage to the Solomon Islands is straightforward, especially as the winds tend to be favourable throughout the SE trade wind season. During July and August the trades blow strongly, making this a fast but rough passage. Both at the beginning and towards the end of the winter season the trades are less consistent and days with calms or W winds are more common. When approaching the Solomon Islands from SE, landfall should be made on Santa Ana Island, a small island lying close to the east of San Cristobal Island. During strong SE winds it is better to continue in the lee of San Cristobal, which offers good shelter along its north coast.

Entry formalities can be completed at the capital Honiara, on the north coast of Guadalcanal.

PS69 *Solomon Islands to Papua New Guinea*

	Honiara to Rabaul 570 m

Best time:	April to November
Tropical storms:	December to March
Charts:	BA: 780
	US: 604
Pilots:	BA: 60
	US: 126, 164

The cyclone season in the Solomon Islands coincides with the NW monsoon which affects most of Papua New Guinea but only the north-western half of the Solomons. Most boats leave the Solomons by early December, to avoid not only the approaching cyclone season, but also the headwinds that can be expected on this route during the NW monsoon. As the majority of those who sail between these two countries will have cruised along the Solomon Islands chain, the crossing to Papua New Guinea is hardly an ocean passage. The best point of departure is Korovou, on Shortland Island, where departure formalities can be completed. Bougainville Island, with its port of entry at Kieta, the nearest island in Papua New Guinea, is only a short sail away. The most popular destination however is Rabaul, on New Britain Island, 260 miles across the Solomon Sea. This well protected harbour is also a port of entry for Papua New Guinea, its main disadvantage being the fact that it lies in the proximity of an active volcano, which has erupted in the past, is expected to erupt again, and is carefully monitored by a team of volcanologists.

From April to October the winds in the Solomon Sea blow mostly from SE. During the transition period between the SE and NW monsoon, the winds are variable and there are also prolonged periods of calm. When negotiating St George's Channel between the islands of New Britain and New Ireland, attention must be paid to the currents, which set to the south during the NW monsoon and to the north during its SE equivalent.

PS70 Routes from Australia and Papua New Guinea

PS71 New South Wales to New Zealand
PS72 New South Wales to New Caledonia
PS73 New South Wales to Fiji
PS74 New South Wales to Vanuatu
PS75 Queensland to New Zealand
PS76 Queensland to New Caledonia
PS77 Queensland to Vanuatu
PS78 Queensland to Fiji
PS79 Queensland to Solomon Islands
PS80 Queensland to Papua New Guinea
PS81 Papua New Guinea to Queensland
PS82 Papua New Guinea to Torres Strait
PS83 Papua New Guinea to Indonesia

PS71 New South Wales to New Zealand

DIAGRAM 66	Sydney to Opua 1220 m

Best time:	November to March
Tropical storms:	December to March
Charts:	BA: 788
	US: 601
Pilots:	BA: 14, 51
	US: 127

This passage across the Tasman Sea can be extremely rough at times and it pays to wait for a favourable forecast before leaving. Lows across the Tasman Sea are accompanied by strong SW winds, often of gale force, and it may be worth leaving on the tail of such a gale, which will ensure several days of favourable winds. Although the proportion of W winds is higher in winter, a passage between May and September is not recommended because of the likelihood of encountering at least one severe gale. The best months for the crossing are January and February, when conditions are often settled and winds are light. Although these months coincide with the cyclone season in the South Pacific, tropical cyclones rarely find their way to these latitudes and even when they do, their force is usually spent. The Tasman Sea is affected more by extratropical cyclones, although these normally only touch its southern part and have a higher frequency in winter, another good reason to avoid a passage during that time.

The route from southern ports is direct, but a stop at Lord Howe Island might be considered by those leaving from Coffs Harbour or more northerly ports. When approaching New Zealand, the route passes to the north of the Three Kings, a group of rocky islets which should be given a wide berth. Having passed North Cape, there are several bays where shelter can be sought in rough weather, before proceeding to Opua, in the Bay of Islands, where entry formalities can be completed by calling customs and immigration from Whangarei.

From ports south of Sydney, a more direct route leads through Cook Strait to Wellington, this more southerly route having a better chance of W winds. See also directions for the reciprocal Route PS51.

PS72 New South Wales to New Caledonia

DIAGRAM 67	Sydney to Noumea 1070 m
	Coffs Harbour to Noumea 870 m

Best time:	April to June
Tropical storms:	December to March
Charts:	BA: 780
	US: 602
Pilots:	BA: 14, 15, 61
	US: 126, 127

Because of the danger posed by cyclones during the summer, this passage should not be undertaken before the end of March. There is always a higher proportion of E winds on this route, but more favourable conditions might be found during the transition period, in April and May, before the onset of the strong easterlies of winter.

The initial course should lead straight offshore to pass quickly through the current that sets strongly south along the Australian coast. As the route from southern ports in New South Wales passes close to Lord Howe Island, a stop can be made there. Most routes also pass close to Middleton and Elizabeth Reefs, which are best avoided, although it is possible to anchor there in very settled weather.

Dumbea Pass, on the SW side of New Caledonia, leads into Noumea, capital and port of entry of the territory.

PS73 New South Wales to Fiji

DIAGRAM 67	Sydney to Suva 1760 m
	Sydney to Lautoka 1710 m

Best time:	April to June
Tropical storms:	December to March
Charts:	BA: 780
	US: 602
Pilots:	BA: 14, 15, 61
	US: 126, 127

The near certainty of encountering contrary winds on the great circle route rules out a direct passage to Fiji from any port in New South Wales. The recommended route stays south of latitude 32°S until longitude 170°E is crossed from where it gradually curves NE so that the islands are approached from due south. The initial course should stay slightly north of east, which would pass well to the south of Middleton and Elizabeth Reefs and close to Norfolk Island. A stop at Norfolk can be convenient to await the easing of strong E winds.

Because a passage to Fiji should be avoided during the cyclone season, the alternative to a direct passage is to sail first to New Zealand, which can be done earlier in the year (see Route PS71), and continue to Fiji in April. This detour has the prospect of better winds on the passage to New Zealand and a better slant through the SE trades on the subsequent leg to Fiji. See also Route PS54.

PS74 New South Wales to Vanuatu

DIAGRAM 67		Sydney to Vila 1380 m
Best time:	April to June	
Tropical storms:	December to March	
Charts:	BA: 780	
	US: 602	
Pilots:	BA: 14, 15, 61	
	US: 126, 127	

Because the islands of New Caledonia straddle the direct route to Vanuatu, a stop in Noumea is almost unavoidable. The route to Vanuatu has two alternatives, either eastabout through the islands of New Caledonia, or to the west of the entire group. The first route is probably easier and directions for it are similar to those for Route PS72.

The direct route leads west of Lord Howe Island and Elizabeth and Middleton Reefs. It then closes with the south coast of New Caledonia to avoid the reefs and dangers to the west of the island. The route passes through Grand Passage north of New Caledonia from where a course can be set for Port Vila, on Efate Island, that leads clear of Petrie Reef. Great caution is necessary when navigating west and north of New Caledonia where the position of some reefs is doubtful and others have not been accurately charted.

PS75 Queensland to New Zealand

DIAGRAM 66		Brisbane to Opua 1200 m
Best time:	April-May, October–November	
Tropical storms:	December to March	
Charts:	BA: 780	
	US: 602	
Pilots:	BA: 15, 51	
	US: 127	

As a passage during the cyclone season is not recommended and one in the middle of winter has few attractions, the best time seems to be between seasons. In April or May, the danger of cyclones is much less, the weather is not yet cold and the SE trades have not reached their mid-winter strength. The passage can be just as pleasant at the end of winter, in October or November, when SW gales are also less frequent.

The route from ports north of Sandy Cape should pass well to the north of Middleton Reef. As the route passes quite close to Norfolk Island, a stop there might be considered. The route from Brisbane stays south of

Elizabeth Reef and passes close to Lord Howe Island, another convenient stop on this route.

For approaches to New Zealand see Routes PS43 and PS71.

PS76 Queensland to New Caledonia

DIAGRAM 67	Brisbane to Noumea 800 m
	Bundaberg to Noumea 820 m

Best time:	April-May, mid-September to October
Tropical storms:	December to March
Charts:	BA: 780
	US: 602
Pilots:	BA: 15, 61
	US: 126, 127

This is a difficult passage at all times because of the certainty of encountering contrary winds for at least part of the voyage, if not the whole of it. It is therefore important to try to wait for a forecast of W winds, which at least ensure a speedy start. The proportion of such winds is higher in winter, but so is that of strong easterlies, so it is better to plan this passage for the intermediate season. Because of the risk of cyclones in the Coral Sea, this passage should not be undertaken after the middle of November or before the end of March.

A direct route can be taken from ports in South Queensland but from ports north of Sandy Cape, either Capricorn or Curtis Channels should be used to reach the open sea before laying a course for Dumbea Pass, in the SW extremity of New Caledonia.

PS77 Queensland to Vanuatu

DIAGRAM 67	Brisbane to Vila 1050 m

Best time:	April-May, mid-September to October
Tropical storms:	December to March
Charts:	BA: 780
	US: 602
Pilots:	BA: 15, 61
	US: 126, 127

Prevailing easterly winds, contrary currents and the many dangers dotted about the southern part of the Coral Sea make this one of the most difficult routes in the South Pacific. From Northern Queensland a direct passage should not even be considered, one alternative being a detour to the south, inside the Great Barrier Reef. Having reached the open sea via the

Capricorn Channel, the route joins that from ports south of Sandy Cape. The route runs south of Cato Island and Bellona Reef and joins Route PS74, if a non-stop passage to Vanuatu is intended. Another alternative is to follow directions for Route PS76 to Noumea and reach Vanuatu by way of the islands of New Caledonia. Such an approach has certain attractions as it avoids the dangerous reefs to the west and north of New Caledonia and offers the possibility of breaking up the voyage in some of the islands of New Caledonia or Southern Vanuatu, if the winds prove too much to cope with.

PS78 Queensland to Fiji

DIAGRAM 67		Brisbane to Suva 1540 m
Best time:	April to June	
Tropical storms:	December to March	
Charts:	BA: 780	
	US: 602	
Pilots:	BA: 15, 61	
	US: 126, 127	

The only feasible way to reach Fiji is by a detour to the south where with luck better winds might be found to make the required easting. Although the recommended practice is to sail south of latitude 32°S, where the chances of finding favourable winds are higher, a slightly more northerly route can be taken should the winds permit this. Ideally one should not set off before a forecast of westerly winds has been obtained. Even with favourable winds, the route should remain close to the latitude of Norfolk Island until past that island. If consistent headwinds are met while in the vicinity of Norfolk, a stop can be made there. It must be stressed, however, that on no account should a detour via New Caldeonia be considered because of the certainty of encountering contrary winds between there and Fiji. From Norfolk Island the route starts curving NE, although this should not be done too soon but only after longitude 170°E has been crossed. See also Routes PS54 and PS73.

PS79 Queensland to Solomon Islands

DIAGRAM 67		Townsville to Honiara 1000 m
		Brisbane to Honiara 1200 m
Best time:	April to October	
Tropical storms:	December to March	
Charts:	BA: 780	
	US: 602, 604	
Pilots:	BA: 15, 60	
	US: 126, 127	

Although this passage can be made at any time outside the cyclone season, the months of July and August also ought to be avoided as it is the time when the SE trades attain their peak. Because of the numerous reefs that have to be avoided in the Coral Sea, there are various routes that leave from the Australian coast. Boats leaving from ports south of Sandy Cape should take the outer route, passing to the east of Cato Island, Wreck and Kenn Reefs. A direct course for the Solomon Islands can be set after Bampton Reef has been safely left to starboard. Boats leaving from ports lying further north should use the Capricorn Channel and then turn NNE, leaving Saumarez and Frederick Reefs to port and Wreck and Kenn Reefs to starboard before gaining the open sea. If setting off from Townsville, there are several passes through which to reach the open sea, either Palm, Magnetic or Flinders Passage. Depending on the direction of the wind outside, it is possible to pass either north or south of Lihou Reef to join the other routes to the Solomons.

PS80 Queensland to Papua New Guinea

DIAGRAM 67	Cairns to Port Moresby 500 m
	Gladstone to Samarai 800 m

Best time:	April to October
Tropical storms:	December to March
Charts:	BA: 780
	US: 604
Pilots:	BA: 15, 60
	US: 127, 164

There are two main routes crossing the Coral Sea from Queensland to Papua New Guinea, one that goes direct to the capital Port Moresby, the other to Samarai, a small island off the SE extremity of New Guinea. The latter route (PS80A) is taken by those who wish to cruise in the outer islands before heading for Port Moresby and beyond. Because Port Moresby is downwind of all destinations, it is a mistake to go there first as it can be very tough sailing against the boisterous SE trades to reach the smaller islands east of New Guinea.

For the direct passage to Port Moresby it is better to stay inside the Great Barrier Reef until almost due south of Port Moresby, Cook's Passage, NE of Cooktown, probably being the easiest way to reach the open sea (PS80B). Unfortunately Cairns is the last port in Northern Queensland where exit formalities can be completed and although it is allowed to day sail inside the Barrier Reef after having cleared out, landing either along the coast or on one of the offlying islands is not permitted.

The alternative route to Samarai (PS80A) can leave the Barrier Reef by a multitude of passes, Grafton Passage just outside Cairns being one of the best. Although most boats leave for Papua New Guinea after having cruised inside the Barrier Reef almost to its northern extremity, for those who have less time and prefer an offshore passage, leaving from one of the more southern ports in Queensland has certain attractions. Because of the direction of the prevailing SE trades, the more northerly the starting point of the passage, the closer the wind. As winter passages across the Coral Sea can be quite rough, this is an aspect that is worth considering when planning this route. The strong trades coupled with the west setting current make it necessary to do some easting whenever the winds permit this. If the destination is Samarai, Bruner Island, off South Cape on the Papuan coast, makes a convenient landfall as it has a light.

PS81 Papua New Guinea to Queensland

DIAGRAM 67	Port Moresby to Cairns 500 m
	Samarai to Cairns 510 m

Best time:	April to November
Tropical storms:	December to March
Charts:	BA: 780
	US: 604
Pilots:	BA: 15, 60
	US: 127, 164

The attraction of a sheltered sail in smooth waters tempts most people to go behind the Great Barrier Reef as soon as they have the Coral Sea behind them. If coming from Port Moresby, the choice is vast as there are many passes that lead through the reef, from Flinders Entrance in the north to Cook's Pass in the south, a distance of some 250 miles. Coming from other parts of Papua New Guinea, probably the most convenient pass is Grafton Passage that leads into Cairns, the nearest port of entry in Northern Queensland. Thursday Island, in Torres Strait, is also a port of entry, but only a few boats take this roundabout way from Port Moresby to Queensland.

Coming south from Samarai, the light on Bougainville Reef makes an excellent landfall. Because of the west setting current and the many reefs lying to leeward, navigation in the Coral Sea must be very accurate and finding the passes through the Great Barrier Reef is often difficult.

The winds in the Coral Sea blow mostly from the E or SE between April and October so that a more easterly departure point in Papua New Guinea normally ensures a better slant across the trades. Between May and September, the trades can become very strong at times, but during the transitional months they are often light and the weather can be squally. NW winds predominate in summer, which is also the cyclone season.

PS82 Papua New Guinea to Torres Strait

| DIAGRAM 67 | Port Moresby to Thursday Island 350 m |
| | Thursday Island to Darwin 700 m |

Best time:	April to October
Tropical storms:	December to March
Charts:	BA: 780
	US: 603
Pilots:	BA: 15, 60
	US: 164

The logical port of departure for this passage is Port Moresby. Because of the various difficulties associated with navigation through the Torres Strait it is essential to carefully plan the time of arrival in the eastern approaches to the strait so as to minimise the risk of passing close to some of the reefs at night. The first danger en route is Portlock Reef, at a distance of 130 miles from Port Moresby. Goldie Reef is 20 miles NNW of Portlock. Ideally one should try to arrive off Portlock Reef in late afternoon, so as to pass between it and Goldie Reef during daylight. The next point to make for is Bramble Cay, lying some 65 miles further west. The distance between Portlock and Bramble Cay can be covered during the hours of darkness and as there is a light with 14 miles visibility on Bramble Cay, this should be sighted before dawn. Such a timing would mean that Bramble Cay is passed in the early morning and that some of the other reefs and islets will also be negotiated in daylight. From Bramble Cay the route enters North East Channel. This well marked channel runs in a SW direction for some 130 miles to the Prince of Wales Channel that finally opens into the Arafura Sea.

Although navigation through this reef-strewn area is not difficult after landfall on Bramble Cay, it is easier to sail in daylight and spend the nights at anchor behind one of the many cays. It must be pointed out, however, that landing on any of the islands is not allowed, as these belong to Australia and legally one should clear in first at Thursday Island.

The winds on this passage are predominantly easterly and between June and August they are often strong. The currents running through the strait have a westerly set at the height of the SE trades, but their rates are unpredictable. The currents are also tidal and in the straits themselves they run WSW on the flood and NE on the ebb. The strongest sets have been recorded in the Prince of Wales Channel, where 5 and 6 knot currents are the order of the day. Another hazard in the eastern approaches is the shallow water that extends far offshore so that the depth sounder cannot give a reliable indication of the actual position. Yet another cause of confusion are the murky waters met far offshore caused by a muddy discharge from the Fly River. The colour of the water gives no indication of its depth.

PS83 New Guinea to Indonesia

DIAGRAM 67	Madang to Jayapura 360 m

Best time:	May to September
Tropical storms:	None
Charts:	BA: 780
	US: 603
Pilots:	BA: 35, 60
	US: 164

The difficulties associated with the passage through the Torres Strait and the long detour to Port Moresby persuade some people to reach Indonesia by sailing along the north coast of New Guinea. This route also gives the opportunity to visit the Hermit and Ninigo Islands before clearing out of Papua New Guinea at Vanimo.

This is a passage that can be done only during the SE trade wind season, as during the NW monsoon, from November to March, both winds and current are contrary. The transitional period is difficult to define, as in some years the NW monsoon comes early, while in others the SE trades do not establish themselves until May. Normally this passage should not be attempted after the middle of November or before the middle of April. Although the weather along this route is governed by the two monsoons, the winds are rarely steady in direction or strength and there are many days when they are light or nonexistent. Calms are particularly frequent during the transitional period. The most constant SE winds usually occur in July and August when there is also a very strong NW setting current, with rates that can exceed 2 knots.

Jayapura, the capital of the Indonesian province of Irian Jaya (Western Irian), is the official port of entry. Yachts without a cruising permit (see Chapter 27) should enquire at the Indonesian Embassy in Port Moresby whether they would be allowed to make an emergency stop in Jayapura before committing themselves to this route.

18 Winds and currents of the North Indian Ocean

Map 2 to 6

The winds and weather of the entire Indian Ocean are dominated by the monsoons which, although affecting primarily the northern half of the ocean, also have a bearing on the weather pattern of the tropical South Indian Ocean. North easterly winds prevail when the sun has a southern declination and south westerlies when the sun's declination is north.

North-east monsoon

A predominantly NE wind blows during the winter months in the North Indian Ocean, Bay of Bengal and the Arabian Sea. The wind is very steady and constant over most parts of the North Indian Ocean, blowing with an average 10–15 knots, its strength diminishing towards the equator. On rare occasions the monsoon can reach gale force, but for most of the time sailing conditions can be described as near as perfect as possible. There are two areas in which the monsoon is less reliable and the winds more variable. In the Arabian Sea, north of latitude 20°N, the weather pattern is sometimes affected by the passage of depressions to the north of the area. The other area lies to the south east of Sri Lanka, between latitude 5°N and the equator, where winds are less constant in strength and direction, the normal direction of the wind being northerly. Further east, in the Malacca Straits, the monsoon is also less pronounced than elsewhere.

The NE monsoon lasts from November to March, beginning earlier in the northern part of the region where it is well established by the middle of November. Towards the equator it does not arrive in full strength until December.

The winter monsoon is preceded and followed by a transitional period as it is replaced by the SW monsoon and vice versa. This transitional period coincides with the movement across the region of the Intertropical Convergence Zone which separates the air masses of the northern and southern hemispheres. The ITCZ is most active in April–May and October–November, which are also the months when most cyclonic storms occur over the North Indian Ocean. During this transitional period the weather is often squally and the winds can reach gale force in these squalls.

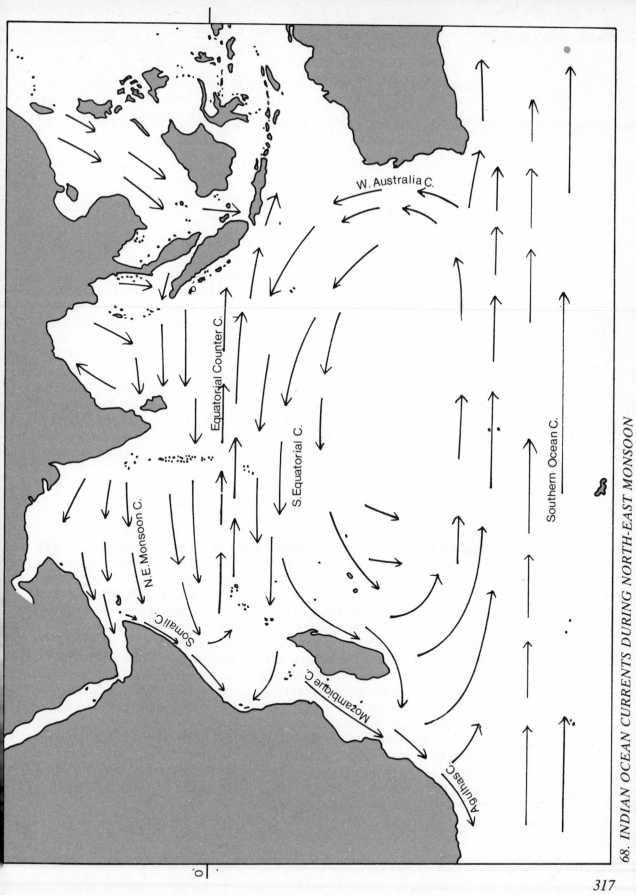

68. INDIAN OCEAN CURRENTS DURING NORTH-EAST MONSOON

W. Australia C.

Equatorial Counter C.

S. Equatorial C.

Southern Ocean C.

N.E. Monsoon C.

Somali C.

Mozambique C.

Aguilhas C.

Otherwise this period can be compared to the doldrums of other oceans, with light winds and calms, which are gradually replaced by the oncoming monsoon. This doldrum belt separating the winds is not so distinctly defined as in the Atlantic and Pacific Oceans.

South-west monsoon

The heating of the Asian land mass during the summer months creates a large area of low pressure over the NW part of the Indian subcontinent. This causes the SE trade wind of the South Indian Ocean to be drawn across the equator, where it joins the general movement of air that flows in an anti-clockwise direction around the area of low pressure lying over India. This is the SW monsoon which is felt from June to September in the same areas as its NE counterpart. The SW monsoon is a consistent wind blowing at an average 20 knots for long periods and frequently reaching gale force. An area lying about 200 miles to the east of Socotra Island is reputed to be the windiest spot in the Indian Ocean, with a frequency of gales in July similar to that of Cape Horn in summer!

The winds gradually diminish in strength during August and by September both the strength of the wind and its direction become less constant. There follows a period of about two months, in October and November, when the winds are often light until the arrival of the NE monsoon. The weather during the SW monsoon is overcast and often unsettled with heavy rainfall.

Tropical storms

Tropical storms or cyclones occur in the Arabian Sea and the Bay of Bengal. The two periods of the year when their frequency reaches a maximum coincide with the transitional period between the two monsoons. The first period of cyclonic activity is at the beginning of the SW monsoon from late May to the middle of June. The second period coincides with the onset of the NE monsoon and lasts from the end of October to the second half of November. Most of these storms form in the vicinity of the ITCZ when it is situated between latitudes 5°N and 15°N.

Most of the storms that occur in May and June are bred in the Arabian Sea from where they move either in a NW and W direction, or in a N direction, recurving towards the NE and the coast. Some of the cyclones that form in October and November in the Bay of Bengal move westward across South India into the Arabian Sea. Both in the Arabian Sea and Bay of Bengal, October has the highest frequency of cyclones. Their frequency decreases in November and they are rare in December and January, none having been recorded in February and March. After the middle of April the likelihood of a cyclone begins to increase.

Currents

The currents of the North Indian Ocean follow a seasonal pattern because of the monsoons, and reverse their direction under their influence. The North-east Monsoon Current occurs during the NE monsoon and reaches its peak in February. It is located between the equator and latitude 6°N and has a westward set (Diagram 68). Its counterpart is the South-west Monsoon Current which occurs from May to September and can be considered to be a continuation of the Somali Current (Diagram 71). This current can attain very high rates, especially off the coast of Somalia and in the vicinity of Socotra, where some of the strongest sets in the world have been recorded, with rates of up to 7 knots. Although the initial set is NE, the current becomes E in the open waters of the Arabian Sea until it hits the land mass of India and turns SE.

At the time of the NE monsoon, the Somali Current flows SW along the African coast as far as the equator where it meets the north flowing East Africa Coast Current. In December and January, the current turns E and becomes the Equatorial Countercurrent.

The Equatorial Countercurrent is the only current of the North Indian Ocean which does not reverse its direction as a result of the monsoons. However, its strength is reinforced during the transitional periods between the two monsoons in April–May and October–November. It sets E throughout the year and lies to the north of the west setting Equatorial Current. The Equatorial Countercurrent reaches its southern limit in February, at the height of the NE monsoon, when it sometimes flows very close to the North-east Monsoon Current. This means that by moving slightly to the north or south, it would be possible to shift from a west setting to an east setting current. The southern limit of the Countercurrent is always south of the equator, regardless of season.

19 Regional weather of the North Indian Ocean

Singapore

Being so close to the equator, Singapore has a hot and humid climate, which varies little throughout the year, 27°C being the average temperature. Calms and light winds occur throughout the year. The NE monsoon begins in November, although the NE winds are deflected and appear at the beginning of this period as a NW monsoon. By January NE winds are established but they do not blow as strongly and steadily as over the China Sea. Heavy monsoon downpours of rain occur in this season from November until February. From April onwards the SE trade winds penetrate from south of the equator, often having a southerly component. Singapore can be affected from April to November by the *sumatras*, thundery storms with strong winds, which blow across from Sumatra and last for several hours.

Malacca Straits and Malaysian west coast

Although within the monsoon areas of the Indian Ocean, the high island of Sumatra and the mountains of the Malay Peninsula block the effect of both the NE and SW monsoons. The weather in the Malacca Straits is highly influenced by local conditions, and variable winds with regular land and sea breezes occur at all times of the year. The daily changes are often more pronounced than the seasonal, which introduces a monotonous element to the hot, humid conditions that prevail all year round. There is no real dry season, but abundant rain at all times with an almost daily routine of thundery squalls.

January to March normally see the best weather, fewer squalls and less rain as the NE monsoon penetrates into the area. Even in this season it is possible to get NW or W winds for some days. March and April are variable and the SW monsoon starts early in May, being strongest in July and August. The SW winds are strongest in the northern portions of the Malacca Straits, variable from SE to SW with calms in the centre and more SE in southern areas towards Singapore.

Sea and land breezes occur on either coast and up to 20 miles offshore. The sea breeze begins about mid-morning and reaches a maximum in the afternoon, dying away at sunset. The strength of the breeze depends on whether it combines with the prevailing monsoon, when it can reach 20 knots, or whether it opposes it, when it remains light and variable. Conditions vary greatly from place to place. On the Malayan coast the night land breeze can be very strong, starting in the evening and sometimes blowing hard all night.

The frequency of thunderstorms is high throughout the region and the year, with Sumatra being one of the most thundery areas in the world. Thunderstorms with lightning, torrential rain and winds of up to 50 knots plague the southern portions of the Malacca Straits particularly, and are called *sumatras*. *Sumatras* are commonest between April and November, usually developing at night and lasting 1-4 hours. The wind is SW to NW with an average of 20-30 knots and in June and August they occur every few days. Similar SW squalls also occur during the SW monsoon in the northern portion of the straits, although these squalls can occur at any time of the day or night and tend to last longer. NW squalls occur at the changeover to the NE monsoon, which is the season of least squalls.

Thailand

The SW monsoon blows more steadily and strongly on the west coast of Thailand than in the Malacca Straits, lacking the shielding effect of the large island of Sumatra. SW winds dominate from May to September with their maximum steadiness in July and August. On the other hand the high land mass of Thailand shelters this coast from the NE monsoon, which tends to have a more northerly component than elsewhere. Very rarely, about once every 50 years, tropical storms track out of the Bay of Bengal and over the Gulf of Thailand.

Bay of Bengal

This area of the Indian Ocean has very typical monsoon weather. The NE monsoon begins in October in northern areas and is established only in November further south. It blows steadily with fine dry weather until April, when the weather becomes hot, still and oppressive over the whole Bay. The SW monsoon only establishes itself around the middle of June, but quickly becomes strong, around 20–25 knots, and blows steadily until August when it starts to decrease, disappearing in October.

Cyclones are more numerous in the Bay of Bengal than in any other area of the Indian Ocean, although they are sometimes shorter and less severe. They can occur from April through to December, but are most frequent in July and October at the change of monsoons.

Sri Lanka

From ancient cities two thousand years old to modern beach resorts of golden sands, Sri Lanka has much to offer the visitor. An equable climate with a temperature deviating little from around 27°C, the two monsoons of the North Indian Ocean dictate the seasons. In neither monsoon are winds as strong as in the Arabian Sea and they vary from coast to coast, the west coast being more sheltered from the NE monsoon, the east coast more sheltered from the SW.

The NE monsoon only sets in at the end of November or even in December, arriving with squally weather and rain. The light to moderate N to ENE winds prevail with fine dry weather until March or April. Heavy rain and stronger winds occur on the more exposed NE coast.

The SW monsoon is longer here than elsewhere, beginning in May and lasting right through until December. The SW monsoon often commences with a 'monsoon burst', a blast of east wind that arrives with rain, thunder and lightning after a week of large clouds and vivid lightning which disappear after sunset. After a few hours of this 'burst', the wind veers to the SW and the monsoon settles in. The SW winds are fairly constant in direction, usually strengthening to 20–30 knots by mid-morning and slackening off in the late afternoon, dropping to around 10 knots during the night. Heavy rain occurs on the SW coast from May to September, although some rain does occur in all months, especially in coastal areas. The south coasts are very affected by heavy swell during the SW monsoon.

Sea and land breezes do blow in coastal areas, their direction depending on the coastal alignment. They are not so pronounced during the SW monsoon.

Although rarely hit by cyclones originating in the Arabian Sea which move to the NW, those which originate in the Bay of Bengal can strike Sri Lanka, most frequently in November and December.

Arabian Sea

It is the seasonal winds of this sea which gave rise to the word 'monsoon' and so it is not surprising that both the NE and SW monsoons blow with strength over this sea. The NE monsoon begins in April and is the time of fair weather. Especially in northern areas it can be more N than NE and even NW, being a very dry wind, as it blows off the continent of Asia. At an average 10–15 knots at the beginning of the season, the winds increase to 15–20 knots in December, but can be stronger still, especially in the north. Temperatures are lower in January and February, the cool season, and increase from March to May, which is the hot season.

The wet season with heavy rains coincides with the SW monsoon, which commences in May in the south and spreads over the whole area by June. There is usually squally weather at the monsoon changeover. On the Indian coast it arrives with a sudden burst of wind from the east, heavy rain and thunder for several hours before the SW winds take over. This burst of the monsoon is preceded by a week of vivid lightning which disappears every day when the sun sets.

The SW winds in the Arabian Sea are very strong and can blow at 30 knots for several days. There is a high frequency of gales, especially near the island of Socotra and during the month of July. In September the winds start weakening and the monsoon breaks up and disappears by October.

Cyclones occur at two periods of the year which coincide with the changeover in monsoon. April to July is one period with the highest frequency in June, while October has the highest frequency in the other period, although cyclones can occur from September through until December. Most cyclones curve NW to strike the shores of the Arabian Peninsula or else tend to recurve to the NE towards India and Pakistan.

Gulf of Aden

This is a hot and arid region, whose coasts are low lying semi deserts. Neither of the monsoons blows as strongly in the Gulf as they do in the Arabian Sea. The NE monsoon lasts from October to April, although the winds are diverted to blow more easterly into the Gulf, turning to blow SE and S through the Bab el Mandeb Straits into the Red Sea. In January and February these easterlies are at their strongest, at 15–20 knots. In May they are more variable, although still mainly easterly but lighter in force.

From June until August the SW monsoon takes over, blowing most strongly in July. The SW winds are very strong, up to 30 knots near the entrance to the Gulf from the Arabian Sea, decreasing to much less at the Aden end. September usually has light variable winds. During the SW monsoon in June, July and August a strong local land breeze called the *Kharif* blows for up to 30 miles off the African coast. Reinforcing the SW wind, it can reach gale force during the night and is very dry, full of dust and sand off Africa. In a similar fashion a strong N or NW wind called the *Belat* blows off the Arabian coast from December to March. Again it starts at night, is full of dust and sand, and can reach 30 knots in some coastal areas. There is sometimes poor visibility due to haze or mist, especially along the Arabian coast during the SW monsoon. From time to time there are dust storms.

Very rarely cyclones do stray into the Gulf from the Arabian Sea in June or October with little warning.

Maldives

This collection of small atolls and coral reefs strung across the equator are rarely more than six feet high, which makes them difficult to see, coconut

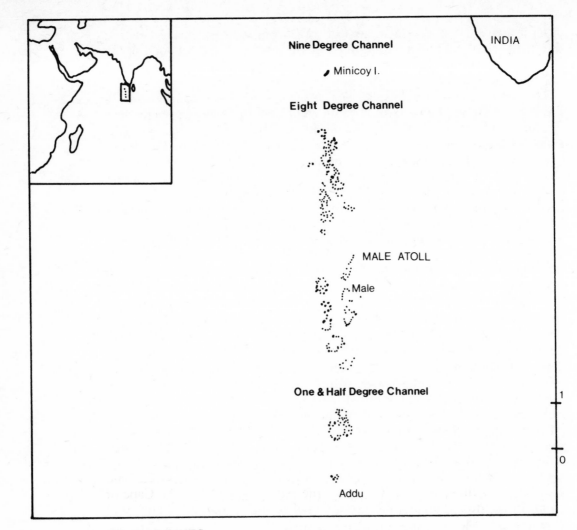

69. MALDIVES

palms rising out of the water being the usual indication that land is there. The winds over this area are much lighter, being on the edge of the monsoon belt. The NE monsoon starts later than elsewhere, in December, and blows until March when it becomes unsteady. This is a mild, dry season.

March to May are hot and dry, the weather becoming very hot and humid before the SW monsoon breaks. From May to October the SW wind blows and thunderstorms, rain and squalls occur during this season, the wind in the squalls sometimes reaching 40 knots.

In the southern areas of the group close to or below the equator, the winds are much more variable even at the height of the monsoon. Here the winds tend to be more N during the NE monsoon and more S or SE during the SW monsoon.

20 Routes in the North Indian Ocean

Compared to the other two great oceans of the world, the Indian Ocean is crisscrossed by a relatively small number of cruising routes. One reason for this is the smaller number of sailing boats that spend any length of time cruising as opposed to crossing this ocean as part of a world voyage. The routes are governed by the predictability of the weather, the seasons being much better defined than anywhere else. The regularity of the monsoons was recognised by early navigators who knew how to take full advantage of the seasonal wind patterns. Because of this regularity it is very easy to plan a voyage well in advance so as to make a particular passage at the optimum time. This applies both to the northern half of the ocean, which is dominated by the NE and SW monsoons, and to its southern half which is under the influence of the SE trade winds.

There are two major routes crossing the Indian Ocean and most people have already made up their minds which one they are likely to follow by the time they have passed through the Torres Strait. For those who wish to cruise in the Mediterranean or intend to reach southern Europe by the shortest route, the logical way leads through the North Indian Ocean and Red Sea. For those who wish to reach the Atlantic by way of the Cape of Good Hope there is no alternative but to sail across the South Indian Ocean to South Africa.

The favourable season for a passage across the North Indian Ocean is during the NE monsoon, when optimum sailing conditions can be expected. Although this season lasts from December to March, passages made in January and February also have the advantage that the Mediterranean is reached after the coldest weather is over and the cruising season is beginning.

For those who plan to take the southern route, there are more factors to be taken into account at the planning stages. The most important factor is to make the passage around the Cape of Good Hope at the most favourable time, which is during the summer months, from January to March. Such a timing means that the crossing of the South Indian Ocean takes place during the safe season, when no cyclones can be expected south of the equator. The cyclone season in the South Indian Ocean lasts from November to March and passages during this time should be avoided. Although cyclones

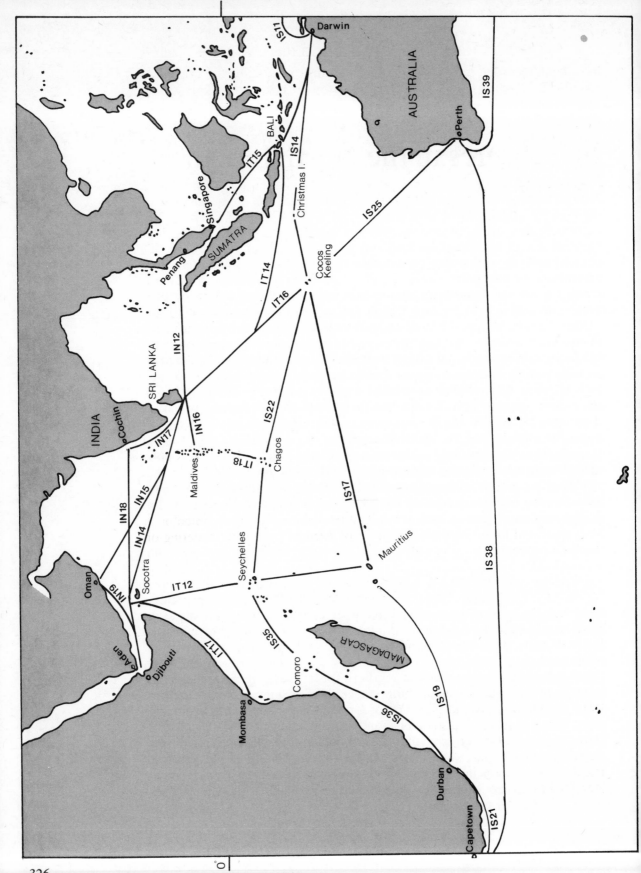

have been recorded in the past in other months too, notably the cyclone of July 1871, which originated south of Sumatra, it is generally agreed that May to October is a perfectly safe time to cross the South Indian Ocean. Because of the conveniently placed islands on the way, most boats that take this route do it in stages by calling at Christmas Island, Cocos Keeling, Mauritius, Reunion and finally Durban. If more time is available a worthwhile detour can be made to the Chagos Archipelago.

A note of warning has to be mentioned regarding the leg around South Africa. Several circumnavigators have encountered the worst weather of their entire voyage along this route where a sudden SW gale can create extremely dangerous conditions when it hits the south flowing Agulhas Current. Every year boats are knocked down, pooped and even lost on this stretch, so it is well worth considering the alternatives before becoming committed to this route.

Most other routes in the Indian Ocean are variations of the above two. For boats sailing in the North Indian Ocean, the harbour of Galle in Sri Lanka is a favourite port of call which does not seem to have been affected by internal troubles in that country. Most boats arrive in Galle from Malaysia and Singapore, although the difficulty in obtaining the Indonesian cruising permit and reports about attacks on yachts in the South China Sea and Malacca Straits have persuaded some people to avoid these areas altogether and sail to Sri Lanka directly from Bali or Christmas Island.

In spite of India's many attractions, most cruising boats continue to bypass this great country, mostly because of the complicated and lengthy formalities to which visiting yachts are submitted by the Indian officials. For similar reasons, few boats venture into any of the Gulf states.

The island groups scattered across the centre of the Indian Ocean attract an increasing number of cruising boats every year. Similarly, more boats are visiting the east coast of Africa, cruising boats being now welcomed or at least tolerated in an increasing number of African countries bordering on the Indian Ocean.

IN10 Routes in the North Indian Ocean

IN11 Singapore to Western Malaysia
IN12 Malaysia to Sri Lanka
IN13 Western Malaysia to Thailand
IN14 Sri Lanka to Red Sea
IN15 Sri Lanka to Oman
IN16 Sri Lanka to Maldives
IN17 Sri Lanka to India
IN18 India to Red Sea
IN19 Oman to Red Sea
IN20 Red Sea to Sri Lanka
IN21 Red Sea to Maldives
IN22 Sri Lanka to Singapore
IN23 Thailand to Singapore

IN11 Singapore to Western Malaysia

| DIAGRAM 70 | Singapore to Port Kelang 180 m |
| | Singapore to Penang 330m |

Best time:	November to April
Tropical storms:	None
Charts:	BA: 4706
	US: 706
Pilots:	BA: 44
	US: 174

There are several ports between Malacca and Penang that can be visited by northbound boats from Singapore. Entry formalities for Malaysia can be completed at Malacca, where it is possible to come alongside other boats moored on the banks of the river.

Although a passage through Malacca Strait can be undertaken throughout the year, the most settled weather is during the NE monsoon, when the frequency of squalls is much lower than during the opposite season. The notorious *sumatras* are more frequent during the SW monsoon and because they are accompanied by heavy rain and gale force winds, they can make navigation difficult, the situation being also complicated by the large amount of shipping.

Another feature of navigation in the Malacca Strait are the strong tidal currents which, combined with the normally light winds, make it more convenient to anchor between tides. This can be done easily as there are anchoring depths all along the sides of the straits and there are sufficient protected places in which to stop for a few hours. The Malaysian side is preferable if this passage is done in shorter stages. Light winds and calms are more frequent during the day, so it is better to sail at night when breezes are steadier and the weather is generally more pleasant. One hazard, however, that is almost impossible to avoid at night are the numerous fish traps that line the two sides of the straits, so it is a good idea to keep out of shallow water during the hours of darkness.

IN12 Malaysia to Sri Lanka

| DIAGRAM 70 | Lumut to Galle 1260 m |
| | Penang to Galle 1200 m |

Best time:	January to March
Tropical storms:	May to December
Charts:	BA: 4706
	US: 706
Pilots:	BA: 44, 38
	US: 173, 174

During the NE monsoon it is preferable to remain on the Malaysian side of Malacca Strait until the north of Sumatra can be fetched on the starboard tack. On leaving the Malacca Strait the route passes between Rondo and Great Nicobar Islands. It is possible to call at Sabang, a small port on the island of Wé, off the northern coast of Sumatra, where yachts are normally allowed to stop briefly even if they are not in possession of an Indonesian cruising permit.

The best passages along this route are made between January and March, when the NE monsoon blows consistently over the North Indian Ocean. The passage should not be undertaken too early, before the monsoon has had time to establish itself, as steady winds can rarely be relied upon before the middle of December. A start from Singapore or Malaysia in early January has the best chance of excellent winds both on the leg to Sri Lanka and on to the Red Sea. Much less favourable conditions will be encountered during the changeover period, in April and October–November, when westerly winds are quite common and there is a higher risk of cyclones in the Bay of Bengal.

This passage is not recommended during the SW monsoon, on account of both the contrary winds and the danger of cyclones in the Bay of Bengal. Although boats have tried to reach Sri Lanka by sailing on a southerly course after passing the northern extremity of Sumatra in the hope of making their westing south of the equator, this is an extremely difficult passage and should be avoided if at all possible. A more logical alternative is to reach the Indian Ocean from Singapore via Sunda Strait and then follow directions for Route IT14.

Because of its convenient situation and good facilities, the port of Galle on the south coast of Sri Lanka is highly recommended for yachts in transit.

IN13 Western Malaysia to Thailand

Penang to Phuket 200 m

Best time:	December to April
Tropical storms:	July
Charts:	BA: 4706
	US: 706
Pilots:	BA: 21, 44
	US: 173, 174

The best season for this route is during the NE monsoon, when the weather is most settled, although winds for a northbound passage are not always favourable. The main cruising attraction on Thailand's west coast is Phuket and the surrounding area. Northbound boats from Penang usually call at Langkawi, a picturesque group of islands close to the Thai border. From Langkawi the route passes east of the Butang group close to the west of Tanga Island. The route runs in a NW direction past several offlying islets and rocks to Phuket harbour.

Some cases of attacks on cruising boats have been reported in this border area. However, it would appear that the main target of the Thai pirates are Malay fishing boats with whom they have a long running feud, and visiting yachts have been caught up inadvertently in this local rivalry.

IN14 Sri Lanka to Red Sea

DIAGRAM 70		Galle to Aden 2130 m
		Galle to Djibouti 2240 m

Best time:	January to March
Tropical storms:	April–May, October–November
Charts:	BA: 4703, 4706
	US: 703, 706
Pilots:	BA: 38, 64
	US: 172, 173

At the height of the NE monsoon, when the average wind strength is between 10 and 15 knots, this passage can be truly delightful. There is also a favourable current and the frequency of gales in the North Indian Ocean is nil. The only problem to worry about is the large amount of shipping, either converging into the Gulf of Aden, or crossing to and from the Persian Gulf.

After leaving either Galle or Colombo, a course should be steered to pass through the Eight Degree Channel, between Ihavandiffulu, the north-ernmost atoll in the Maldive Archipelago, and Minicoy Island. The course leads from there to a point north of Socotra Island which should be avoided due to the apparent unfriendliness of its inhabitants. After the middle of March it may be necessary to pass south of Socotra and between it and the African coast, if SW winds are experienced near the island. From Socotra a direct course can be steered for either Aden or Djibouti.

This passage is not normally undertaken against the SW monsoon and it should not even be considered. The only alternative during the SW monsoon is to cross the equator and make one's westing with the help of the SE trades, possibly south of the Chagos Archipelago, before recrossing the equator. As this route passes NE of the Seychelles, directions are similar to those for Route IT12.

IN15 Sri Lanka to Oman

DIAGRAM 70	Galle to Raysut 1680 m

Best time:	January to March
Tropical storms:	May–June, October–November
Charts:	BA: 4705, 4706
	US: 705, 706
Pilots:	BA: 38, 64
	US: 172, 173

Although the Sultanate of Oman does not encourage tourism, cruising boats that make the detour to stop there are treated courteously, even if they are only allowed to stop in Raysut. The course after leaving Sri Lanka leads through the Nine Degree Channel, where a short stop is possible at Sueli Par, the atoll on the north side of the channel. The weather during the NE monsoon is very pleasant and the passage from Sri Lanka usually enjoys excellent winds. The passage should not be made before the end of the year, to allow the monsoon to establish itself.

IN16 Sri Lanka to Maldives

DIAGRAM 70	Galle to Male 420 m

Best time:	January to March
Tropical storms:	None
Charts:	BA: 2898
	US: 707
Pilots:	BA: 38
	US: 173

Tropical storms very rarely touch the Northern Maldives and the danger of encountering a cyclone along this route is remote. The passage is best made during the NE monsoon when winds are mostly favourable. Contrary winds and a strong east setting current are the order of the day for a passage during the SW monsoon and even during the transitional months the winds are often westerly. If heading straight for the capital Male, landfall should be made on Mirufenfushi and Diffushi, two low islets marking the easternmost point of North Male Atoll.

The Maldives should be approached with great caution, both because they are all low lying islands and because of the strong unpredictable currents which sweep through them.

IN17 Sri Lanka to India

DIAGRAM 70	Galle to Cochin 350 m

Best time:	December to February
Tropical storms:	May–June, October–November
Charts:	BA: 4706
	US: 706
Pilots:	BA: 38
	US: 173

Mainly because of considerable bureaucratic hurdles, only a small number of yachts cruise in India. Although the NE monsoon has more settled weather, the high proportion of NW winds make it difficult to reach most ports on the west coast of the Indian subcontinent during this monsoon. Coastal navigation is made somewhat easier between December and February by alternating land and sea breezes which make it possible to take long tacks along the coast. When sailing along the coast at night it is almost impossible to avoid the numerous fishing nets and boats without lights that are a permanent feature of this coast. It is better to stay a few miles offshore during the hours of darkness.

The northbound passage is not easier during the SW monsoon when the weather is often unsettled. One alternative is to reach NW India towards the end of the SW monsoon, in September, and sail down the coast with the help of the NW winds and south going current that occur at the change of seasons.

During the NE monsoon few boats venture further north than Cochin, where it is possible to leave the boat under guard and travel inland.

IN18 India to Red Sea

DIAGRAM 70	Cochin to Aden 1850 m
Best time:	December to February
Tropical storms:	May–June, October–November
Charts:	BA: 4705
	US: 705
Pilots:	BA: 38, 64
	US: 172, 173

A direct route to the Red Sea can be taken from anywhere on the west coast of India at the height of the NE monsoon, from December to the beginning of March. After the middle of March the winds are less constant and there is a higher percentage of calms in the Arabian Sea. During March it is better to set a course that would pass to the south of Socotra Island, where SW winds can be expected. Towards the end of the NE monsoon choosing the best route becomes even more crucial as there is an increased chance of contrary winds close to Socotra Island. In April it is advisable to steer for a point 50 miles south of Socotra so as to clear Ras Asir on the next tack as the current is also setting north towards Socotra at this time.

The direct passage is virtually impossible during the SW monsoon, from May to September, when the only alternative is to make a long detour south of the equator via the Chagos Archipelago. This route passes NE of the Seychelles and recrosses the equator in about longitude 53°E. See also Route IT12.

IN19 Oman to Red Sea

DIAGRAM 70	Raysut to Aden 600 m
	Raysut to Djibouti 720 m

Best time:	January to March
Tropical storms:	May–June, October–November
Charts:	BA: 4705
	US: 705
Pilots:	BA: 64
	US: 172

Excellent sailing conditions prevail during the NE monsoon, January and February being the best months to head for the Red Sea. Because of a higher percentage of calms near land, the initial course from Raysut should lead offshore. The proportion of SW winds increases towards the end of March when a contrary current also starts making itself felt parallel to the coast. The passage should not be undertaken during the SW monsoon, when strong headwinds make it almost impossible to reach the Red Sea along this route. During the transitional period between monsoons, the area is subject to tropical storms.

IN20 Red Sea to Sri Lanka

DIAGRAM 77	Aden to Galle 2130 m

Best time:	September
Tropical storms:	May–June, October–November
Charts:	BA: 4705, 4706
	US: 703, 706
Pilots:	BA: 38, 64
	US: 172, 173

Choosing the time for this passage presents a major dilemma, as the cyclone free months of July and August also have the highest frequency of gales. In fact the frequency of gales in July just to the east of Socotra is similar to that off Cape Horn in summer. As passages across the Arabian Sea can be extremely rough at the height of the SW monsoon, only September offers the prospect of a more comfortable voyage. The transitional months between the two monsoons cannot be recommended either because of the risk of cyclones, although an April passage has a good chance of fair winds and a lower risk factor.

The course from either Djibouti or Aden passes well to the north of Socotra to avoid the strong west setting current along the African coast. Sri Lanka can be approached through either the Nine or Eight Degree

Channels, which are separated by Minicoy Island. Whichever channel is used it should be approached with caution, especially at night or in thick weather, which is sometimes associated with the SW monsoon.

The small port of Galle, on the south west coast of Sri Lanka, is much more suitable for yachts than Colombo.

IN21 Red Sea to Maldives

DIAGRAM 77	Aden to Male 1780 m
	Djibouti to Male 1860 m

Best time:	September
Tropical storms:	May–June, October–November
Charts:	BA: 4703
	US: 703
Pilots:	BA: 38, 64
	US: 173

Directions are very similar to those for Route IN20 and a course for Male, the capital and port of entry for the Maldives, should only be set after having passed well to the north of Socotra. The low lying Maldives should be approached with extreme caution because of the strong current that sets on to the islands during the SW monsoon.

IN22 Sri Lanka to Singapore

DIAGRAM 77	Galle to Penang 1200 m
	Galle to Singapore 1450 m

Best time:	July to September
Tropical storms:	May to November
Charts:	BA: 4706
	US: 706
Pilots:	BA: 38, 44
	US: 173, 174

Although the cyclone season in the Bay of Bengal extends over the entire SW monsoon period, at the height of the monsoon the development of tropical storms is opposed by the strong monsoon and the few cyclones that occur between July and September normally stay well to the north of the area crossed by this route. The route enters the Malacca Strait north of Sumatra, between Great Nicobar and Rondo Islands. The SW monsoon is usually blocked by the land mass of Sumatra and better winds are therefore found on the Malaysian side of the strait. Because of the strong tidal currents in Malacca Strait, it is usually better to anchor between tides. (See also Route IN11.)

Those who wish to cruise in Malaysia before continuing to Singapore can clear in at Penang Island. This is also a good starting point for a cruise to Langkawi and Phuket on the west coast of Thailand, both popular destinations for cruising boats (see Route IN13).

IN23 Thailand to Singapore

Phuket to Singapore 520 m

Best time:	December to April
Tropical storms:	None
Charts:	BA: 4706
	US: 706
Pilots:	BA: 21, 30, 44
	US: 161, 173, 174

The west coast of Thailand south of Phuket can be cruised throughout the year as it is not affected by the cyclones that originate in the Bay of Bengal, although the NE monsoon has the more pleasant weather. During the SW monsoon the weather is sultry and hot and the frequency of squalls is higher. Coming south into Malaysia, Langkawi and Penang Islands are other favourite cruising spots. Sailing conditions in the Malacca Strait are also better during the NE monsoon (see Route IN11). In both seasons the main current has a northerly set.

Although most cruising boats prefer the west coasts of Malaysia and Thailand, a number of yachts have ventured recently along the east coasts of these two countries which face the South China Sea. Because the east coast is exposed to easterly winds, it is better to sail there during the SW monsoon. There are many attractive fishing harbours along the coast from Singapore to the Gulf of Thailand. The border area between Malaysia and Thailand should be avoided as several cases of piracy have been reported. The situation seems to have improved with the reduction in the number of refugee boats from Vietnam, who used to be the main target for the pirates, but cruising in this area cannot be regarded as entirely safe.

21 Transequatorial routes in the Indian Ocean

IT11 Maldives to Chagos Archipelago
IT12 Seychelles to Red Sea
IT13 Chagos Archipelago to Sri Lanka
IT14 Bali to Sri Lanka
IT15 Bali to Singapore
IT16 Cocos Keeling to Sri Lanka
IT17 Kenya to Red Sea
IT18 Chagos Archipelago to Maldives
IT19 Red Sea to South Indian Ocean

IT11 Maldives to Chagos Archipelago

DIAGRAM 77	Male to Salomon 600 m

Best time:	January to March
Tropical storms:	None
Charts:	BA: 4707
	US: 707
Pilots:	BA: 38, 39
	US: 170, 171

The best time to make this passage is during the NE monsoon when favourable winds will be found both north and south of the equator. From May to November the predominant direction of the winds is southerly and even during the transitional period boats have experienced a high proportion of southerly winds, so the only time when one can be sure of fair winds is at the height of the NE monsoon. After leaving Male, on North Male Atoll, it is better to keep to the east of all islands including Felidu Atoll, which has a light. Permission must be obtained from the authorities in Male if one wishes to visit the southern Maldives and clear out at Addu, the southernmost atoll of the group.

Diego Garcia is a military base leased by the British government to the USA and a stop in the main island is only permitted for emergency purposes. However, boats can stop in most other islands of the Chagos Archipelago, Peros Banhos and the Salomon Islands being convenient stops for those arriving from the north.

IT12 Seychelles to Red Sea

DIAGRAMS 70, 77	Mahé to Aden 1460 m
	Mahé to Djibouti 1570 m

Best time:	September to mid-October
Tropical storms:	May–June
Charts:	BA: 4703
	US: 703
Pilots:	BA: 3, 39, 64
	US: 170, 171, 172

The optimum time for this passage is towards the end of the SW monsoon, in September or early October, when the strength of the winds begins to subside in the north western part of the Indian Ocean. At this time of year the SE trades extend to the equator from where the winds become gradually SW and blow with increasing force as one approaches Socotra Island. This area is notorious for its high frequency of gales during the SW monsoon and this is the reason why an earlier passage, during July or August, is not recommended. Even towards the end of the SW monsoon winds can be very strong and this fact combined with the strong currents usually produce rough seas around the Horn of Africa.

On leaving the Seychelles a NW course should be steered to cross the equator west of longitude 51°E. This avoids a strong current that sets SE during the transitional period between monsoons. Closer to the African coast, the Somali Current sets strongly to the north and can reach rates as high as 170 miles per day in the area south of Socotra Island.

During the transitional period, the SE trades blow as far as the equator and favourable winds can be held into the Gulf of Aden. However, the passage must not be left too late as NE winds start to predominate north of the equator after the second half of October. Thick haze and poor visibility make navigation hazardous along the African coast and a safe distance should be kept off the coast both at night and in daytime.

If the passage is attempted during the NE monsoon, all easting must be made south of the equator and the equator crossed between longitudes 66°E and 68°E. From that point the course turns NW to pass on the windward side of Socotra. However, boats that have made the passage towards the end of the NE monsoon, in late February or March, have been able to lay a more northerly course after leaving the Seychelles, crossing the equator around longitude 63°E. From this point the tack is chosen which allows the most northing to be made. During the NE monsoon winds in the Gulf of

Aden are mostly easterly, but during the transitional period, particularly in October, they are either S or SW.

IT13 *Chagos Archipelago to Sri Lanka*

DIAGRAM 77		Peros Banhos to Galle 860 m
Best time:	May to September	
Tropical storms:	December to July	
Charts:	BA: 4707	
	US: 707	
Pilots:	BA: 38, 39	
	US: 170, 171, 173	

The strategy for this passage depends entirely on the state of the monsoon north of the equator. During the SW monsoon, from April to September, it is probably best to try to sail a direct course for Sri Lanka and only compensate for the set of the current after having crossed the equator. Attention should be paid to the strong currents that flow around the northern part of the Chagos Archipelago. Although the winds can be expected to be light at the beginning, the effect of the monsoon should make itself felt on nearing the equator with winds veering gradually from S to SW and finally W.

During the NE monsoon it is essential to make as much easting as possible south of the equator, which should be crossed in about longitude 82°E, so as to approach Sri Lanka from slightly east of south.

IT14 *Bali to Sri Lanka*

DIAGRAM 70		Benoa to Galle 2320 m
Best time:	September to mid-October	
Tropical storms:	December to July	
Charts:	BA: 4071	
	US: 632, 706	
Pilots:	BA: 34, 38, 44	
	US: 163, 173, 174	

This is a more direct route to Sri Lanka than Route IT15 and is used mainly by those who are on their way to the Red Sea and are not interested in sailing through Singapore and the Malacca Straits. If the port of departure is Benoa it is best to head immediately offshore and sail south of Java. In September or early October the SE trades will provide favourable winds to about latitude 5°S but because winds tend to be more consistent further south, it is advisable not to set a direct course for Sri Lanka until longitude

95°E has been reached as both contrary winds and currents are more likely to be encountered closer to Sumatra.

This passage is not recommended during the NE monsoon when mostly contrary winds will be met both south and north of the equator. The transitional period from the SW to the NE monsoon provides the best conditions. If the passage is made at the height of the SW monsoon, all necessary westing should be made south of latitude 5°S, as strong westerly winds would make it very difficult to reach Sri Lanka on a direct course. Directions for Route IT16 should also be consulted as they refer to the same area of the Indian Ocean.

IT15 Bali to Singapore

DIAGRAMS 70, 76	Benoa to Singapore 990 m

Best time:	May to September
Tropical storms:	None
Charts:	BA: 1263
	US: 632
Pilots:	BA: 34, 36
	US: 163, 174

There are two main ways to sail to Singapore from Bali, either direct through the Karimata Strait (IT15A), or by the more indirect route via Bangka and Riouw Straits (IT15B). The first route is faster and can be done non-stop as it is mostly offshore; the second route is usually slower and offers the possibility of overnight stops if winds are not favourable. The second route is not recommended for those who do not possess an Indonesian cruising permit. For both routes the best time is during the SE/SW monsoon. During the transitional months of April, October and early November, winds are more variable and calms frequent. During these months there is also a high frequency of rain squalls, often of torrential proportions, that make it difficult to anchor every night in safety and make the offshore route more attractive.

On leaving Benoa, the course leads NE through the Lombok Strait where extremely strong currents can be experienced. During the SE monsoon the main direction of the currents is southerly, although at certain times a favourable current sets NE along the coast of Bali. This current occurs approximately at the time of the moon's transit and lasts for two or three hours so it is worth timing a departure for two hours before the transit and leaving at slack water. North of Bali the route leads into the Java Sea through one of the passes between Madura and Kangean islands, Sapudi Strait being the easiest to negotiate as it has lights.

In the Java Sea, the two routes split. Route IT15A leads through the Karimata Strait keeping to the east of all dangers that lie off the coast of Belitung (Billiton) Island. The course is altered to pass north of Ontario reef and close to Seroetoe (Serutu) Island. A NW course leads from there into the China Sea, crossing the equator in about longitude 105°E. Coming from this direction it is easier to make a landfall on the NE coast of Bintan island and approach Singapore through either the middle or south channel of Singapore Strait, keeping clear of the rocks and reefs north of Bintan.

Route IT15B leads through Bangka Strait, the narrows between Sumatra and Bangka islands. The direction of the wind in the strait is usually parallel to the coast, although strong SW winds can be experienced towards the end of the SE monsoon. Because of the nature of the tidal currents in the strait, it is better to stay close to the coast of Sumatra during the SE monsoon. North of Bangka Strait it is possible to follow either a direct or an indirect route. The former leads outside Lingga island to Riouw Strait and because it is easily navigable is used by most boats. The indirect route follows the coast of Sumatra through Berhala and Pengelap Straits and joins the direct route for the final approach to Singapore through Riouw Strait. A slightly more indirect route leads to Singapore from SW through Durian Strait and Phillip Channel.

IT16 Cocos Keeling to Sri Lanka

DIAGRAM 70	Cocos to Galle 1490 m

Best time:	September
Tropical storms:	December to July
Charts:	BA: 4707
	US: 706
Pilots:	BA: 38, 44
	US: 163, 173

Although this passage can be made at any time of the year, most people who undertake it intend to continue their voyage towards the Red Sea and therefore plan to arrive in Sri Lanka on the eve of the NE monsoon. However, passages that are made later risk encountering northerly winds north of the equator. It is therefore advisable to make this passage while the SW monsoon is still in force in the North Indian Ocean, September being probably the best month. Boats that made the passage in the second half of October encountered light variable winds and erratic currents between latitude 3°S and the equator. Similar conditions were experienced north of the equator all the way to Sri Lanka.

The most difficult aspect of this route is the fact that it crosses three different currents, none of which can be fully predicted. The route runs first through the west setting South Equatorial Current, its effect likely to be cancelled out on nearing the equator by the east setting Equatorial Countercurrent. The currents north of the equator depend on the state of the monsoon, setting east during the SW monsoon, west during the NE monsoon. However, it does appear that the combined set of the currents is usually to the east and all boats making this passage found themselves further east than expected.

Yet another factor to be borne in mind on this route is that it crosses the doldrums, although the belt of calms or light winds between the SE trades and the monsoon prevailing north of the equator is not too wide and sometimes the wind systems merge into each other almost without a break. During August and September the SE trades reach as far as latitude 5°S. The recommended procedure is to make for a point in 4°S, 80°E, then sail north along the 80°E meridian until the equator is crossed.

If this passage is made during the NE monsoon, from December to March, as much northing as possible should be made after leaving Cocos Keeling so as to cross the equator in about longitude 90°E and approach Sri Lanka from a better angle.

IT17 *Kenya to Red Sea*

| DIAGRAM 70 | Mombasa to Aden 1640 m |
| | Mombasa to Djibouti 1750 m |

Best time:	April–May, September
Tropical storms:	June, October
Charts:	BA: 4701, 4703
	US: 71
Pilots:	BA: 3, 64
	US: 170, 171, 172

The classic route of the Arab traders benefits from favourable winds throughout the SW monsoon, from April to October. However, as the winds often attain gale force during the months of July and August in the vicinity of Socotra and the Horn of Africa, the voyage is more comfortable either at the beginning or end of the SW monsoon. Good passages on this route have been made in September, when the winds are favourable both south and north of the equator and the strong Somali Current also gives a considerable boost to daily runs. The course runs parallel to the African coast, but because of the thick haze and poor visibility associated with the SW monsoon, particular attention must be paid to navigation. The most dangerous area is when approaching Ras Hafun, which has claimed many boats whose navigators had wrongly identified this headland.

The time of departure is critical, as the transitional period is very short and the NE monsoon can arrive before the middle of October, when both winds and current change direction. Alternatively, the passage can be made at the beginning of the SW monsoon, when winds might be lighter. If the passage is made at the height of the SW monsoon, in July or August, one must be prepared to put up with very strong winds and rough seas.

If this passage is made during the NE monsoon it is better to wait until the end of March, so as to arrive north of the equator at the change of monsoons. On leaving Mombasa, easting should be made south of the equator, which should be crossed in about longitude 53°E. The best tack should be sailed from there northwards so as to pass between Socotra and Cape Guardafui.(See also IT12.)

IT18 Chagos Archipelago to Maldives

DIAGRAM 70	Peros Banhos to Male 600 m

Best time:	May to September
Tropical storms:	None
Charts:	BA: 4707
	US: 707
Pilots:	BA: 38, 39
	US: 171

The most favourable sailing conditions can be expected during the SW monsoon when southerly winds predominate south of the equator. Winds are much lighter and there are long periods of calm during the changeover period. During the NE monsoon the winds south of the equator are mostly NW.

Currents in this region can be very strong and their set is difficult to predict, particularly in the transitional period between monsoons. The strongest current during the SW monsoon is the Indian Monsoon Current which sets strongly east on both sides of the equator.

The course from Peros Banhos or the Salomon Islands is almost due north and there are no dangers en route until the Maldives archipelago is approached. The capital Male is at the southern extremity of North Male Atoll where entry formalities must be completed by all vessels.

IT19 Red Sea to South Indian Ocean

DIAGRAM 77	Bab el Mandeb to Mombasa 1730 m
	Bab el Mandeb to Seychelles 1550 m
	Bab el Mandeb to Diego Garcia 2200 m

Best time:	November to March
Tropical storms:	May–June, October
Charts:	BA: 4071
	US: 702, 703
Pilots:	BA: 3, 38, 64
	US: 170, 171, 172

Although most yacht traffic in the Red Sea is from south to north, every year an increasing number of boats sail to various destinations in the South Indian Ocean by a more direct route from Europe and the Mediterranean.

Kenya and other points along the east coast of Africa are most easily reached during the NE monsoon. The major difficulty usually occurs at the beginning of the route when consistent easterly winds make it difficult to get out of the Gulf of Aden. Once Ras Asir has been weathered, favourable winds and current ensure a fast sail along the coast of Africa. The same holds true for a passage to the Seychelles during the NE monsoon as the islands can also be reached by a direct route from the Gulf of Aden. The next leg of the voyage to destinations further south should be postponed until after the end of the cyclone season in the South Indian Ocean. (See also Route IS27.)

During the SW monsoon the coast of Africa can only be reached by taking a roundabout route via the Seychelles. Having passed north of Socotra, the course leads SE and crosses the equator as far west as the winds will permit. Having met the SE trades in between latitudes 2°S and 4°S, the course is shaped to pass north of the Seychelles and on to Kenya, or alternatively a stop can be made in the Seychelles. (See also Routes IS28 and IS34.)

The SW monsoon route from the Red Sea to Chagos and Mauritius crosses the equator between longitudes 70°E and 72°E. From Chagos the same directions apply as for Route IS29. A September passage from the Red Sea would also benefit from more favourable sailing conditions for the next leg to Mauritius.

22   Winds and currents of the South Indian Ocean

Maps 2 to 6

The weather in the tropical zone of the South Indian Ocean is greatly influenced by the advance of the North Indian monsoon south of the equator during the northern winter and its corresponding retreat during summer. Outside of the tropics the weather follows a normal pattern.

South-east trade winds

These winds blow on the equatorial side of the anticlockwise circulation of air that exists around the area of high pressure situated in about latitude 30°S. Compared to the other oceans, the South Indian high rarely consists of a single cell and often contains a succession of east moving anticyclonic systems. The trade winds blow on their north side and form a wide belt that stretches across the ocean from Western Australia to Madagascar and the coast of Africa. Between July and September this belt spreads over a very large area and becomes continuous with the SE trade winds of the South Pacific. The entire belt moves north and south throughout the year, its northern limit varying from latitude 2°S in August to latitude 12°S in January. The fluctuation of the southern limit is less pronounced, from 24°S in August to 30°S in January.

The average strength of these trades is between 10 to 15 knots in summer and 15 to 20 knots in winter. Over the central region, the wind blows steadily from SE or ESE, especially from May to September when the SW monsoon is in force north of the equator.

North-west monsoon

From November to March, when the ITCZ is situated south of the equator, the NE monsoon of the North Indian Ocean is drawn into the southern hemisphere. Because of the rotation of the earth it is deflected to the left and becomes a NW wind in the northern part of the South Indian Ocean. Winds are generally light and vary considerably both in direction and strength during this period. The weather is often squally and unsettled.

Monsoons of the Indonesian Archipelago

The weather pattern of the Indonesian Archipelago is more seasonal than that of the adjacent areas, being dominated by the two monsoons. The SE monsoon generally lasts from April to September and is replaced by a NW monsoon from October till March. Though neither of them is very strong, the SE monsoon is the more consistent both in strength and direction, particularly during July and August when it becomes continuous with the SE trade winds of the South Pacific and Indian Oceans. During the NW monsoon, the direction of the winds is predominantly NW, although their strength and consistency diminish further south. South of latitude 4°S the weather is often squally alternating with calms, variable winds and rain.

Variables

On the polar side of the SE trade wind belt there is an area of light variable winds which coincides with the high pressure region. The axis of these highs is situated in about latitude 30°S in winter, moving further south towards latitude 35°S during the summer. The weather varies greatly within this zone which has similar characteristics to the Horse Latitudes of the Atlantic Ocean.

Westerlies

South of the Indian Ocean high pressure region westerly winds prevail. The almost continuous passage of depressions from west to east causes the wind to vary considerably in direction and strength. Particularly in the higher latitudes of the Roaring Forties and beyond, the frequency of gales is high, the weather cold and the seas rough.

Tropical storms

The cyclone season of the South Indian Ocean lasts from November to May, although December to April are considered to be the dangerous months, as cyclones occur only rarely in November and May. The month with the highest frequency of storms is January.

The willy-willies that affect the coasts of W and NW Australia occur mostly between December and April. They can extend as far as the Timor Sea and Arafura Sea, the latter being also subject to South Pacific cyclones that occasionally hit Northern Australia. Their season is from December to March.

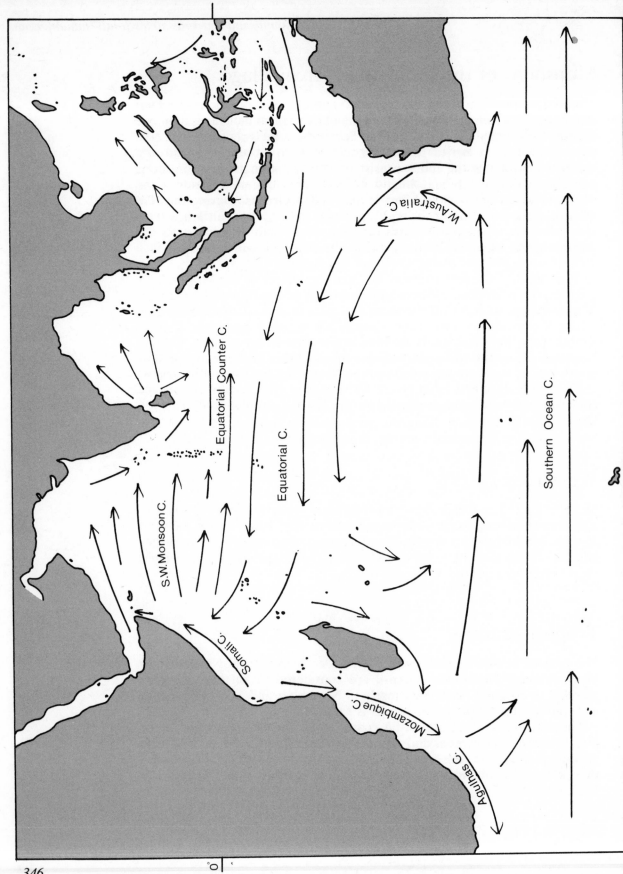

Equatorial Counter C.

Equatorial C.

W.Australia C.

Southern Ocean C.

S.W.Monsoon C.

Somali C.

Mozambique C.

Agulhas C.

Currents

The main surface circulation of the South Indian Ocean is anticlockwise but because of the monsoons of the North Indian Ocean, there is only one Equatorial Current. The west flowing Equatorial Current always lies south of the equator, its northern limit varying between latitudes 6°S and 10°S depending on longitude and season. The limit is nearer the equator during the SW monsoon of the North Indian Ocean. On the western side of the ocean, the northern part of the current flows past Madagascar until it reaches the coast of Africa. The current splits in two, one branch following the coast in a northerly direction, the other setting south into the Mozambique Channel. This becomes the Mozambique Current which further south alters its name to that of the Agulhas Current.

The Agulhas Current contains not just the waters of the Mozambique Current but also those of the southern branch of the Equatorial Current. The two currents meet off the coast of Africa in about latitude 28°S from where the combined current sets strongly SW before it passes the Cape of Good Hope into the South Atlantic. One part of the Agulhas Current branches off to the SE where it joins the Southern Ocean Current. The south side of the main circulation of the South Indian Ocean is formed by this current which sets in an E and NE direction. The eastern side of this anticlockwise movement is formed by the West Australia Current, which sets in a NW direction along the west coast of Australia. Eventually it passes into the Equatorial Current, thus completing this giant cycle.

23　Regional weather of the South Indian Ocean

Northern Australia

From May through until September this area falls in the area of steady SE trade winds that form a belt across both the South Pacific and Indian Oceans. The steadiest winds blow in July and August, although the strength of the wind often drops at sunset and freshens at sunrise. After September the winds lighten and tend to come from the north, often falling away at night. From December to January the ITCZ moves south and lies over this region bringing unsettled weather.

Conditions along the coast vary from place to place. In the Gulf of Carpentaria winds from February to May are mostly ENE, while between Cape Wessel and Cape Van Diemen both monsoons are irregular and near the coast land and sea breezes alternate. Between Cape Van Diemen and North West Cape the NW monsoon prevails from October to April.

Cyclones can strike along the entire northern coast from December until March.

Arafura and Timor Seas

These seas stretching from the north coast of Australia to the Indonesian Archipelago have a typical monsoon climate. The convergence zone marking the boundary between the SE and NW monsoons passes through this area on its way to lie over the north of Australia in January and passes through again to reach its apogee north of Borneo in July. As the ITCZ moves across the seas in February to March and again in November to December, it brings typical doldrum weather of squalls and thunderstorms.

After March the SE monsoon establishes itself and blows steadily through until October or November, with the strongest SE winds between 10 and 20 knots in June, July and August. This season is dry and pleasant. The NE monsoon blows from December to February, but is not so settled and winds can be from W and SW as well as NW. This season is accompanied by heavy rain in squalls and thunderstorms and the sky is often overcast.

These seas border on the cyclone area, but only about one storm a year affects the Timor region. As a rule the cyclones move SW and WSW and those which recurve to SE only do so S of latitude 13°S. Boats on passage through these seas passing south of Indonesia towards the Indian Ocean between January and April should therefore be on the alert.

Indonesia

Indonesia is one of the last countries in the world where a major proportion of transport, trading and fishing is still carried out under sail. These often very colourful sailing craft cover long distances between the islands, shaping their courses to take full advantage of the diurnal pattern of land and sea breezes.

The climate in the entire archipelago is hot and humid with a high rainfall. The area is under the influence of the NW and SE monsoons, although the high mountains of some islands and irregular coastlines cause significant modifications to local weather conditions. The high islands often block the monsoons completely. Strong winds are quite rare, although some squalls can be violent and as these often develop suddenly, can be quite dangerous to those caught unaware. Tropical cyclones are also very rare, the only area affected being near Timor and Flores Islands, with less than one storm per year, in the period from January to April.

Although conditions may vary locally, as the archipelago stretches over a considerable portion of the ocean, it can be assumed that the SE monsoon will last from April to October and the NW monsoon from November to March.

Among the islands to the east of Java, the SE monsoon blows strongly from the ESE, being at its height during June, July and August. This period coincides with the dry season, lasting from May until November, although rain can be expected to fall in all months of the year. The NW monsoon sets in about December and attains its maximum in January. The period of the NW monsoon is the wet season, having the highest rainfall in December and January, when squalls are most frequent.

Along the northern shores of these islands, winds in both seasons are steadier during the night hours, being influenced by land and sea breezes. For this reason most Indonesian sailing craft tend to make their passages at night, keeping close to the shore. Land and sea breezes are very important for those planning to sail in these waters and are very evident along the coasts of larger islands, although weaker on smaller islands. These breezes are at their strongest when the monsoons are weak. The change from land to sea breeze occurs in the middle of the morning, while that from sea to land occurs shortly after sunset near mountainous coasts and later in the night near flat country. The force of the breezes decreases with distance from the shore but can be felt up to 20 miles offshore. The breezes are strongest near mountainous country sloping gradually to the sea, and are also stronger on clear days.

On steep coasts facing E or SE, rainfall is spread over the entire year, with the heaviest rains during the SE monsoon, whereas on other coasts and in the open sea, the rainy season is from November to March, the heaviest rain falling in the middle of the day or afternoon.

The seas around the Indonesian Archipelago and particularly the Banda Sea are prone to spectacular displays of phosphorescence. In July and August a luminous ocean often occurs so that the water appears like snow or milk giving off a very strong light, which can be quite eery when sailing at night.

Cruising in Indonesia is not allowed without a cruising permit, which must be obtained beforehand (see Chapter 27).

Western Australia

Although not a common destination for the world voyagers, sailing conditions off this coast attracted the world's attention with the Australian capture of the America's Cup. In the overall pattern of wind circulation, the westerlies of the southern ocean turn up the West Australian coast, eventually to become the SE trades. Along the coast the weather comes mostly from the south with S and SW winds prevailing even higher up the coast in the trade wind belt. The more northerly parts of this coast are subject to cyclones from December to March.

Christmas Island

The SE trade wind blows over this island almost continuously from May until December, but in the first months of the year when the NW monsoon is established to the north of the island, it makes itself felt with occasional heavy rains, strong winds and thunderstorms. In January and February winds can blow strongly from the west or north. The island is normally spared the cyclones which affect the area between it and North West Australia.

Cocos Keeling

This group is made up of North Keeling Island to the north and the Cocos Islands within a lagoon to the south. The SE trades prevail for most of the year, the low land providing no obstacle to their passage. The trades do vary slightly between south and east and are at their strongest in August. At the height of the cyclone season, the trade wind is less steady, being interrupted by calms, variable winds and the occasional storm. During this season, fine days are often followed by gales, thunderstorms and heavy showers.

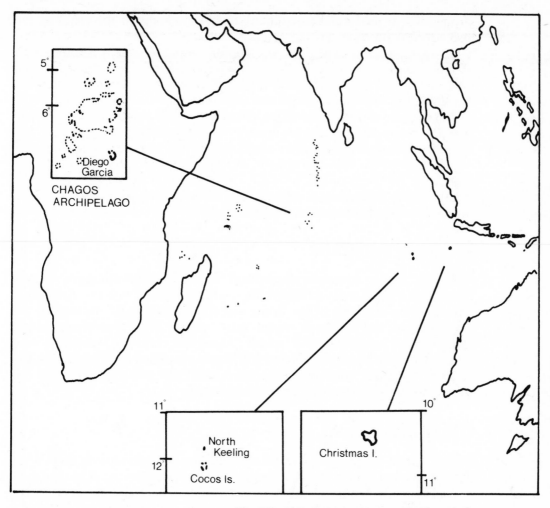

72. ISLANDS IN THE SOUTH INDIAN OCEAN

Chagos Archipelago

A British possession, these islands have been leased to the USA, who use Diego Garcia, the largest island, as a military base. It is forbidden to anchor near or land on Diego Garcia, although it is permitted in other islands to the north of this group.

Chagos enjoys South Indian Ocean weather with SE trades from April to November, but as the islands are close to the upper limit of the trades, they can be light and more variable. From December to March when the ITCZ moves south, the NE monsoon is deflected to a give a NW flow of wind.

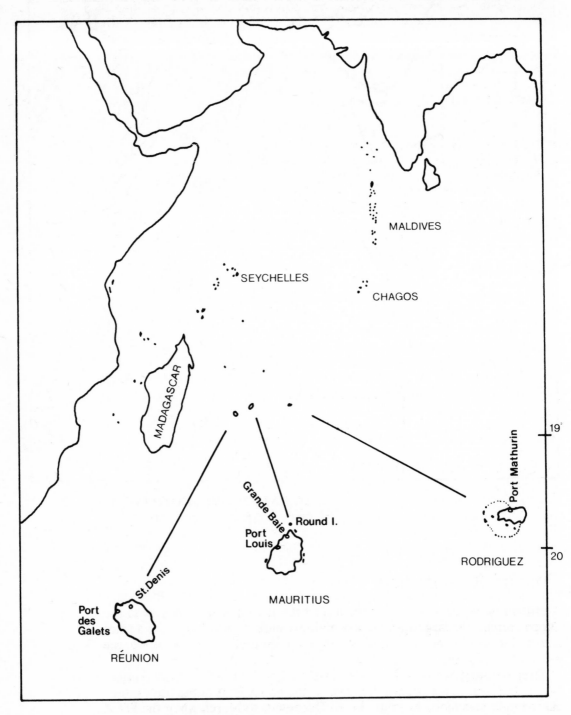

MALDIVES

SEYCHELLES

CHAGOS

MADAGASCAR

Port Mathurin

19°

Grande Baie

Round I.

Port Louis

RODRIGUEZ

20

St.Denis

MAURITIUS

Port des Galets

RÉUNION

73. MASCARENE ISLANDS

This NW monsoon is not so reliable and brings rain. It blows most strongly in January and February. This NW monsoon period is the cyclone season, but these storms normally form south of Chagos and move on a southerly track. They almost never track north towards the equator.

Rodriguez

The least visited of the Mascarene Islands, Rodriguez comes under Mauritius for administrative purposes. This island lies in the SE trade winds more or less all the year round. The season with the most settled weather is from June to October. From November to May the cyclone season prevails over this area, bringing with it unsteady weather, the wind sometimes drawing round to the NE and staying there for several days. Calms also occur during this period, although they seldom last long.

Mauritius

Port Louis is the capital of this now independent state, largest of the Mascarene Islands. Lying in the trade wind belt, the SE trade winds reach their maximum strength in July and August, being less in the months preceding and following this period. December to April is the hottest time on this island and also the rainy season when NE winds are common. Mauritius lies well in the cyclone region of the South Indian Ocean, November to May being the critical months.

Réunion

A French overseas territory, Réunion completes the trio of Mascarene Islands in the south-west Indian Ocean, which are convenient staging posts for those on transindian voyages. From April to November the SE trades blow almost continuously, usually freshening by mid-morning and growing lighter by mid-afternoon. The wind often dies away at night under the influence of the land, and if it does not go calm at night, it will normally blow hard the following morning. The SE trades are at their strongest in June, July and August. In the cyclone season, which is the most inclement time of year, lasting from November to May, SE winds are still the most common wind, but they are more moderate in strength and are subject to interruptions by winds from W or NW or by calms.

Madagascar

This large island off the coast of Africa receives the full force of the SE trade winds blowing across the Indian Ocean and they can rise to gale force in the latter part of the year. The strongest SE trades are in July, August and September. The SE trades influence the island all year, although the southern limit of these trades moves up the coast from August to November. During this period variable winds are experienced in the southern half of the island, although winds are usually from an easterly or north-easterly direction. These other winds can still blow quite strongly. In March, when the ITCZ is further south, the northern tip of the island loses the SE trade to NE and NW winds.

The island is within the cyclone belt, although cyclones are not so frequent here as in the Mauritius area. Madagascar enjoys abundant rain and spectacular lightning when thunderstorms occur near the coast. The South Equatorial Current splits at the centre of the island and runs north and south along the island. At the edge of the Agulhas Current, where there is a change in sea temperature, there is the usual problem of fog forming quite frequently.

Comoro Islands

This cluster of small islands off the NW coast of Madagascar are part of the triangular cruising route between Kenya and the Seychelles. The prevailing winds are the NW and SE monsoons, the latter varying so much between SW and SE as to be also known as the SE trade wind. The NW monsoon commences at the end of October or early in November and lasts until April. This is the hot and rainy season, which is characterised by irregular winds and squally weather.

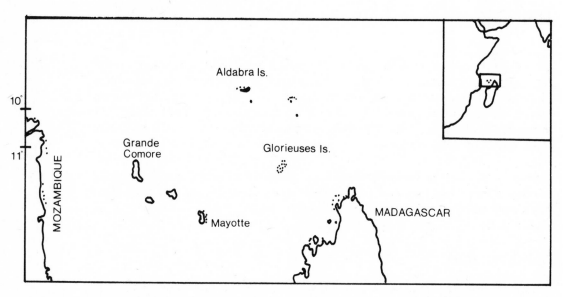

74. COMOROS

In the SE season winds blow more regularly, although never too strongly, their strength broken by the mass of Madagascar. The changeover between the seasons is marked by calms, variable winds and squally weather. Occasionally cyclones do reach the Comoro Islands in the season from February to April.

Seychelles

This group of small islands are famed for their beautiful reefs, and the diving can tempt yachtsmen to make a detour to visit them. The SE trade winds prevail from May to the middle of October, although in some years they are not established until June or even July. The SE season is the fine weather period, with steady SE winds blowing in July, August and September. In November the changeover to the NW monsoon occurs, marked with heavy squalls and rain. The NW monsoon is the wet season and lasts through until April. During these months winds blow from the NW, W or WSW. Cyclones are practically unknown and if they do pass through the area of the Seychelles, it is usually around 200 miles to the south of the capital, Mahé.

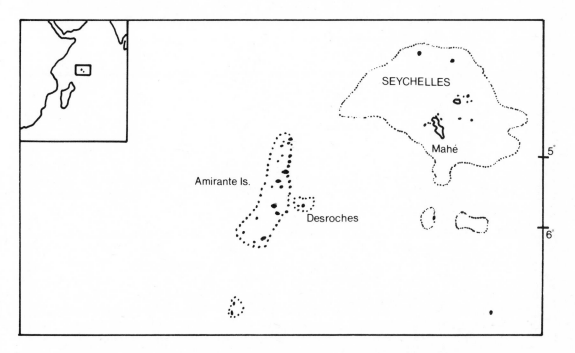

75. SEYCHELLES

East Africa

For centuries Arab dhows have sailed from the Persian coast to this coast to trade, sailing down with one monsoon and back with the other, although in present-day Kenya and Tanzania they are becoming a rare sight. The SE trade winds blow steadily from April to October and rarely exceed 20 knots. The wide band of northbound current runs close to the shore and can be augmented by these SE trades so as to reach 4 knots, which makes it very difficult to sail south in this region. Therefore it makes sense if planning to include this area in a cruise to commence at the most southerly point and work one's way northward. During the NE monsoon, when winds from the NE and E prevail, this current is slacker and can reverse its direction altogether. Along the Tanzanian coast it is possible to sail inside the reefs and islands. The climate is generally warm and fine, being cooler in July and August, hot and muggy in February and March.

South Africa

For the regional weather of South Africa see page 134 in Chapter 9.

24 Routes in the South Indian Ocean

For an overall view of cruising routes in the South Indian Ocean, refer to the beginning of Chapter 20, where these are discussed together with those of the North Indian Ocean

IS11 Torres Strait to Darwin
IS12 Torres Strait to Bali
IS13 Darwin to Bali
IS14 Darwin to Christmas Island
IS15 Bali to Christmas Island
IS16 Christmas Island to Cocos Keeling
IS17 Cocos Keeling to Mauritius
IS18 Mauritius to Réunion
IS19 Mauritius to Durban
IS20 Réunion to Durban
IS21 Durban to Cape Town
IS22 Cocos Keeling to Chagos Archipelago
IS23 Chagos Archipelago to Seychelles
IS24 Christmas Island to Chagos Archipelago
IS25 Western Australia to Cocos Keeling
IS26 Indonesia to Chagos Archipelago
IS27 Seychelles to Mauritius
IS28 Seychelles to Kenya
IS29 Chagos Archipelago to Mauritius
IS30 Kenya to Seychelles
IS31 Mauritius to Comoros
IS32 Comoros to Kenya
IS33 Mauritius to Seychelles
IS34 Seychelles to Comoros
IS35 Comoros to Seychelles
IS36 Comoros to Durban
IS37 Durban to Mauritius
IS38 Cape Town to Western Australia
IS39 Western Australia to Bass Strait

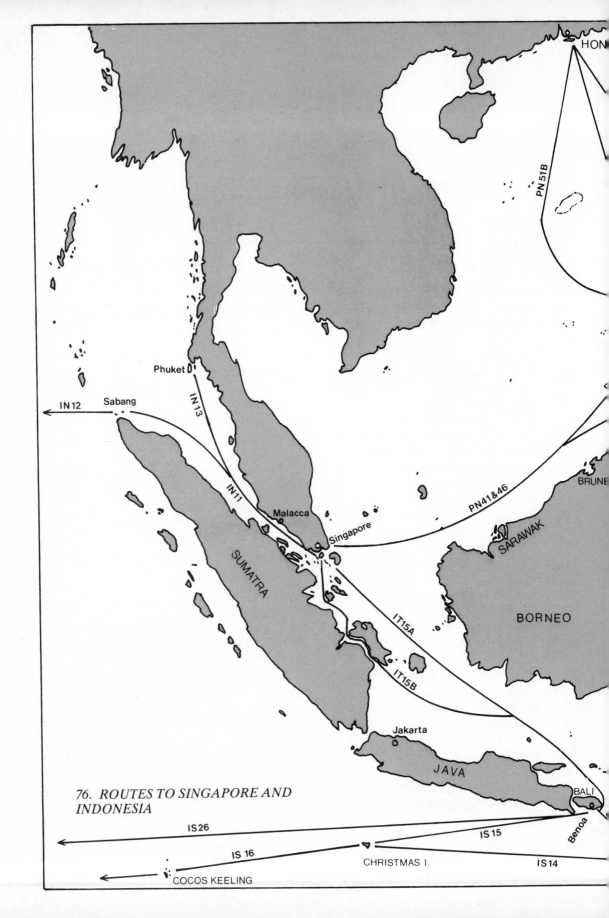

76. *ROUTES TO SINGAPORE AND INDONESIA*

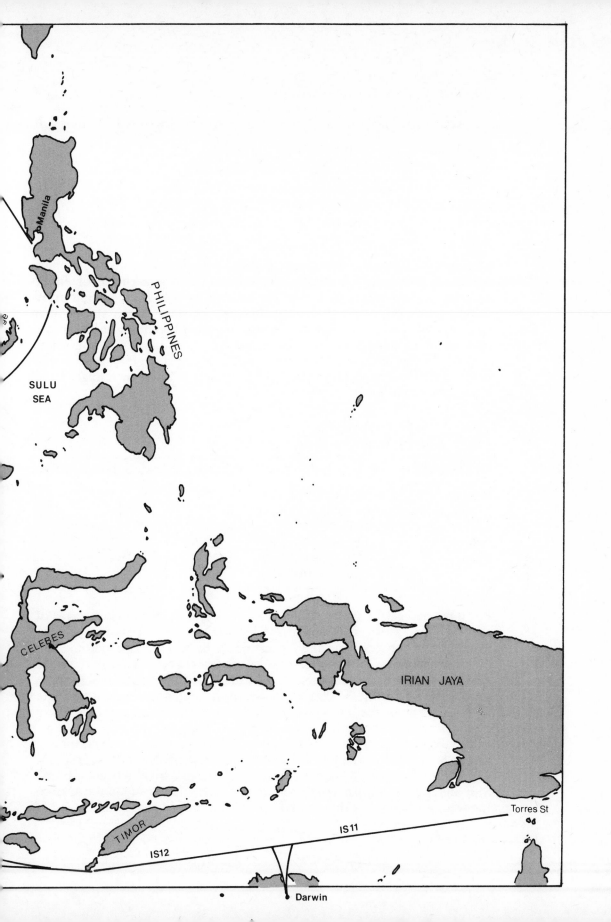

SULU
SEA

PHILIPPINES

Manila

CELEBES

IRIAN JAYA

TIMOR

Torres St

IS 11

IS 12

Darwin

IS11 Torres Strait to Darwin

DIAGRAMS 70, 76		Thursday Island to Darwin 700 m

Best time:	May to October
Tropical storms:	December to March
Charts:	BA: 4603
	US: 603
Pilots:	BA: 15, 17
	US: 164, 175

During the SE monsoon, from the middle of April to the end of October, winds on this route are mostly favourable. There is a choice of either reaching Darwin by taking a short cut through the Van Diemen Gulf or by sailing around the west of Bathurst Island. Because of the strong tidal streams in Dundas and Clarence Straits and the difficult navigation in the approaches to Darwin, the roundabout route is often quicker, although it is longer. Those who have more time available might prefer to cover the entire distance in daily stages as there are plenty of good anchorages from Cape Arnhem onward.

IS12 Torres Strait to Bali

DIAGRAM 76		Thursday Island to Benoa 1600 m

Best time:	May to October
Tropical storms:	December to April
Charts:	BA: 4603
	US: 603
Pilots:	BA: 15, 34, 35
	US: 163, 164

For most people the timing of this passage is crucial for the later stages of their voyage. Most boats bound for the Indian Ocean pass through the Torres Strait between June and August when the best sailing conditions can be expected on this route. After the Arafura Sea has been crossed, the same directions apply as for those setting off from Darwin (Route IS13). If one is too late in the season, the best way to avoid encountering a cyclone en route is by sailing along the north coast of the southern Indonesian islands where cyclones are not known to occur.

The direct route from Torres Strait to Bali crosses both the Arafura and Timor Seas, whose weather is dominated by the SE and NW monsoons. The trade winds blow strongly from May till August from between SE and SSE and there is a considerable sea. At the start and the end of the season, the wind is often E backing to ENE. The SE monsoon lasts until the end of

October or even November. It is then followed by variable winds and calms. As the NW monsoon coincides with the cyclone season, passages during this time are best avoided.

The seasons in the Timor Sea follow almost the same pattern. Sometimes during the SE monsoon the air is laden with dust brought from the Australian desert, and visibility can be poor. In the vicinity of land, the winds are generally influenced by the contour of the islands, while in the channels between the islands the winds often blow with great force. The currents in the Lombok Strait run at considerable rates and can produce dangerous conditions in the approaches to Benoa harbour when a strong wind is blowing against the current. During the SE monsoon, the main direction of the current is southerly.

IS13 Darwin to Bali

DIAGRAM 76	Darwin to Benoa 960 m

Best time:	May to October
Tropical storms:	December to April
Charts:	BA: 4603
	US: 603
Pilots:	BA: 17, 34
	US: 163, 175

This route leads south of all Indonesian islands. The only dangers on the direct route are the Hibernia and Ashmore Reefs to the south of Timor Island. Some people break the trip at Ashmore Reef, especially if the winds are light. The green reflection or blink of the shallow water can often be seen in the sky long before the actual reef is sighted. Currents in the area are usually strong. The best recommended anchorage is in the NW corner of the reef, off a small cay. In good visibility it is fairly easy to thread one's way among the coral heads. The reef is often visited by Indonesian fishermen.

During the SE monsoon the prevailing winds both in the Arafura and Timor Seas are from the SE or E. The only difficulty likely to be encountered is the very strong currents in the Lombok Strait in the approaches to Benoa harbour. Because of the currents and the meandering entrance channel to Benoa, this port should only be entered in daylight.

Best passages on this route are made during July and August, when the SE winds are most regular. At the beginning and especially at the end of the SE monsoon the winds become irregular, SSW winds sometimes being encountered in the Timor Sea in October. The south side of the Indonesian islands should not be approached until close to Bali on account of contrary currents. During April and also in November and December winds on this route are often light and there are prolonged periods of calms.

A cruising permit is required for all sailing boats wishing to visit Indonesia (see Chapter 27). However, on some occasions skippers arriving in Benoa without a permit have been allowed by the Harbour Master to stay a few days for reprovisioning.

IS14 Darwin to Christmas Island

DIAGRAMS 70, 76		Darwin to Christmas Island 1500 m
Best time:	May to October	
Tropical storms:	December to April	
Charts:	BA: 4603, 4070	
	US: 70, 603	
Pilots:	BA: 17, 34	
	US: 163, 175	

This is normally a fast sail in 15–25 knot SE winds if the passage is timed for July or August. If it is left later than the beginning of September, the trade winds can be less reliable and there is a greater chance of calms and light variable winds. Occasionally strong squalls have been encountered on this run, with sudden winds of up to 50 knots.

The anchorage at Christmas Island can be uncomfortable when the trades are at their strongest, a good incentive to up anchor and sail the 500 miles to Cocos Keeling, where there is a much better selection of safe and beautiful anchorages.

IS15 Bali to Christmas Island

DIAGRAM 76		Benoa to Christmas Island 580 m
Best time:	May to October	
Tropical storms:	December to April	
Charts:	BA: 4071	
	US: 70	
Pilots:	BA: 34	
	US: 163, 170	

Generally pleasant sailing conditions can be expected during the months when the majority of boats make this passage, which is August and September. The trades blow strongly in July and August, but there are years when the trades fail to establish themselves and winds are either light or can blow with gale force for several days.

IS16 Christmas Island to Cocos Keeling

DIAGRAM 76	Christmas Island to Cocos 530 m

Best time:	May to October
Tropical storms:	November to April
Charts:	BA: 4070
	US: 70
Pilots:	BA: 34, 44
	US: 163

During the SE trade wind season the winds on this route are almost always favourable. Occasionally the trades cease to blow for a day but periods of calms or light winds are usually short lived. The one unpleasant feature of this route is the large swell from the south or south-west. Because the wind is blowing from the SE and the swell is almost at right angles to the direction of the wind, the motion can be very uncomfortable and it can also be tough on selfsteering gears which have sometimes broken under the strain of the violent motion.

IS17 Cocos Keeling to Mauritius

DIAGRAM 77	Cocos to St Louis 2850 m
	Cocos to Rodriguez 2500 m
	Rodriguez to Mauritius 350 m

Best time:	June to October
Tropical storms:	November to April
Charts:	BA: 4070
	US: 70
Pilots:	BA: 39, 44
	US: 163, 170, 171

This long haul across the width of the South Indian Ocean has the full benefit of the SE trades during the southern winter months, from May to October. However, the winds often blow at 20–25 knots for days on end and sometimes reach gale force. The pleasure of a fast passage is often marred by a uncomfortable cross-swell which rolls in relentlessly from the Southern Ocean. The weather is generally rougher in the proximity of Cocos Keeling and both winds and seas usually moderate after the half-way mark to Mauritius has been passed. The trade winds continue to blow consistently in October, but the weather becomes more squally and the chances of encountering gale force winds are greater. Although it would appear that by making a sweep to the north it would be possible to avoid the area with the highest frequency of gales, this does not seem to be the case.

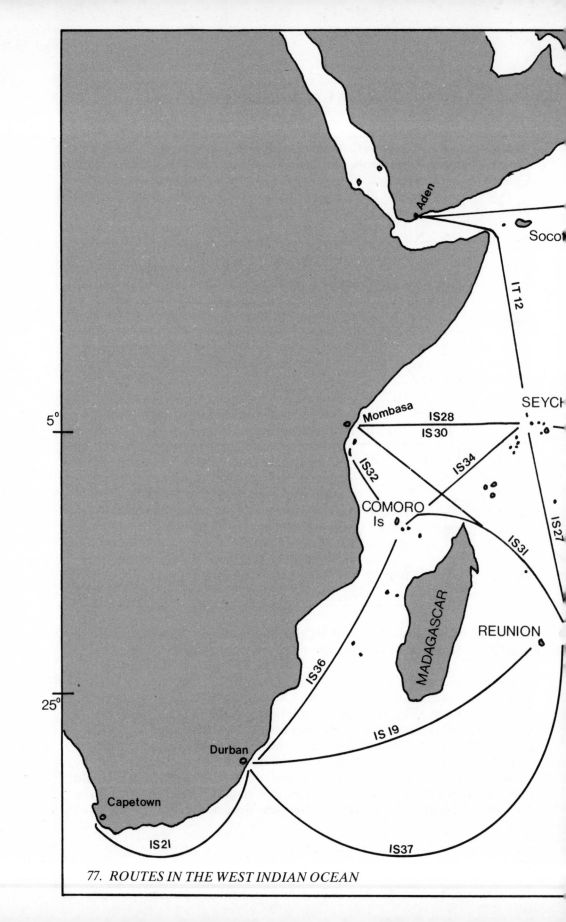

5°

25°

Aden

Soco

IT 12

SEYCH

Mombasa

IS28

IS30

IS32

IS34

IS27

COMORO
Is

IS31

MADAGASCAR

REUNION

IS36

IS 19

Durban

Capetown

IS21

IS37

77. ROUTES IN THE WEST INDIAN OCEAN

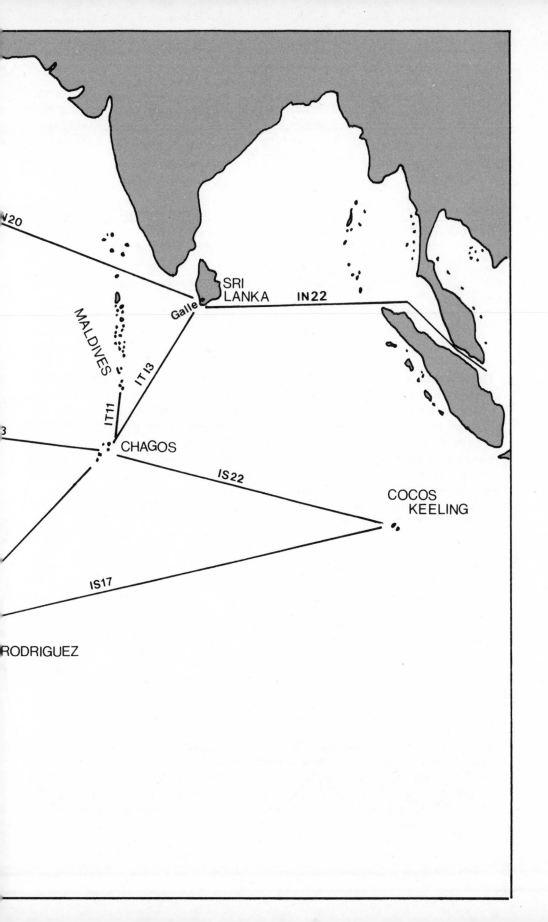

Boats that have arrived in Mauritius by a more roundabout way have encountered equally rough conditions to those which sailed a direct course.

Some boats break the journey to Mauritius by calling in at Rodriguez, 350 miles to the east, where cruising boats are welcome and local boats sometimes sail out to guide the visitors in.

IS18 Mauritius to Réunion

DIAGRAM 77		Port Louis to Port des Galets 120 m
Best time:	May to October	
Tropical storms:	November to April	
Charts:	BA: 4070	
	US: 700	
Pilots:	BA: 39	
	US: 170, 171	

This short passage between the largest two of the Mascarene Islands can be made at any time outside the cyclone season. Most boats stop at this French overseas territory on their way to South Africa either in October or November. Many of those who stop in Réunion do so to stock up with French goods and to obtain a South African visa, as there is a South African Consulate in the capital, St Denis. Although such visas are not compulsory for sailors who do not leave their boats while in South Africa, they are recommended for those who intend to travel inland.

Entry formalities for Réunion can be completed at Port des Galets, on the north-western side of the island.

IS19 Mauritius to Durban

DIAGRAMS 70, 77		St Louis to Durban 1550 m
Best time:	October–November	
Tropical storms:	November to May	
Charts:	BA: 4070	
	US: 700	
Pilots:	BA: 3, 39	
	US: 170, 171	

There are few other areas in the world that have such a bad reputation among cruising boats as the south western corner of the Indian Ocean. The strong south flowing Agulhas Current can create extremely rough conditions when hit by a SW gale, similar to conditions encountered off Cape Hatteras when the Gulf Stream is hit by a violent norther. Every year there are cases of boats rolled over and dismasted either on the passage from Mauritius to Durban or on the next leg to Cape Town.

The best time to leave Mauritius is early in November when the frequency of spring gales around latitude 30°S is getting lower and the chances of an early cyclone are remote. The recommended procedure is to try to keep between 100 and 150 miles off the southern tip of Madagascar as the weather in the vicinity of this island is often unsettled. This course also avoids a reputed freak wave area on the extended continental shelf off Madagascar. Yet another reason why it is recommended to keep to at least 150 miles south of Madagascar is because the South Equatorial Current splits here, half of it merging with the Agulhas Current, the other half flowing north into the Mozambique Channel. By closing too early with the African coast several boats have been pushed north by the northern branch of the current, while hoping for a southerly boost from the Agulhas Current. The winds up to this point can be expected to be favourable, although not necessarily trade wind conditions as encountered earlier on.

It is impossible to predict the kind of weather to expect when closing with the South African coast and the only solution is to keep an eye on the barometer. If there is a marked drop, the wind will shift to the SW and blow hard for anything from one hour to several hours until that particular low has passed. The weather of the entire area between Madagascar and the Cape of Good Hope is dominated by the presence of frontal systems which are created by Antarctic lows moving eastward. The approach of a cold front is usually heralded by a gradual change in the appearance of the sky, with cirrus clouds marching in from the west. These are replaced by dense banks of cumulus, while the wind is backing slowly from E to NW, freshening all the time. After a brief interlude the gale arrives from the SW, its severity and duration depending on the nature and extent of the front. During the passing of a front, when the wind shifts suddenly from E or NE to SW, conditions in the Agulhas Current can become hazardous, especially around the 100 fathom line. In such a situation it is best to head immediately for the coast as the waves are smaller in the shallower water near the coast. Alternatively, one should try to keep well offshore in deeper water and only approach the coast when close to the destination.

A local method of forecasting the approach of a SW *buster* is to watch the fall in the barometer, when the winds are probably NE. As the barometer stops falling, the wind becomes light and then ceases altogether. The moment the barometer starts rising one has between half an hour and one hour before the arrival of the SW gale, which may be enough warning to quickly leave the 100 fathom line.

Most boats have encountered very mixed weather on this route, with winds blowing at anything from 0 to 50 knots. However, very few are spared the SW gales that occur south of Madagascar and which succeed each other at two- to three-day intervals. After the area south of Madagascar has been passed, a new course should be laid to a point 200 miles ENE of Durban. Depending on wind and weather, a direct course can be steered from there to Durban. A common mistake is to allow too much for leeway, trying to make landfall north of Durban, expecting to be taken south by the current. However, should a SW gale arrive while close to the coast, one would be pushed even further north and in that case the alternative is to seek shelter in Richards Bay. This port is also recommended if landfall is made too far north of Durban. The subsequent 90 mile leg to Durban can be made later with a favourable weather forecast.

Note: Although it has been suggested that boats bound for South Africa from Mauritius should sail direct to Port Elizabeth in order to avoid the worst of the Agulhas Current, rather than stop at Richards Bay or Durban en route, experienced local sailors strongly advise against such a course of action. The Agulhas Current reaches its maximum width and strength close to the latitude of Port Elizabeth, making this the most dangerous area during bad weather. Furthermore, the chances of encountering the centre of the lows which are moving parallel with the coast are much greater in these latitudes than if the coast is approached north of Richards Bay, where the Agulhas Current is also narrower. It is therefore better to make landfall after a passage from either Mauritius or Réunion in about latitude 28°S and continue south only with a favourable weather forecast.

IS20 Réunion to Durban

DIAGRAMS 70, 77		Port des Galets to Durban 1420 m
Best time:	October–November	
Tropical storms:	November to May	
Charts:	BA: 4070	
	US: 700	
Pilots:	BA: 3, 39	
	US: 170, 171	

The same directions apply as for Route IS19 from Mauritius. Several of those who have made this passage described it as the toughest leg of their entire voyage. It is therefore essential to prepare the boat thoroughly for the trip to Durban and although conditions en route might be more favourable than those described in IS19, one should be prepared for the worst.

IS21 Durban to Cape Town

DIAGRAMS 70, 77		Durban to Cape Town 735 m
Best time:	January to March	
Tropical storms:	None	
Charts:	BA: 4204	
	US: 61003, 61000	
Pilots:	BA: 2, 3	
	US: 171, 123	

Few people attempt to make this passage in one go without seeking shelter in one of the few good ports en route. In fact the lack of sheltered anchorages is only one of three factors that make sailing along this section particularly difficult, the other two being the Agulhas Current and the unpredictable weather pattern. The Agulhas Current runs in a SW direction following the 100 fathom (200 metres) contour of the continental shelf and can attain up to 6 knots in places. The weather around the southern extremity of the African continent is greatly influenced by pressure systems moving NE from the Southern Ocean. As mentioned in Route IS19, a SW gale combined with the strong south flowing current can create giant waves up to 60 ft in height and even higher.

It has been established from research carried out into the formation of these freak waves that in all cases the dominant waves came from the SW. This always appears to coincide with a specific weather pattern, when areas of low pressure move along the coast in a NE direction. It is not uncommon during such conditions for the wind to suddenly change from a near NE gale to a full SW gale, the wind reinforcing the existing wave pattern which acts against the Agulhas Current.

Usually the largest waves occur between the edge of the continental shelf and an area 20 miles to seaward and this is the reason why mariners are advised to move inshore inside the 100 fathom line as soon as there is a sign of an approaching SW gale. Although coastal passages are outside the scope of this book, the area under discussion has created so many nightmares to small boat voyagers that it may be worthwhile looking at the Durban to Cape Town route in sections.

Durban to East London 250 m
As there is absolutely no safe shelter along this stretch of coast, it is essential to leave Durban with a good forecast. It is recommended to leave Durban at the end of a SW gale when the barometer has topped out around 1020 millibars. On leaving Durban one should head straight for the 100 fathom line to take full advantage of the strong south setting current. Should the weather deteriorate en route, one must close with the shore immediately so as to avoid the worst of the waves.

East London to Port Elizabeth 120 m
The same rules for leaving apply as for the run from Durban south, with the proviso that if the weather is still favourable when level with East London and the barometer is not falling dramatically, it is better to continue to Port Elizabeth. In case of a sudden deterioration of the weather, the same kind of avoiding action should be taken as described earlier. It must be stressed that the Agulhas Current is very strong between these two ports and also that there are inshore setting currents into some of the bays en route.

Port Elizabeth to Mossel Bay 170 m
This section presents fewer problems than the previous ones as there are several places en route where one can shelter from a gale. One of the first of these ports is Knysna, although the entrance is quite difficult because of the strong tidal currents and can become hazardous during a SW gale when heavy swells break across the entrance. Shelter can also be found in Mossel

Bay, near Cape Seal in Plettenberg Bay and close to Cape St Francis, where one should beware of uncharted reefs.

Mossel Bay to Cape Town 195 m

There are several places where one can anchor safely during unfavourable weather and on no account should Cape Agulhas be rounded in bad weather. There are onshore setting currents near all headlands on this route, which are also fronted by reefs, making navigation very difficult, especially in poor visibility.

IS22 Cocos Keeling to Chagos Archipelago

DIAGRAMS 70, 77	Cocos to Salomon Islands 1520 m

Best time:	June to September
Tropical storms:	April
Charts:	BA: 4070
	US: 70
Pilots:	BA: 39, 44
	US: 163, 170, 171

For the duration of the SE monsoon, both winds and current are favourable along this route. Occasionally in July and August the trades blow very strongly south of latitude 10°S, but these conditions are less common further north. Better sailing conditions are often encountered at the beginning and end of the SE monsoon, September being considered to be the best month. The influence of the NE monsoon makes itself felt as far south as latitude 10°S. Between January and April, winds are less constant in direction and usually have a northerly component. The weather in the transition period between monsoons is often unsettled, with overcast skies and rain squalls, which are often accompanied by violent winds.

Because of the restrictions that apply to boats arriving in Diego Garcia it is better to make straight for the Egmont Islands on the north side of the archipelago, unless an emergency call at Diego Garcia can be justified. (See Chapter 27.)

IS23 Chagos Archipelago to Seychelles

DIAGRAMS 70, 77	Peros Banhos to Mahé 1160 m

Best time:	May to September
Tropical storms:	None
Charts:	BA: 4071
	US: 702
Pilots:	BA: 39, 44
	US: 171

The SE monsoon should be favoured for this route, with its best weather between May and September, when both winds and current are favourable. Near perfect sailing conditions have been encountered by boats making this passage in May and June. Later in the year the NE monsoon starts making itself felt in the South Indian Ocean, the transitional months of October and November being associated with light winds, calm seas and the occasional violent rain squall.

The route is clear of dangers, but the Seychelles should be approached with caution because of the rocks and reefs that surround them. The islands are best approached from SE on a course that passes close to the southern extremity of Mahé, the main island and port of entry.

IS24 Christmas Island to Chagos Archipelago

DIAGRAM 70	Christmas to Salomon Islands 2010 m
Best time:	May to September
Tropical storms:	November to April
Charts:	BA: 4070
	US: 70
Pilots:	BA: 34, 39, 44
	US: 163, 170, 171

There are few boats which bypass Cocos Keeling Island and sail direct from Christmas Island to Chagos. However, in unsettled weather it might be preferable to sail a direct course, rather than make the detour to the south. The winter months of May to September provide both favourable winds and current. The weather on this route is similar to that on Routes IS16 and IS22, to which reference should be made. It should also be noted that Diego Garcia is a restricted military island and anchorage must be sought elsewhere in the Chagos Archipelago (see Chapter 27).

IS25 Western Australia to Cocos Keeling

DIAGRAM 70	Fremantle to Cocos 1580 m
Best time:	May to October
Tropical storms:	November to April
Charts:	BA: 4070
	US: 70
Pilots:	BA: 17, 44
	US: 163, 175

Tropical storms affect this region during the summer months, from the middle of November to April, and a passage during these months is therefore not recommended. Better sailing conditions usually occur in May–June and September–October, when the SE trade winds either have not reached their full strength or have started to diminish.

IS26 Indonesia to Chagos Archipelago

DIAGRAM 76	Benoa to Salomon Islands 2570 m

Best time:	May to October
Tropical storms:	None
Charts:	BA: 4071
	US: 70
Pilots:	BA: 34, 39
	US: 163, 170, 171

This more direct route is preferred by those who are not tempted by the usual detour via Christmas and Cocos Keeling Islands. The route from Bali runs slightly north of latitude 10°S where good sailing conditions can be expected throughout the SE monsoon and the risk of cyclones is almost nonexistent. The route can be joined south of Sumatra by boats that have reached the Indian Ocean through the Sunda Strait. Although the route is under the general influence of the SE trade winds, strong winds from the southern quarter are not unusual during the winter months and they are often accompanied by a big swell. Rough seas have been encountered especially around longitude 90°E, the disturbance being apparently caused by a submarine mountain ridge.

Because of the special regulations affecting visitors to Diego Garcia, where only genuine emergency stops are allowed, it is better to make straight for either the Salomon Islands or Peros Banhos in the north of the Chagos Archipelago.

IS27 Seychelles to Mauritius

DIAGRAM 77	Mahé to St Louis 940 m

Best time:	May–June, October
Tropical storms:	November to April
Charts:	BA: 4070
	US: 702
Pilots:	BA: 39
	US: 170, 171

A windward passage most of time, this route offers few alternatives, as the season when northerly winds are more frequent also coincides with the cyclone season. If the passage is made during the SE trade wind season, but outside of the blustery months of July and August, better conditions can be expected in May and early June or in October, when the winds can be more easterly.

IS28 Seychelles to Kenya

DIAGRAM 77		Mahé to Mombasa 940 m
Best time:	May to September	
Tropical storms:	None	
Charts:	BA: 4071	
	US: 70	
Pilots:	BA: 3, 39	
	US: 170, 171	

Favourable winds can be expected on this route throughout the SE trade wind season, from April till October, the months with the most consistent winds being May to September. During this period the current is also favourable, setting westward, but it turns northward before reaching the African coast.

On leaving Mahé Island, the course should lead well to the north of the Amirante Islands as they are low and the light on the most northerly island is reported to be out of action occasionally.

IS29 Chagos Archipelago to Mauritius

DIAGRAM 77		Peros Banhos to Port Louis 1220 m
Best time:	May–June, September–October	
Tropical storms:	November to April	
Charts:	BA: 4070	
	US: 702	
Pilots:	BA: 39	
	US: 170, 171	

A windward passage during most of the SE trade wind season, this route can benefit from better winds at the beginning and end of winter when the trades do not have too much south in them. It has been noticed that the stronger the SE trades, the more south there is in them, and vice versa. Therefore it may be worth avoiding this route in July and August when the trades are known to be quite blustery. Boats that have made the passage in October have reported pleasant sailing conditions. If the winds are easterly, it is possible to call in first at Rodriguez Island before continuing to Mauritius (see Route IS17).

IS30 Kenya to Seychelles

DIAGRAM 77	Mombasa to Mahé 940 m

Best time:	January to March
Tropical storms:	None
Charts:	BA: 4071
	US: 70
Pilots:	BA: 3, 39
	US: 170, 171

The NE monsoon makes itself felt along this route between January and March, when conditions for an eastbound passage are favourable, even if the winds are often light. Between December and April, the current along this route is also favourable. Although this is the cyclone season in other parts of the South Indian Ocean, cyclones very rarely reach the latitude of the Seychelles. But even if a cyclone came this way, it would pose no threat to a boat on passage from Africa as it could turn north at the first sign of an approaching storm and move quickly out of its way.

IS31 Mauritius to Comoros

DIAGRAM 77	St Louis to Glorieuses 840 m

Best time:	May to October
Tropical storms:	November to April
Charts:	BA: 4070
	US: 701, 702
Pilots:	BA: 39
	US: 170, 171

This is a downwind run to the northern tip of Madagascar during the SE trade wind season and on to the Comoros, a group of small islands spread out between Madagascar and the African coast. The first stop can be made at Iles Glorieuses, two small islands surrounded by a reef. The passage can also be interrupted at Tromelin Island, a tiny French possession lying half-way between Mauritius and the northern tip of Madagascar.

IS32 Comoros to Kenya

DIAGRAM 77	Grande Comoro to Mombasa 570 m

Best time:	May to October
Tropical storms:	November to April
Charts:	BA: 4701
	US: 701
Pilots:	BA: 3, 39
	US: 171

Favourable winds prevail along this route in the SE monsoon and there is also a northbound coastal current throughout the year, which can reach as much as 4 knots at the peak of the SE monsoon, but is only slight during the NE monsoon. The most pleasant weather is in July and August, when the temperature is cooler and humidity low.

The route passes Tanzania where it is possible to take an inshore route inside the reefs. Clearance formalities can be effected in the Tanzanian ports of Dar es Salaam, Tanga and Zanzibar. The island of Pemba is closed to visitors on security grounds and as there are several sensitive areas in Tanzania, skippers are urged to check the situation with the authorities in Dar es Salaam to avoid trouble with local officials.

Kenya has a more relaxed attitude towards visiting yachts. There are several protected ports along the Kenyan coast; clearance formalities can be carried out in Shimoni, Mombasa, Kilifi, Malindi and Lamu.

IS33 Mauritius to Seychelles

DIAGRAM 70		Port Louis to Mahé 940 m

Best time:	June to September
Tropical storms:	November to April
Charts:	BA: 4071
	US: 702
Pilots:	BA: 39
	US: 170, 171

The SE trade winds provide fair winds on this route from May to October, although the weather tends to be occasionally squally. Cyclones affect the area around Mauritius from the middle of November until the beginning of May, during which time it is best to avoid being in this area.

As the route passes fairly close to the Cargados Carajos Reefs, some boats take the opportunity to stop at one of these small islands. They belong to Mauritius and permission to stop there should be obtained beforehand from the Fisheries Department in Mauritius.

IS34 Seychelles to Comoros

DIAGRAM 77		Mahé to Glorieuses 640 m

Best time:	May to October
Tropical storms:	November to April
Charts:	BA: 4070
	US: 70
Pilots:	BA: 39
	US: 171

Because of the likelihood of headwinds during the SE monsoon, it might be better to make this voyage in shorter stages by calling in at some of the island groups en route. After leaving the main island of Mahé, the course should lead west of Platte Island unless a stop is intended in the Amirante Islands lying further west. These have several good anchorages, the one behind Desroches Island being the most convenient for a southbound trip from the Seychelles. Similar stops can be made at Alphonse or St François Islands before continuing towards the Comoros.

IS35 Comoros to Seychelles

DIAGRAM 70		Grande Comoro to Mahé 820 m
Best time:	May to October	
Tropical storms:	November to April	
Charts:	BA: 4070	
	US: 70	
Pilots:	BA: 39	
	US: 171	

Because the area around the Comoros is subject to tropical storms, this passage should not be undertaken during the cyclone season. From May to October winds are mostly SSE or SE and there is also a favourable current. The course from Iles Glorieuses should lead clear of Wizard Reef lying to the north of Providence Island. There are several island groups north of Madagascar that can be visited en route to the Seychelles and all of them have protected anchorages.

IS36 Comoros to Durban

DIAGRAMS 70, 77		Grande Comoro to Durban 900 m
Best time:	October–November	
Tropical storms:	November to May	
Charts:	BA: 4070	
	US: 70	
Pilots:	BA: 3, 39	
	US: 171	

The direct route to Durban or other South African ports leads through the Mozambique Channel, where the north setting Mozambique Current can create very difficult sailing conditions. Although the winds that blow between Madagascar and the African mainland often come from a favourable direction, strong NE winds blowing against the current produce rough seas. This passage should not be made before the middle of

September when the chances of encountering contrary winds in the Mozambique Channel are greater than later in the year. South of the Channel, similar directions apply as for Route IS19.

Because of political considerations, it is not advisable to sail too close to the coast of Mozambique, nor to enter any port. This advice is especially intended to the crews of boats flying the flag of a nation not regarded as 'friendly' by the government of Mozambique.

IS37 Durban to Mauritius

DIAGRAM 77	Durban to Port Louis 1550 m
Best time:	May
Tropical storms:	November to April
Charts:	BA: 4070
	US: 70, 700
Pilots:	BA: 3, 39
	US: 170, 171

Few boats attempt to follow the rhumb lines between these two points because of the strong Agulhas Current and the probability of encountering equally contrary winds. The recommended course is to make easting with the help of the prevailing westerly winds of higher latitudes. On leaving Durban, a SE route is taken so that easting is made between latitudes 38°S and 40°S. Strong westerlies are going to be encountered in these latitudes and also frequent squalls. Having sailed about 800 miles in an easterly direction, a northerly course can be set which leads into an area of variable winds and calms. The SE trades can sometimes be found as far south as 30°S. The best month for this passage is considered to be May as the cyclone season has come to an end in the South Indian Ocean and the winter gales of higher latitudes are only about to begin.

IS38 Cape Town to Western Australia

DIAGRAM 70	Cape Town to Fremantle 4700 m
Best time:	October to February
Tropical storms:	November to April
Charts:	BA: 4204, 4070
	US: 70
Pilots:	BA: 2, 3, 17, 39
	US: 123, 170, 175

As most of this passage will be made in the Roaring Forties or even higher latitudes, it is recommended to sail in the southern summer when the frequency of gales is lowest, the weather warmer and there is little risk of encountering icebergs. Although the recommended time coincides with the season of tropical storms, these very rarely reach high latitudes and the only area where they might be encountered is close to Western Australia.

On leaving Cape Town, a southerly course should be steered to avoid the area of the Agulhas Bank which has a high frequency of gales and also has a contrary current. Even if the course made good is SW because of SE winds, the lost ground can be made up later when the area of westerly winds has been reached. In October and November the northern limit of icebergs extends to latitude 39°S in the area comprised between longitudes 20°E and 30°E, so the course should become easterly before this area is reached. For vessels going to Western Australia, the route runs between latitudes 39°S and 40°S, where the proportion of westerly winds is relatively high during the summer months and the weather considerably warmer than if one went south to about latitude 50°S where the predominance of westerly winds, and gales, is indeed higher. It must be stressed that a reluctance to go far enough south in search of westerlies, and staying around latitude 35°S, usually means a greater proportion of SE winds. Course should be altered for Fremantle or any other West Australian destination only after meridian 100°E has been crossed.

IS39 Western Australia to Bass Strait

DIAGRAM 70	Fremantle to Bass Strait 1700 m

Best time:	December to March
Tropical storms:	None
Charts:	BA: 4709, 4601
	US: 709, 601
Pilots:	BA: 13, 14, 17
	US: 127, 175

Sailing along the south of Australia can be done either in one long leg to Bass Strait or in easy coastal stages by stopping at various places en route. The offshore route has the advantage of more constant winds as the Great Australian Bight is renowned for its baffling winds in summer. If the transocean route had been left for a detour to Western Australia, it is advisable to regain that route after rounding Cape Leeuwin. The route runs along latitude 40°S and after crossing meridian 140°E the course is altered to pass north of King Island. Extreme caution must be exercised when approaching Bass Strait from westward, especially at night or in bad visibility, because of the strong currents that sweep through the straits.

For vessels bound for Sydney direct from Cape Town the passage through Bass Strait is only recommended in winter. During the summer better conditions are met by keeping south of Tasmania. After passing Tasmania, the course should only turn north after longitude 155°E, so as to avoid the full effect of the south setting Australia Current and to approach Sydney from offshore where the current is much weaker and the winds steadier.

25 Winds, currents and routes in the Red Sea

Winds and weather

The distinctive long shape of the Red Sea, bordered by low arid coasts with high mountains rising some twenty miles inland, dictates in some measure the direction of winds, which tend to blow parallel to these coasts, either from a NW or SE direction. These winds differ markedly in the southern and northern areas of the Red Sea and in the south show a seasonal variation due to the movement of the convergence zone between the wind systems of the northern and southern hemispheres.

Although the Red Sea is well to the north of the equator, the ITCZ moves into this area to reach its farthest position north, around 12°N approximately, in July. At this time of year it marks the boundary between the SW monsoon of the Indian Ocean and the prevailing NW winds of the northern Red Sea. During these summer months NW winds blow down the entire length of the Red Sea merging into the SW monsoon in the Gulf of Aden.

In winter the ITCZ lies well to the south of this region, but there is another unrelated convergence zone which lies around 18°N from October to May and marks the boundary between the SE winds of the southern Red Sea and the NW winds of the northern section. This convergence zone is usually marked by cloudy skies in contrast to the ubiquitous sunshine prevailing in the region as a whole. This zone is associated with rain and drizzle.

SE winds predominate from October to January in all areas south of the convergence zone. From January to May the SE winds may not penetrate quite as far as the zone itself, but still predominate in the most southerly areas and in the Straits of Bab el Mandeb. These winds are strongest from November to February, averaging around 20 knots, but gale force winds of 30 knots and over occur fairly frequently. September and May are transitional months with lighter winds. In the Straits of Bab el Mandeb, a funnelling effect occurs which increases the wind speed at all times of the year, but especially in the winter months, November to March, when it is frequently 25 knots and over.

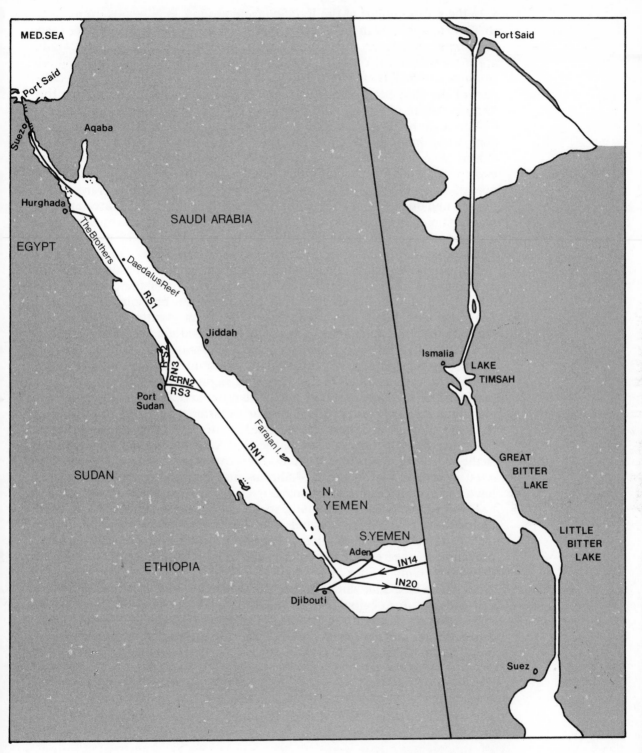

78. ROUTES IN THE RED SEA
THE SUEZ CANAL

In the northern part of the Red Sea from around 20°N, winds from the N to NW predominate in all months of the year, being stronger in winter than in summer. However, in the most northerly part, the Gulf of Suez, winds are more frequently over 20 knots from April to October with the highest frequency of gale force winds during this time. The Gulf of Suez is the only part of the Red Sea to be affected by depressions moving east across the Mediterranean.

Although the Red Sea winds are on average light to moderate, periods of complete calm do occur, sometimes for several days at a time. No tropical storms have been recorded in any part of the Red Sea. There are however two special winds occurring in this region. The *haboob* is a short squall of over 35 knots blowing off the coast of Sudan between S and W, raising lots of sand and dust. *Haboobs* occur particularly in the Port Sudan area and are most common between July and September. The other wind is the *khamsin*, a strong dry S to SE wind similarly blowing off the land in Egypt causing sandstorms, most commonly between February and May.

All of these winds which bring sand and dust reduce visibility considerably, often to less than 100 feet, especially near the coast. On the other hand, due to the special refraction conditions prevailing in the Red Sea, land and lights are often visible for much greater distances than normal, up to 100 miles away. This effect can also affect the horizon, raising or lowering it, which can produce errors in astronavigational observations, up to 20' error in longitude and 10' error in latitude. This phenomenon can affect observations taken before and after noon in different ways and can produce the impression of an apparent cross-current. It is thought that refraction is less at twilight and in the early morning, so therefore the taking of star sights has been recommended in this region. A brilliant luminescence sometimes occurs in the Red Sea, making the water appear shallower. With the presence of unlit reefs extending considerably from the coast in several places, these conditions may explain why so many yachts have come to grief in this region.

The Red Sea area is a hot, arid region with a low rainfall. The average temperature is very high, around 30°C, but often reaches over 40°C in the day, and even temperatures exceeding 50°C are not uncommon. Temperatures are lowest in winter in the more northerly part, dropping to 18°C in the Gulf of Suez on a winter night. This contrasts with the southern areas of the Red Sea, where in August the temperature is over 40°C by day and does not drop below 32°C even at night, which can easily lead to heat exhaustion in unclimatised people. Care must be exercised in this area, especially on metal yachts, because the temperature of a steel deck can easily rise to a blistering 70°C.

Currents

The overall direction of flow of current in the Red Sea is influenced by the monsoons in the Indian Ocean. From November until April while the NE monsoon is blowing, water is pushed into the Red Sea and there is a predominantly N to NW setting current along the axis of the Red Sea. From May until October when the SW monsoon prevails over the Indian Ocean, water is drawn out of the Red Sea and a S to SE setting current prevails. Due to the narrowness and shape of the Red Sea, there is a great variability in the currents and many lateral currents run out and in from the main stream, particularly near islands and reefs. These cross-currents occur in all months and are very variable. They are not, however, as strong as was first believed, because many apparent cross-currents were found to be due to errors in astronavigation produced by the refraction effect on the horizon. The strongest current is experienced in the Straits of Bab el Mandeb, reaching 2 knots during the NE monsoon. In the transitional months between monsoons, April and May or October, there is little or no current.

Routes

Diagram 78

Charts:	BA: 6, 8, 63, 138, 141
	US: 62081, 62191, 62195, 62230, 62250, 62290
Pilots:	BA: 64
	US: 172

In spite of its many attractions, good anchorages, excellent fishing and magnificent diving, the Red Sea has just as many disadvantages from the cruising point of view and therefore most people try to pass through it as quickly as possible. In most cases the problems are of a political nature, the eastern shore being virtually barred to visiting yachts, while in its southern part, the continuing troubles in Ethiopia make that country's coastline extremely dangerous for small boats. This leaves only the coasts of Egypt and Sudan to be explored and even here, foreign yachts cannot always rely on a friendly reception from the authorities. The only alternative for boats bound either for the Indian Ocean or the Mediterranean is a passage up or down the middle of the Red Sea, but even this is not such an easy task because of the large amount of shipping and often unfavourable wind.

Because of all these factors, most sailing boats that pass through the Red Sea combine the two possibilities, alternating long offshore legs with coastal cruising in daily hops. The method has much to recommend it as it is less trying for the crew than a non-stop passage and is also safer, because many of the numerous navigational hazards can be avoided in this way. The average time in which the entire length of the Red Sea can be navigated in this manner is three weeks.

Reefs and other dangers are well marked on British Admiralty charts particularly, and navigation among the reefs is not difficult in good light. When seeking an anchorage for the night, it is advisable not to leave this until too late in the afternoon because the lower sun casts a sheen over the water obscuring dangers which are otherwise easily seen.

RN Northbound routes

Regardless of the time of year, northbound boats usually have to contend with contrary winds for at least half their passage up the Red Sea. Therefore it is difficult to recommend a preferred time of year, especially as the Red Sea passage is usually a continuation of a voyage, the timing of which has been decided by other factors. Most boats undertake their northbound voyage at the end of winter, between February and April, usually after crossing the North Indian Ocean during the NE monsoon. Although NW winds prevail in the northern half of the Red Sea throughout the year, these tend to be lighter in spring than in winter, making April one of the best months for the northbound voyage. Another advantage of a late March or April passage is that the Mediterranean is reached as the weather starts getting warmer and the cruising season begins. Although the headwinds of the Red Sea have become something of a legend among sailors, it must be pointed out that winds do not always follow the axis of the sea and although forced to tack, boats can usually choose a more favourable tack. Another observation worth bearing in mind is that the wind tends to shift with the sun, being more NE in the morning and NW in the afternoon.

RN1

Aden to Bab el Mandeb 100 m
Djibouti to Bab el Mandeb 70 m
Bab el Mandeb to Jabal Attair 200 m
Jabal Attair to Masimirit 270 m

When heading for the Red Sea from the Gulf of Aden, whether coming from Djibouti or Aden, boats passing through the Straits of Bab el Mandeb (Gates of Sorrow) should do so west of Perim Island. A traffic separation zone is in operation in the straits and northbound vessels must keep to the starboard side. Perim Island should not be passed unnecessarily close, because it is a restricted area and yachts have been fired on by the military in the past. For the same reason, Small Strait east of Perim Island should only be used in an emergency.

The next 200 miles to Jabal Attair Island (15°32′N, 41°50′E), which has a powerful light on it, can be made either non-stop or in shorter stages by anchoring in the two island groups en route. If the winds continue to be favourable, it is advisable to make as much northing as possible while the wind lasts, rather than stop in the islands. Both Hanish and Zubair Islands belong to North Yemen and although anchoring by yachts in transit is usually tolerated by the authorities, landing is prohibited. In poor visibility or heavy weather, it is better to pass to the east of the Hanish Islands, where clearer landmarks make it easier to avoid the various dangers. Zubair Islands should be passed on their west side where there are no offlying dangers. If they are passed on the east side, attention must be paid to East Rocks, a cluster of rocks north of Jabal Zubair.

Jabal Attair is an excellent landfall from where a new course can be laid to pass safely between the dangers that front both shores of the Red Sea, the width of the fairway being about 60 miles in this area. From Jabal Attair the course should cross latitude 17°N in 40°40′E, to avoid both the Farasan Islands on the Saudi Arabian side and the Dahlach Bank off the Eritrean coast. For those who do not wish to stop in Sudan, the next landfall is Masamirit Islet (18°50′N, 38°45′E), which should be approached from the SE and passed to the east because of the dangerous area south of it.

RN2   Jabal Attair to Khor Nawarat 260 m

For those who prefer to cover the remaining distance in shorter stages by sailing inside the reefs, there are three ways of approaching the Sudanese coast. The first option is to make for Khor Nawarat, an anchorage lying very close to the Ethiopian–Sudanese border. Because of this position, the dangerous reefs and islets in the Suakin Group and the reportedly unpredictable currents, Khor Nawarat should be approached with extreme caution and only if the vessel's position has been confidently established. Ethiopian territorial waters must not be entered on any account and if in any doubt it is safer to remain offshore and attempt to make landfall on Masamirit light.

An alternative way to reach the Sudanese coast is to pass close to the south of Masamirit Islet and make for Trinkitat harbour by threading a passage carefully through the various reefs. An inshore passage, reasonably well beaconed, leads both from Khor Nawarat and Trinkitat to Port Sudan. The latter can also be reached by an offshore route which passes east of all dangers in the Suakin Group and turns west at Hindi Gider light.

RN3   Port Sudan to Suez 700 m

Northward from Port Sudan, the alternatives are the same, as boats can either stay inside the reefs or sail offshore. Compared to the southern half of the Red Sea, the north has fewer dangers and the offshore route has a clear run all the way to Daedalus Reef (24°56′N, 35°52′E). A useful landfall en route is Gezirat Zabargad, a high rocky islet off Foul Bay, an area which is best avoided even by those who have been coastal sailing to this point. Longer offshore legs become increasingly necessary as there are fewer safe anchorages along the Egyptian coast. After The Brothers (26°19′N, 34°51′E), a safe, all-weather anchorage can be found at Hurghada or nearby. The Gulf of Suez can then be reached via Tawila Channel, which avoids a detour past Shaker Island and the Strait of Gubal. Navigation through the narrow Gulf of Suez can be daunting, due to the numerous oil rigs, heavy shipping and the usually contrary wind.

If Suez Bay is reached during the night, it is recommended to anchor off the main channel and wait for daylight before passing among the heavy commercial traffic. A shipping agent or his representative will arrive in his launch soon after Suez Bay has been entered, offering to make arrangements for transiting the Suez Canal. Agency fees are extremely competitive and skippers are advised not to accept an offer before the going rate has been established. See also notes on the passage through the Suez Canal in Chapter 27.

The recommended yacht anchorage for yachts intending to transit the canal is in Port Ibrahim, just inside the southern breakwater of the main harbour. The breakwater can be passed either west or east and the anchorage is at its eastern end, close to the entrance into the North Basin. The Port Authority and other offices are on the north side of the Canal entrance (see Diagram 84).

RS Southbound routes

The best time for a southbound passage through the Red Sea depends on just as many factors as a northbound voyage. The most pleasant time to head south is probably during the spring months, from February to April, when the weather is becoming warmer in the northern areas and is not too hot in the southern section. At this time favourable winds can be expected to last at least as far as the latitude of Port Sudan. From May onwards winds from the NW should be carried the entire length of the Red Sea. The timing of this passage usually depends on the destination after the Red Sea, and the weather in the North Indian Ocean must be taken into account. For an eastbound passage across the North Indian Ocean, the SW monsoon which blows from May to October ensures the most favourable winds, although these may be too strong at the height of the monsoon in July and August when a high proportion reach gale force. These months are best avoided because of the unbearable heat. See also Routes IN20, IN21 and IT19.

RS1

Suez to Hurghada 200 m
Hurghada to Port Sudan 500 m

Although anchorage can be sought each night as for the northbound route, it is more common for boats to head south in longer offshore legs taking advantage of favourable winds. At the southern end of the Gulf of Suez, several miles can be saved by sailing through either Zeit or Tawila Channels which lead to the anchorage at Hurghada. The course then leads offshore passing close to The Brothers (26°19'N, 34°51'E) and Daedalus Reef (24°56'N, 35°52'E), both of which have powerful lights.

RS2

Ras Hadarba to Port Sudan 150 m

If an inshore passage is preferred south of Foul Bay, a convenient place to go behind the reefs is at Ras Hadarba, close to the border between Egypt and Sudan. The entire distance from there to Port Sudan can be covered mostly in sheltered waters where safe anchorages are easily found every night.

RS3

Port Sudan to Khor Nawarat 120 m
Khor Nawarat to Bab el Mandeb 460 m

The inshore route can be continued beyond Port Sudan as far as either Trinkitat or Khor Nawarat. From Trinkitat the open sea is reached via a pass which leads due east through the reefs and islets of the Suakin Group. From Khor Nawarat, all dangers of the Suakin Group are left to port and a safe course is laid as soon as open water is reached so as to move quickly out of Ethiopian waters. As stressed earlier, the territorial waters of Ethiopia must be avoided and therefore Khor Nawarat is the last place on the western shore of the Red Sea where shelter should be sought.

South of latitude 18°N, the only alternative is to steer a course down the middle of the Red Sea. The coasts of Saudi Arabia and North Yemen should not be approached, nor should anchorage be sought in any of their offlying islands, except in a real emergency. From Masamirit Islet the course leads half-way between the Dahlach Bank, on the Ethiopian side, and the Farasan Islands, on the Saudi side, to Jabal at Tair, a conspicuous island situated in 15°32′N, 41°50′E. Two groups of islands lying south of it, Zubair and Hanish Islands, offer shelter in heavy weather. Both island groups should be approached with caution as there are some offlying dangers. Zubair Islands are best passed on their western side, while Jabal Zuqar and the Hanish Islands should be passed to the east, paying careful attention to the various rocks in their vicinity. When passing through the Bab el Mandeb Straits, Perim Island should be kept to port, but the island should not be passed too close as it is a restricted military area.

26 Winds, currents and routes in the Mediterranean

Winds and weather

The Mediterranean climate is on the whole extremely pleasant, marked by long fine summers, hot but not too hot, and mild winters that are not too cold. Most gales and rain occur in winter months, few storms interrupting the long summer. Local conditions vary considerably, stronger winds and squalls often resulting from local phenomena and not due to the overall weather pattern. Tropical storms do not affect this region.

The Mediterranean can be divided into two halves, western and eastern, corresponding to the two deeper basins which are separated by a ridge, running through Italy, Sicily and Malta to the African coast. In the summer the Western Mediterranean comes under the influence of the Atlantic high pressure area centred near the Azores, while the Eastern Mediterranean is influenced by the low pressure area east of the Mediterranean, which is an extension of the Indian Ocean monsoon. As a rule, weather systems move across the Mediterranean from west to east and this is particularly true of depressions in the winter months. The commonest winds over the entire area are from the northerly sector, more from the NW in the western basin, N in the Aegean and NE in the easterly areas.

Well chronicled down the centuries are the various regional winds, which are a notable feature of Mediterranean weather.

Mistral

'Magistralis', meaning masterful, was the name originally given to the cold dry NW wind which holds masterly sway over the Western Mediterranean in both frequency and strength. Now corrupted to *mistral* or *maestral*, these NW winds are formed when cold air flowing down over France is blocked by the heights of the Alps and is diverted to pour into the Mediterranean via the Rhone valley. The *mistral* blows strongly in the Gulf of Lions and the Gulf of Genoa, while the Rhone delta area and Marseille receive the full force of the *mistral* on almost 100 days a year. On average 20 knots, the *mistral* is frequently stronger and can reach 50–60 knots on occasion. The *mistral* often reaches the Balearics and Sardinia and on occasion can be felt as far as Malta and North Africa. The French Riviera east of Marseille is sheltered by the mountains behind the coast and the *mistral* is felt less there.

The *mistral* blows at intervals throughout the year, although it is commonest in the winter half, normally lasting from 3 to 6 days, and is typified by clear skies. Along the Spanish coast this NW wind is called the *Tramontana*, being strong, cold and dry with many local variations.

Vendavales

These are strong SW winds which blow between North Africa and the Spanish coast, especially in the late autumn and early spring. These winds, which do not last long, can reach gale force and are associated with depressions moving across Spain and Southern France. The *vendavales* are associated with squalls and thunderstorms, but are less strong near the African coast and the NE coast of Spain. They are much stronger when funnelled through the Straits of Gibraltar. Hitting the west coast of Sardinia and the Gulf of Genoa, these strong SW winds are called *libeccio* in Italian.

Sirocco

This name is used generally for any winds from the south bringing hot air off the continent of Africa. Due to depressions moving east across the desert, the *sirocco* blows off the north coast of Africa very hot and dry, often laden with sand and dust, thus reducing visibility.

As these winds pass across the sea, they pick up some moisture and so in Spain, Malta, Sicily, Sardinia and Southern Italy, the *sirocco* arrives at a lower temperature and with a higher humidity than off the African coast. In those places it is a warm hazy wind associated with a low layer of continuous cloud. Rain falling through the dust carried by these winds can sometimes be red or brown.

A similar wind blows off the Arabian peninsula to affect Israel, Lebanon, Cyprus, Crete and other southern islands in the eastern Mediterranean, particularly in the transitional periods between seasons, from April to June, September and October. In Egypt the *sirocco* is called the *khamsin*, which means 50 in Arabic, because it occurs most frequently in the 50 days following the Coptic Easter. It usually blows at gale force for about one day and is most common from February to April. Later in May and June the *khamsin* is less frequent but can last longer. Other local names for the *sirocco* are *leveche* in SE Spain and *chihli* in North Africa.

Levante

These NE winds blow near the Spanish coast, reaching gale force in spring (February to May) and autumn (October to December). In summer months from June to September, the *levante* are shorter and with less wind. The *levante* are formed when a depression is situated between the Balearics and North Africa, usually when there is a high pressure area over the European land mass to the north.

The *levante* are commonest along the central region of the Spanish coast, being less frequent to the south. These winds continue into the Straits of Gibraltar, where they are funnelled to become easterly and are known as *levanter*. The *levante* bring lower temperatures and rain, which is often heavy near to the coast, while the long fetch produces heavy seas.

Gregale

These strong winds also from the NE are felt in the central Mediterranean, on the coasts of Sicily and Malta and especially in the Ionian Sea. They flow out of high pressure areas situated over the Balkans and are common in the winter half of the year, especially February. These winds usually blow at gale force, are cold and produce a heavy swell. The NE coast of Malta is particularly vulnerable as the main harbours are open to the NE. It was a *gregale* that wrecked St Paul on the Maltese coast in the first century AD.

Meltemi

This wind is more commonly known by its Turkish name *meltemi* than as the *etesian* wind, which is taken from the Greek word meaning annual. These regular winds blow steadily over the eastern basin of the Mediterranean all summer, commencing in May or early June and continuing until September or even October. The *meltemi* is at its strongest and steadiest in July and August. Even when the *meltemi* is not blowing or while it is being established in the earlier months, it is rare to get winds from any other direction during this time. Periods of calm can occur, particularly at the beginning of the season. The *meltemi* has many similarities with a monsoon and in some respects it can be regarded as an extension of the Indian monsoon caused by the low pressure area east of the Mediterranean.

The *meltemi* blows from the north in the central Aegean, tending to be more NE in the northern Aegean and NW in the southern areas, extending across the whole eastern basin of the Mediterranean, although it peters out before reaching the southern shores. The *meltemi* is a fresh wind, on average 15–20 knots, and associated with fine clear weather. Often it blows up to 30 knots, especially in the afternoons, and occasionally it reaches 40 knots. It is less strong in the most northerly areas and strongest in the S and SW Aegean. The wind does tend to decrease at night.

The overall weather picture is summarised as follows.

Western Mediterranean

Summers are fine with few storms. Gale force winds do occur, but these are often generated by local depressions over a limited area. Because of this they are difficult to predict and give little warning of their onset, as an impending gale is rarely preceded by a meaningful change in barometric pressure. Strong winds such as *vendavales, sirocco* or *levante* are more common in the transitional months of spring and autumn. The *mistral* can blow in summer but is much less frequent than at other times of the year. The commonest wind over this area is from the NW, except in the most southerly areas near the African coast, where winds from the E and NE are more frequent. There can be calm periods for several days at a time. There is little rain over this area in summer months, except for summer and autumn thunderstorms near some of the coasts.

In winter winds are much more variable and gales more frequent. Depressions from the Atlantic track in from the west, either across France or Spain or through the Straits of Gibraltar. Also some local depressions form in the Gulf of Lions or the Gulf of Genoa and track to the south, bringing strong winds and squally weather. The *mistral* gales are more frequent in winter months and NW winds predominate over this area. *Vendavales* and *libeccio* blow especially in late autumn and early spring. In spite of the increased frequency of gales in winter, there are also some quiet periods. Although most rain falls during winter as showers, temperatures are mild and there are a reasonable number of clear sunny days.

Eastern Mediterranean

The summers are dominated by the seasonal winds from the northern quarter, which blow strongly, but are associated with clear skies and fine weather. Rainfall is scanty and almost nonexistent on the southern shores. The climate of the eastern basin is a little more continental than the western or central areas, which means fewer fronts, less rain and a lower humidity. It is noted for long hot summers and short winters. Most of the rain falls in winter months.

In winter, depressions track in an easterly direction either SE towards Cyprus or NE towards the Black Sea. Although small in size, these depressions can be very violent as they develop rapidly and with little warning. Some violent storms in this area are dangerous as they are local in character, arriving quickly out of a clear sky. Although winds from the northerly sector are commonest in winter too, winds from all directions do occur and there are strong gale force winds from the south particularly. Both S and N winds are more prolonged than E or W winds, which do not last so long. November to February are the worst months with cold dry N to NE gales and warm moist SE to SW gales which bring dust. When a depression passes there can be a change from S to N within a few hours. At the transitional period between seasons, such as in April and May, calms can occur for several days.

Coastal weather

Close to the coast, the weather is greatly affected by the height of the land and other topographical features. Local conditions vary enormously, any prevailing wind usually being lighter near the coast, while land and sea breezes have a strong effect. The land and sea breezes are particularly marked in summer months and reach 20–30 knots in some places. The direction of the wind changes not only with the time of day, but also with the orientation of the coast. A reversal in the direction of the wind usually occurs between early morning and late afternoon. Local squalls are more frequent where the coast is mountainous and wind is frequently accelerated down valleys or between islands. These effects are particularly true for high islands. For example in summer a strong sea breeze blows onshore in the daytime in Sicily, being NE at Palermo, NE to S at Syracuse and S to SW at Agrigento and so on, around the island. It is impossible to describe all local conditions in detail, but a few brief points will be made.

Gibraltar

Winds tend to be funnelled either W or E in the straits. At Gibraltar W winds predominate in winter and E in summer. *Levanters* are more frequent from July to October and can blow for up to 15 days at a time, although not always too strongly (15 knots). In winter the *levanter* is shorter but stronger, bringing rain, clouds and haze. *Vendavales* also occur most frequently from November to March. In the lee of the Rock of Gibraltar the wind causes eddies blowing strongly from different directions only a short distance apart.

Gulf of Lions

This area is especially noted for sudden changes in wind and weather, with very different conditions in places near together. After the *mistral*, the next common wind is the *marin*, which blows warm and moist, SE to SW off the sea, and although not as strong as the *mistral*, it raises a heavy sea.

Straits of Messina

The wind tends to blow either in a N or S direction along the straits, depending on prevailing conditions. Sometimes the wind will be NE on the eastern side, NW on the western side and very light in the middle.

Alternatively it can be S to SE in the southern approaches, changing abruptly to NW in the northern approaches, which creates a heavy sea. Violent squalls come off the high ground, which together with strong tidal currents and a number of small whirlpools and eddies contribute to these straits retaining the flavour of Scylla and Charybis of the time of Odysseus. A line of bores called *tagli* can occur at the change of tide. Mirages of a multiple image type are sometimes seen in these straits.

The Aegean

When the *meltemi* is blowing strongly offshore, sudden squalls often occur in the lee of high ground. Accelerated down the land, this can produce 40–50 knots of wind very suddenly in an area previously calm. This effect occurs particularly on steep southern coasts, both of islands and the mainland. The *meltemi* is also funnelled through straits, ravines and between islands. When sheltering on a southerly coast during a N gale, this squally effect must be allowed for.

African coast

The *sirocco* or *khamsin* is strongest near to the coast of North Africa and there is also a daily change in wind direction due to strong land and sea breezes. Thunderstorms are very frequent along this coast, especially in late summer and early autumn. Temperatures can be very hot when the *sirocco* is blowing.

Black Sea

The Black Sea enjoys a climate very similar to the Mediterranean in summer, being mainly fine and sunny, with winds predominantly from the NW or W formed by the same system which generates the *meltemi*. In winter, however, the weather is much colder, especially in more northerly parts where ice can occur. Very variable conditions prevail in the transition months, April–May and September–October, the winds changing very quickly both in force and direction. Local effects as well as land and sea breezes are well marked. In the Dardanelles and Bosporus, NE winds are the most frequent as there is a general airflow from the Black Sea into the Aegean. If the wind is not blowing from the NE in these narrows, it is usually from the opposite SW direction.

Currents

As the Mediterranean loses more water by evaporation than it receives from rivers emptying into it, there is a general inflow of water from the

Atlantic Ocean at all times of the year. This east setting current is strongest through the Straits of Gibraltar and along the North African coast, where it averages around 2 knots. After passing through the channel between Sicily and Tunisia it gradually loses its strength as it flows eastward. There is a weaker anticlockwise circulation in both of the two basins of the Mediterranean joined by an east setting current in the Malta channel between the two areas. In the western basin, this current flows north up the Italian west coast turning west along the south coast of France and flowing south down the Spanish coast. In the eastern basin, the eastward flowing current turns north along the coast of Israel and Lebanon, west along the Turkish coast, completing the circle along the northern coast of Crete. A branch makes an anticlockwise circulation of the Aegean Sea, joined in its southward movement by water flowing out of the Black Sea and into the Mediterranean via the Bosporus and Dardenelles. Another branch makes an anticlockwise circulation of the Adriatic.

Excepting the steady current along the North African coast, the actual currents are very variable and are affected considerably both by the direction and force of the wind and local conditions. For example, when the *meltemi* is blowing, a S to SW setting current predominates in the central and western Aegean. The strongest currents are experienced in the Straits of Gibraltar, the Bosporus and Dardanelles. Other straits, such as the Straits of Messina, are strongly affected by tidal currents.

Routes

Sailing conditions in the Mediterranean have been reviled and ridiculed more than in any other part of the world by modern sailors and the most repeated saying is that 'in the Mediterranean one either gets too much wind or not at all, and what one gets is on the nose'. Fortunately this is not always true and although the winds encountered in this inland sea cannot be compared in constancy to the trade winds of the Caribbean or Indian Ocean, most offshore passages can be made under sail. The Mediterranean has been plied for many centuries by all kinds of wind-driven craft and some of the voyages of ancient time have become legend. Being aware of the capricious nature of Mediterranean winds, ships used to be provided with a set of sturdy oars and although slaves have gone out of fashion, modern diesel engines can take their place just as well.

Because of its long maritime history, the weather of the Mediterranean is well known and this simplifies the task for those intending to do some forward planning. As the sailing season stretches over almost nine months of the year, from early March to the end of November, a lot of ground can be covered if an early start is made. This is recommended especially for those planning to make west to east passages as westerly winds are more common during early spring and late autumn. However, because weather patterns are less clearly defined in the Mediterranean than in other parts of the world, a 'best time' to make a particular passage cannot be given. With a few exceptions, the weather can rarely be regarded as dangerous in the Mediterranean and the most violent storms almost invariably occur in winter, January and February being the worst months.

The multitude of good harbours throughout the Mediterranean coupled with the unparalleled richness and variety of places to visit ashore means that most people prefer coastal cruising and therefore only the most frequented offshore routes have been described.

M10 West to east routes

M11 Gibraltar to the Balearic Islands
M12 Balearic Islands to the French Riviera
M13 French Riviera to Corsica
M14 Corsica to Messina Strait
M15 Balearic Islands to Messina Strait
M16 Messina Strait to Greece
M17 Gibraltar to Malta
M18 Malta to Greece
M19 Routes in the Adriatic Sea
M20 Routes in the Aegean Sea
M21 Routes in the Marmara and Black Seas
M22 Rhodes to Cyprus
M23 Cyprus to Israel
M24 Cyprus to Port Said
M25 Rhodes to Port Said
M26 Malta to Port Said

M11 Gibraltar to Balearic Islands

DIAGRAM 79	Gibraltar to Ibiza 380 m
	Ibiza to Palma de Mallorca 70 m

Charts:	BA: 2717
	US: 301
Pilots:	BA: 45
	US: 130, 131

The route runs parallel to the Spanish coast keeping 15–20 miles offshore, where steadier winds will be found. The favourable east setting current is felt at least as far as Cabo de Gata, where the route turns NE passing close to Cabo de Palos. Along the entire length of the Spanish coast there are

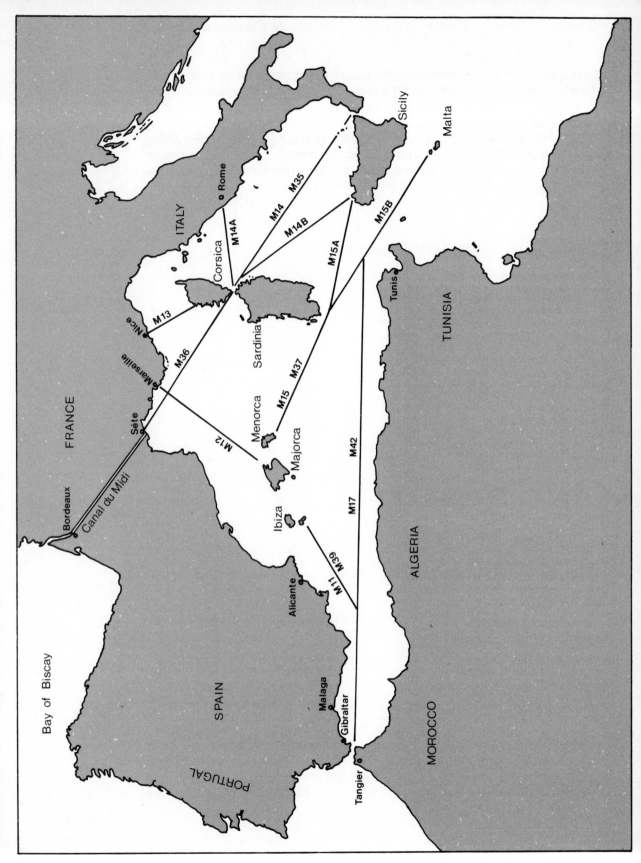

several good harbours in which shelter can be sought in bad weather. From Cabo de Palos, the route for Ibiza passes west of Formentera Island. There are several deep water channels between the southern extremity of Ibiza and Espalmador Islet, lying close to the northern tip of Formentera. The currents in the channels are strong and usually set against the prevailing wind, which can result in rough seas in strong winds. Under such circumstances it is better to pass east of Formentera, which is also the recommended procedure if one is bound direct for Palma de Mallorca.

M12 Balearic Islands to French Riviera

DIAGRAM 79	Mallorca to Marseille 300 m
	Menorca to Nice 280 m

Charts:	BA: 1780, 2717
	US: 301
Pilots:	BA: 45, 46
	US: 131

During the summer months the prevailing wind on this route is NW. The worst thing that can affect a vessel bound for the French coast is to encounter a *mistral*, which can be very violent in the Gulf of Lions. Even if the destination lies further east, it is advisable to close with the coast in the vicinity of Hyères Island as there are plenty of ports where it is possible to stop should the weather deteriorate.

M13 French Riviera to Corsica

DIAGRAM 79	Nice to Calvi 100 m
	St Raphael to Ajaccio 130 m

Charts:	BA: 1780
	US: 301
Pilots:	BA: 46
	US: 131

Because the west coast of Corsica is more attractive and has a number of good harbours, most boats leaving the Riviera make straight for Calvi or Ajaccio. Favourable winds can be expected during the summer months and even the *mistral* blows from the right direction, although it is usually associated with rough seas.

M14 Corsica to Messina Strait

DIAGRAM 79	Bonifacio to Messina 360 m
	Bonifacio to Anzio 160 m
	Porto Cervo to Palermo 260 m

Charts:	BA: 165
	US: 301
Pilots:	BA: 45, 46
	US: 131

The Bonifacio Strait, separating Corsica from Sardinia, is an intricate waterway dotted with rocks and islets, although navigation through the channels that transverse it is not too difficult. Having passed through the strait, there is a choice of routes and few boats take the direct route to Messina Strait (M14). The more attractive alternative is Route M14A which closes with the Italian mainland at either Civitavecchia, Fiumicino or Anzio. The route then follows the coast although stops can be made at the Pontine Islands, Ischia or Capri, as well as ports on the mainland, before reaching Messina Strait. The alternative Route M14B makes a detour via Porto Cervo and the west coast of Sardinia and reaches Messina via Palermo and the north coast of Sicily or direct via the Aeolian Islands.

The currents through the Messina Strait depend on the state of the tide and can attain over 4 knots at springs. The south going stream has a longer duration and this can be further increased by a northerly wind. Each turn of the tide is accompanied by one or more tidal bores. These waves are only dangerous to small craft if a strong wind is blowing against the tide. The times of the tides are described in detail in the relevant Sailing Directions.

M15 Balearic Islands to Messina Strait

DIAGRAM 79	Menorca to Messina 560 m
	Mallorca to Malta 620 m

Charts:	BA: 165, 2717
	US: 301
Pilots:	BA: 45
	US: 131

The route from either Mallorca or Menorca passes so close to Sardinia that most boats make a small detour to visit at least the southern part of this island. Route M15A continues towards the north coast of Sicily before reaching Messina Strait.

Boats bound for the Eastern Mediterranean can avoid Messina Strait by taking Route M15B which passes south of Sicily and calls in at Malta. This route is recommended especially in summer, when there is a better chance of favourable winds than along Route M15A, where calms are more frequent.

M16 *Messina Strait to Greece*

DIAGRAM 80	Messina to Zante 290 m
	Zante to Patras 60 m
	Messina to Pylos 330 m

Charts:	BA: 1439
	US: 302
Pilots:	BA: 45, 47
	US: 131, 132

Having passed through the Straits of Messina, boats bound for the Aegean can either reach it through the Corinth Canal (M16A), or by rounding the southern tip of the Peloponnesus (M16B). Neither route presents any problems as the Ionian Sea is free of dangers. If the northern alternative is chosen, landfall will be made between the islands of Cephalonia and Zante, which lie in the approaches to the Gulf of Patras. This leads into the Gulf of Corinth and the canal which cuts across the narrow isthmus separating the Greek mainland from the Peloponnesus. The Corinth Canal provides a convenient short cut to the Saronic Gulf and ports close to Athens.

Route M16B is more advantageous for islands in the southern Aegean, but also has a better chance of favourable winds than the northern route. A convenient port of call after the crossing of the Ionian Sea is Pylos, from where the route continues around the three fingers of the Peloponnesus into the Aegean.

M17 *Gibraltar to Malta*

DIAGRAM 79	Gibraltar to La Valetta 1020 m

Charts:	BA: 165, 2717
	US: 301
Pilots:	BA: 45
	US: 130, 131

During the summer months, from May to September, the route passes close to the north of Alboran Island before closing with the African coast. The route follows the African coast closely as far as Galita Island to take advantage of the east setting current. Galita Island should be passed to the north. Along the entire North African coast, vessels should keep outside of territorial waters and also pay attention to local fishing boats, especially at night, as they are often unlit. From Cape Bon the route passes north of both Pantelleria and the Maltese islands.

Westerly winds are more likely to be encountered along this route during the remaining months of the year, from October to April, and therefore this passage is best planned either at the beginning or the end of the season. During summer it is usually better to make the voyage in stages, stopping either in Spain and the Balearics, or along the African coast. This coast should be avoided in winter when strong northerly gales make it a dangerous lee shore. If easterly winds persist after leaving Gibraltar, either in summer or winter, it is normally better to stay close to the Spanish coast and make easting possibly as far as Sardinia before tacking across to pass between Cape Bon and Sicily.

M18 Malta to Greece

DIAGRAM 80	La Valetta to Zante 340 m
	La Valetta to Khania 480 m

Charts:	BA: 1439
	US: 302
Pilots:	BA: 45, 47, 48
	US: 130, 131, 132

Winds on this eastbound route across the Ionian Sea are variable throughout the year with the highest frequency of W winds in winter. There is a preponderance of N winds in summer, with light winds and calms being more common at the beginning and end of summer. The most direct route to the Aegean (M18A) passes south of the Peloponnesus and approaches the Cyclades from the SW. Any of the three channels separating Cape Malea from Crete can be used, although the northernmost Elafonisos Channel, between Kithera Island and Cape Malea, is usually favoured as it is the most sheltered. Boats bound for Crete or Rhodes should use the Andikithira Channel, south of the small island of the same name.

Because of the constancy of N winds in the Aegean during summer, it is more convenient to approach the Cyclades from the NW rather than SW and therefore Route M18B is recommended between June and August. On this route, landfall should be made on Zante and the island rounded from the south. From Zante the route continues into the gulfs of Patras and Corinth and reaches the Aegean through the Corinth Canal.

M19 Routes in the Adriatic Sea

Charts:	BA: 1440
	US: 301
Pilots:	BA: 47
	US: 131

For many years hardly any boats ventured north of the Ionian Islands as there were few cruising attractions in the Adriatic Sea. All this has changed with the opening up of the Yugoslav coast to cruising, with a great variety of anchorages and harbours from Kotor in the south to Trieste in the north. Compared to the diversity of Yugoslavia, the east coast of Italy has very little to offer and there are only a limited number of safe harbours along the entire coast. For political reasons, the coast of Albania should not be approached and its territorial waters must be avoided.

Because of its narrowness and other specific factors, weather conditions in the Adriatic tend to be very localised. The most dangerous wind is the *bora*, a violent northerly wind that occurs mostly in winter. There is a north setting current along the eastern shore which can be used to advantage when making northbound passages. It is generally advisable to favour the Yugoslav coast when bound in either direction, because of the availability of sheltered anchorages.

M20 Routes in the Aegean Sea

Charts:	BA: 180
	US: 302
Pilots:	BA: 48
	US: 132

The islands of the Grecian archipelago and the Turkish coast of Asia Minor offer a great variety of cruising opportunities and this is reflected in the steep increase in the number of sailing boats that ply the Aegean each summer. Navigation rarely presents any real problems, there are countless safe harbours and anchorages, all dangers are clearly marked on charts and even the traditional rivalry between Greece and Turkey affects visiting sailors only in a tangential way.

Ideally, the Aegean should be cruised from north to south and because of the prevailing N wind of summer, it is recommended to try to arrive in the northern Aegean before the end of May so as to benefit from a favourable wind for the following three months. The ever-increasing popularity of these cruising grounds makes most ports very crowded during the peak holiday months of July and August, when more secluded anchorages should be sought out. As the safe cruising season extends from March to November, it is possible to visit most harbours either before or after the great summer invasion. This may also be the time to visit some of the adjacent areas, such as Istanbul or the Black Sea.

M21 Routes in Marmara and the Black Sea

Charts:	BA: 2214
	US: 302
Pilots:	BA: 24
	US: Not available

Most boats reach this area from the SW, island hopping through the Aegean, although a few boats arrive in the Black Sea from the Danube. The passage through the Aegean should be undertaken in spring, before the onset of the *meltemi*, when winds are either light or nonexistent, and one must be prepared to motor. Because of the strong outflowing current in the Dardanelles, tacking against a NE wind is almost impossible, the task made even more difficult by the large amount of shipping. A weak countercurrent is usually felt on the European side of the straits, which should be favoured as far as Chanakkale, where it is compulsory to cross to the Asian side to clear into Turkey. The rest of the Dardanelles and the crossing of the Sea of Marmara is best done in daily stages because of the shipping and also the frequent lack of wind at night. A convenient anchorage for yachts in transit in Istanbul is on the Asian side, in Moda Bay.

Passing through the Bosporus should only be attempted in daylight and the European side of the strait should again be favoured, where a weaker countercurrent will be found. A thick haze often occurs on summer mornings, which makes navigation very difficult in the straits due to the large number of ships. Clearance procedures in or out of Turkey must be effected at Büyükdere, on the European side of the Bosporus, close to the Black Sea end.

Cruising in the Black Sea is limited to a few Turkish ports and the designated ports of entry of the other countries: Bulgaria, Romania and the Soviet Union. For these three countries, permission to visit them by boat must be obtained beforehand as well as tourist visas for every crew member. None of these countries actively encourages visits by yachts, although entry is not forbidden. However, because of several restricted areas, the authorities should be informed well in advance if a visit to one of their ports is intended.

M22 Rhodes to Cyprus

DIAGRAM 80	Rhodes to Paphos 190 m
	Rhodes to Kyrenia 220 m

Charts:	BA: 183
	US: 302
Pilots:	BA: 48, 49
	US: 132

The most direct route from Rhodes (M22A) leads to Paphos, a small port on the SW coast of Cyprus from where it is easy to reach the two major ports in Southern Cyprus, Limassol and Larnaca. The alternative Route M22B leads to Northern Cyprus, from where ports in the southern part of the island can be reached by rounding its eastern extremity. An easterly current sets along the coast of Cyprus and because of it Cape Andreas, its NE extremity, should be approached with caution. As it is less direct than M22A, the latter route is recommended only if one intends to call in at ports along the coast of Southern Turkey before crossing over to Cyprus.

While the separation of Cyprus remains unresolved, it must be pointed out that yachts are not permitted to clear into Southern Cyprus if they have already called in at ports in the northern half of the island. The authorities insist that yachts must arrive in Southern Cyprus from an overseas port. The reverse is not the case and a boat can proceed directly from Southern to Northern Cyprus.

M23 Cyprus to Israel

DIAGRAM 80	Larnaca to Haifa 150 m
	Larnaca to Tel Aviv 180 m

Charts:	BA: 183
	US: 302
Pilots:	BA: 49
	US: 132

The best point of departure for the short passage to Israel is Larnaca, where up-to-date information should be obtained from the port authorities concerning sensitive areas to be avoided. As long as the troubles in the Lebanon are continuing, the boundary between it and Israel should be approached with greatest caution. As Haifa is so close to the border with Lebanon, this large commercial harbour is best avoided and it is preferable to sail directly from Larnaca to Tel Aviv. Landfall on the Israeli coast should be made in daytime. The small boat harbour in Tel Aviv should not be entered with an onshore wind as the swell breaking over the harbour entrance makes manoeuvring extremely difficult.

M24 Cyprus to Port Said

| DIAGRAM 80 | Larnaca to Port Said 230 m |
| | Limassol to Port Said 210 m |

Charts:	BA: 183
	US: 302
Pilots:	BA: 49
	US: 132

There is a clear run from either Larnaca or Limassol to a point 10 miles north of the entrance into Port Said, which is the recommended anchorage for commercial shipping waiting to transit the Suez Canal. Because of the low, featureless coast and the shallow depths which extend several miles offshore, the position of Port Said is very difficult to ascertain if landfall is made either too far east or west. The situation is further complicated by the unpredictability of the currents in the area. The cluster of ships at anchor is usually the first indication of the approaches to Port Said.

The approach channel to Port Said extends far offshore and is well marked by buoys. It should be entered at its seaward extremity and no short cuts taken because of the large number of wrecks lying in the approaches. Small vessels are allowed to proceed into the harbour without a pilot and all formalities can be completed after the vessel has berthed at the Port Fouad Yacht Club. This is situated on the eastern side of the harbour, immediately past a shipyard (see Diagram 83).

M25 Rhodes to Port Said

| DIAGRAM 80 | Rhodes to Port Said 350 m |

Charts:	BA: 183
	US: 302
Pilots:	BA: 48, 49
	US: 132

Favourable winds can be expected along this route for most of the year. Because the current normally sets eastward along the Egyptian coast, landfall should be made to the west of Port Said. As the water is shallow throughout the area, the coast should not be approached beyond the 20 fathom line which can be followed as far as Damietta. Port Said can be approached from there in safety and directions are the same as for Route M24.

M26 *Malta to Port Said*

DIAGRAM 80	La Valetta to Port Said 940 m

Charts:	BA: 183, 1439
	US: 302
Pilots:	BA: 45, 49
	US: 130, 132

The direct route is recommended in summer, when landfall should be made as advised in Route M25. If the passage is made in winter or in strong N winds, it may be advisable to pass closer to Crete, as there are several good harbours along its south coast where shelter can be found in bad weather. However, when sailing close in the lee of Crete, attention must be paid to the squalls which occasionally blow with great force down the steep mountain slopes towards the sea.

M30 East to west routes

M31 Port Said to Cyprus
M32 Cyprus to Rhodes
M33 Port Said to Rhodes
M34 Greece to Messina Strait
M35 Messina Strait to Corsica
M36 Corsica to Sète
M37 Sicily to the Balearic Islands
M38 Greece to Malta
M39 Balearic Islands to Gibraltar
M40 Israel to Port Said
M41 Port Said to Malta
M42 Malta to Gibraltar

M31 *Port Said to Cyprus*

DIAGRAM 80	Port Said to Paphos 210 m
	Port Said to Limassol 210 m
	Port Said to Larnaca 230 m

Charts:	BA: 183
	US: 302
Pilots:	BA: 49
	US: 130, 132

A direct route for any port on the south coast of Cyprus can be laid as soon as the long entrance channel to Port Said has been left behind. As Cyprus

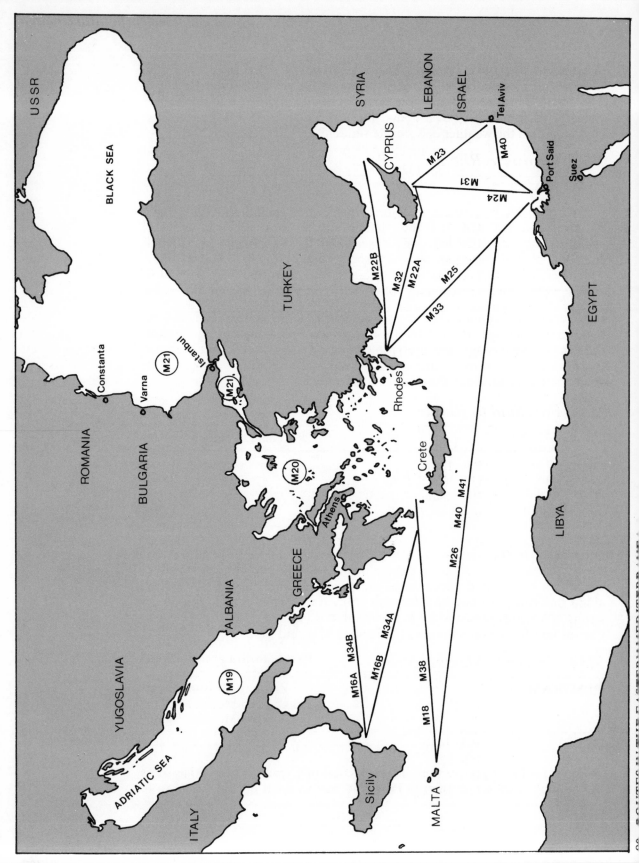

lies almost due north of Port Said, the island is often used as a first Mediterranean stop by boats arriving early in the year from the Red Sea. The small harbour of Paphos, on the SW coast of Cyprus, is a convenient point of departure for boats bound for Rhodes and can also be used for shelter should the weather deteriorate suddenly.

M32 Cyprus to Rhodes

DIAGRAM 80		Paphos to Rhodes 190 m
		Kyrenia to Rhodes 220 m
Charts:	BA: 183	
	US: 302	
Pilots:	BA: 48, 49	
	US: 130, 132	

It is generally recommended to wait for a spell of E or SE winds before making this passage. If persistently strong W or NW winds spring up after the start of the passage, it is preferable to go on the port tack and head for the Turkish coast where either a change in the weather can be awaited or shorter tacks taken along the coast.

M33 Port Said to Rhodes

DIAGRAM 80		Port Said to Rhodes 350 m
Charts:	BA: 183	
	US: 302	
Pilots:	BA: 48, 49	
	US: 130, 132	

Should the weather deteriorate soon after leaving Port Said, shelter can be sought in Alexandria where a change in the weather and more favourable winds can be awaited. Because of the preponderance of contrary winds along this route, it may be necessary to motor in calm or light winds. If strong NW winds persist while in Port Said, it is better to make a detour via Cyprus and follow directions as for Routes M31 and M32.

M34 Greece to Messina Strait

DIAGRAM 80		Zante to Messina 290 m
		Iraklion to Messina 520 m
		Pylos to Messina 330 m
Charts:	BA: 1439	
	US: 302	
Pilots:	BA: 45, 48, 49	
	US: 130, 131, 132	

Two main routes cross the Ionian Sea to Messina, their choice depending on the point of departure in Greece. For boats coming from islands in the Northern Aegean or from ports in the vicinity of Athens, the short cut provided by the Corinth Canal can be very convenient, especially if one is short of time at the end of the season. Route M34B continues through the Gulf of Patras and reaches the Ionian Sea between the islands of Zante and Cephalonia.

Route M34A is more convenient for boats leaving from the Southern Aegean or Crete. A direct course for Messina can be set from northern Crete, but for boats coming from the Cyclades it is easier to pass close to the southern extremity of the Peloponnesus and make a last stop in Pylos before bidding farewell to Greece.

M35 Messina Strait to Corsica

DIAGRAM 79	Messina to Bonifacio 360 m

Charts:	BA: 165
	US: 301
Pilots:	BA: 45, 46
	US: 131

The direct route passes through the Aeolian Islands and traverses the Tyrrhenian Sea to the Straits of Bonifacio. There are several channels leading through the straits, the main passage (Boca Grande) being the easiest to negotiate.

Because of the difficulties associated with a passage through the Straits of Messina from south to north, an alternative route for boats sailing from Greece to Corsica and Southern France is to pass south of Sicily, thus avoiding Messina Strait altogether. After crossing the Ionian Sea, landfall can be made at Syracuse, in the SE extremity of Sicily, from where the south coast of this island can be sailed either non-stop or in several smaller stages along the coast. In a similar way, the onward passage from Sicily to Corsica can either be made non-stop or by calling in at ports on the east coast of Sardinia.

M36 Corsica to Sète

DIAGRAM 79	Bonifacio to Sète 270 m

Charts:	BA: 1780
	US: 301
Pilots:	BA: 46
	US: 131

This route is usually taken by boats heading for the Canal du Midi at the end of their Mediterranean cruise. With persistent NW winds it is better to make straight for the French coast and make westing by shorter tacks along the coast. This is also the recommended practice to avoid a strong *mistral*, when conditions can become very rough in the Gulf of Lions and it is better to wait for an improvement in the weather in one of the many harbours along this coast.

M37 Sicily to the Balearic Islands

DIAGRAM 79	Palermo to Menorca 450 m
	Trapani to Mallorca 470 m

Charts:	BA: 165, 2717
	US: 301
Pilots:	BA: 45
	US: 131

The route from Northern Sicily passes so close to Sardinia that few boats go by without stopping. Boats that have sailed along the south coast of Sicily are advised to cross over to Sardinia after the western extremity of Sicily has been passed to avoid the east setting current in the vicinity of Cape Bon.

M38 Greece to Malta

DIAGRAM 80	Iraklion to La Valetta 540 m

Charts:	BA: 1439
	US: 302
Pilots:	BA: 45, 47, 48
	US: 130, 131, 132

The most convenient route from the Aegean to Malta passes through one of the channels that separate Crete from the Peloponnesus. Alternatively, the Ionian Sea can be reached via the Corinth Canal, although such a route is only recommended for boats leaving from ports in the Saronic Gulf, as both from the Cyclades and the Dodecanese, the route south of the Peloponnesus is shorter.

M39 Balearic Islands to Gibraltar

DIAGRAM 79	Ibiza to Gibraltar 380 m
	Mallorca to Gibraltar 450 m

Charts:	BA: 2717
	US: 301
Pilots:	BA: 45
	US: 130, 131

The route from Mallorca passes east of Ibiza and makes for a point about 20 miles off Cabo de Gata. The Spanish coast should be approached only after Cabo de Gata has been passed as the east going current is strongest in the vicinity of this cape. The route then follows the coast of Spain closely so as to avoid the stronger current offshore. If strong W winds are encountered when approaching Gibraltar it is usually better to seek shelter in a Spanish port and wait for a change rather than try to make headway against both contrary wind and current.

M40 Israel to Port Said

DIAGRAM 80		Tel Aviv to Port Said 140 m
Charts:	BA: 183	
	US: 302	
Pilots:	BA: 49	
	US: 132	

A contrary current usually makes itself felt along this route and it is therefore preferable not to follow the coast too closely, where the current is strongest. If landfall is made too far east of Port Said, it may be impossible to identify any coastal features and the approaches to Port Said will only be indicated by the large number of ships lying at anchor in the recommended waiting area. See also Route M24 for further details.

M41 Port Said to Malta

DIAGRAM 80		Port Said to La Valetta 940 m
Charts:	BA: 183, 1439	
	US: 302	
Pilots:	BA: 45, 49	
	US: 130, 131, 132	

Contrary winds are predominant on this route and every shift of wind should therefore be used to advantage. A good supply of fuel should also be loaded in Port Said to be able to motor if necessary in calms or light winds. On leaving Port Said the initial course should make for the south coast of Crete, where shelter can be sought in strong W or NW winds. Such a course also avoids passing too close to the coast of Libya. If shelter is sought in the lee of Crete or if passing close to the island, attention must be paid to the strong squalls blowing down the steep mountains. In a similar way, the lee of Sicily can be used for shelter if strong winds are encountered when approaching Malta.

M42 Malta to Gibraltar

DIAGRAM 79	La Valetta to Gibraltar 1020 m

Charts:	BA: 165, 2717
	US: 301
Pilots:	BA: 45
	US: 130, 131

Depending on the direction of the wind, the route after leaving Malta can pass either N or S of Pantelleria Island. If strong NW winds are encountered SW of Sicily, shelter should be sought in the lee of Pantelleria. With persistent contrary winds, better progress can be made by heading from Malta straight across to the Tunisian coast and staying close to it as far as Cape Bon. After Cape Bon has been cleared, the coast of Africa should be avoided because of the east setting current. It is therefore recommended to sail across to the Spanish coast to Cabo de Palos and follow directions as for Route M39.

27 Canals and cruising regulations

1 Panama Canal

DIAGRAMS 81, 82
Pilots: BA: 7A
       US: 148, 153

The handing over of the Panama Canal to the Panamanian authorities by the United States does not appear to have affected the actual operation of the Canal in the least and transiting procedures are just as straightforward and easy to accomplish as before.

Arriving on the Atlantic side, yachts enter the breakwater and proceed in a southerly direction to the recommended anchorage, which is located to the east of Channel buoy No. 4 and to the south of Cristobal Mole. The yacht anchorage, called the Flats, is marked by red and amber buoys. Clearance instructions can be requested on VHF Channel 16. Both at Cristobal and Balboa, on the Pacific side, yachts are boarded by a Panamanian boarding officer, who has many functions and will perform customs, quarantine and immigration duties. After the yacht has cleared, the skipper and crew may go ashore. At Cristobal one can either remain at anchor at the Flats, or proceed to the nearby Panama Canal Yacht Club, where cruising yachts are welcome. A fee of about 30 cents per foot per day is charged, which includes both mooring fees and the use of club facilities. The Club monitors Channel 64 during office hours. Those who prefer to remain at anchor can come to the Club by dinghy and use its facilities, provided permission has been obtained beforehand. The use of outboard engines is no longer prohibited between the anchorage and shore facilities.

Yachts arriving at the Pacific side of the Canal have three options. For those who intend to transit the Canal as soon as possible, the recommended procedure is to fly the Q flag and anchor at Flamenco Island. Clearance instructions can be obtained on Channel 16. For those who intend to spend longer in the Balboa area, a mooring can be rented at the Balboa Yacht Club. The club office is open all day on weekdays and until noon on Saturday, and monitors Channel 63. Clearance formalities and the transiting of the Canal can be arranged at the Club. On no account should a yacht arriving off the Club attempt to anchor, as the currents are very strong and the ground is foul. One should pick up a vacant mooring and then hail the Club launch, which operates 24 hours a day. Although one can provision in Balboa, it is more convenient on the Atlantic side, where the shops are closer to hand.

The third possibility on the Pacific side is to clear into Panama at Taboga Island, about 7 miles from Flamenco Island. The Guardia Nacional Office on Taboga should be contacted first. The formalities have to be completed in Balboa, which can be reached by ferry.

On either side of the Canal, if a yacht does not intend to transit in the first 48 hours, a cruising permit has to be obtained from the Panamanian authorities. Similarly, a permit has to be obtained if a yacht does not leave Panama within 48 hours after transiting the Canal. This also applies to those wishing to visit the San Blas Islands on the Atlantic side or the Las Perlas Islands on the Pacific side. Cruising without a permit runs the risk of a heavy fine. A permit is valid for one month. An additional permit has to be obtained for the San Blas Islands at Porvenir, where one is required to stop and check in before proceeding to the islands. The Panama cruising permits are issued by the Direccion General Consular y de Naves. At Balboa the office is in Building 101, close to the Immigration gate at Pier 18, while in Cristobal the office is in room 107 on the second floor of Building 1303, close to the Police Station.

Those wishing to transit the Canal must take the following steps once clearance formalities have been completed:

1. The skipper must call the Admeasurers office (Tel: 246-7293 on the Atlantic side; Tel: 252-4571 on the Pacific side) to make arrangements for the yacht's Panama Canal tonnage to be determined.

   In Cristobal, the Admeasurers office is on the second floor of the Administration Building No.1105. In Balboa, the office is on the first floor of Building 729, Marine Bureau Building.
2. After admeasurement, the skipper has to report to the Senior Canal Port Captain's office (Building 1105, third floor, Cristobal, or Building 910, La Bola). The skipper will be informed about the requirements for transiting the Canal, such as four mooring lines not less than 100 ft long, four linehandlers in addition to the skipper, and adequate fenders. The vessel is also required to be able to maintain a speed of 5 knots under her own power. Transiting fees and tolls are paid in this office.
3. The skipper is then allotted a provisional pilot time for his scheduled transit, prior to which he will be required to call Marine Traffic Control (Tel: 252-3629) to confirm the time.

There are three types of lockage for yachts under 125 ft (38 m) LOA when transiting the Canal: centre chamber, sidewall or alongside a tug. The Canal Port Captain decides on the type of lockage for each yacht. Because of the roughness of the walls and the turbulence created during the filling of the chambers, yachts usually transit centre chamber or alongside a Commission tug. Yachts that cannot maintain a speed of 5 knots will need a change of

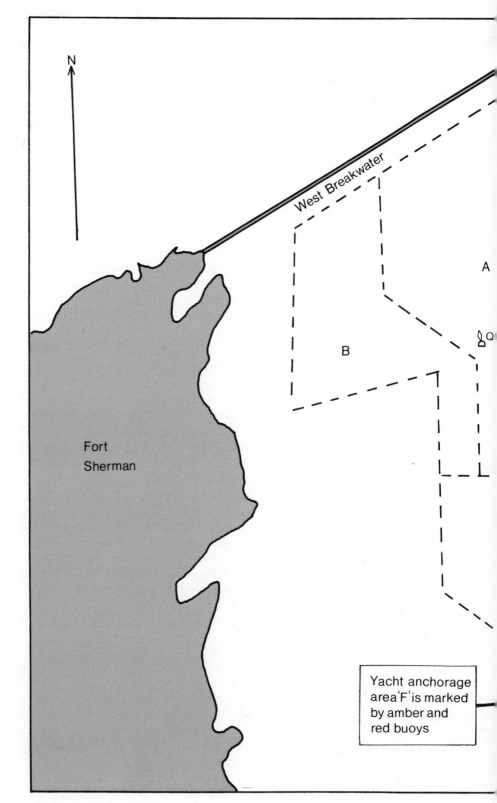

81. PANAMA CANAL ATLANTIC OCEAN ENTRANCE

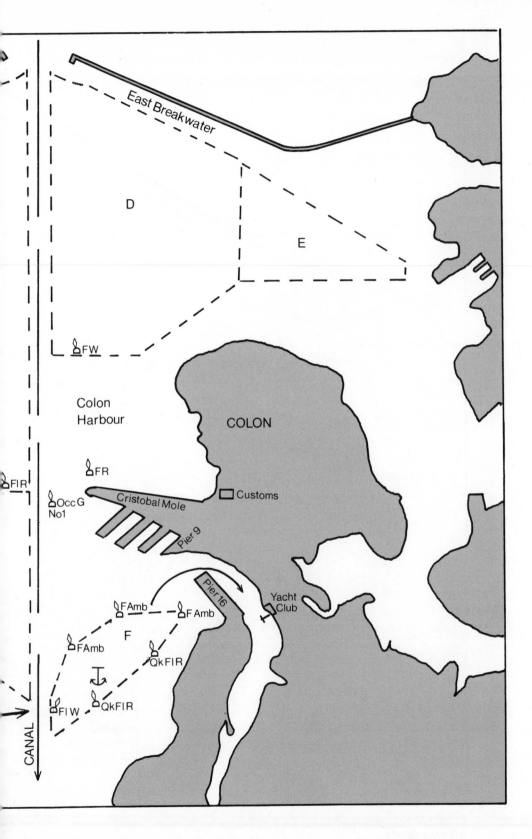

East Breakwater

D

E

FW

Colon
Harbour

COLON

FR

FIR

Occ G
No1

Cristobal Mole

Pier 9

Customs

Pier 16

Yacht
Club

FAmb

F Amb

F

FAmb

QkFlR

FlW

QkFlR

CANAL

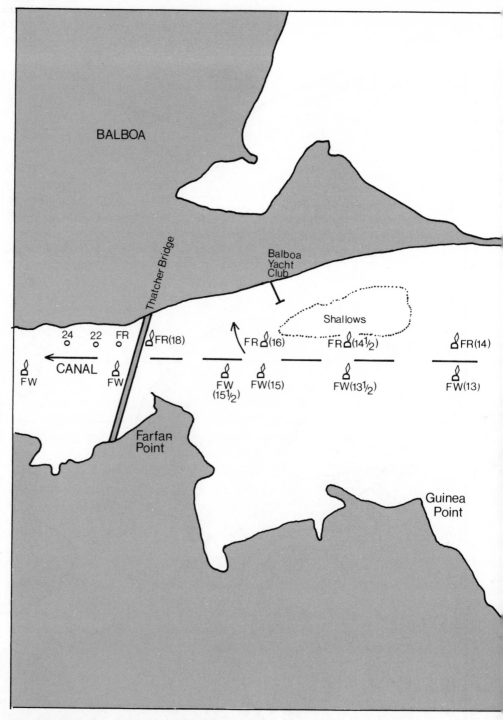

BALBOA

Thatcher Bridge

Balboa
Yacht
Club

Shallows

24   22   FR
○   ○   ○   FR(18)   FR(16)   FR(14½)   FR(14)

← CANAL

FW   FW   FW   FW(15)   FW(13½)   FW(13)
                          (15½)

Farfan
Point

Guinea
Point

82. *PANAMA CANAL PACIFIC OCEAN
ENTRANCE*

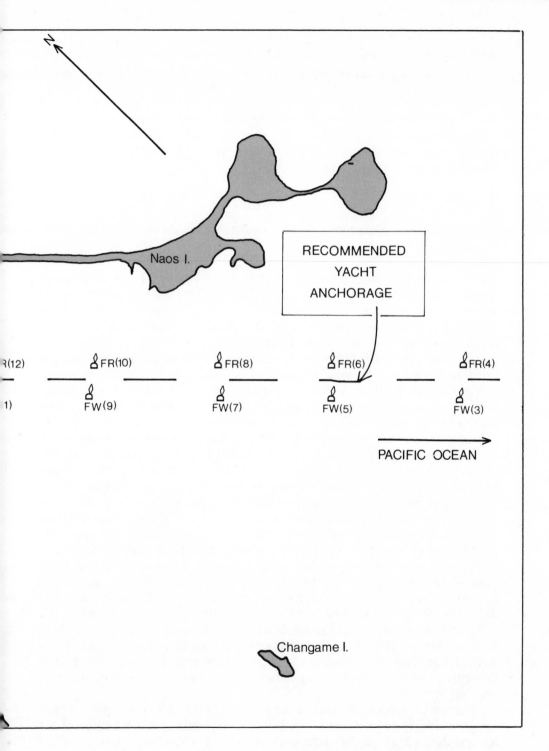

N

Naos I.

RECOMMENDED
YACHT
ANCHORAGE

R(12)   FR(10)   FR(8)   FR(6)   FR(4)

1)   FW(9)   FW(7)   FW(5)   FW(3)

PACIFIC OCEAN

Changame I.

pilot at Gamboa, half way through the Canal. However, if one has indicated that a speed of 5 knots could be maintained and this was not achieved, the yacht will be delayed at Gamboa until a second pilot becomes available the following day. All additional expenses for this will be paid by the owner. Yachts that cannot maintain more than 4 knots have to be towed through the Canal by a Commission launch, for which a fee is charged.

For communications in the Canal area, all yachts are now required to have a radio with channels in the marine band, although pilots normally bring their own portable transceivers.

2 Suez Canal

DIAGRAMS 78, 83, 84
Pilots: BA: 64
       US: 132, 172

The 87.5 mile long canal links the Mediterranean and the Red Sea by way of several lakes and without any locks. Its opening in 1869 had a tremendous impact on international shipping as it halved the distance between Europe and the Far East. In its long history, the canal has been closed twice as a result of war, in 1956 for a year and in 1967 for seven years. It is now used regularly by about 100 ships per day and its recent upgrading has made it possible for the canal to be transited by vessels of up to 200,000 tons.

Vessels under 300 tons are allowed to use the canal free of charge, although there are some additional fees that have to be paid by all users, including the smallest yacht. The masters of small vessels intending to transit the canal are allowed by the Suez Canal Authority to complete the necessary formalities on their own, but as they are fairly complicated, the use of a shipping agent is strongly recommended. Both in Port Said and Suez there are several firms which specialise in handling small boats and their representatives are usually on station in the approaches to the canal offering their services, sometimes rather forcefully. If the services of a local agent are employed, all additional costs must be specified by the agent and fees agreed in advance. Agent fees and transit costs all have to be paid in US dollars, therefore it is advisable to carry some funds in notes, including smaller denominations. If attempting to complete formalities alone this appears to be easier in Port Said, where the Suez Canal Company will give directions about the various formalities that must be complied with.

Small vessels arriving at the Mediterranean entrance to the Canal in Port Said must berth at the Port Fouad Yacht Club, which is situated on the east side of the harbour, immediately after a shipyard. Because of the high density of traffic and intricate approaches, Port Said harbour should not be entered at night.

Whether completing formalities alone or with the help of an agent, a pilot appointed by the Canal Authority will join the yacht on the morning of the agreed day, either at the yacht club or more likely at the Customs wharf close to the entrance to the canal, on the west side of the harbour. Because

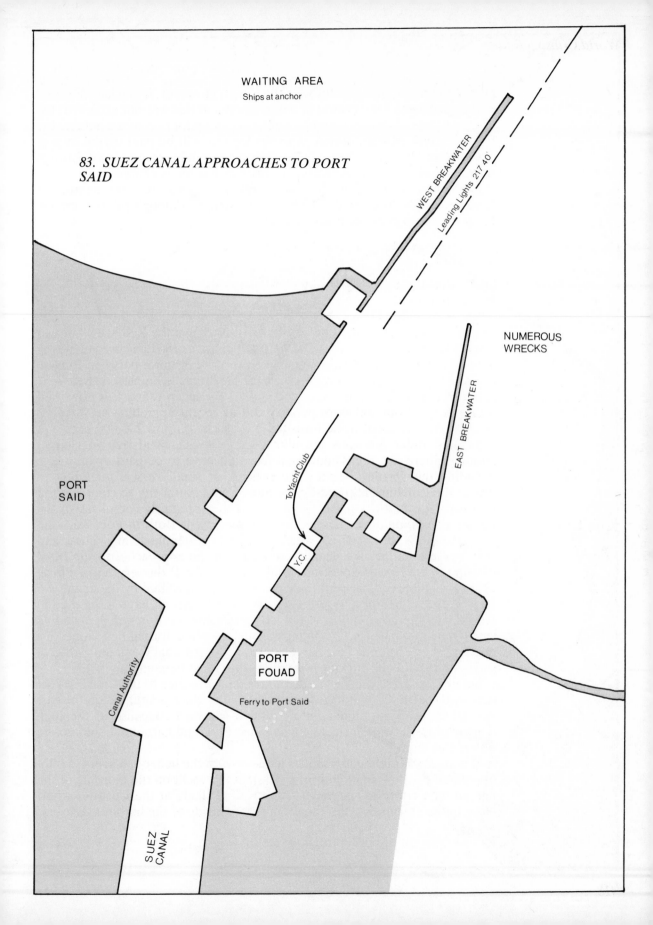

WAITING AREA
Ships at anchor

83. SUEZ CANAL APPROACHES TO PORT SAID

WEST BREAKWATER

Leading Lights 217 40'

NUMEROUS WRECKS

EAST BREAKWATER

To Yacht Club

PORT SAID

Y.C.

Canal Authority

PORT FOUAD

Ferry to Port Said

SUEZ CANAL

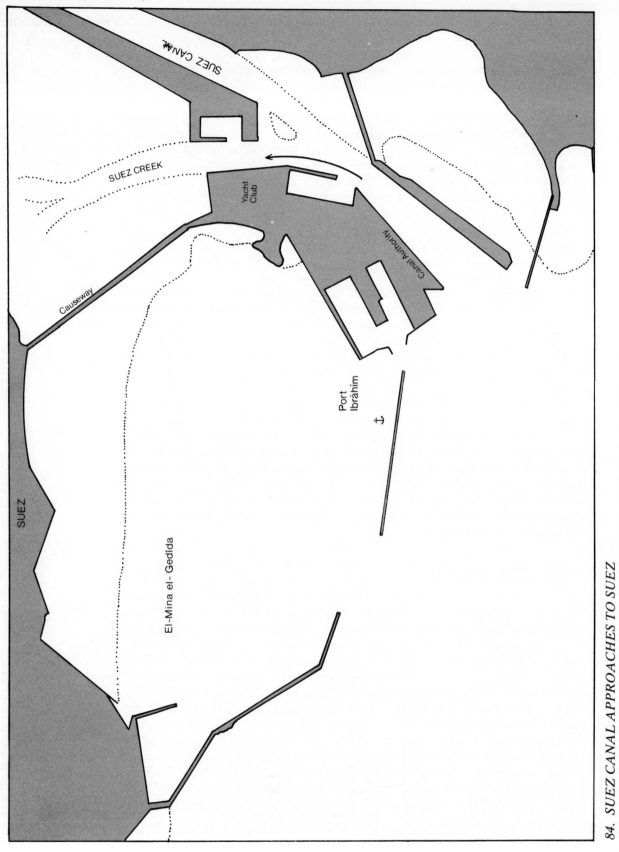

84. *SUEZ CANAL APPROACHES TO SUEZ*

of the length of the canal, very few yachts are able to transit the canal in one day. Small vessels are not permitted to use the canal at night and it is therefore necessary to anchor overnight at Ismailia, in the NW corner of Lake Timsah. The pilot will be taken ashore by a launch, but the crew is not allowed to land. Another pilot will join the yacht at dawn to complete the journey to Suez. The use of sails is not permitted in the canal, although with the pilot's permission the mainsail may be run up while crossing the Bitter Lakes if the weather warrants this. In Suez, yachts usually moor at the Suez Yacht Club, situated in a creek on the western bank, close to the southern end of the canal. The pilot will give instructions how to reach the club and he can be dropped there.

Vessels approaching the Canal from southward must anchor in Port Ibrahim, in the NE corner of Suez Bay, close to the north of the canal entrance. After formalities have been completed, the boat can move to the Suez Yacht Club, or remain at anchor. A pilot will join the boat at dawn on the day of transit and will take the vessel as far as Ismailia, where the night will be spent at anchor. As in the case of southbound vessels, there will be a change of pilot at Ismailia. If the vessel is delayed for any reason and Ismailia cannot be reached before nightfall, the skipper may be required to anchor for the night in a place where the yacht does not impede the passage of larger vessels.

Skippers who do not wish to be delayed after transiting the canal can request outward clearance from either Port Said or Suez while completing formalities for their transit. They can proceed on their way as soon as they have dropped the pilot at the end of the canal. Those wishing to visit inland areas of Egypt either before or after passing through the canal need a tourist visa, which is best obtained in advance from an Egyptian embassy abroad. Every crew member must also exchange a certain amount of foreign currency on arrival in Egypt. During a trip inland, the boat can be left in the care of either yacht club.

3 Galapagos Islands

The islands which inspired Charles Darwin to write his *Origin of Species* are much more difficult to visit by boat than in the days of the *Beagle* when sailing ships used to call there regularly. The Ecuadorian government, which administers the archipelago, is determined to preserve the unique nature of these islands, whose flora and fauna were badly damaged during the last century. The entire archipelago has been declared a National Park and sailing to any island without a cruising permit is strictly forbidden.

The procedure for obtaining a cruising permit is rather lengthy and the chances of obtaining one are slim, because permits are allocated according to a quota system, with only a limited number of permits being granted to cruising yachts each year. However, persistent skippers have managed to obtain a permit by writing well in advance to the Ministry of Defence in Quito. By application to the Ecuadorian Embassy in one's country of origin, a detailed list of the necessary documents and relevant papers can be obtained, as well as the text in Spanish of the letter which has to be submitted to the Ministry of Defence in Quito. The signed lettter should be returned to the Embassy together with photocopies of the vessel's registration document, skipper's certificate of competence and the first and second pages of all crew members' passports. Those who do obtain a cruising permit will be able to visit most islands, but will have to be accompanied by a licensed guide. The fee for an English speaking guide is about 30 US dollars per day.

Both yachts possessing a cruising permit and those without must call in first at one of the two ports of entry: Puerto Baquerizo Moreno (Wreck Bay) on San Cristobal Island, or Puerto Ayora (Academy Bay) on Santa Cruz Island. Neither the skipper nor the crew should go ashore until the boat has been inspected by the Navy, after which the skipper can carry out the formal clearance procedures at the Port Captain's office. The clearance fee charged for arrival and departure is about 60 US dollars from 0800 to 1800 hours on weekdays, twice as much after midnight, on Sundays and public holidays. The higher rate is charged according to the time of arrival, not when the formalities are completed, so it is a good idea to plan the arrival during daylight hours from Monday to Saturday.

In the case of boats arriving without a cruising permit, an official decree states: 'Small vessels with a crew of less than six people, sailing towards the islands of the South Pacific, are allowed to stop at Puerto Baquerizo Moreno on San Cristobal Island in order to provision with fuel, food and water. The maximum time granted by the Port Captain will be 72 hours'. However, some boats have managed to clear in at Academy Bay as well and at both ports skippers have been allowed to stay up to one week by claiming an emergency.

Some people who have managed to obtain a longer extension to their stay from the Port Captain have visited the islands on one of the many local tour boats, which charge from 25 to 150 dollars per person per day depending on their degree of comfort. An additional fee of 30 US dollars is charged by the Galapagos National Park from every person who visits the islands.

Most boats stop in the Galapagos Islands en route to the South Pacific, but for those who plan only to stop for reprovisioning, it is probably better to bypass the islands and allow for more stores when provisioning in Panama. Fuel, fresh water and provisions are often difficult to obtain in these islands. However, if one is determined to visit these unique islands, it is wise to start the procedure for obtaining a permit at least one year before the planned visit.

There have been reports recently that the Ecuadorian authorities are gradually easing the restrictions imposed on cruising yachts.

4 French Polynesia

Every member of the crew of visiting yachts, including the skipper, and also children, who intends to spend any length of time in the islands of French

Polynesia must be in possession of a valid airline ticket to their country of origin, or deposit the equivalent sum of money in a bank in the capital Papeete. Letters of credit are not accepted and the bond must either be paid over the counter in cash or travellers cheques or transferred by telex from the applicant's personal bank to the Banque Indo-Suez, Papeete, Tahiti, French Polynesia.

A short visa for up to 30 days can be obtained on arrival in most outlying islands of French Polynesia, such as the Marquesas or the Austral Islands, but longer visas or extensions of this visa will not be issued without the posting of a bond. Even if a visa has been obtained beforehand from a French Consular office, this cannot be extended unless a bond has been deposited. Lately the authorities have started taking stern measures to discourage cruising boats from remaining in the territory during the cyclone season. Extensions to visas are no longer granted if they stretch into the cyclone season and visiting boats are expected to be on their way by 1st November, the official start of the cyclone season.

The money is returned before departure when commencing clearing out procedures and can be obtained in other islands which have banks, such as Bora Bora. It is not necessary to return to Papeete. No interest is paid on the money deposited at the bank, in fact an additional charge is made by the bank for handling the bond.

5 Chagos Archipelago

The British Indian Ocean Territory consists of Diego Garcia and some 55 islands in the Chagos Archipelago including Peros Banhos and the Salomon Islands which are increasingly popular among yachts cruising in the South Indian Ocean. All these islands are a British dependency and are administered by the Royal Navy who are responsible for the maintenance of law, customs and immigration. The US presence in Diego Garcia, which remains under British sovereignty, is the result of an arrangement reached between the two governments in 1966. The US and UK reserve the whole of the Chagos Archipelago for military purposes, although the main installations are on Diego Garcia. Access to this island is only allowed for emergencies and yachts are discouraged from even trying to stop there. All boats that attempt to enter Diego Garcia are stopped outside the main pass on the north side of the island and are searched by British naval personnel.

Cruising boats are permitted to stop in all islands that are not used for military purposes. The islands are regularly patrolled by an official boat from Diego Garcia that will check the papers of visiting yachts making sure that certain rules are not infringed. These are mainly concerned with nature conservation. Turtles, live coral, live shells and all the flora and fauna of the islands are protected. The heart of palm must not be taken and the coconut crabs are also protected. Fishing is allowed only with a line, not with spear guns, as these are prohibited, as are all offensive weapons.

6 Indonesia

Indonesia is one of the countries where it is strictly forbidden to cruise without a cruising permit. In the past this permit was obtained through one's embassy in Jakarta, but the procedure has been changed and now applications can only be forwarded to the Indonesian authorities via an officially appointed agent.

One of the agencies offering this service is B.P. Bhati Pertiwi Sejarti, located at 20 Jl. Taman Pluit Kencana Dalam, Jakarta 14440, Telephone 6991383, Telex 42768 ARECBAM IA. The agent's fee is $US 300, which must be sent with the application form. The agent, Mr A.V. Chandra, can usually obtain the permit within two months and it is then sent to the applicant together with the appropriate letters of approval from the Departments of Foreign Affairs, Defence and Security, and also from the Directorate General of Sea Communications. If the application is turned down, $US 100 will be refunded and the letter of refusal from the Department of Defence forwarded to the applicant.

A tourist visa must also be obtained before sailing to Indonesia. The first step, however, is to write to Mr Chandra and ask for the appropriate form. Although the formalities seem daunting, the Indonesian Archipelago is an attractive cruising ground and the harbour of Benoa particularly has always been a popular base for those wishing to visit Bali.

Bibliography

Asia and Pacific Review 1985, World of Information, Saffron Waldon (1985).

ALLEN Philip, ed. *The Atlantic Crossing Guide*, W.W. Norton & Co., New York (1983).

BROWN Alexander Crosby, *Horizon's Rim*, Arrowsmith, London (1935).

BASS George F., ed., *A History of Seafaring*, Book Club Associates, London (1974).

CHICHESTER Francis, *Gipsy Moth Circles the World*, Pan Books, London (1969).

CORNELL Jimmy *Modern Ocean Cruising*, Adlard Coles, London (1983).

CORNELL Jimmy *Ocean Cruising Survey*, Sheridan House, Dobbs Ferry, New York (1985).

DEBENHAM Frank *Discovery and Exploration*, Paul Hamlyn, London (1968).

DENHAM H.M. *The Aegean*, John Murray, London (1970)

DENHAM H.M. *The Ionian Islands to Rhodes*, John Murray, London (1969).

DENHAM H.M. *Southern Turkey, the Levant and Cyprus*, John Murray, London (1973).

DENHAM, H.M. *The Tyrrhenian Sea*, John Murray, London (1972).

FAGAN Brian M. *California Coastal Passages*, Capra Press, Santa Barbara, California (1981).

FINDLAY Alexander George *Memoir of the Northern Atlantic Ocean,* 13th edition (1873).

FITZROY Rear Admiral *The Weather Book: A Manual of Practical Meteorology*, Longman Green, London (1863).

GIESEKING Ilsemarie *Zwischen Brückendeck und Kochtopf*, Gieseking, Elmshorn (1982).

GRENFELL PRICE A., ed. *The Explorations of Captain James Cook in the Pacific*, Dover Publications, New York (1971).

Guide Afrique 1984–85, UTA French Airlines (1984).

HART Jerrems C. and STONE William T. *A Cruising Guide to the Caribbean and the Bahamas*, Dodd, Mead & Co., New York (1982).

HENDERSON Richard *Sea Sense*, Second Edition, International Marine Publishing Co., Camden, Maine (1979).

HEYERDAHL Thor *Sea Routes to Polynesia*, Futura, London (1974).

HISCOCK Eric *Voyaging Under Sail*, 2nd edition.
Incorporated in *Cruising Under Sail*, Third Edition. Oxford University Press, (1974). Published in the US by International Marine Publishing Co., Camden, Maine (1986).

HORSBURGH James *Directions for Sailing to and from the East Indies, Africa and South America Vol. I*, 57th edition, London (1841).

KLINE Harry, ed. *Cruising Guide to the Bahamas*, Tropic Isle Publishers, Miami (1982).

LUCAS Alan *Cruising the Coral Coast*, Horwitz, Sydney (1980).

LUCAS Alan *Red Sea and Indian Ocean Cruising Guide* Imray Laurie Norie and Wilson, Huntingdon (1985).

MAURY M.F. *Sailing Directions Vol. I*, William Harris, New York (1858).

MAURY M.F. *Sailing Directions Vol. II*, Cornelius Wendel, New York (1859).

MOITESSIER Bernard *Cape Horn: The Logical Route*, Adlard Coles, London, (1973).

NEALE Tom *An Island to Oneself*, Collins, London (1966).

NORWOOD Richard *The Seaman's Practice*, London (1637).

Ocean Passages for the World, Hydrographer of the Navy (1895)
    1923 edition.
    1973 edition.

Pacific Business Guide 1986, World of Information, Saffron Waldon (1986).

Pacific Islands Yearbook, Pacific Publications, Sydney (1985).

RANTZEN M.J. *Little Ship Navigation*, Herbert Jenkins, London (1969).

Reed's Ocean Navigator, 3rd Edition, Thomas Reed Publications, London (1977).

Reed's Nautical Almanac & Coastal Pilot East Coast, Gulf Coast and Islands (USA), Better Boating Association, Needham, Massachusetts (1982).

Reed's Nautical Almanac & Coastal Pilot West Coast, Canada, Mexico, Hawaiian Islands, Thomas Reed Publications, London (1985).

RIDGELL Reilly *Pacific Nations and Territories*, Guam Community College, (1982).

ROBB Frank *Handling Small Boats in Heavy Weather*, Adlard Coles, London (1972).

ROSSER W.H. *Navigation of the Atlantic, India and Pacific Oceans*, 3rd edition (1868).

ROSSER W.H. and IMRAY J.F. *Sailing Directions for the Indian Ocean* (1866).

Royal Cruising Club Bulletins.

Sailing Directions Vols 1, 7a, 24, 34, 38, 44, 45, 46, 48, 60, 64, 67, 70, 71, Hydrographic Department.

Seven Seas Cruising Association Commodores' Bulletins 1976–86.

South Seas Guide 1985–86, UTA French Airlines (1985).

SOUTHBY-TAILYOUR Ewen *Falkland Island Shores*, Conway Maritime, London (1985).
STREET Donald M.Jr. *Street's Cruising Guide to the Eastern Caribbean*, W.W. Norton & Co., New York (1981).
TATE Michael *Blue Water Cruising*, Temple Press, London (1964).
TAVERNIER Bruno *Great Maritime Routes*, MacDonald, London (1970).
WALTER Richard *Anson's Voyage Around the World*, Penguin Books, London (1947).
WILENSKY Julius M. *Yachtman's Guide to the Windward Islands*, Wescott Cove Publishing Co., Stamford, Connecticut (1973).

Chart and Pilot Sources

British Admiralty Charts: These can be obtained from good chandlers. The following are just 4 who stock them: J.D. Potter Ltd, The Minories, London EC3; Kelvin Hughes, 31 Mansell Street, London E1; Captain O.M. Watts Ltd, 45 Albermarle Street, London W1; London Yacht Centre, 13 Artillery Lane, London E1.

United States National Ocean Survey charts: May be purchased by mail from the Distribution Branch, N/CG33, National Ocean Service, 6501 Lafayette Avenue, Riverdale, Maryland 20737. A chart catalog is available from the National Ocean Survey or at local chart outlets.

British Admiralty Sailing Directions: These pilot books cover the world in many volumes and can be obtained from the above London addresses.

U.S. Sailing Directions: Like their British equivalent, these pilots cover the world in many volumes. There is close cooperation between the British and U.S. governments in the publication of the pilots, which are available in the U.S. from the Defense Mapping Agency, Office of Distribution Services (DDCP), 6500 Brookes Lane, Washington, D.C. 20315. A catalog is available.

Index of Routes

In numerical order

A = Atlantic; P = Pacific; I = Indian; R = Red Sea; M = Mediterranean; N = North; S = South; T = Transequatorial.

AN10 Routes from Northern Europe
AN11 Europe to North America, 62
AN12 Southbound from Northern Europe, 64
AN13 Routes across the Bay of Biscay, 65
AN14 Northern Europe to Madeira, 66
AN15 Northern Europe to Canary Islands, 66
AN16 Madeira to Canary Islands, 67
AN17 Northern Europe to Azores, 67
AN20 Routes from Portugal
AN21 Portugal to Gibraltar, 69
AN22 Portugal to Canary Islands, 69
AN23 Portugal to Madeira, 70
AN24 Portugal to Azores, 70
AN25 Portugal to Northern Europe, 71
AN30 Routes from Gibraltar
AN31 Gibraltar to Madeira, 71
AN32 Gibraltar to Canary Islands, 72
AN33 Gibraltar to Lesser Antilles, 72
AN34 Gibraltar to Northern Europe, 73
AN40 Routes from the Canary Islands and West Africa
AN41 Canary Islands to Lesser Antilles, 74
AN42 Canary Islands to Cape Verde Islands, 76
AN43 Canary Islands to West Africa, 77
AN44 Canary Islands to Bermuda, 77
AN45 Cape Verde Islands to Lesser Antilles, 78
AN46 West Africa to Lesser Antilles, 79
AN50 Routes from the Azores
AN51 Azores to Gibraltar, 79
AN52 Azores to Portugal, 80
AN53 Azores to English Channel, 80

AN54 Azores to Ireland, 81
AN55 West Africa to Azores, 83
AN60 Routes from Bermuda
AN61 Bermuda to Northern Europe, 84
AN62 Bermuda to Azores, 84
AN63 Bermuda to Lesser Antilles, 85
AN64 Bermuda to Virgin Islands, 86
AN65 Bermuda to USA, 88
AN70 Routes from USA
AN71 USA to Northern Europe, 89
AN72 USA to Azores, 90
AN73 USA to Bermuda, 90
AN74 USA to Virgin Islands, 91
AN75 USA to Bahamas, 92
AN76 USA to Panama, 93
AN80 Routes from the Bahamas and Virgin Islands
AN81 Bahamas to Bermuda, 94
AN82 Bahamas to Virgin Islands, 95
AN83 Bahamas to Panama, 97
AN84 Puerto Rico and Virgin Islands to Bermuda, 97
AN85 Virgin Islands to USA, 98
AN86 Virgin Islands to Bahamas, 100
AN87 Virgin Islands to Jamaica and the Gulf of Mexico, 100
AN88 Virgin Islands to Panama, 101
AN90 Routes in the Caribbean Sea and from Panama
AN91 Panama to Central America and the Gulf of Mexico, 104
AN92 Panama to the Windward Passage, Jamaica and Hispaniola, 105
AN93 Panama to Hispaniola, 106
AN94 Panama to Virgin Islands, 107
AN95 Panama to Lesser Antilles, 107
AN96 Panama to Venezuela and the ABC Islands, 108
AN100 Routes from the Lesser Antilles
AN101 Lesser Antilles to ABC Islands and Venezuela, 109

AN102 Lesser Antilles to Panama, 111
AN103 Lesser Antilles to USA and Canada, 112
AN104 Lesser Antilles to Bermuda, 112
AN105 Lesser Antilles to Azores, 113
AN110 Routes from the ABC Islands
AN111 ABC Islands and Venezuela to Lesser Antilles, 114
AN112 ABC Islands and Venezuela to Virgin Islands, 115
AN113 Northward from Venezuela and the ABC Islands, 115
AN114 ABC Islands and Venezuela to Panama, 116

AT10 Transequatorial routes in the Atlantic
AT11 Europe to Cape Town, 121
AT12 Canary Islands to Cape Town, 122
AT13 US east coast to Cape Town, 123
AT14 Canary Islands to Brazil, 124
AT15 Cape Verde Islands to Brazil, 124
AT16 West Africa to Brazil, 125
AT17 Brazil to Lesser Antilles, 126
AT18 Brazil to Europe, 126
AT19 Cape Town to the Azores, 127
AT20 Cape Town to US east coast, 128
AT21 Cape Town to Lesser Antilles, 128
AT22 Cape Horn to Europe, 129
AT23 Cape Horn to US east coast, 130

Routes in the South Atlantic
AS11 Cape Town to St Helena, 143
AS12 St Helena to Ascension, 144
AS13 St Helena to Brazil, 144
AS14 Cape Town to Brazil, 144
AS15 Brazil to Tristan da Cunha, 145
AS16 Tristan da Cunha to Capetown, 146
AS17 South America to Falkland Islands, 147
AS18 South America to Magellan Strait, 147

AS19 Magellan Strait to Falkland
   Islands, 147
AS20 Falkland Islands to South America,
   148

*PN10 Routes from the west coast of North
   America*
PN11 California to Hawaii, 174
PN12 California to Panama, 174
PN13 Northward from California, 175
PN14 California to British Columbia, 175
PN15 Alaska to British Columbia, 176
PN16 British Columbia to California, 176
PN17 British Columbia to Hawaii, 177
PN20 Routes from Panama
PN21 Panama to Central America, 178
PN22 Panama to California, 179
PN23 Panama to British Columbia, 180
PN24 Panama to Alaska, 181
PN25 Panama to Hawaii, 181
PN26 Central America to Hawaii, 182
PN27 Central America to Panama, 182
*PN30 Routes from Hawaii, Marshalls and
   Kiribati*
PN31 Hawaii to Alaska, 186
PN32 Hawaii to British Columbia, 186
PN33 Hawaii to California, 187
PN34 Hawaii to Line Islands, 188
PN35 Line Islands to Hawaii, 189
PN36 Hawaii to Marshall Islands, 189
PN37 Hawaii to Japan, 190
PN38 Marshall Islands to Hawaii, 190
PN39 Kiribati to Hawaii, 191
*PN40 Routes from the Philippines and
   Singapore*
PN41 Philippines to Singapore, 194
PN42 Philippines to Hong Kong, 195
PN43 Philippines to Japan, 195
PN44 Philippines to Guam, 196
PN45 Philippines to Palau, 196
PN46 Singapore to Philippines, 197
PN47 Singapore to Hong Kong, 198
PN50 Routes from Hong Kong
PN51 Hong Kong to Singapore, 198
PN52 Hong Kong to Philippines, 199
PN53 Hong Kong to Japan, 200
PN54 Hong Kong to Guam, 201
PN55 Taiwan to Guam, 201
PN60 Routes from Japan
PN61 Japan to Alaska, 202
PN62 Japan to British Columbia, 202
PN63 Japan to California, 203
PN64 Japan to Hawaii, 203
PN65 Japan to Guam, 204
PN66 Guam to Japan, 204
PN67 Japan to Hong Kong, 205
PN70 Routes in Micronesia
PN71 Guam to Palau, 206
PN72 Palau to Guam, 206

Transequatorial Routes in the Pacific
PT11 California to Galapagos, 212

PT12 California to Marquesas, 213
PT13 California to Tahiti, 213
PT14 British Columbia to Marquesas,
   214
PT15 Central America to Marquesas, 215
PT16 Central America to Easter Island,
   215
PT17 Panama to Galapagos, 216
PT18 Panama to Marquesas, 216
PT19 Southbound from Panama, 217
PT20 Marquesas to Hawaii, 218
PT21 Tahiti to Hawaii, 219
PT22 Tahiti to Panama, 220
PT23 Cook Islands to Hawaii, 220
PT24 Hawaii to Tahiti, 221
PT25 Hawaii to Marquesas, 222
PT26 Tuvala to Kiribati, 222
PT27 Kiribati to Tuvala, 223
PT28 New Guinea to Philippines, 223
PT29 New Guinea to Guam, 224
PT30 Palau to New Guinea, 225

PS10 Routes in the Eastern South Pacific
PS11 Galapagos to Marquesas, 263
PS12 Marquesas to Tahiti, 264
PS13 Galapagos to Easter Island, 265
PS14 Galapagos to Gambier Islands, 265
PS15 South America to Easter Island, 266
PS16 Easter Island to Pitcairn, 266
PS17 Pitcairn to Gambier Islands, 267
PS18 Easter Island to Magellan Straits or
   Cape Horn, 267
*PS20 Routes from the Society and Cook
   Islands*
PS21 Society to Cook Islands, 271
PS22 Tahiti to Austral Islands, 272
PS23 Tahiti to Cape Horn, 272
PS24 Cook Islands to Samoa, 273
PS25 Cook Islands to Tonga, 273
PS26 Cook Islands to New Zealand, 274
PS30 Routes from Samao and Tonga
PS31 Samoa to Tonga, 277
PS32 Samoa to Fiji, 277
PS33 Samoa to Wallis, 279
PS34 Samoa to Society Islands, 279
PS35 Tonga to Society Islands, 280
PS36 Tonga to Samoa, 280
PS37 Tonga to Fiji, 281
PS38 Tonga to New Zealand, 282
PS40 Routes from Fiji, Tuvala and Wallis
PS41 Fiji to Samoa, 282
PS42 Fiji to Tonga, 282
PS43 Fiji to New Zealand, 284
PS44 Fiji to New Caledonia, 285
PS45 Fiji to Vanuatu, 285
PS46 Wallis to Fiji, 286
PS47 Tuvalu to Fiji, 286
PS48 Tuvalu to Wallis, 287
PS49 Wallis to Tuvalu, 288
PS50 Routes from New Zealand
PS51 New Zealand to New South Wales,
   292

PS52 New Zealand to Queensland, 293
PS53 New Zealand to New Caledonia,
   294
PS54 New Zealand to Fiji, 295
PS55 New Zealand to Tonga, 296
PS56 New Zealand to Cook Islands, 296
PS57 New Zealand to Tahiti, 297
PS58 New Zealand to Cape Horn, 298
*PS60 Routes from New Caldonia,
   Vanuatu and Solomon Islands*
PS61 New Caledonia to Fiji, 299
PS62 New Caledonia to New Zealand,
   302
PS63 New Caledonia to New South
   Wales, 302
PS64 New Caledonia to Queensland, 303
PS65 New Caledonia to Torres Strait, 303
PS66 Vanuatu to New Caledonia, 304
PS67 Vanuatu to Torres Strait, 304
PS68 Vanuatu to Solomon Islands, 305
PS69 Solomon Islands to Papua New
   Guinea, 305
*PS70 Routes from Australia and Papua
   New Guinea*
PS71 New South Wales to New Zealand,
   307
PS72 New South Wales to New
   Caledonia, 307
PS73 New South Wales to Fiji, 308
PS74 New South Wales to Vanuatu, 309
PS75 Queensland to New Zealand, 309
PS76 Queensland to New Caledonia, 310
PS77 Queensland to Vanuatu, 310
PS78 Queensland to Fiji, 311
PS79 Queensland to Solomon Islands,
   311
PS80 Queensland to Papua New Guinea,
   312
PS81 Papua New Guinea to Queensland,
   313
PS82 Papua New Guinea to Torres Strait,
   314
PS83 Papua New Guinea to Indonesia, 315

IN10 Routes in the North Indian Ocean
IN11 Singapore to Western Malaysia, 328
IN12 Malaysia to Sri Lanka, 328
IN13 Western Malaysia to Thailand, 329
IN14 Sri Lanka to Red Sea, 330
IN15 Sri Lanka to Oman, 330
IN16 Sri Lanka to Maldives, 331
IN17 Sri Lanka to India, 331
IN18 India to Red Sea, 332
IN19 Oman to Red Sea, 333
IN20 Red Sea to Sri Lanka, 333
IN21 Red Sea to Maldives, 334
IN22 Sri Lanka to Singapore, 334
IN23 Thailand to Singapore, 334

*Transequatorial routes in the Indian
   Ocean*
IT11 Maldives to Chagos Archipelago,
   336

IT12 Seychelles to Red Sea, 337
IT13 Chagos Archipelago to Sri Lanka, 338
IT14 Bali to Sri Lanka, 338
IT15 Bali to Singapore, 339
IT16 Cocos Keeling to Sri Lanka, 340
IT17 Kenya to Red Sea, 341
IT18 Chagos Archipelago to Maldives, 342
IT19 Red Sea to South Indian Ocean, 342

Routes in the South Indian Ocean
IS11 Torres Strait to Darwin, 360
IS12 Torres Strait to Bali, 360
IS13 Darwin to Bali, 361
IS14 Darwin to Christmas Island, 362
IS15 Bali to Christmas Island, 362
IS16 Christmas Island to Cocos Keeling, 363
IS17 Cocos Keeling to Mauritius, 363
IS18 Mauritius to Réunion, 366
IS19 Mauritius to Durban, 366
IS20 Réunion to Durban, 368
IS21 Durban to Cape Town, 368
IS22 Cocos Keeling to Chagos Archipelago, 370
IS23 Chagos Archipelago to Seychelles, 370
IS24 Christmas Island to Chagos Archipelago, 371
IS25 Western Australia to Cocos Keeling, 371
IS26 Indonesia to Chagos Archipelago, 372
IS27 Seychelles to Mauritius, 372
IS28 Seychelles to Kenya, 373
IS29 Chagos Archipelago to Mauritius, 373
IS30 Kenya to Seychelles, 374
IS31 Mauritius to Comoros, 374
IS32 Comoros to Kenya, 374
IS33 Mauritius to Seychelles, 375
IS34 Seychelles to Comoros, 375
IS35 Comoros to Seychelles, 376
IS36 Comoros to Durban, 376
IS37 Durban to Mauritius, 377
IS38 Cape Town to Western Australia, 377
IS39 Western Australia to Bass Strait, 378

Routes in the Red Sea
RN Northbound routes, 384
RS Southbound routes, 386

Routes in the Mediteranean
M11 Gibraltar to the Balearic Islands, 395
M12 Balearic Islands to the French Riviera, 397
M13 French Riviera to Corsica, 397
M14 Corsica to Messina Strait, 398

M15 Balearic Islands to Messina Strait, 398
M16 Messina Strait to Greece, 399
M17 Gibraltar to Malta, 399
M18 Malta to Greece, 400
M19 Routes in the Adriatic Sea, 401
M20 Routes in the Aegean Sea, 401
M21 Routes in the Marmara and Black Seas, 402
M22 Rhodes to Cyprus, 403
M23 Cyprus to Israel, 403
M24 Cyprus to Port Said, 404
M25 Rhodes to Port Said, 404
M26 Malta to Port Said, 405
M31 Port Said to Cyprus, 405
M32 Cyprus to Rhodes, 407
M33 Port Said to Rhodes, 407
M34 Greece to Messina Strait, 407
M35 Messina Strait to Corsica, 408
M36 Corsica to Sète, 408
M37 Sicily to the Balearic Islands, 409
M38 Greece to Malta, 409
M39 Balearic Islands to Gibraltar, 409
M40 Isreal to Port Said, 410
M41 Port Said to Malta, 410
M42 Malta to Gibraltar, 411

In alphabetical order

Acapulco to Balboa, 182
Acapulco to Hiva Oa, 215
Aden to Bab el Mandeb, 384
Aden to Galle, 333
Aden to Male, 334
Aitutaki to Niue, 273
Aitutaki to Pago Pago, 273
Aitutaki to Tongatapu, 273
Aitutaki to Vava'u, 273
Antigua to Aruba, 109
Antigua to Bermuda, 112
Antigua to Cristobal, 111
Antigua to Horta, 113
Antigua to New York, 112
Antigua to St John, 112
Apia to Mata Uta, 279
Apia to Neiafu, 277
Apia to Niuatoputapu, 277
Apia to Suva, 277
Aruba to Cristobal, 116
Aruba to St Thomas, 115
Aruba to Windward Passage, 115
Auckland to Cape Horn, 298
Auckland to Nuku'alofa, 296
Auckland to Papeete, 297
Auckland to Rarotonga, 296
Auckland to Suva, 295

Bab el Mandeb to Diego Garcia, 342
Bab el Mandeb to Jabal Attair, 384
Bab el Mandeb to Mombasa, 342

Bab el Mandeb to Seychelles, 342
Balabac Strait to Singapore, 194
Balboa to Acapulco, 178
Balboa to Callao, 217
Balboa to Guayaquil, 217
Balboa to Hilo, 181
Balboa to to Kodiak, 181
Balboa to to Nuku Hiva, 216
Balboa to Puntarenas, 178
Balboa to San Diego, 179
Balboa to Vancouver, 180
Balboa to Wreck Bay, 216
Bashi Channel to Guam, 201
Beaufort to Bermuda, 90
Beaufort to Mayaguana, 92
Beaufort to San Salvador, 92
Beaufort to St Thomas, 91
Beaufort to Windward Passage, 93
Benoa to Christmas Island, 362
Benoa to Galle, 338
Benoa to Salomon Islands, 372
Benoa to Singapore, 339
Bermuda to Antigua, 85
Bermuda to Beaufort, 88
Bermuda to Boston, 88
Bermuda to Falmouth, 84
Bermuda to Horta, 84
Bermuda to New York, 88
Bermuda to St Thomas, 86
Bernardino Strait to Yokohama, 195
Bonaire to Antigua, 114
Bonaire to Mona Passage, 115
Bonaire to St Croix, 115
Bonifacio to Anzio, 398
Bonifacio to Messina, 398
Bonifacio to Sète, 408
Bora Bora to Aitutaki, 271
Bora Bora to Penrhyn, 271
Bora Bora to Rarotonga, 271
Bora Bora to Suvorov, 271
Brisbane to Honiara, 311
Brisbane to Noumea, 310
Brisbane to Opua, 309
Brisbane to Suva, 311
Brisbane to Vila, 310
Bundaberg to Noumea, 310

Caicos Passage to Bermuda, 94
Cairns to Port Moresby, 312
Callao to Hangaroa, 266
Cape Cod to Cape Wrath, 89
Cape Horn to Bermuda, 130
Cape Horn to Falmouth, 129
Cape Horn to Gibraltar, 129
Cape Horn to New York, 130
Cape North to Brisbane, 293
Cape North to Lord Howe, 292
Cape North to Sydney, 292
Cape Town to Barbados, 128
Cape Town to Fremantle, 377
Cape Town to Horta, 127

Cape Town to Martinique, 128
Cape Town to New York, 128
Cape Town to St Helena, 143
Cape Virgins to Stanley, 147
Cape Wrath to Cape Cod, 62
Christmas Island to Cocos, 363
Christmas to Hilo, 189
Christmas to Salomon Islands, 371
Cochin to Aden, 332
Cocos to Galle, 340
Cocos to Rodriguez, 363
Cocos to Salomon Islands, 370
Cocos to St Louis, 363
Coffs Harbour to Noumea, 307
Costa Rica to Easter Island, 215
Cristobal to Antigua, 107
Cristobal to Aruba, 108
Cristobal to Caracas, 108
Cristobal to Grand Cayman, 104
Cristobal to Grenada, 107
Cristobal to Kingston, 105
Cristobal to Martinique, 107
Cristobal to Mona Passage, 107
Cristobal to Santo Domingo, 106
Cristobal to St Croix, 107
Cristobal to Swan Island, 104
Cristobal to Windward Passage, 105

Dakar to Banjul, 77
Dakar to Barbados, 79
Dakar to Horta, 83
Dakar to Martinique, 79
Dakar to Salvador, 125
Darwin to Benoa, 361
Darwin to Christmas Island, 362
Djibouti to Bab el Mandeb, 384
Djibouti to Male, 334
Durban to Cape Town, 368
Durban to Port Louis, 377

Falmouth to Cape Town, 121
Falmouth to Funchal, 66
Falmouth to Horta, 67
Falmouth to La Coruna, 65
Falmouth to Las Palmas, 66
Falmouth to Lisbon, 65
Falmouth to Newport, 62
Falmouth to Vilamoura, 65
Fanning to Hilo, 189
Fremantle to Bass Strait, 378
Fremantle to Cocos, 371
Funafuti to Mata Utu, 287
Funafuti to Suva, 286
Funafuti to Tuvalu, 222
Funchal to Las Palmas, 67

Galle to Aden, 330
Galle to Cochin, 331
Galle to Djibouti, 330
Galle to Male, 331
Galle to Raysut, 330

Gibraltar to Ibiza, 395
Gibraltar to Antigua, 72
Gibraltar to Barbados, 72
Gibraltar to Cape Town, 121
Gibraltar to Falmouth, 73
Gibraltar to Gran Canaria, 72
Gibraltar to La Valetta, 399
Gibraltar to Madeira, 71
Gladstone to Samarai, 312
Gran Canaria to Antigua, 74
Gran Canaria to Barbados, 74
Gran Canaria to Bermuda, 77
Gran Canaria to São Vicente, 76
Grande Comoro to Durban, 376
Grande Comoro to Mahé, 376
Grande Comoro to Mombasa, 374
Grenada to Cristobal, 111
Grenada to Margarita, 109
Guam to Palau, 206
Guam to Yokohama, 204

Hangaroa to Cape Horn, 267
Hangaroa to Cape Pillar, 267
Hangaroa to Pitcairn, 266
Hilo to Christmas, 188
Hilo to Fanning, 188
Hilo to Kodiak, 186
Hilo to Majuro, 189
Hilo to Nuku Hiva, 222
Hilo to Papeete, 221
Hilo to San Diego, 187
Hilo to San Francisco, 187
Hilo to Vancouver, 186
Hilo to Yokohama, 190
Hong Kong to Guam, 201
Hong Kong to Manila, 199
Hong Kong to Nagasaki, 200
Hong Kong to Singapore, 198
Honiara to Rabaul, 305
Horta to Crookhaven, 81
Horta to Falmouth, 80
Horta to Gibraltar, 79
Horta to Lisbon, 80
Horta to Vilamoura, 80
Hurghada to Port Sudan, 386

Ibiza to Gibraltar, 409
Ibiza to Palma de Mallorca, 395
Iraklion to La Valetta, 409
Iraklion to Messina, 407

Jabal Attair to Khor Nawarat, 385
Jabal Attair to Masimirit, 384

Khor Nawarat to Bab el Mandeb, 387
Kiel Canal to Dover Straits, 64
Kodiak to Prince Rupert, 176
Kyrenia to Rhodes, 407

La Valetta to Gibraltar, 411
La Valetta to Khania, 400

La Valetta to Port Said, 405
La Valetta to Zante, 400
Larnaca to Haifa, 403
Larnaca to Port Said, 404
Larnaca to Tel Aviv, 403
Las Palmas to Cape Town, 122
Las Palmas to Dakar, 77
Las Palmas to Nouadhibou, 77
Las Palmas to Salvador, 124
Lautoka to Noumea, 285
Lautoka to Vila, 285
Lifuka to Suva, 281
Limassol to Port Said, 404
Lisbon to Falmouth, 71
Lisbon to Funchal, 70
Lisbon to Gibraltar, 69
Lisbon to Horta, 70
Lumut to Galle, 328
Luzon Strait to Okinawa, 195

Madang to Guam, 224
Madang to Jayapura, 315
Madang to Palau, 223
Madang to San Bernardino, 223
Mahé to Aden, 337
Mahé to Djibouti, 337
Mahé to Glorieuses, 375
Mahé to Mombasa, 373
Mahé to St Louis, 372
Majuro to Hilo, 190
Majuro to Tarawa, 190
Male to Salomon, 336
Mallorca to Gibraltar, 409
Mallorca to Malta, 398
Mallorca to Marseille, 397
Manila to Hong Kong, 195
Manzanillo to Hilo, 182
Maragarita to Grenada, 114
Martinique to Bonaire, 109
Martinique to Cristobal, 111
Mata Utu to Funafuti, 288
Menorca to Messina, 398
Menorca to Nice, 397
Messina to Bonifacio, 408
Messina to Pylos, 399
Messina to Zante, 399
Mombasa to Aden, 341
Mombasa to Djibouti, 341
Mombasa to Mahé, 374
Mona Passage to Bermuda, 97
Montevideo to Cape Virgins, 147
Montevideo to Stanley, 146

NE Providence Channel to Bermuda, 94
Neiafu to Apia, 280
Neiafu to Pago Pago, 280
Neiafu to Suva, 281
New York to Bermuda, 90
New York to Cape Town, 123
New York to St Thomas, 91
Newport to Falmouth, 89

Newport to Horta, 90
Nice to Calvi, 397
Norfolk to Horta, 90
Noumea to Bramble Cay, 303
Noumea to Brisbane, 303
Noumea to Bundaberg, 303
Noumea to Coffs Harbour, 302
Noumea to Lautoka, 299
Noumea to Opua, 302
Noumea to Suva, 299
Noumea to Sydney, 302
Noumea to Whangarei, 302
Nuku Hiva to Hilo, 218
Nuku Hiva to Papeete, 264
Nuku'alofa to Auckland, 282
Nuku'alofa to Opua, 282
Nuku'alofa to Suva, 281
Nuku'alofa to Tahiti, 280
Nuku'alofa to Whangarei, 282

Okinawa to Bungo Strait, 195
Opua to Lautoka, 295
Opua to Noumea, 294

Pago Pago to Neiafu, 277
Pago Pago to Suva, 277
Pago Pago to Tahiti, 279
Palau to Guam, 206
Palau to Madang, 225
Palau to Manus, 225
Palau to Menorca, 409
Papeete to Balboa, 220
Papeete to Hilo, 219
Paphos to Rhodes, 407
Penang to Galle, 328
Penang to Phuket, 329
Penrhyn to Hilo, 220
Peros Banhos to Galle, 338
Peros Banhos to Mahé, 370
Peros Banhos to Male, 342
Peros Banhos to Port Louis, 373
Phuket to Singapore, 335
Pitcairn to Mangareva, 267
Port des Galets to Durban, 368
Port Louis to Mahé, 375
Port Louis to Port des Galets, 366
Port Moresby to Cairns, 313
Port Moresby to Thursday Island, 314
Port Said to La Valetta, 410
Port Said to Larnaca, 405
Port Said to Limassol, 405
Port Said to Paphos, 405
Port Said to Rhodes, 407
Port Sudan to Khor Nawarat, 387
Port Sudan to Suez, 385
Porto Cervo to Palermo, 398
Puntarenas to Balboa, 182
Puntarenas to Hilo, 182
Puntarenas to Hiva Oa, 215

Rarotonga to Nuie, 273
Rarotonga to Opua, 274

Rarotonga to Pago Pago, 273
Rarotonga to Tongatapu, 273
Rarotonga to Vava'u, 273
Ras Hadarba to Port Sudan, 387
Raysut to Aden, 333
Raysut to Djibouti, 333
Rhodes to Kyrenia, 403
Rhodes to Paphos, 403
Rhodes to Port Said, 404
Rio de Janeiro to Barbados, 126
Rio de Janeiro to Gibraltar, 126
Rio de Janeiro to Falmouth, 126
Rio de Janeiro to Stanley, 146
Rio de Janeiro to Tristan da Cunhua, 145
Rodriguez to Mauritius, 363

Salvador to Gibraltar, 126
Salvador to Tobago, 126
Samarai to Cairns, 313
San Bernardino to Guam, 196
San Bernardino to Palau, 196
San Diego to Balboa, 174
San Diego to Hilo, 174
San Diego to Hiva Oa, 213
San Diego to Papeete, 213
San Diego to Wreck Bay, 212
San Francisco to Hilo, 174
San Francisco to Hiva Oa, 213
San Francisco to Vancouver, 175
San Juan to Bermuda, 97
Santo to Honiara, 305
São Vincente to Antigua, 78
São Vincente to Barbados, 78
São Vincente to Martinique, 78
São Vincente to Rio de Janeiro, 124
São Vincente to Salvador, 124
Singapore to Balabac Strait, 197
Singapore to Hong Kong, 198
Singapore to Penang, 328
Singapore to Port Kelang, 328
St Barts to Beaufort, 112
St Croix to Cristobal, 101
St Helena to Ascension, 144
St Helena to Fernando de Noronha, 144
St Helena to Salvador, 144
St Louis to Durban, 366
St Louis to Glorieuses, 374
St Raphael to Ajaccio, 397
St Thomas to Beaufort, 98
St Thomas to Bermuda, 97
St Thomas to Charlestown, 98
St Thomas to Cristobal, 101
St Thomas to Galveston, 100
St Thomas to Kingston, 100
St Thomas to New York, 98
Stanley to Montevideo, 148
Stanley to Rio de Janeiro, 148
Suez to Hurghada, 386
Suva to Apia, 283
Suva to Auckland, 284
Suva to Neiafu, 283
Suva to Noumea, 285

Suva to Nuku'alofa, 283
Suva to Opua, 284
Suva to Pago Pago, 283
Suva to Vila, 285
Suva to Whangarei, 284
Suvorov to Pago Pago, 273
Sydney to Lautoka, 308
Sydney to Noumea, 307
Sydney to Opua, 307
Sydney to Suva, 308
Sydney to Vila, 309

Tahiti to Cape Horn, 272
Tahiti to Raivavae, 272
Tahiti to Rapa, 272
Tahiti to Tubuai, 272
Tarawa to Funafuti, 223
Tarawa to Hilo, 191
Tel Aviv to Port Said, 410
Tenerife to Barbados, 74
Tenerife to Martinique, 74
Thursday Island to Benoa, 360
Thursday Island to Darwin, 314, 360
Townville to Honiara, 311
Trapani to Mallorca, 409
Tristan da Cunha to Cape Town, 146

Valparaiso to Hangaroa, 266
Vancouver to Hilo, 177
Vancouver to Hiva Oa, 214
Vancouver to San Francisco, 176
Vila to Bramble City, 304
Vila to Honiara, 305
Vila to Noumea, 304
Vilamoura to Falmouth, 71
Vilamoura to Funchal, 70
Vilamoura to Gibraltar, 69
Vilamoura to Horta, 70
Vilamoura to Los Palmas, 69

Wallis to Futuna, 286
Wallis to Suva, 286
Wellington to Syndey, 292
Whangarei to Noumea, 294
Whangarei to Nuku'alofa, 296
Whangarei to Papeete, 297
Whangarei to Rarotonga, 296
Whangarei to Suva, 295
Windward Passage to Cristobal, 93
Windward Passage to Cristobal, 97
Wreck Bay to Hangaroa, 265
Wreck Bay to Mangareva, 265
Wreck Bay to Nuku Hiva, 263

Yokohama to Guam, 204
Yokohama to Hilo, 203
Yokohama to Hong Kong, 205
Yokohama to Kodiak, 202
Yokohama to San Francisco, 203
Yokohama to Vancouver, 202

Zante to Messina, 407
Zante to Patras, 399

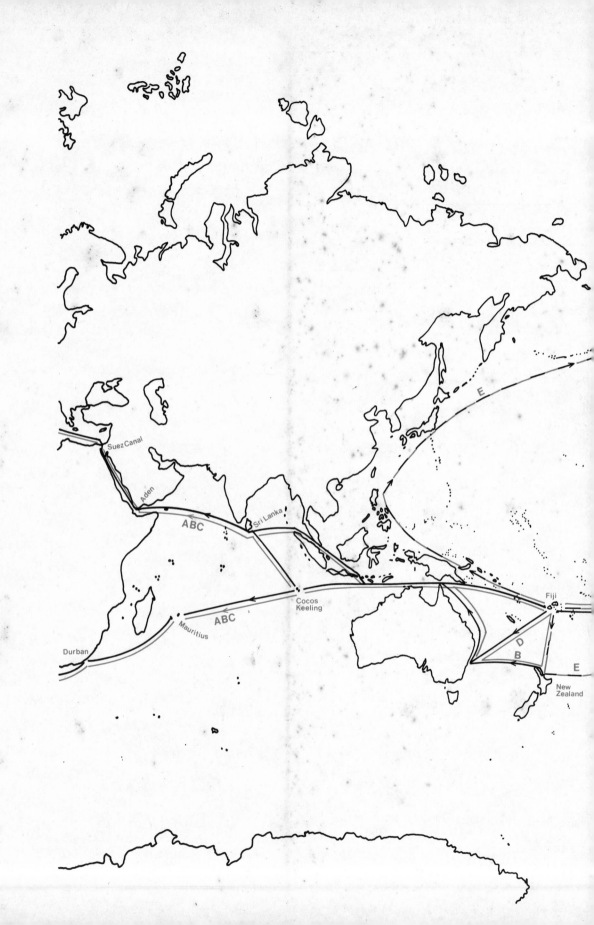

Suez Canal

Aden

ABC

Sri Lanka

ABC

Durban

Mauritius

Cocos
Keeling

Fiji

D

B

E

E

New
Zealand